Prima's Official Strategy Guide

David S J Hodgson

Prima Games
A Division of Random House, Inc.

3000 Lava Ridge Court
Roseville, CA 95661
(800) 733-3000
www.primagames.com

Product Development Manager: Jennifer Crotteau
Project Editor: Carrie Ponseti
Design and Layout: Graphic Applications Group, Inc.

ISBN: 0-7615-4517-4
Library of Congress Catalog Card Number: 2003114648
Printed in the United States of America

04 05 06 07 JJ 10 9 8 7 6 5 4 3 2 1

Acknowledgments
Special thanks to Epic Games: This guide would not have been possible without the extraordinary help and support of Ben Beckwith, Scott Bigwood, Cliff Bleszinski, Phil Cole, Laurent Delayen, Stuart Fitzsimmons, Dave Hagewood, Michiel Hendriks, Tim Lang, Jeff Morris, Matt Oelfke, Rogelio Olguin, Nate Overman, Steve Polge, Ron Prestenback, Mark Rein, Peter Respondek, David Sirmons, Tim Sweeney, and Steve Wenninger.

Author Special Thanks: My beautiful wife Melanie; Mum, Dad, Ian and Rowena; Bryn and Rachel; Bryan and Steve Stratton; Jen and Carrie; Laibach, Kraftwerk, and Synaesthesia; and "L" for Leo, who swallowed some tacks.

CONTENTS

Tournament Introductions

The ultimate team sport is back and better than ever in *Unreal Tournament 2004*. Forget any notions of a fair fight. There's little honor in this competition, so survive by any means necessary. And yet, the finest players are those who balance their pleasure in shedding blood with supreme team comradeship in the matches that demand squads of like-minded warriors.

Unreal Tournament 2004: Prima's Official Strategy Guide contains everything from massive weapons strategies to every nook, cranny, and power-up point in the entire series of all-new levels.

"The Players Club" section offers official biographies of this season's competition. The "Tournament Training" section covers the basics. It explains the controls and every technique you must master to stand a hope of placing well. Next is "Inventory and Ordnance", with exhaustive information on every weapon and item. The "Vehicle and Turrets" section covers the larger tanks, armored personnel carriers, and guard turrets. There's also a "Single-Player Strategies" section.

Then comes the map section, which features 50 all-new tournament maps, complete with item placements and complex strategies. This includes all the stages for the new Assault and Onslaught events. Finally find console commands, screen tips, and easter eggs.

But don't get too cocky, rookie. You have a long way to go before becoming the point leader. Strap on that body armor, shine that grenade launcher, fire the Raptor's retro thrusters, and get into that arena. The crowd goes crazy for new meat....

The Player's Club

Tournament Character Listings

The expanded motley crew of fiends, genetic mutants, powerful alien races, and killing automatons has left this season's Tournament organizers giddy with excitement; and with a total of 86 combatants flexing their trigger fingers, there are more choices than ever before! Below is a list of all the competitors along with a brief bio, any combat enhancements they possess, and any species advantages they have (accessible only via the Species Statistics Mutator), along with visual evidence of the player. Additional advice, such as picking teammates or specific body types, is detailed in the "Training" section.

Combat Enhancements

If you are playing against Bots, or through the single-player game, often you'll encounter various non-player controlled entities. Through complex AI routines, some of the characters faced (or brought into your team) have acquired specific combat enhancements or preferences; if these are available, they are listed under that character. Aside from Favorite Weapon and Bot Use, these statistics show minor but recognizable variations from a "normal" style of play; the stats show abilities or deficiencies for each kind of combat potential, detailed below.

The statistics range from -2.0 to 2.0. The higher the ability, the more the character will use or be proficient in it. Note that player characters do not have any enhancements—your avatar is based solely on your own style of play! Study these enhancements if you are about to challenge a team or if you want to learn the preferences of a specific character on your side. Why? Because you can understand the character's needs in the combat zone, and help them out (or hinder if you're facing them) as described here:

Accuracy

A natural ability above or below the norm to consistently strike an enemy with any weapon. Place characters with good Accuracy with you or in defensive positions.

Aggressiveness

An innate ability to challenge all comers in the combat zone while shrugging off or haphazardly ignoring wounds. These make good offensive teammates or those you know will quickly come to your aid.

Bot Use

This statistic ranges from 1 to 3 and shows the preference for placing a particular character as a Bot in Instant Action games or those with Bots in them. There is a slight chance that a Bot will be chosen over the random norm if it has this stat.

Combat Style

This shows you whether the character has learned more complex combat techniques, such as side-stepping or dodging attacks, and attacks with cunning and relish. Leave these types to Roam or keep them close by.

Favorite Weapon

This shows the character's weapon preference; it attempts to secure and use this item over all others, meaning you should learn where the appropriate weapon is in each zone before you give orders. The favored weapon brings about different combat situations (a sniper rifle-wielding friend should guard your base, while a rocket launcher fan may want to be pushed to the front).

Jumpiness

This shows how likely the character is to use jumping as part of its repertoire, either to cut corners or leap in combat.

Tactics	Strafing Ability
Similar to Combat Style, but related to overall conduct (rather than fighting techniques), those with tactical skill will, for example, quickly learn how your team is playing and act to help or hinder you (i.e., by guarding or moving to Double Domination points to secure a win).	If the character can move from side to side while in combat or maneuvering, it's more likely to be skilled in close-quarter fighting and should be used offensively.

Once all of the different characters are listed, all the known variants of the characters are shown—characters that have a different name but appear in the guise of a particular type. Unless otherwise stated, these have no combat enhancements—they are simply composite automatons of existing warriors in that group.

Aliens (Gen Mo'Kai)

The Gen Mo'Kai are a ruthless race of alien warriors that found a home in the Tournaments. The Gen Mo'Kai are among the most graceful and agile characters. When you enable Species Statistics, the Gen Mo' Kai are 20 percent more maneuverable in the air and 30 percent faster on the ground, and they accelerate 10 percent faster than the average human character. They also have a 10 percent higher jump and a 10 percent higher aerial dodge speed. The downside is a maximum health that is 20 percent lower than average and weapons that inflict 10 percent less damage than average.

Mokara

Age: 20

Race: Gen Mo'Kai

Combat Enhancements

Accuracy: 0.5

Aggressiveness: 0.2

Bot Use: 1

Combat Style: -0.3

Favorite Weapon: Shock Rifle

Data: Damarus's sister, and second in line to the scepter of Mobeth, Mokara feels that her brother is unworthy of the title and seeks to usurp it by proving herself the better in battle. Quiet and reserved, she watches her enemies closely for hidden weaknesses.

Makreth

Age: 24

Race: Gen Mo'Kai

Combat Enhancements

Aggressiveness: 0.3

Bot Use: 1

Combat Style: 0.3

Favorite Weapon: Flak Cannon

Strafing Ability: 1

Data: A warrior maiden of the Yellow Bone clan, Makreth proudly wears the death mask handed down through generations of her family. Her bared fangs and slitted eyes have caused more than one opponent to freeze in fear for their lives.

Faraleth

Age: 28

Race: Gen Mo'Kai

Combat Enhancements

  Aggressiveness: 0.4

  Bot Use: 1

  Combat Style: 0.3

  Favorite Weapon: Rocket Launcher

  Strafing Ability: 1

Data: When the human plague known as the Crimson scourge annihilated her tribe, the healer Faraleth went mad with grief, sickened by her own impotence to combat the disease. Now every death she suffers in the Tournaments is one small step toward redemption.

Nebri

Age: 26

Race: Gen Mo'Kai

Combat Enhancements

  Accuracy: 0.3

  Bot Use: 1

  Strafing Ability: 0.5

Data: Her face permanently disfigured by the venom of an Arborean predator, Nebri signed up for the Tournaments rather than face further rejection by those who were once her suitors. Little does her compatriot Damarus know that her feelings for him are considerably less than hostile.

Damarus

Age: 23

Race: Gen Mo'Kai

Combat Enhancements

  Bot Use: 1

  Favorite Weapon: BioRifle

  Strafing Ability: 0.5

  Tactics: 0.7

Data: The son of Mobeth tribe leader Gik Ma, Damarus has made quite a name for himself in the arenas. As a volunteer, he enjoys many physical pleasures, but those who think his hedonistic lifestyle has made him soft haven't seen him from the wrong end of a biorifle.

Komek

Age: 27

Race: Gen Mo'Kai

Combat Enhancements

  Bot Use: 1

  Favorite Weapon: Flak Cannon

  Strafing Ability: 1.0

Data: Like Makreth, Komek prefers to wear the death mask of his family into battle. This has earned him the disdain of Motig who prefers to instill fear into his enemies with displays of skill rather than gaudy facial art.

Motig

Age: 19

Race: Gen Mo'Kai

Combat Enhancements

  Accuracy: 0.2

  Bot Use: 1

  Strafing Ability: 1

  Tactics: 0.5

Data: The youngest of the Gen Mo'Kai players, Motig is also the most enthusiastic and outgoing of the recruits. He plays the crowd like a finely tuned instrument, using finesse and style to impress, while crushing his enemies underfoot. Underestimating his abilities in combat may be the last mistake you'll ever make.

Selig

Age: 25

Race: Gen Mo'Kai

Combat Enhancements

  Accuracy: 0.1

  Bot Use: 1

  Favorite Weapon: Rocket Launcher

  Strafing Ability: 1.0

Data: Unlike his flashy young friend Motig, Selig prefers to keep to himself. Between competitions he likes to explore the worlds he visits and document the interesting things he finds, or play a lethal game of cat and mouse with the interesting things that find him.

Additional Competitors

Name	Strafing Ability	Accuracy	Name	Strafing Ability	Accuracy
Caskuli	1.0	0.3	Pelosin	1.0	0.3
Delara	1.0	0.3	Rathik	1.0	0.3
Gramatik	1.0	0.3	SeeSeela	1.0	0.3
Napaket	1.0	0.35	Timrit	1.0	0.3

Artificial Lifeforms (Robots)

These metal combatants were designed to be the ultimate killing machines. There's no doubt that their creators succeeded on every level. Many of these artificial lifeforms have organic components inside their hard exoskeletons, but hearts are not among them. When you enable Species Statistics, the robots have 10 percent more health and a 60 percent higher dodging ability on the ground than the average human character. However, they suffer a 20 percent penalty to walking speed, a 30 percent penalty to crouching movement speed, and a 30 percent penalty to aerial dodging speed.

Thorax

Age: N/A

Race: Artificial Lifeform

Combat Enhancements

   Accuracy: 0.3

   Bot Use: 1

   Favorite Weapon: Rocket Launcher

   Tactics: 1.5

Data: Relentless in competition and possessive of a digital immortality that even the organics are incapable of understanding, Thorax seeks only one goal: victory.

Mandible

Age: N/A

Race: Artificial Lifeform

Combat Enhancements

   Bot Use: 1

   Favorite Weapon: Flak Cannon

   Tactics: 1.5

Data: Mandible's programmer thought it would be interesting to have his creation contemplate the meaning of life. Three days and 76 bodies later, the automaton still lacked an answer but had gained extensive knowledge of human physiology.

Widowmaker

Age: N/A

Race: Artificial Lifeform

Combat Enhancements

   Accuracy: 0.3

   Bot Use: 1

   Jumpiness: 0.8

   Strafing Ability: 1.5

Data: Widowmaker is one of the few battle drones confirmed to be wholly inorganic. Advanced threat detection and onboard evasive logic make this being a force to be reckoned with.

Syzygy

Age: N/A

Race: Artificial Lifeform

Combat Enhancements

   Bot Use: 1

   Strafing Ability: 0.35

   Tactics: 1.3

Data: Syzygy takes the term "bleeding edge" to a whole new level.

Cobalt

Age: N/A

Race: Artificial Lifeform

Combat Enhancements

Accuracy: 0.2

Bot Use: 1

Strafing Ability: 0.8

Tactics: 1.5

Data: Every soldier trains for combat using drones to perfect his targeting skills. But what if the drone was smarter and stronger, and you were the target?

Rapier

Age: N/A

Race: Artificial Lifeform

Combat Enhancements

Accuracy: 0.3

Bot Use: 1

Tactics: 1.5

Data: It slices, it dices, eviscerates, and decapitates, sees in the dark, and can track you by your DNA.

Corrosion

Age: N/A

Race: Artificial Lifeform

Combat Enhancements

Accuracy: 0.1

Bot Use: 1

Tactics: 1.1

Data: Beneath an exterior of cold metal burns a soul as bright as a dying star, the essence of a being who sought to rule the galaxy at the Emperor's side. With his dreams stripped away from him as easily as his dying flesh, Corrosion now exists only to seek his revenge.

Renegade

Age: N/A

Race: Artificial Lifeform

Combat Enhancements

Accuracy: 0.3

Bot Use: 1

Favorite Weapon: Link Gun

Tactics: 1.5

Data: No mercy will be granted by the drone, as this feature was removed in the last operating system update.

Virus

Age: Unknown

Race: Cybernetic

Combat Enhancements

Aggressiveness: -0.2

Bot Use: 3

Combat Style: 0.2

Favorite Weapon: Shock Rifle

Jumpiness: 1.0

Strafing Ability: 0.5

Data: A remorseless killing machine, Virus specializes in dealing death with the shock rifle.

Cyclops

Age: Unknown

Race: Cybernetic

Combat Enhancements

Aggressiveness: 0.2

Bot Use: 3

Combat Style: 0.2

Favorite Weapon: Flak Cannon

Strafing Ability: 0.5

Data: Cyclops must be kept in stasis between matches, as he has trouble recognizing the difference between Tournament matches and normal life.

Axon

Age: Unknown

Race: Cybernetic

Combat Enhancements

Accuracy: 0.15

Aggressiveness: -0.2

Bot Use: 3

Combat Style: -0.2

Jumpiness: 1.0

Strafing Ability: 1.0

Data: Axon was the first Liandri warrior outfitted with the BioMech Mark III body armor and augmentation system, made legendary by Xan Kriegor.

Xan Kriegor

Age: Unknown

Race: Cybernetic

Combat Enhancements

Accuracy: 1.0

Aggressiveness: -0.2

Bot Use: 1

Combat Style: -0.2

Jumpiness: 1.0

Strafing Ability: 2.0

Data: Attention! This character is only available once certain criteria are met in the Single Player Tournament! Former Tournament champion Xan Kriegor is an almost mythical figure. His return from several years of isolation has been greeted with great trepidation by other Tournament competitors.

Cathode

Age: Unknown

Race: Cybernetic

Combat Enhancements

  Accuracy: 0.09

  Aggressiveness: 0.15

  Bot Use: 3

  Combat Style: -0.25

  Favorite Weapon:
Link Gun

  Jumpiness: 0.2

  Strafing Ability: 0.6

Data: Liandri Corporation has released no information about this competitor.

Matrix

Age: Unknown

Race: Cybernetic

Combat Enhancements

  Accuracy: 0.05

  Aggressiveness: 0.1

  Bot Use: 3

  Combat Style: -0.3

  Favorite Weapon:
Shock Rifle

  Jumpiness: 0.6

  Strafing Ability: 0.8

Data: Liandri Corporation has released no information about this competitor.

Divisor

Age: Unknown

Race: Cybernetic

Combat Enhancements

  Aggressiveness: -0.15

  Combat Style: -0.15

  Favorite Weapon:
Rocket Launcher

  Jumpiness: 0.4

  Strafing Ability: 0.8

Data: Liandri Corporation has released no information about this competitor.

Enigma

Age: Unknown

Race: Cybernetic

Combat Enhancements

  Accuracy: 0.05

  Aggressiveness: 0.1

  Bot Use: 3

  Combat Style: -0.3

  Favorite Weapon:
Shock Rifle

  Jumpiness: 0.6

  Strafing Ability: 0.8

Data: Liandri Corporation has released no information about this competitor.

Additional Competitors

Name	Strafing Ability	Accuracy	Name	Strafing Ability	Accuracy
Cyclone	1.5	0.35	Seeker	1.5	0.35
Incisor	1.5	0.3	Shard	1.5	0.35
Katana	1.5	0.3	Torque	1.5	0.3
Predator	1.5	0.35	Vector	1.5	0.3

Egyptians (Anubans)

As settlers on a distant planet, a race of humans based its culture on ancient Egyptian civilization. These characters have very high maneuverability (150 percent better control in the air, 30 percent higher jump, and 50 percent higher aerial dodging ability) when you enable Species Statistics. However, they suffer a 15 percent maximum health penalty, a 10 percent inflicted damage penalty, a 20 percent acceleration penalty, and a 10 percent dodging penalty on the ground.

Diva

Age: 18

Race: Human

Combat Enhancements

  Aggressiveness: 0.4

  Bot Use: 1

  Combat Style: 0.4

  Favorite Weapon:
  Rocket Launcher

  Jumpiness: 0.5

  Strafing Ability: 0.5

Data: Known for her charm and charisma off the Tournament floor, Diva takes advantage of her reputation by being exceedingly vicious in her pursuit of victory. She takes great amusement in having sympathy notes delivered to her opponents prior to a match.

Memphis

Age: 21

Race: Human

Combat Enhancements

  Aggressiveness: -0.05

  Bot Use: 1

  Strafing Ability: 0.4

  Tactics: -0.35

Data: Once a beautiful daughter of the aristocracy who had grown tired of her pampered existence and taken to the arena, Memphis has become a battle-hardened warrior addicted to the adrenaline high of combat and self-preservation.

Asp

Age: 25

Race: Human

Combat Enhancements

  Accuracy: 0.25

  Aggressiveness: -0.05

  Bot Use: 1

  Combat Style: -0.1

  Favorite Weapon:
  Sniper Rifle

  Strafing Ability: -0.3

  Tactics: -0.2

Data: Beautiful and deadly, Asp is as quick to strike as her namesake, and more likely to ensure that her victims don't recover from her bite.

Cleopatra

Age: 25

Race: Human

Combat Enhancements

  Bot Use: 1

  Combat Style: 0.1

  Tactics: 0.5

Data: If you think Cleopatra and Asp have something going on, then you may be right. But it's not something you want to show up for unarmed.

Scarab

Age: 24

Race: Human

Combat Enhancements

  Accuracy: -0.4

  Bot Use: 1

  Combat Style: -0.1

  Favorite Weapon:
  Link Gun

  Strafing Ability: 0.4

  Tactics: 1.0

Data: A lieutenant in the Desert Legion and veteran of three tribal wars, Scarab is a cold and calculating tactician who prefers to draw his enemies out into the open where he can kill them at his leisure.

Horus

Age: 28

Race: Human

Combat Enhancements

  Aggressiveness: 0.05

  Bot Use: 1

  Favorite Weapon:
  Shock Rifle

  Strafing Ability: -0.35

  Tactics: 0.7

Data: Three generations of arena combat have made Horus's bloodline a force to be reckoned with, and one that's very popular with the crowd.

Roc

Age: 27

Race: Human

Combat Enhancements

Accuracy: -0.1

Aggressiveness: 0.25

Bot Use: 1

Tactics: 0.4

Data: A former officer in the Temple Guardians, Roc found the position to be less than rewarding. The extremely low incidence of crime within the city proper made it a very dull career. It was the encouraging words of an Imperial recruiter that finally convinced him to take leave of his world and venture out into the galaxy.

Hyena

Age: 27

Race: Human

Combat Enhancements

Accuracy: -0.25

Bot Use: 1

Combat Style: -0.1

Favorite Weapon: Minigun

Tactics: 1.0

Data: To the warriors of the Northern Waste, the display of emotions is a sign of weakness. Hyena has never shed a tear in his life, every drop of water more precious than his blood. Born to do battle on the desert sand, he now fights to return there.

Additional Competitors

Anat	Isis	Maat	Osiris	Sphinx
Arachne	Jackyl	Nafiret	Ramses	Sunspear
Bastet	Khepry	Natron	Sayiid	Tefenet
Hathor	Lexa	Nekhbet	Sekhmet	Tranquility
Imhotep	Luxor	Nephthys	Seth	

Juggernauts

Juggernauts are genetically modified (gene-boosted) humans and are the toughest characters in the Tournament. If you enable Species Statistics from the Mutator menu, you'll see that Juggernauts have approximately 90 percent more health than the average human character. Their power comes from their size, but their bulk has a downside. Their ground speed, jump height, acceleration, and aerial dodging abilities are all slightly below average (10–20 percent less than the average character).

Rylisa

Age: 32

Race: Homo sapiens (gene boosted)

Combat Enhancements

Aggressiveness: 0.05

Bot Use: 1

Strafing Ability: 0.5

Data: Former Union Leader of Ore Miners' Local #732G, Rylisa found the bribes offered to her by an Imperial official to be an insult, so she cut off his hands and used his subdermal ID chips to access his accounts, netting her life in the Allerian Ice Mines.

Reinha

Age: 29

Race: Homo sapiens (gene boosted)

Combat Enhancements

Accuracy: -0.15

Bot Use: 1

Tactics: 1.0

Data: After her husband was killed in a mining accident, Reinha had nothing left to live for, so she adopted the nickname her spouse had given her in his native Portuguese and set out to find meaning in death.

Ambrosia

Age: 26

Race: Homo sapiens (gene boosted)

Combat Enhancements

Bot Use: 1

Tactics: 0.5

Data: A gene-boosted weightlifter who strangled a judge in a fit of adrenaline induced rage, Ambrosia has resigned herself to a life in the Tournaments, and the unthinkable horror of dealing with her teammate Gorge's sexual innuendos for the foreseeable future.

Siren

Age: 27

Race: Homo sapiens (gene boosted)

Combat Enhancements

Accuracy: -0.4

Aggressiveness: 0.3

Bot Use: 1

Favorite Weapon: Flak Cannon

Jumpiness: 0.75

Tactics: 1.0

Data: Not only is she a victim of a severe beating with the ugly stick, she's had DNA from the tree spliced directly into her genes. There's nothing pretty about Siren and she'll be the first to admit it. Because if you mention it, she'll kick your ass.

17

Gorge

Age: 34

Race: Homo sapiens (gene boosted)

Combat Enhancements

Aggressiveness: 0.1

Bot Use: 1

Combat Style: 0.1

Tactics: 0.5

Data: It takes a special kind of person to survive the harsh environment of the Allerian Penal Colony. It takes another kind of person altogether to revel in it. Gorge is more than just a survivor; he's a predator with a sweet tooth for suffering. Once incarcerated, Gorge took to the Tournaments like a fish to water, honing his combat skills both on and off the arena floor. The lack of firepower in the prison mines doesn't affect his training regimen in the least. Who needs a gun when you've got hands and teeth?

Frostbite

Age: 37

Race: Homo sapiens (gene boosted)

Combat Enhancements

Accuracy: -0.2

Bot Use: 1

Favorite Weapon: Rocket Launcher

Strafing Ability: 0.6

Tactics: 0.5

Data: You can feel his cold gaze at a distance, like gangrene crawling beneath your flesh. It devours you, seeks to turn your blood to ice and your heart to stone. Imagine what he'll do when he actually gets his hands on you.

Cannonball

Age: 28

Race: Homo sapiens (gene boosted)

Combat Enhancements

Accuracy: 0.3

Aggressiveness: 0.1

Bot Use: 1

Favorite Weapon: Sniper Rifle

Strafing Ability: -1.0

Tactics: 0.5

Data: If a trash compactor and a tank had offspring, then Cannonball would be the result. He's big, ugly, and has the personality of a rabid grizzly, and only the suicidal would voluntarily share a cell with this career criminal.

Arclite

Age: 24

Race: Homo sapiens (gene boosted)

Combat Enhancements

Accuracy: -0.15

Aggressiveness: 0.3

Bot Use: 1

Combat Style: 0.2

Favorite Weapon: Minigun

Strafing Ability: 0.8

Data: Unlike his male counterparts, Arclite is neither a criminal nor a killer by nature. His presence in the Tournaments is simply a byproduct of his genetic makeup. But watch your step around him. He's not happy to be here.

Additional Competitors

Name	Strafing Ability	Accuracy	Name	Strafing Ability	Accuracy
Avalanche	—	—	Matriarch	0.2	—
Brutus	0.2	—	Medusa	0.2	—
Bulldog	—	—	Misery	0.2	—
Bullseye	0.2	—	Molotov	—	—
Chaos	0.2	—	Obsidian	0.2	0.5
Clangor	0.2	—	Odin	0.2	0.5
Earthquake	0.2	—	Outrage	0.2	—
Fury	0.2	0.5	Perdition	—	—
Hydra	0.2	—	Rampage	0.2	0.5
Jackhammer	0.2	—	Sorrow	—	—
Jezebel	—	—	Titania	0.2	—
Lockdown	—	—	Vengeance	—	—

Mercenaries

Mercenaries, or "Mercs," are unmodified humans trained in the combat arts. Their training has made them as tough as nails, but they don't carry around excessive bulk. When you enable Species Statistics from the Mutator menu, all Mercs have approximately 30 percent more health than the average character and no loss in any other statistic.

Prism

Age: 26

Race: Human

Combat Enhancements

Accuracy: -0.1

Bot Use: 1

Favorite Weapon: Link Gun

Tactics: 0.5

Data: Raised on the crippled Capships of the 7th Mercenary fleet, Prism is part engineer, part gun for hire. She takes her name from the custom eyepiece she designed while inspecting bulkheads for micro-fractures.

BlackJack

Age: 26

Race: Human

Combat Enhancements

Accuracy: 0.45

Bot Use: 1

Favorite Weapon: Sniper Rifle

Strafing Ability: -1.5

Tactics: -1.0

Data: Don't let those pretty eyes fool you. She's hard as steel and holds her own in the arena better than most men. As a scout for Merc raiding parties, she earned a reputation for dependability and courage while she was still a kid. But then nobody's really a kid anymore. They took that away too.

19

Sapphire

Age: 27

Race: Human

Combat Enhancements

Accuracy: 0.25

Bot Use: 1

Strafing Ability: -0.5

Tactics: -0.5

Data: Soft spoken, intelligent, and attractive, yet extremely brutal in the arena, Sapphire sets the hearts of many combatants racing—often for many different reasons.

Satin

Age: 24

Race: Human

Combat Enhancements

Bot Use: 1

Favorite Weapon: Shock Rifle

Strafing Ability: -0.5

Tactics: -0.3

Data: It was only two years ago that an Imperial Dreadnought captured her clan's vessel and brought its human cargo to the slave docks of Briggan IV. The dockmaster thought her a pretty one and kept her for himself but his unwanted attentions earned him a crushed larynx and a swift visit to the light at the end of the tunnel. Overseer Driak, who had always despised the dockmaster, took an instant liking to the girl and trained her for the Tournaments, where she has been ever since.

Lauren

Age: 34

Race: Human

Combat Enhancements

Accuracy: 0.5

Bot Use: 1

Strafing Ability: 1.5

Tactics: 1.5

Data: Fierce, loyal, and technically capable. Her frame may be slim but she has the most incredible reflexes. Born into a poor asteroid miner family, she became notorious by stealthily eradicating her parents' competitors in space before becoming a full-time Tournament warrior. Her soft side? It has been rumored she'd do anything to defend her high-school sweetheart, Brock.

Wraith

Age: 27

Race: Human

Combat Enhancements

Accuracy: -0.1

Aggressiveness: 0.2

Bot Use: 1

Favorite Weapon: Rocket Launcher

Jumpiness: 0.9

Strafing Ability: 0.5

Tactics: -0.2

Data: A participant in the Tournaments since the age of 19, Wraith has taken part in some of the most savage battles fought on the arena floor. Considering his long history of combat, and the injuries he has incurred, it begs the question of which may be more scarred: his body or his mind.

Torch

Age: 28

Race: Human

Combat Enhancements

  Accuracy: -0.35

  Aggressiveness: 0.1

  Bot Use: 1

  Strafing Ability: 0.9

  Tactics: 0.75

Data: He's not much for talking, but when you need to give orders, you don't want to be yelling over your men. If there's a point to be made, Torch prefers to make it with raw firepower.

Romulus

Age: 26

Race: Human

Combat Enhancements

  Accuracy: -0.3

  Aggressiveness: 0.25

  Bot Use: 1

  Favorite Weapon: Flak Cannon

  Strafing Ability: 0.7

  Tactics: 0.5

Data: Supported by his twin brother, Romulus has proven that with the right team behind you a good leader can go anywhere. So what if his brother feels a little jealous now and then, and maybe they start taking shots at each other. That's what the cloning tank's for, right?

Remus

Age: 26

Race: Human

Combat Enhancements

  Accuracy: -0.3

  Bot Use: 1

  Favorite Weapon: BioRifle

  Strafing Ability: 0.75

  Tactics: 0.85

Data: Being a twin in the Tournaments isn't so bad, as long as you're on the same side. If you think it's hard to have to face a brother in the arena, try it when he's also got your face. One thing makes it easier though. He's a real jackass.

Brock

Age: 45

Race: Human

Combat Enhancements

  Accuracy: 0.5

  Bot Use: 1

  Strafing Ability: 1.0

  Tactics: 2.0

Data: Fresh from the interstellar academy, a scion from a rich Martian family. It is rumored he killed his mentor during training but had his father bribe the authorities. Can be a hothead, but mostly tends to do things by the book.

Malcolm (ThunderCrash)

Age: 42

Race: Human

Combat Enhancements

Accuracy: 0.5

Bot Use: 1

Strafing Ability: 2.0

Tactics: 2.0

Data: Attention! This character is only available once certain criteria are met in the Single Player Tournament! Needs no introduction—most famous veteran of the Tournaments, recognized on every planet. With the typical calm pride of the Earth-born, and strong sense of loyalty, Malcolm is a true survivor and born leader.

Othello (ThunderCrash)

Age: 34

Race: Human

Combat Enhancements

Accuracy: -0.1

Bot Use: 3

Combat Style: 0.1

Favorite Weapon: Flak Cannon

Strafing Ability: 0.3

Tactics: 0.5

Data: Othello's superior combat abilities were evident at an early age, and he was trained to become a member of the elite ThunderCrash force from the age of nine.

Jakob (ThunderCrash)

Age: 31

Race: Human

Combat Enhancements

Bot Use: 2

Combat Style: -0.4

Favorite Weapon: Shock Rifle

Data: Little is known about Jakob's origins, except that he grew up in the fringe mining worlds along the Centaur Rim.

Azure (ThunderCrash)

Age: 39

Race: Human

Combat Enhancements

Accuracy: -0.05

Bot Use: 3

Combat Style: -0.3

Favorite Weapon: BioRifle

Strafing Ability: 0.65

Tactics: 0.5

Data: Born into an extremely rich family, Azure has had the benefit of training from the top fighters of her time. Physical engineering from the best hospitals has enhanced her abilities to the limit of perfection.

Aryss (ThunderCrash)

Age: 27

Race: Human

Combat Enhancements

  Accuracy: 0.05

  Bot Use: 3

  Combat Style: -0.1

  Favorite Weapon:
  Minigun

  Strafing Ability: 0.45

  Tactics: 0.3

Data: A former hot-shot pilot, Aryss found that her skill and agility worked well on the battlefield, earning her a spot on the ThunderCrash team.

Riker (ThunderCrash)

Age: 31

Race: Human

Combat Enhancements

  Bot Use: 3

  Combat Style: -0.1

  Favorite Weapon:
  Rocket Launcher

  Tactics: 1.0

Data: Riker is a walking fusion of tactics and style. He always tries to find new ways of killing his opponents and has won multiple awards for creative improvisation.

Annika (ThunderCrash)

Age: 28

Race: Human

Combat Enhancements

  Accuracy: 0.2

  Bot Use: 3

  Combat Style: -0.2

  Favorite Weapon:
  Sniper Rifle

  Strafing Ability: -0.65

  Tactics: -0.1

Data: Annika's sister, a miner, was killed due to incompetent Liandri management in the depths of Vulcana 32. She joined the ThunderCrash to help win the Tournament so she can bring a class action lawsuit against the Corporation and make them pay for the death of her sibling.

Tamika (ThunderCrash)

Age: 25

Race: Human

Combat Enhancements

  Accuracy: -0.2

  Bot Use: 3

  Combat Style: 0.2

  Favorite Weapon:
  Rocket Launcher

  Strafing Ability: 0.75

  Tactics: 0.8

Data: Tamika's mother left her at an early age, and she was raised in a house full of men where she was hardened by years of abuse. Bitter beyond belief, she is a hard combatant with a penchant for obliterating male contestants.

Unreal TOURNAMENT 2004

Outlaw (Hellions)

Age: 32

Race: Human

Combat Enhancements

Accuracy: 0.15

Bot Use: 3

Combat Style: 0.1

Favorite Weapon:
Flak Cannon

Jumpiness: 0.2

Strafing Ability: -0.1

Tactics: 0.2

Data: Outlaw was recruited into the Hellions after he reputedly went on a cross-galaxy crime spree in which he murdered nearly 300 civilians.

Garrett (Hellions)

Age: 37

Race: Human

Combat Enhancements

Accuracy: 0.15

Bot Use: 3

Combat Style: -0.1

Favorite Weapon:
Rocket Launcher

Jumpiness: 0.8

Strafing Ability: 0.3

Tactics: 0.7

Data: Garrett has been a Hellion since birth. A real ladies man, he attracts quite a bit of non-Hellion fans due to his gruff demeanor.

Zarina (Hellions)

Age: 24

Race: Human

Combat Enhancements

Accuracy: -0.1

Bot Use: 3

Strafing Ability: 1.0

Tactics: 0.7

Data: Zarina is the original wild child. She's a regular party machine and she often fights while intoxicated. She believes it gives her an edge.

Kaela (Hellions)

Age: 28

Race: Human

Combat Enhancements

Bot Use: 2

Strafing Ability: 0.4

Tactics: 0.9

Data: Kaela is as nasty as they come. If her foul language doesn't kill you, her weapon will do the job.

Kane (Hellions)

Age: 29

Race: Human

Combat Enhancements

  Accuracy: 0.1

  Bot Use: 3

  Combat Style: 0.3

  Jumpiness: 0.7

  Strafing Ability: -0.3

  Tactics: -0.2

Data: Not only is Kane psychotic but he's got multiple personalities that change his fighting style instantly.

Baird (Hellions)

Age: 26

Race: Human

Combat Enhancements

  Accuracy: -0.1

  Bot Use: 3

  Combat Style: 0.1

  Jumpiness: 0.35

  Strafing Ability: 0.3

  Tactics: 0.2

Data: They say it's the quiet ones you have to look out for. Baird is unusually quiet until the time comes to fight. He then turns into a raging motormouth until he's decimated every single opponent.

Rae (Hellions)

Age: 23

Race: Human

Combat Enhancements

  Accuracy: -0.2

  Bot Use: 3

  Strafing Ability: 0.6

  Tactics: 0.2

Data: Rae and her sister Greith were found as infants by the Hellions, who were scavenging a destroyed colony suspected to have been ransacked by the Skaarj.

Greith (Hellions)

Age: 23

Race: Human

Combat Enhancements

  Accuracy: -0.2

  Bot Use: 3

  Favorite Weapon: Shock Rifle

  Tactics: 0.8

Data: Greith and her sister Rae were found as infants by the Hellions, who were scavenging a destroyed colony suspected to have been ransacked by the Skaarj.

Ophelia (Hellions)

Age: 23

Race: Human

Combat Enhancements

Accuracy: 0.05

Bot Use: 3

Favorite Weapon:
Link Gun

Strafing Ability: 0.4

Tactics: -0.1

Data: Ophelia has risen quickly to a prominent position with the Hellions and was the youngest Hellion selected for participation in the Tournament team. She is already credited with the development of important new tactics using her favorite weapon, the link gun.

Additional Competitors

Ariel	Dragon	Janus	Perish	Tiberius
Charisma	Faith	Kain	Phantom	Xantares
Cinder	Gaul	Mystique	Rust	Xargon
Cipher	Gryphon	Nemesis	Silhouette	
Despair	Huntress	Nova	Stargazer	

Nightmares

Nightmares are human experiments that have gone horribly wrong. These human-alien hybrids aren't easy on the eyes, and they're not easy on their opponents either. When Species Statistics is enabled, the Nightmares suffer a small (10 percent) penalty to their ground speed and jump height, but their walking and crouching movement speeds are 50 percent and 20 percent higher than the average, respectively.

Domina

Age: 54

Race: Homo sapiens Medusae

Combat Enhancements

  Accuracy: 0.3

  Bot Use: 1

  Strafing Ability: 0.5

Data: A walking deathtrap that preys on the compassion of her victims, Domina prowls the dark corners of a thousand worlds seeking enemies of the Empire. Like all members of the Vigilance Force, Domina possesses the unique ability to ferret out treason where none has been committed. Some say she can hear guilty thoughts, others say she can find the threads of dissent woven deep into the DNA. Whatever it may be, if the shadows speak to you in a child's voice one day, run, and never stop running as long as you have breath in your body.

Subversa

Age: 38

Race: Homo sapiens Medusae

Combat Enhancements

  Accuracy: 0.2

  Bot Use: 1

Data: Her eyes are devoid of life, empty orbs that take in the world with an unfeeling gaze. A thin trail of spittle runs untended from her tightly gagged mouth, yet she never rubs it away. Only one thing brings a spark of vitality to this tortured soul: the suffering of others.

Lilith

Age: 19

Race: Cybernetic Human

Combat Enhancements

  Bot Use: 1

  Jumpiness: 0.8

  Strafing Ability: 0.5

Data: Having lost her legs during an attack on an Imperial medical supply transport, Lilith was captured and sentenced to deletion of personality at the Purgatory penal facility. With her mind and body rebuilt from the ground up, she now serves as a bounty hunter for the Empire.

Fate

Age: Unknown

Race: Cybernetic Human

Combat Enhancements

  Accuracy: 0.3

  Bot Use: 1

  Tactics: 0.5

Data: As a child, her dreams were filled with ghoulish monstrosities, nightmares that craved the sustenance of human suffering. Decades later only the nightmare remains, and the innocence of childhood is a fairy tale for the weak.

Brutalis

Age: 24

Race: Homo sapien Taratis

Combat Enhancements

Accuracy: 0.3

Bot Use: 1

Tactics: 1.0

Data: As strong as he is ugly, Brutalis was part of an experiment to hybridize Human and Taratic prisoners into a highly intelligent killing machine. The project was scrapped after proving to be more successful than anyone could have imagined.

Ravage

Age: Unknown

Race: Homo sapien Taratis

Combat Enhancements

Aggressiveness: 0.4

Bot Use: 1

Favorite Weapon: Flak Cannon

Data: If League regulations allowed for unarmed combat, then the competition would be quite brief with Ravage involved, and very, very messy.

Mr. Crow

Age: Approx. 36

Race: Homo sapiens Medusae

Combat Enhancements

Bot Use: 1

Favorite Weapon: Rocket Launcher

Jumpiness: 0.6

Data: Mr. Crow brings culture and style to a sport as brutal and decadent as any in history. The fact that he is a raving lunatic with a taste for the bizarre only adds to his charms in the eyes of the public.

Harlequin

Age: 34

Race: Homo sapiens Medusae

Combat Enhancements

Accuracy: 0.3

Bot Use: 1

Strafing Ability: 0.7

Data: Ever wonder why children are afraid of clowns? Now you know.

Abaddon

Age: 31

Race: Human

Combat Enhancements

Accuracy: 0.2

Bot Use: 3

Favorite Weapon: Minigun

Strafing Ability: 0.5

Tactics: 1.0

Data: Abaddon, the leader of the Black Legion, is the result of extensive genetic manipulation experiments. The sponsoring corporation considered the experiment a failure, because although he is a highly efficient killer, the constant pain wracking his body is expected to considerably shorten his lifespan, reducing the commercial potential for the technology.

Additional Competitors

Name	Jumpiness	Strafing Ability	Accuracy	Name	Jumpiness	Strafing Ability	Accuracy
Avarice	—	0.5	0.3	Mortis	—	0.5	0.35
Circe	0.9	0.8	0.3	Samedi	—	0.8	0.3
Darkling	—	0.5	0.3	Septis	—	0.8	0.3
Jigsaw	0.75	0.8	0.3	Succubus	—	0.5	0.3

Skaarj

The Skaaj are a fierce, muscular, and incredibly savage hybrid race of which little is known. However, tournament watchers have been keen to view the ferociousness the Skaaj bring to even the smallest skirmish. In spite of their weighty appearance, the Skaaj are extremely agile (thanks in part to their incredible lower body structure). With Species statistics enabled, Skaaj speed up 10 percent faster, are 20 percent more maneuverable while airborne, and 20 percent quicker along the ground than the average human. This is backed up by an enhanced aerial dodge of 10 percent, and a 10 percent higher jump. All this maneuverability comes at a price though; damage inflicted is around 10 percent less, and their large target size means their maximum health is 20 percent lower.

Dominator

Age: Unknown

Race: Skaarj

Combat Enhancements

Aggressiveness: 0.4

Bot Use: 3

Combat Style: 0.4

Favorite Weapon: Rocket Launcher

Jumpiness: 1.0

Strafing Ability: 0.5

Data: Brutal and cunning, Dominator exemplifies the Skaarj warrior code.

Guardian

Age: Unknown

Race: Skaarj

Combat Enhancements

Aggressiveness: 0.4

Bot Use: 3

Combat Style: 0.2

Favorite Weapon: Rocket Launcher

Jumpiness: 1.0

Strafing Ability: 0.5

Data: Disdainful of inferior species, Guardian seeks to demonstrate the superiority of the Skaarj. In his spare time, he enjoys hunting Nali and other servant races.

Skakruk

Age: Unknown

Race: Skaarj

Combat Enhancements

Accuracy: -0.1

Aggressiveness: 0.35

Bot Use: 3

Combat Style: 0.5

Favorite Weapon: Flak Cannon

Jumpiness: 0.3

Strafing Ability: 0.7

Data: Freakishly strong even for a Skaarj, Skakruk attributes his power to eating the marrow of his enemies.

Kraagesh

Age: Unknown

Race: Skaarj

Combat Enhancements

Accuracy: -0.1

Aggressiveness: 0.25

Bot Use: 3

Combat Style: 0.14

Jumpiness: 0.5

Strafing Ability: 0.2

Data: Kraagesh, "Lord of the Krall" in the Skaarj language, is famed for his effective use of Krall in subjugating other servant races.

Clan Lord

Age: Unknown

Race: Skaarj

Combat Enhancements

Accuracy: 1.0

Aggressiveness: 0.4

Bot Use: 1

Combat Style: 0.4

Jumpiness: 0.7

Strafing Ability: 1.0

Data: Attention! This character is only available once certain criteria are met in the Single Player Tournament! The Iron Skull Clan Lord is feared and revered by the Skaarj for his unmatched fighting prowess.

Drekorig

Age: Unknown

Race: Skaarj

Combat Enhancements

Aggressiveness: 0.4

Bot Use: 3

Jumpiness: 1.0

Strafing Ability: 1.0

Data: Drekorig fights in the Tournament for the honor of his Clan, which was disgraced during the Human/Skaarj Wars when the Skaarj Mothership was destroyed.

Gaargod

Age: Unknown

Race: Skaarj

Combat Enhancements

Accuracy: 0.3

Aggressiveness: 0.15

Bot Use: 3

Combat Style: 0.24

Jumpiness: 0.7

Strafing Ability: 0.3

Data: From what was once a high-status family in the Iron Skull clan, Gaargod aspires to use success in the Tournament as a springboard to crush his enemies on the Home World.

Gkublok

Age: Unknown

Race: Skaarj

Combat Enhancements

Accuracy: 0.35

Aggressiveness: 0.3

Bot Use: 3

Combat Style: 0.4

Jumpiness: 0.4

Strafing Ability: 0.4

Data: Gkublok was named "Walking Death" by the Nali during his stay on Na Pali.

Tournament Training
Basic Training

Game Types

The seven game types in *Unreal Tournament 2004* are listed below, with basic tactics for each of the main gameplay modes. We provide expert strategies from top players. Peruse the Deathmatch section for Deathmatch mode strategies.

Assault: An attacking team has a series of objectives and the defending team tries to stop them. Then the roles are reversed. The team to complete all (or more) objectives in the fastest time wins.

Onslaught: Each team starts at a base and must link PowerNodes to chain to their opponents' core, inside the enemy base. The first team to destroy the other's core wins.

Deathmatch: In this multiplayer free-for-all, the player with the most kills wins.

Capture the Flag: Your team steals the flag from your opponents' base and brings it back to your own headquarters. The first team to complete a certain number of captures wins.

Team Deathmatch: This variant is identical to Deathmatch, except you're on a team. The first team to rack up the specified number of kills wins.

Double Domination: Your team must occupy both team bases for 10 consecutive seconds to score a point. The team with the most double-occupations by the end of the time limit wins.

Bombing Run: Your goal is to carry a bomb into your opponents' base. Picture football with no downs and plenty of explosions.

Mutant: In this Deathmatch variant, the first player to kill another becomes a Mutant with superhuman powers. All other players must defeat the Mutant; the player to do this becomes the Mutant. Additionally, the player with the least points becomes the Bottom Feeder: a normal player with the ability to kill all players. The highest score wins.

Invasion: In this Deathmatch variant, the player, teamed with human or Bot colleagues, must stop continuous waves of monsters. The highest score wins.

Last Man Standing: Each player has the same number of lives in this Deathmatch. Once your lives are used up, you become a spectator. The last player alive wins.

Assault Basics

This classic match type returns. The two teams are split up into Attackers and Defenders. The Attackers try to complete a series of objectives. After this first objective is completed, the spawn point usually moves farther into the level, and a second objective appears. Objectives appear until a final objective completes the level. The Attackers' aim is to finish the final objective in the fastest possible time.

The Defenders must hold each objective as long as possible, and retreat if their current objective is compromised. Then the Defenders move to the next objective, and attempt to hold that. This continues until the time runs out or all objectives have been overrun.

Once a match finishes, a second match begins, with the Attackers and Defenders switching sides. There are two criteria for victory: if the Attackers didn't complete all objectives, the other team must reach at least that point within the time limit. Otherwise, complete all objectives with a faster overall time.

Levels usually consist of multiple zones with the Attackers at one end and the objective at the other, with the Defenders. Usually you have one objective, but sometimes there are two. In addition, some maps have bonus objectives that don't need to be completed and don't affect victory conditions, but do aid in the Attackers' overall strategy.

Objectives appear as triangles within circular targets. Regular objectives are shown as a line triangle. Bonus objectives are shown as a filled-in triangle. If you are on the same level or above your objective, the triangle is your team color. If you are underneath your objective, the triangle changes to yellow. When anyone from the attacking side comes within 50 meters of the objective, a large exclamation point appears inside the triangle. When you are within a few meters of the objective, the triangle turns into an icon. The icon shape depends on what needs to be done to complete the objective, as shown below:

Icon	Remarks
Triangle	Objective to reach
! Triangle	Objective within 50 meters of Attackers
Hand	Enter this opening to complete objective
Large Target	Shoot this to complete objective
Human Outline	Stand and wait at this point to complete objective
Use Command	Press Use to complete this objective
Ball	Pick up this object to complete this objective
Red Car	Location of a vehicle

Basic Assault strategy varies wildly from map to map, but Attackers need teammates on both offense and defense and should learn creative methods of completing each objective. Find multiple routes throughout the level and know each subsequent objective location.

Defenders should know where they will spawn and how to reach subsequent spawn points. Learn when to give up holding a location and move on (or suicide) to the next. Have camping or sniping spots lined up. Work as a team, with perhaps one maniac who waylays the Attackers. Grab all the good power-ups so the Attackers cannot use them.

Onslaught Basics

Onslaught matches involve the most players and the largest levels. Each team begins equidistant from the other, in similar bases. The bases feature vehicles and a central core. Defending the core is paramount, as the first team to destroy the other's base wins. However, an impenetrable energy field shields both cores from attack. The only way to drop the energy field is to divert power away from the core, by rerouting a series of PowerNodes.

If neither team has destroyed the other team's PowerCore before the round ends, the round goes into Overtime. During Overtime, each team's PowerCore loses energy based on how many PowerNodes are captured. If your team controls most of the PowerNodes in the map, then your PowerCore will lose much less energy. If your team can control all the PowerNodes on the map, your PowerCore won't lose any energy, but the enemy teams will lose energy very quickly. There is an incentive to win before Overtime, however—your team scores two points for a win before Overtime and only one point for a win during Overtime. By default, Onslaught matches require three team points to win a full match.

A map in the screen's top right shows the bases and available PowerNodes. White nodes haven't been captured yet. Your side owns nodes in your team's colors, and your enemy controls those in the opponents' colors. When the action begins, claim PowerNodes nearest your base. To capture a node, run over it. After the PowerNode's energy level rises (help this with the link gun), the node changes to your team's color. When this happens, a few vehicles specific to each node spawn. Only your team can access these, unless a teammate drives, then leaves, a vehicle.

After you claim and activate the initial node, the line to your base changes to your team's colors, and you can continue to claim nodes that are attached to any you own. These flash on your map. You can't claim other PowerNodes until there's a direct link between them and nodes you control. Continue until there's a direct link from one of your nodes to an enemy node. Attack the enemy PowerNode by shooting its central energy column until it becomes neutral. Pour energy into it until it changes to your color.

Continue until you reach the node that links to your opponents' base. Claim this node, and the base's core becomes vulnerable—blast it with all available ordnance. If your core is attacked, either wipe out the attackers, or sever the link by reclaiming or destroying the node linked to the base. The action continues until a core is destroyed.

After you understand the premise of capturing and keeping PowerNodes, learn how the enemy can gain access to your base (where is the most important node?). Check the node link routes; some aren't apparent. Push a recon group to the next node you intend to claim so that when your main force powers up a previous node, you can claim and link to it.

Learn which weapons and vehicles appear near your node (out-of-the-way nodes often spawn more impressive vehicles). Learn the strengths and weaknesses of the vehicle types, such as the Raptor's flying capabilities (but lack of armor). Watch the maps and formulate a coherent team strategy.

Deathmatch Basics

Deathmatch games are free-for-alls where the goal is to rack up as many kills as possible in the time limit. Each time you manage to kill an opponent, you earn a point (a "frag"). Each time you accidentally kill yourself, you lose a point.

Win a Deathmatch game in one of two ways: Be the first player to earn the number of points specified in the Score Limit on the Round Settings Menu, or be the player with the highest number of points when the time limit expires. Hiding in corners keeps you alive, but it also keeps you from earning points.

Capture the Flag Basics

Capture the Flag is a classic team-versus-team mode in which each team has a base at one end of the level. Each base contains a flag in the team's color. Run into the enemy base, pick up that flag by running over it, and bring it to your base. Your team scores one point for each time you capture the opposing team's flag, if your own team's flag is in your base when you return with the enemy flag.

If you are killed while carrying a flag, the flag remains on the level where you died. To recover your team's flag, kill the opposing player carrying it, then run over the flag to return it to your base.

Work as a team. Keep at least one player guarding your base to kill any opponent trying to take your flag. Send at least two players after an opponent's flag so they can cover each other. If the level has high ground, send a player with a lightning gun to snipe at any opponent who runs across open ground to grab your flag.

If the opposing team grabs your flag, hunt down the flag carrier. Send a player or two to the enemy base to grab that flag, because your opponents can't score if they don't possess their own flag.

The team that reaches the score limit first wins. If the time limit expires before the score limit is reached, the team with the higher score wins. If both teams are tied, you go into sudden death overtime and the first team to score wins.

Team Deathmatch

In Team Deathmatch, the first team to reach the score limit with all members' combined scores is the winner. Unless you have enabled the Friendly Fire option under Game Settings, you cannot injure your teammates.

Travel in packs because it's easier to kill opponents when you can pin them down with crossfire. However, sticking too close to your teammates leaves you vulnerable to rocket and other splash damage attacks.

Double Domination

Like Capture the Flag and Bombing Run matches, Double Domination matches place two teams on a level with two bases. At each base's center is a trigger colored red or blue depending on which team owns the base. Run over this trigger to take possession of the base. Hold both bases for 10 seconds to score a point.

Simultaneously play offense and defense. Split your team in two, with each half responsible for one base. Don't waste time running around—only the bases matter. Dig in around a base and destroy any enemy who tries to take it.

The first team to reach the score limit wins. If the time limit expires, the team with the most points wins. If both teams are tied at the end of the time limit, the next team to score is the winner.

Bombing Run

Bombing Run is like football with heavy artillery. Pick up the yellow ball, carry it into the enemy's base, and either run or fire the ball through that goal. You score three points for firing the ball through the enemy goal and seven points for running it in.

When you are holding the ball, two things happen: You automatically equip the ball launcher (which appears only during Bombing Run games) and you cannot switch to any other weapon. Also, your health regenerates at about three points per second, enough to withstand moderate fire, but not enough to save you from a rocket or a lightning gun blast.

Pass the ball by firing it to a teammate. Have a teammate lurk around the enemy goal to receive passes, but also protect your own goal and maintain a good mid-field presence so you can get the ball.

35

If a player is killed while carrying the ball, the ball remains where the player was killed and any other player can pick it up. If the ball is dropped or fired off of the level, it reappears in its original location, around the middle of the level.

When your team has the ball, move your players down the field to pick off enemy players, and clear a path for the ball carrier, or receive a pass. When the opposing team has the ball, fall back to your own goal, because that's where the ball carrier will head.

The first team to reach the score limit wins. If the time limit expires before the score limit is reached, the team with more points wins. If both teams are tied at the end of the time limit, the first team to score in sudden death overtime wins.

Basic Controls

Know your controls. The game has a default control scheme, but customize your control setup to your play style. The game has more than three dozen commands, so try a few setup layouts and come up with a setup that works for you. To customize your control scheme or view the default commands, see the Controls section under Settings.

Movement

You must keep moving to survive. Master the art of moving quickly.

Running

By default, your character always runs. Run forward or backward with the Move Forward/Move Backward buttons. You run in the direction you're facing. Good choices for Run buttons are the up and down arrow keys or the classic "W" and "S" keys.

> **NOTE**
>
> This guide uses generic terms for actions—such as fire, alt-fire, and jump—instead of giving you the default button for the action and expecting you to translate that into your own control setup.

Walking

Use the Walk button in conjunction with the Move Forward and Move Backward buttons to move around narrow ledges and similar areas where it's better to be safe than speedy. You cannot fall off ledges while walking.

Strafing

Strafing—moving to the right or left while facing forward—separates pros from rookies. Use the Strafe Right/Strafe Left buttons to move from side to side while battling opponents or when rounding corners. This keeps you targeted on your foes and allows you to dodge your enemies' attacks. A moving target is harder to hit. Many players map the Strafe Right/Strafe Left commands to the right and left arrow keys.

Jumping

Use the Jump button to hop. If you're moving, you jump horizontally as well as vertically. Jump over small obstacles, jump repeatedly up slopes, and jump while running from enemies so it's harder for them to hit you. To double jump, hit the Jump button at the apex of your jump.

Dodging

Press the Strafe Right/Strafe Left keys twice to dodge. Dodging is faster than strafing. To wall dodge, jump against a wall and double-tap the Strafe button that propels you away from the wall.

Crouching

The crouch is invaluable when you are camped out with a lightning gun to snipe careless enemies. Stand behind a short obstacle, then press and hold the Crouch button to duck behind it for cover. Release the button to pop up and shoot someone in the head. You can move forward and backward slowly while crouching.

Driving

In Onslaught matches, you can pilot various vehicles. The Inventory and Ordnance chapter details the vehicles and their abilities. Pressing your Use button while near a vehicle places you at the wheel. If a vehicle has side doors and multiple seats, or players already occupying positions, you need to approach from an empty side. In some vehicles you can fire a weapon while driving. Switch between available seats (such as the driver, passenger, and turret gunner) by pressing the 1, 2, or 3 keys.

Respawning

When an opponent pummels the health out of you, you die. Death is temporary. Hit the Fire button to respawn elsewhere in the level with full health. You lose your weapons and ammunition.

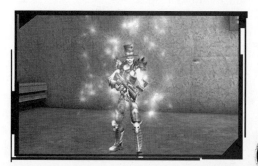

Adrenaline Combos

As you kill opponents, capture flags, and pick up adrenaline capsules, the adrenaline meter fills. When it is full, the adrenaline pill in the top right of the HUD blinks. This means you can perform an adrenaline combo. See the table for more information on how to perform adrenaline combos.

Adrenaline Combos		
Button(s)	**Combo Name**	**Effect**
Move forward (x4)	**Speed**	A short burst of speed helps you catch up to or run away from enemies
Right, right, left, left	**Invisibility**	Makes your character temporarily invisible, though not invulnerable
Move back (x4)	**Booster (Defense)**	Your character briefly regenerates health
Move forward (x2), move back (x2)	**Berserk**	Allows your character to shoot more quickly

After you activate an adrenaline combo, your adrenaline starts counting down from 100. At zero, the adrenaline combo wears off. Picking up adrenaline capsules and killing opponents increases your adrenaline.

Looking

Getting a good view of the arena is important. Use the mouse to control your view. Get used to looking around you as you move.

With Mouse

Using the mouse is the quickest and easiest way to look around. Adjust the sensitivity of the mouse to your own taste. Unless you have enabled the Invert Mouse Y setting (see Input Settings), you look in the direction you move the mouse.

With Keyboard

You can control your view with the keyboard as well—configure the look up, down, right, and left keys in the Looking submenu of the Control Settings menu.

 **CAUTION**

The four directions allowed by the keyboard can't match the 360 degrees offered by the mouse.

Weapons

Having the right weapon and being able to equip it instantly is important. See Inventory and Ordnance for information on each weapon in the game.

Fire

The Fire button is one of the most-used buttons, and most players assign it to the left mouse button. Clicking it fires your equipped weapon's primary attack. Many weapons fire continuously if you hold down the button. See the individual weapon descriptions for details on each weapon's primary fire mode.

Alt-Fire

Many weapons have a secondary (or alternate) fire mode. See each weapon's description to learn their alt-fire commands. The right mouse button is a natural choice for the alt-fire function.

Equipping Weapons

Every weapon you pick up is available in your weapon inventory if you have ammunition for it. You can equip one weapon at a time. Use the Next Weapon/Previous Weapon buttons to cycle through them in the order of preference you determined in the Weapons-Priorities submenu. If you have a mouse wheel, consider using wheel up and wheel down to switch weapons.

The Best Weapon button brings up your favorite, as determined in the Priorities submenu. You can assign each weapon a number key in the Weapons-Bindings submenu of the Control Settings menu. Press that number key to equip that weapon.

Weapons, Items, and Lockers

The Inventory and Ordnance chapter details these. Weapons float above spawning points around every map. You cannot possess two identical weapons (with the exception of the Assault Rifle). Items include health or ammunition. New to this season are weapon lockers (available in Assault and Onslaught), which allow you to pick up one to six weapons, depending on what is hooked on the locker.

Throw Weapon

When you run out of ammo for a weapon, throw the weapon in the enemies' path as bait. In cooperative multiplayer games, toss a weapon on the ground so a buddy can pick it up. You can't replenish your ammunition by picking up a weapon from a weapon spawn point or locker, so throw the weapon away and pick up a fully loaded one.

39

Environmental Assets and Hazards

You have a couple of environmental assets and various environmental hazards to worry about.

Jump Pads and Teleports

White or red pads with shimmering arrows allow you to leap larger distances than normal. Use jump pads to reach areas you can't double jump to. Teleports move you to a different location. You can double jump off a jump pad, but not a teleport, although you can telefrag an enemy only after teleporting.

Sloping Boards

Many levels have stone or wooden boards leaning against walls. Use a wall jump to leap onto this board and again off it, onto an upper platform or ledge above. This maneuver isn't easy!

Falling and Bottomless Ravines

Don't drop more than one story or you'll lose a few health. This amount increases the farther you fall, and at around 10 stories, you'll splat when you hit unless you whip out your shield gun. The larger the level, the better the chance of a long fall (such as if your Raptor is struck in mid-flight). Be careful when moving around ravines, especially if you can't see the bottom. Falling into a bottomless ravine means death unless you translocate as you fall, aiming the pod at terra firma. Always blast an opponent off a ledge or ravine; the shock combo is great for this attack.

Lava

Step in a lava pool, and you sizzle to death in two seconds, although you can leap out quickly and survive if you're near a low ledge. Push enemies into lava with shock combos.

Water

You can dive into water and use weapons. However, you move slowly and can be attacked easily as you surface and climb out. Don't spend more than 30 seconds in water or you begin to drown, losing around two to five health a second.

Fast-Moving Ground

If you're on a vehicle skimming the surface, such as the giant convoy in the Assault map, don't fall off; these vehicles move so fast that you're flayed alive as you land.

Communication

Communication with your teammates is essential. If you're playing a LAN game, your teammates might be in the same room. In internet games, you use the game's built-in communication features. *Unreal Tournament 2004* also introduces real-time radio microphone chatter, which is a godsend in the heat of combat. Refer to your instruction manual for full details.

Say

The Say button brings up a prompt at the bottom of the screen. Type in a message and press Enter to send it to every player in the game. Vocal recognition software then transforms your typing into actual words.

Team-Say

Team-say works the same as Say, except the message goes only to your teammates. Send quick strategy notes to your teammates without worrying about your opponents intercepting them.

Speech Menu

The Speech menu key brings up a list of preset phrases. Warn off a teammate who's mistaken you for an enemy, taunt a fallen adversary, and much more.

Gestures

To silently send a message to nearby teammates, use a gesture. It requires only one keystroke, and your teammate doesn't have to take their eyes off the action. Available gestures include Throat Cut, Ass Smack, Halt, and Cheer.

Spectator

Spectator mode allows you to watch the action without taking part in it. It's a good way for new players to watch the pros at work and pick up some new and nasty ideas.

Toggle Follow-View

The Toggle Camera button switches your camera view from first person to third person.

Switching Characters

Switch between different characters' perspectives with the Follow Next and Previous Perspective buttons. This lets you see the game through your competitors' eyes so you can analyze their play styles. Find a character who is pulling off impressive moves and jump into that character's perspective.

HUD

The heads-up display (HUD) is a screen overlay that contains relevant information about your character (health, ammo levels, and adrenaline) and your game performance.

Toggle HUD

By default, HUD is visible. To turn it off and on, press the Toggle HUD button.

Grow/Shrink HUD

Use the Shrink HUD button to keep the information from taking up too much screen space. Press the Grow HUD button to return it to its original size.

Toggle Weapon

By default, your weapon appears onscreen from a first-person perspective. To hide the weapon and clear more screen space, press the Toggle Weapon button. This does not affect your weapon or its accuracy, because the crosshairs still appear in the screen's center.

Miscellaneous

Pause

The Pause button freezes the action. This only works in single player.

Screenshot

The Screenshot button takes a snapshot of the screen and saves it in your computer's *Unreal Tournament 2004* system folder. Capture images of frantic battles and mess around with them.

Console

You can set the Console button to another Button via INI editing.

Show Menu

The Show menu button brings up an in-game menu that allows you to continue or forfeit the game, switch teams in mid-game, or access the Settings menu.

Scores

The Scoreboard button brings up the scores list that appears automatically after you get killed. It lets you check your progress without having to eat a rocket.

Main Menu

The main menu has seven options:

Single Player: Begin a single-player game with Bots as allies against computer-controlled opponents.

Join Game: Join an existing Deathmatch, CTF, Bombing Run, or Double Domination game through LAN or internet.

Host Game: Start a multiplayer game and invite other online gamers to join.

Instant Action: Jump right into a Deathmatch, play a quick round of Capture the Flag, or fire up one of several other quick games.

Community: Receive the latest news, modifications, gameplay enhancements, and other interesting information from the *Unreal Tournament* community.

Settings: Configure controls, audio and video settings, and network options. Refer to your instruction manual for further details.

Exit: Quits you out of the game.

Single Player

Single-player mode puts you in charge of a team of Bots with one mission: to defeat and humiliate every other team in Capture the Flag, Double Domination, Team Deathmatch, Assault, and Bombing Run matches. As you complete matches, your team rises or falls in the tournament rankings depending on your performance.

Success depends not only on your own running and gunning skills, but also on your ability to build a solid team. Between matches, you can hire and fire team members or reassign them to different positions. For more information on single-player mode, refer to the Single-Player Strategies chapter.

Playing Online

Choosing to Join Game from the main menu takes you to the Server Browser menu, where you can look for online games in progress and join any that has room for an additional player. Play a quick round of Deathmatch/Team Deathmatch, Capture the Flag, Bombing Run, Assault, Onslaught or Double Domination with up to 32 human players. The Server Browser menu offers important info about the game you're joining, so read it carefully.

If you want total control over your online play experience, choose Host Multiplayer Game from the main menu. The Multiplayer Host menu allows you to determine which type of game you want to host, which maps you want to play on, various unique rules and mutators for the game, and many more options. Refer to your instruction manual for more details.

Instant Action

Instant Action mode allows you to jump straight into a single-player game, without setting up a team. It is essentially the single-player version of Join Game. Instant Action mode offers seven games and three Deathmatch variations: Deathmatch (plus Invasion, Mutant, and Last Man Standing), Team Deathmatch, Capture the Flag, Bombing Run, Assault, Onslaught, and Double Domination. There are no rankings in Instant Action—it's all about quick matches, furious action, and reducing Bots to bite-sized chunks. Refer to your instruction manual for further details.

Game Strategies

The basic premise is simple: Shoot everyone who isn't on your side while avoiding getting killed. That's easier said than done. Learn the basic game strategies and practice. Knowing how to perform these maneuvers is one thing; pulling them off is another.

Keep Moving

The game may seem fast and overwhelming at first, but don't stand still and carefully set up shots. Moving is the best way to pick up weapons and ammunition, and the only way to avoid enemy fire.

Strafe

Strafing is the key to victory. Strafe to the sides so you can keep your crosshairs pointed on an enemy as you dodge their fire. Strafe around blind corners so your weapon is pointed in the right direction when you come around the corner.

Side-to-Side Strafing

Strafing from side to side is an effective basic strategy. Vary the length of time you move in each direction so your moves aren't predictable. Try to dodge incoming fire. Also, keep the crosshairs trained on your enemies and blast them into oblivion. When you can do both, you're becoming a true *Unreal Tournament 2004* player.

Circle-Strafing

Circle-strafing is an advanced technique, but players who master it gain a huge advantage. Using the Strafe Right/Strafe Left buttons, strafe in a circle around enemies, keeping your crosshairs trained on them.

Use the Move Forward/Move Backward buttons to keep distance between you and the enemy, and vary the direction of your circle-strafe to keep your opponent from predicting your movements. This allows you to inflict maximum damage on your opponent while staying mobile enough to be a difficult target.

To pick off a circle-strafing enemy, put some distance between you and aim carefully.

Run Backward

If an opponent attacks you with a weapon designed for close-range use, such as the minigun or the flak cannon, use the Move Backward button to run backward, and keep your crosshairs trained on your foe. While running backward, use a more precise weapon, such as the lightning gun or shock rifle, to pick them off. Use this in areas without pits or gaps; it's easy to backpedal off the arena and fall to your doom.

Steep Climbs

Some inclined surfaces are too steep to run up. You can scale some by pressing the Jump button repeatedly as you run up the incline. Don't stop jumping before reaching the top, or you will slide back down.

Duck and Cover

If you have the lightning gun and plan to do some camping, pick a location with a short, solid obstacle between you and your target. Fire a shot or two, then duck behind the obstacle. Most weapons fire in a straight line, so keep a solid barrier between you and the enemies.

Watch Your Ammo

When the action gets fast, it's easy to hold down the Fire button and waste your ammunition. Pick your shots carefully, fire in bursts, and switch to a new weapon when your ammo count gets low.

When all your weapons are low on ammunition, go on an ammo hunt. If you keep moving through the level, and know where the ammo pickups are, you should get all the ammo you need.

Elevator Jumps

Many levels have elevator platforms. Get on a rising elevator and jump just as you reach the top to perform an elevator jump. This propels you much farther than a normal jump.

Creative Weapon Use

Most of the weapons have alt-fire modes, but some of them can be used in unconventional ways. For example, if

you point the shield gun down and fire its primary weapon mode, you propel yourself into the air. Additional maneuvers are shown below, and in the Inventory and Ordnance chapter.

Announcing Fervor

The announcer will congratulate you on incredible shows of skill, bravado, and downright lunacy. In fact, the announcer speaks a few choice words after certain circumstances are met. Here's what it means:

Kill Skills

If you mow down two targets within around two seconds, the announcer mentions this "combo." If you "chain" your kills together, your

associated kills grow higher, and the announcer gets more giddy:

Combo Kill Chains (Enemies Defeated)	Kill Skills
2	Double Kill
3	Multi Kill
4	Mega Kill
5	Ultra Kill
6	MONSTER KILL!!!
7	LUDICROUS!!!
8	HOLY S#@T!

To achieve a higher combo kill chain, you need a good deal of health, supreme aiming, a room overly populated with enemies (such as a one-on-one Deathmatch level with 30 spawned foes), and a safe spot to demolish from. Close combat, ideally with the flak cannon in a small chamber, is the easiest way.

Cheating Death

Continuously cut down the enemy during a match without dying, and the announcer lets everyone know how impressive your death-cheating skills are with the following:

Enemies Killed Without Dying	Death Cheating Accolade
Causing First death	First Blood
5	Killing Spree!
10	Rampage!
15	Dominating!

Enemies Killed Without Dying	Death Cheating Accolade
20	Unstoppable!
25	GODLIKE!
30	WICKED SICK!

Cheat death with the cunning use of sniping and camping, and by returning to the most powerful weapons and items. Don't overstretch yourself.

Vehicular Manslaughter

During Onslaught matches only, the announcer barks cool phrases if you've achieved something special using vehicles:

Explanation	Hollering
Combo kills from airborne Raptor	**TOP GUN**
Using specifically designed vehicle armaments to kill infantry	**ROADKILL**
Simple ramming of enemy infantry with vehicle	**ROAD RAGE**
Landing on enemy with vehicle	**PANCAKE**
Stealing opposing flying vehicle	**HIJACK**
Stealing opposing ground vehicle	**CARJACK**
Performing an airborne stunt	**DAREDEVIL**

Advanced Training: Complex Strategies

It's time to learn the techniques that separate the "very best" from the "quite good." These maneuvers take time to learn, and some are tricky to attempt. However, once learned, they mean game survival when you're playing against the best.

Double Jumping

Jump forward and you land quicker than if you ran to the same spot. Tap the Jump button again (double jump) and you boost farther while still airborne. Double jumping allows you to move faster and is the main way to reach objects that connect you to shortcuts to upper areas. Vary the speed of your second jump tap to vary the length of your jump. Use this technique instead of running until you perfect the dodge jump.

Dodge Jumping

Dodge jumping is how all professional tournament players get around a map. Press the directional button forward to run. But double-tap the same button to dodge. Jump immediately after the dodge to complete the technique. This allows you to cover more ground than running or double jumping, and you gain extra height to land on upper or raised areas. Combine this with other techniques (such as circle-strafing), and other directions (dodge jump to the sides or backward) to become almost impossible to predict or hit!

Wall Jumping

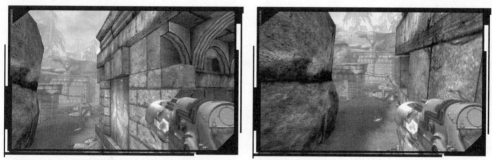

This is difficult, but it enables you to scale walls up to platforms above. Jump at a wall, or a plank leaning against the wall, then jump off it. Combine this with a dodge jump to scale sides of levels. Time the jump to coincide with the instant your feet touch the wall sides.

Air Dodging

When you're in the air, use the directional buttons to adjust your flight trajectory. This can mean the difference between being struck by rockets or dodging them, or landing on the edge of a lava pool instead of in it.

Shield Jumping

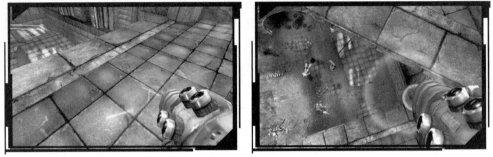

Point your shield gun at the ground, fill up the power meter, and release it as you jump. This allows you to bounce onto higher ledges than you could reach normally. You take some damage using this maneuver, but you can grab powerful items using otherwise impossible routes.

Assault Strategies

Every Assault map has its own series of objectives. Otherwise most of the main and Deathmatch strategies apply to these matches. Stick together, splitting up only when necessary. Use the willo-the-wisp function (M or N) to show the most direct route to the next objective as you learn the maps. This glowing route marker doesn't show optional objectives.

Onslaught Strategies

- Your overall plan is to split into three forces. A main team lands and links the first PowerNode. A second infantry and ground vehicle force heads for the second node, ready to link it to the first when it goes online. The third team gets any available Raptors and lands on a third node to start linking as ground forces arrive. Otherwise, the Raptors should seek out superweapons or interfere with the enemy.

- Staying at extreme range with an instant-hit ranged weapon or the Hellbender's main turrets is a cheap but effective way to capture enemy PowerNodes.

- Note the range of your weapon; the link gun's alt-fire stream attack has a shorter range than you can see, so don't aim it at distant enemies. Rockets have a range too, although they travel longer.

- If your Onslaught match drags into overtime, the match continues until one team overloads the core.

- Heal your PowerNodes with the link gun's alt-fire. While you're healing, run about collecting ammo and power-ups nearby.

- All vehicles and nodes can be link-healed and chain-link healed. All enemy vehicles can be chain-linked into a fiery explosion. PowerNodes heal twice as fast with two of you healing it!

- If you're low on link gun ammo, throw the gun away and head into a weapons locker for a new, fully loaded weapon.

- Your team can pick up weapons next to PowerNodes you don't own.

- Steal a march on the enemy by grabbing a vehicle at your home's base while the rest of the team tackles the first node. Move the vehicle to the second connected node so you can link this as soon as the first one comes online.

- The Raptor is the best vehicle for flying over the landscapes, zipping to the other side of the map, and landing at PowerNodes you need to link.

- Land the Raptor on top of mountains, and look out to snipe.

- While in a vehicle, use the number keys to toggle through positions within that vehicle.

- When attacking a turret on foot, get close so the turret can't pivot down to you, and the turret gunner can't see you; then take it out.

- Your mouse wheel or right mouse button usually zooms in when manning a turret; use this!

- For a classic tank strategy, while the rest of your team stands behind the tank and links heals, poke the tank over a hill, fire the main turret at your target, then retreat down the hill a few meters to use the hillside as cover. Repeat the process.

- Try this strategy in the Raptor too. Peek over a mountain, fire at your target, and duck below. This makes avoiding AVRiL rockets easier.

- Check the Cartographical Evidence chapter for the vehicles and weapons that PowerNodes spawn; out-of-the-way nodes usually have more impressive vehicles.

- Usually, each Onslaught map has a superweapon. Learn its position, fly the Raptor to it as the match begins, and use it on a cluster of enemies (usually trying to link their first node). You can win in minutes if you halt enemy progress early enough.

- Beware of falling vehicle husks! Destroyed vehicles or vehicles tumbling into you will kill you. Ram enemies if all else fails, but the vehicle takes falling damage, which usually makes lightly armored vehicles explode.

- You'll get a special pat on the back if shoot down a Raptor with your tank turret.

- Demoralize the opposition by "bullfighting" with enemy Mantas or Scorpions. Dodge jump out of the way of a charging vehicle, then pummel it.

- Learn when to fight and when to flee. Communicate with your team constantly.

- Snipers should have a field day against drivers and passengers of opposing vehicles and turrets. Headshots are the best way to bring them to a halt (Raptor and Tank drivers notwithstanding).

- Use Mantas to ferry additional personnel. Stand on either wing fan and hitch a ride. Watch out for opposing gunfire and rough landings!

- Use friendly vehicles to push teammates up hills.

- Try out convoys of the same vehicles. Back this up with smooth action between vehicles. A great example is multiple Hellbenders firing their main turrets with a group of shock balls that are then comboed into a line of destruction with the regular turret fire. You can decimate a stronghold or a line of troops with this tactic.

- Powerful gunfire can push enemy vehicles back, and weighty vehicles such as the Goliath tank can crash into lighter enemy vehicles. Don't underestimate the power of a tank when ramming an enemy vehicle near a precipice!

- When you are charging up a PowerNode with your link gun, point your weapon at the base and not the floating target above. This makes you less visible to the enemy. The same rule applies when you are attacking the node.

- Don't rule out a tactical suicide. If your power core is being attacked, and you're nowhere near a PowerNode, bind a key to suicide. Kill yourself and respawn at the enemy base to prevent defeat.

- If you're manning a turret, expect to be forcefully tossed out if the node associated with it is taken by the enemy.

Unreal
TOURNAMENT
2004

- Each vehicle has a secondary horn. The default key for the horn is the colon (:). Set input playvehi-clehorn_1 or _0 switches between the two horn types. Many of the horn sounds are amusing. Use these as code for your team to perform an action or show a position.

- When you are attacking a PowerNode, hit it with rapid-fire ordnance from multiple sources. Enemies can spawn at this node only if it isn't being attacked.

- Use the scenery to your advantage. You can fire through leaves at targets, even if the leaves block your view. Learn the level so you can target enemy nodes and areas without visual representation.

- Place grenades on your vehicle, run it toward an enemy area, then get out and find cover. If an enemy tries to enter the vehicle, detonate the grenades! This is also great if you're attempting a suicide run into a group of enemies. Leap out at the last second, and even if you die, your grenades go off, with impressive results!

- Attain the same effects by plastering grenades all over your body, your teammate, or an enemy, then detonating them in an enemy stronghold. Create suicide kamikaze units!

- Lower the gravity, and launch from various hills using the Scorpion (and to a lesser extent, the Hellbender). Spin in the air. Crouch and jump just before you leap for more airborne effects. Point your vehicle back or down while in the air for back or front flips. Jump, then duck for other interesting effects. Handbrake before a jump, and hold out the Scorpion's razor arms for a different trajectory. Then when you land, check your Daredevil skills! These don't affect the game, but mess around with the airborne antics of each vehicle.

- Use your tanks to demolish and hold enemy nodes nearest the core; their strength and armor help you immeasurably. Meanwhile, the rest of the team attacks the core. The enemy is stuck between facing down a tank to sever the core link or attacking all your forces at the core, and they usually mill about in confusion.

- Always look on your map for nodes being attacked. Your side isn't playing well together if you didn't know an enemy node was being taken.

- Don't passively defend nodes the enemy cannot attack. It's better to have larger forces at critical nodes.

- Don't give up if someone is destroying your core. Move your forces to the connecting node and retake that rather than chase and destroy enemies at your core. Enemies keep returning to your core, but capturing the node gives you new vehicles and severs the link.

- The Manta is the easiest vehicle to squash enemies with; perform airborne hops, then land on them. Aim the Manta at an enemy, leap out, and watch the Manta run over the enemy (an excellent tactic if your Manta is about to explode).

- When you reach a node in a fast-moving vehicle, tap the brakes and leap out at the node, or ram a piece of scenery to stop the vehicle. Don't let the vehicle trundle off while you power up the node.

- The Hellbender's cannon's extreme range is its best feature. Zoom in from a great distance (you can aim through the horizon fog at node targets or vehicles you can't see, but know their location). Plug enemies as they race to you. You can destroy them easily due to your range and power of attack.

- If you must move around on foot, dodge jump to move faster.

Deathmatch, Team Deathmatch, and Main Strategies

Dozens of professional competitions and the finest players have contributed these main factors in Deathmatch success. Try these tips in other match types too:

- Use a mixture of chasing and careful checking of all exits when following an enemy (Deathmatch).
- Use corridor edges (which are usually in shadow) to hide for a second when in combat.
- Landing on your opponent's head causes two damage and can kill!
- Invasion Deathmatches are usually easier to battle through with the link gun. Keep yourself armored up and full of ammo.
- InstaGib matches are an excellent way to learn how to fire the shock rifle, lightning gun, or sniper rifle. Hold down fire and aim instead of tapping the Fire button when the enemy is in your sights (the split second reaction delay means less chance of a hit).
- Your matches are all about controlling the power-ups; learn their location and make sure you get them.
- The double damage, for example, respawns after 30 seconds, so run to the location just as it appears instead of waiting for it. Time your routes through a level so you have a 30-second route that takes you into combat and back just as the DD appears.
- Try wounding your opponent, then translocating away if you're in a spawning area. Otherwise you face the healthy foe you just killed (Team Deathmatch).
- With the translocator, fire it, alt-fire, then press fire again to switch to your weapon and prepare for incoming enemies. Learn how to flick between the translocator and a weapon.
- Bind a key to the translocator cam to see where you're going, where the camera currently is, or if it's damaged (meaning you'll die if you warp); react accordingly.
- Learn how to kill the enemy using the lightning gun and sniper rifle while both weapons are zoomed out. Perfect your single-hit tagging.
- Your dodge jump allows you to dodge backward, which is especially good against rockets and the shock rifle.
- Elevator jump just before the lift platform reaches the top of the shaft to sail farther.
- When you double jump, vary the time to jump the second time to leap farther. This is useful in areas of low gravity.
- When double jumping up a series of platforms or wall areas, continuously tap Jump.
- Hide and/or center your weapons. The left and right-handed weapon points fire slightly to the side of the middle crosshairs. This is important when you're aiming with a shock rifle.
- Complete a circuit of all major pick-ups continuously, unless you need health. Guard and take them, and let no one else grab them. Learn a couple of good camping spots during the circuit.
- Standing around is the quickest way to die. Even when you're camping, move around.
- Use unfamiliar tactics to mix it up a little. Alternate methods to retrieve items confuse the enemies and give you a surprise advantage (shield jump up to the double damage in DM-one-on-one-ALBATROSS, for example).
- Switch from fast-firing weapons (such as the link gun's primary bolts) to a slow-firing weapon (such as the lightning gun) and continue to battle the enemy. They'll be off balance and unable to predict your attacks.
- Learn where your enemies are going and the routes they travel, then camp out or intercept them. Looking up is worse than looking down. Peering down at an enemy allows you to see the ground and victim, and usually means you'll get off the first shot.

51

- Jump over rockets as they head toward you, especially in tight corners, and run straight at the enemy if you're nimble enough!
- Headshots always result in more damage; specific weapons are excellent for decapitations.
- Shoot off a few bullets if your chosen gun is full and you're near more of the same ammo type. Then pick up the ammo so the enemy can't grab it.
- Try out the goo shield jump. Plaster the ground with biorifle ooze, then shield jump off that. You'll take more damage, but boost vertically much farther than ever!

Capture the Flag Strategies

Although most of the main strategies are relevant to Capture the Flag, here are some specific tactics:

- Segment your teams into defense and offense, then keep to your chosen job. Stay alert, and take one for the team every time. Use the translocator to travel to your opponent's base.
- Instead of trying to attack more than one enemy when you're carrying the flag, get a couple of bodyguards. Use your shield to fend off incoming fire.
- Dropping the translocator device down the hole in the flag stand is not allowed. Instead, place the translocator in an unused corner near the flag base so you can translocate back into play near your foe's flag just after you score!
- Jump in front of the flag carrier to stop the carrier from being hit.
- Find a good hiding spot in the enemy base, and wait for your friend to grab the flag. Watch him go, then hunt the enemies in the flag base to clear it. When your hapless flag-carrying chump dies, steal the flag.
- If enemies are attacking you far from their base, wound them. If you're translocating back to the flag after being killed, you don't want a healthy enemy appearing nearby, when you could leave them wounded in your own territory.
- Be patient. Never go for the flag without fully equipping yourself.
- When getting out of an enemy flag base, lay down suppressing fire with biorifle goo, flak, or rockets.
- While playing defense, leave the translocator in your base, ideally on a path of an incoming enemy (next to the flag). Use the remote camera to check incoming foes, then telefrag an enemy. Even if you miss the telefrag, you're near the foe.
- Hang out in a dark corner and shoot enemies as they arrive.

Bombing Run Strategies

All the necessary Double Domination strategies are contained within the main strategy tips above, or the DD area of the Cartographical Evidence chapter. However, the Bombing Run mode has its share of expert tactics:

- Throw the ball a huge distance away so the opponent can't find it. Then translocate to the ball and grab it.
- Try to telefrag the ball carrier. Aim and fire your translocator pod under the ball, use the camera or watch for an enemy to pick it up, then telefrag.
- Throwing to a teammate happens automatically. If there's no available teammate to pass to, you hear a beep. Throw to a teammate even if you can't see him.
- Shoot at a horizontal goal from below or above.

- Pick a goalie on your team to guard the base and goal.

- Make sure you're powered up before you attempt a bombing run.

- Hang around for others to come to your aid and set up a good passing game, so the enemy doesn't know which teammate the ball is going to next.

- Use the adrenaline power of "speed up" when you're heading to the goal.

- Use superweapons to incredible effect! In BR-SERENITY, have one player translocate to the redeemer. When the teammate has the ball, aim the redeemer at the thrown ball, and as the redeemer is en route to the target, have your teammate pick it up and get blasted in the sky while the enemies explode below! This is a classic "cheese" tactic.

- Beware, balers: You lose your translocator charge when you throw the ball, so you can't keep throwing and translocating.

Unreal Tournament 2004 Glossary

Alt-fire: A weapon's secondary fire function (the plasma shaft on the link gun, for example)

Bot: A computer-controlled player

Camping: Hiding in a secluded location with a long-range weapon, remaining still and picking off enemies from a distance

Cheese: Performing an unbelievable stunt or violent act that results in the demise of others, while you remain unscathed

Console: A command prompt from which you can enter cheat codes or other command information to change aspects of the game

Frame rate: A measure of the smoothness of the game, measured in frames per second (FPS). A high frame rate means the game is running smoothly, with little choppiness. This requires more processing power.

Gib: A kill, used in reference to one-shot kills

HUD: Heads-up display; information about your character displayed on the screen

LAN: Local area network, a direct cable connection between two or more computers

Newbie: A new player; a rookie

Resolution: The amount of game information displayed on your screen. Higher resolutions show more and require more processing power

Respawn: The reappearance of a weapon, item, or character

Spectator: A player who is observing the action but is not involved in the match

Strafe: Moving from side to side while facing forward

Spawn-camping (a.k.a. spawn whoring): Staying at a particular spot with a good view of an enemy spawn point, and defeating enemies before they can arm themselves and retaliate

System resources: Your computer's ability to process the technical aspects of the game; generally determined by your processor speed, your graphics card, and the amount of RAM

Telefrag: Using a translocator to teleport "into" an enemy standing over the translocator pod, killing him instantly

Toggle: Turning a feature on and off with the same button, like a light switch

Inventory and Ordnance

Each map contains a supply of items, weapons, and power-ups. This section reveals all the weaponry and ammunition, plus health, shielding, and other power-ups. This section also includes comprehensive hit and damage tables. Finally, players who prefer the "classic" versions of some of the weapons can choose them in the Settings menu.

Items

Adrenaline

Find orange and white adrenaline capsules scattered around most levels. They add two points of adrenaline to your adrenaline meter. When your adrenaline meter hits 100, the pill icon starts blinking and you can perform adrenaline combos (see Tournament Training for more information on adrenaline combos). Take these adrenaline pills wherever you see them, but save the combos for special situations, such as getting extra speed to reach a goal in Bombing Run or a berserk boost to destroy an enemy objective in Assault.

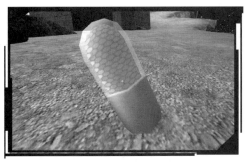

Health

The three varieties of health pick-ups all restore some of your health. Cross-shaped health packs +25 restore your health, but they do not raise it above 100 points.

Health vials +5 look like blue test tubes. They can raise your health meter above 100 points, to a maximum of 199 points.

Pick up a big keg–o-health +100 to instantly restore 100 points of health. Like health vials +5, they raise your health to the 199-point maximum.

Pick up health whenever possible. If you know a wounded enemy might try to grab this health, wound yourself lightly with the shield gun and then take the health pack. Take vials and kegs immediately.

Double Damage

Purple double damage (DD) icons spin slowly as they float above the ground. A double damage modifier doubles your weapons' power for 30 seconds. Use double damage with weapons that have a fast fire rate (such as the minigun or assault rifle) or weapons that do splash damage (such as the rocket launcher). A weapon powered up with double damage glows purple. Remember that you can grab a DD, then leap into a vehicle and power up the weapon inside (excellent when you're in a tank!). Secure the DD immediately, before your opponents do.

Shield Pack

The yellow shield packs give you shields, which act as a second health bar. Any damage you suffer is first subtracted from your shields and you lose health only after your shields are fully depleted. Shield packs come in +50 and +100, and you can have up to 150 shield points at any time. Check the map section for their whereabouts.

Weapons Detail

Weapon's List Legend

Damage - How much damage each firing inflicts

Head Special - If weapon can strike target's head

Instant Hit - If weapon can instantly strike target

Ranged Fire - If weapon fires in an arc or has limited range

Range - The weapon's range of fire

Splash Damage - When the ordnance detonates, does it inflict damage over a wide area?

Combo Ability - Can multiple firings be strung together into a more powerful attack?

Starting Ammo - How many firings before the weapon empties (the secondary value depletes at the same rate as the primary value)

Maximum Ammo - Maximum ammunition capacity

Ammo Depletion Time (in seconds) - How long it takes to empty the weapon's starting ammunition

Rate of Fire - How quickly the weapon can fire off a single shot

Trajectory Affected by Gravity - If the weapon's ordnance is affected by gravity

An asterisk (*) indicates a note that is explained at the bottom of the table.

The Head Stomp

	Primary Fire	Secondary Fire
Damage*	2	N/A
Head Special	No	N/A
Instant Hit	Yes	N/A
Ranged Fire	No	N/A
Range	Close	N/A
Splash Damage	No	N/A
Combo Ability	No	N/A
Starting Ammo	N/A	N/A
Maximum Ammo	N/A	N/A
Ammo Depletion Time	N/A	N/A
Rate of Fire	N/A	N/A
Trajectory Affected by Gravity	Yes	N/A

* This attack has no secondary fire capabilities

Tournament Official Info-tag

Tournament Regulation Combat Boots*

Ammunition: Ammunition Not Applicable

(*Skaarj feet or automaton appendages also valid)

Utilization of the head stomp in the combat zone is not recommended by the Liandri Corporation. Extensive battle simulations have shown that there are more accurate and effective methods to defeat an opponent than this lucky strike.

Ordnance Tactics

Execute the head stomp by jumping or falling and landing on your competitor's head. If you fall correctly, your foe suffers two points of damage and slight confusion. Any weapon is much more useful, but for ultimate humiliation, try stomping your opponent to death!

Translocator

	Primary Fire	Secondary Fire		Primary Fire	Secondary Fire
Damage	N/A	Telefrag	Starting Ammo	6	N/A
Head Special	No	No	Maximum Ammo	6	N/A
Instant Hit	No	Yes	Ammo Depletion Time	N/A	N/A
Ranged Fire	Yes	No	Rate of Fire	Medium	Very Fast
Range	Close	Medium	Trajectory Affected by Gravity	Yes	No
Splash Damage	No	No			
Combo Ability	Yes	N/A			

Tournament Official Info-tag

The translocator was originally designed by Liandri Corporation's R&D sector to facilitate the rapid recall of miners during tunnel collapses. However, rapid deresolution and reconstitution can have several unwelcome effects, including increases in aggression and paranoia. In order to prolong the careers of today's contenders, limits have been placed on translocator use in the lower-ranked leagues. The latest iteration of the translocator features a remotely operated

Translocator

Ammunition: Translocator Homing Device

camera, exceptionally useful when scouting out areas of contention. It should be noted that while viewing the camera's surveillance output, the user is effectively blind to their immediate surroundings.

Ordnance Tactics

The translocator's primary fire shoots out a small, blinking homing device that arcs through the air and lands on the ground. Should it fall into a dangerous area or at a location that gives you an unfair advantage or is out of the tournament zone, then the device disappears. You can re-fire another five times before the weapon requires recharging. Press the primary trigger to launch the beacon device (also known as a probe or pod), and press the secondary fire to warp to its location (whether it is still moving or has finished landing). Equip, fire, and equip again to switch to a 3D camera view.

Used primarily in Capture the Flag and Bombing Run exercises, the translocator lets you move faster than running allows, while dodging attacks due to your constant teleporting. It also lets you reach areas that are normally out of bounds, such as rafters and high sniping positions. If you try to use the translocator when you have the flag or ball, you teleport without the item.

You maintain momentum even when you've teleported to the probe or pod location. So if you fall for a bit, then shoot your pod and teleport, you keep your falling velocity and aren't spared the falling damage. Shoot and warp as soon as you fall to avoid damage.

You can use the device to constantly ascend, although this usually works better in areas of low gravity as you keep gaining speed until you hit the ground, even when you keep teleporting upward. Move to the highest location in a map, translocate up once, then again. That's the highest point you can reach before your dropping velocity outpaces your teleport ascending speed.

Use the translocator to dodge (for example, fire the probe off a balcony into space, and when you start to fall, aim back at the balcony), but don't shoot out more than six shots in succession or you'll have to wait for the device to charge.

Crouching and translocating allows you to appear inside nooks and crannies you couldn't reach if you were standing, but make sure you crouch before you fire. An option in the Settings/game tab makes the beacon trajectory higher. This arc travels higher, then falls faster. Choose your preferred arc (fire at torso level, and the probe can arc across an entire level).

Telefrag enemies by waiting for a foe to stand close to your translocator pod. Use the camera to watch the position of your foe before you telefrag them.

If you see an enemy translocator beacon, shoot it so sparks arc from it. This damages the pod so a teleporting enemy is immediately destroyed. Check your pod for damage by using the camera to look for sparks. Equip, fire, and equip again to launch the camera, which has a three-dimensional view. The signal degrades the farther away you are from it, but it's a great way to look around an enemy base and direct troops or see how your defenses are holding up. Fire your beacon, then switch to any weapon and attack a foe, and switch back; the beacon is still active and can be teleported to, or the beacon can be returned and fired again.

> **NOTE**
>
> For further information on the translocator's usefulness, check the overviews of Capture the Flag and Bombing Run in the Training section.

Shield Gun

	Primary Fire	Secondary Fire
Damage	150	N/A
Head Special	No	No
Instant Hit	Yes	N/A
Ranged Fire	No	No
Range	Close	N/A
Splash Damage	Yes	N/A
Combo Ability	No	N/A
Starting Ammo	None	N/A
Maximum Ammo	None	N/A
Ammo Depletion Time	3*	15**
Rate of Fire	Slow	Very Fast
Trajectory Affected by Gravity	Yes	N/A

* Time taken to charge primary attack
** Time shield can function before depletion

Tournament Official Info-tag

Kemphler DD280 Riot Control Device (Shield Gun)

Ammunition: Ammunition not applicable

The Kemphler DD280 Riot Control Device has the ability to resist and reflect incoming projectiles and energy beams. The plasma wave inflicts massive damage, rupturing tissue, pulverizing organs, and flooding the bloodstream with dangerous gas bubbles. This weapon may be intended for combat at close range, but when wielded properly should be considered as dangerous as any other armament in your arsenal.

Ordnance Tactics

The shield gun is useful in many ways. It is always with you and constantly replenishes ammo. Its primary attack can be deadly, although it has a very short range. Although many other weapons are better, the plasma wave can pulp opponents who haven't seen you. Also try it to pulverize a foe with a flak cannon. However, it inflicts pain on the user in conjunction with a jump, in a technique known as a shield jump (detailed in the Training chapter). Charge up as the wave is launched automatically and run straight at your foe as last resort.

The actual shield (secondary attack) is useful in Assault and Capture the Flag matches. When you have the flag and you can't return fire for some reason, use the shield to absorb some of the punishment. In Assault maps, it's useful when you have to wait at an objective. Power up the shield, run into the fray, and access the objective before you die. When you have extra shield packs, you can concentrate on objectives and shrug off enemy fire with your shields up.

If you're falling, point the weapon down and bring up the shields, and you won't take as much damage when you land. If you see someone at the edge of a cliff, tap the primary fire to shove him off. The damage you inflict depends on how long you hold the Fire button down. This includes yourself when shield jumping; point your gun down and hit yourself, and you'll take 45 damage. A small boost causes only 12 points of damage, but doesn't propel you as far. The maximum height and minimum distance occurs when you point the gun straight down, so hold the weapon at a 45 degree angle (or a little lower) for best jumping results. For long distances, try a dodge shield jump.

The primary attack doesn't use energy, but the secondary one counts down as long as you hold it, to a maximum of 15 seconds before needing a recharge. Don't flick the shield on and off as this wastes energy. Note that the shield can't protect against energy weapons (such as the shock rifle).

Assault Rifle

	Primary Fire	Secondary Fire
Damage	4*	70
Head Special	No	No
Instant Hit	Yes	No
Ranged Fire	No	Yes
Range	Medium	Short
Splash Damage	No	Yes
Combo Ability	No	No
Starting Ammo	100	4
Maximum Ammo	100	4
Ammo Depletion Time	14	1 or 4**
Rate of Fire	Very Fast	Medium
Trajectory Affected by Gravity	No	Yes

*Bullets are fired three per second for 12 damage per second.

** Grenades can be instantly fired or charged for greater distance; figure shows charge time/empty time.

Tournament Official Info-tag

AR770 Assault Rifle Mk.1 Classic (with optional M355 Grenade Launcher)

AR770 Assault Rifle Mk.2 (with optional M355 Grenade Launcher)

Ammunition: Box of Grenades and Bullets (20 Bullets, 4 Grenades)

Inexpensive and easily produced, the AR770 provides a lightweight 5.56mm combat solution that is most effective against unarmored foes. With low-to-moderate armor penetration capabilities, this rifle is best suited to a role as a light support weapon. The optional M355 Grenade Launcher provides the punch that makes this weapon effective against heavily armored enemies.

Ordnance Tactics

Your default starting weapon is available in classic or new models and can be wielded in each hand. With two assault rifles (grabbed from a dead body or a weapons locker), you fire twice as many bullets but still have the same ammo limits and grenade lobbing skills. Its impressive rate of fire and ability to stay accurate even at medium distances means this is a reasonable weapon at close and mid-range melees. If you're reacting to the weapon, dodge jump or strafe left and right so the enemy wastes bullets.

Hold down the primary fire button for a continuous stream of bullets, or tap for a short burst. There's no advantage to hitting an opponent in the head with this weapon, so aim for the larger torso area. You start with an assault rifle, and these weapons are useful only in matches where weapons aren't readily accessible. Get proficient with this gun and wipe out tournament newcomers searching for weapons as a match starts.

Mix and match bullets and grenades in a barrage attack; charge up the grenade and lob it into a nearby enemy, then finish with bullets for a confusing but surprisingly potent attack. If you're charging an enemy, build up your grenade lob, let it fly so it lands on your foe, then as you close, lob a second grenade to complete the job. Unless you're attacking at close quarters, launch the grenades with maximum power so they travel faster and more accurately. Play with your pitch (hold the gun slightly above center to increase the arc of the grenade lob), and don't underestimate the grenades—they bounce and are difficult to see. Their splash damage is mediocre.

BioRifle

	Primary Fire	Secondary Fire
Damage	39	154*
Head Special	No	No
Instant Hit	No	No
Ranged Fire	Yes	Yes
Range	Short	Short
Splash Damage	No	Yes
Combo Ability	Yes	Yes
Starting Ammo	20	10**
Maximum Ammo	50	50
Ammo Depletion Time	6	6
Rate of Fire	Fast	Medium
Trajectory Affected by Gravity	Yes	Yes

* 154 is the damage inflicted by the largest possible goo ball. Smaller goo balls have the following number/ damage ratios: 2 = 58, 3 = 77, 4 = 96, 5 = 115, Max = 154

** Refers to the number of ammo points taken to fire the largest goo ball

Tournament Official Info-tag

GES BioRifle

Ammunition: BioRifle Ammo (20)

The GES BioRifle continues to be one of the most controversial weapons in the tournament. Loved by some, loathed by others, the biorifle has long been the subject of debate over its usefulness. Some tournament purists argue that it is the equivalent of a cowardly minefield. Others argue that it enhances the tactical capabilities of defensive combatants. Despite the debate, the weapon provides rapid-fire wide-area coverage in primary firing mode, and a single-fire variable payload secondary firing mode. In layman's terms, this equates to being able to pepper an area with small globs of biosludge, or launch one large glob at the target.

Ordnance Tactics

Subtle, understated, and usually forgotten about, this gun has shocking power. It's strictly for short-range combat, and the tighter and more enclosed the environment, the more fun you'll have. If you're on the receiving end of bio ooze, dodge jump to avoid the incoming blobs.

The primary attack shoots out small green blobs of toxic goop. These hurt enemies when they step on them, if the ooze hits them. The blobs also stick to walls and explode after around 10 seconds or if a foe touches it. Against a running enemy, hit the foe with half the shots, and place the rest on the floor to be stepped on. Remember the sludge can also damage you!

The secondary attack allows you to build up a larger ball of ooze that explodes into multiple smaller segments. Each is as deadly as a primary blob, but if you manage to strike a foe with a secondary blob, you'll kill him. Even if the blob misses, it creates a wide blast zone, so try dropping it into the middle of a group, then fire primary shots at any survivors.

This is a great weapon to fire on enemies from above and is almost as fearsome as the flak cannon if the secondary fire is used in small spaces. Try coating the grounds of well-traveled areas (ideally around blind corners) so a dashing enemy treads into a goopy ambush. Try coating the ceiling of a corridor you're running down, especially if pursued by an enemy, as the sludge drops onto the floor. Point the weapon directly at your feet (as low as you can) and run forward, dropping goop on the floor. If you're quick, this leaves a trail behind you making it another effective way to thwart chasers. Finally, if you keep your primary fire trained at a single blob, it eventually explodes with a force of a secondary fire explosion.

Mine Layer

	Primary Fire	Secondary Fire
Damage	200	N/A
Head Special	No	N/A
Instant Hit	No	N/A
Ranged Fire	Yes	N/A
Range	Short	N/A
Splash Damage	Yes	N/A
Combo Ability	Yes	N/A
Starting Ammo	8	N/A
Maximum Ammo	30	N/A
Ammo Depletion Time*	6	N/A
Rate of Fire	Medium	N/A
Trajectory Affected by Gravity	Yes	N/A

* It takes six seconds to lay the maximum of eight mines. Lay more than eight and the first mine you laid explodes.

Tournament Official Info-tag

Quad-fill Mine Layer

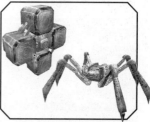

Ammunition: Parasite Mines (8)

The spider mine layer is used for deploying spider mines, autonomous mobile mines that are highly effective for both foot soldiers and vehicles.

Ordnance Tactics

This weapon is used mainly in Onslaught matches (and to a lesser extent, Assault maps). The primary fire throws out up to eight of these scuttling mines that drop where you aim them and remain stationary unless near an enemy. Then they move and explode on the enemy. You cannot have more than eight of your own mines on the ground at once; explode some so there are fewer than eight before you fire off more.

Your secondary fire "shepherds" the spider mines to whatever direction you aim. So, you can use them as remote mines or as a swarm to overrun an enemy vehicle, turret, or infantry member. To use them as remote mines, try sneaking up near the enemy base or PowerNode, on the other side of a hill or road you know the enemy will traverse, and drop them just over the lip so the enemy can't see them before they detonate. To swarm with them, deposit the eight mines around a corner, then dash out with the mines in tow and point to the enemy you want them to swarm. Mines also destroy enemy vehicles that a foe has exited, so don't use them if you're carjacking.

For a kamikaze tactic (to charge an enemy encampment or if you're being overrun), launch as many mines as you can because they all explode when you die. Mines are useful when defending a small location. Don't guide them up ledges or steep hills or they explode. You can place them on friendly vehicles and then charge an enemy base.

Defeat spider mines by outrunning them, and at an appropriate range, blast them all with a single rocket or flak cannon shot. Spider mines also leap for you; dodge jump out of the way, turn, and destroy them.

Advanced tactics include the following: You can place spider mines on vehicles. Try loading a Manta with spider mines on the wings and fly near an enemy player or vehicle. They will jump off and attack the enemy. This tactic, however, will make your Manta highly explosive. One shot from most weapons at an attached spider mine will cause a chain reaction that will destroy you.

If you want to make your spider mines even more powerful, attach a couple grenades to them. However, the grenades will weigh down the spider mines; the more you attach, the slower they move. You can use the above two tactics together to deliver some serious destruction. It takes time to attach the spider mines and grenades, though, and you risk blowing yourself up in the process!

Shock Rifle

	Primary Fire	Secondary Fire
Damage	45	45*
Head Special	Yes	No
Instant Hit	Yes	No
Ranged Fire	No	Yes
Range	Infinite	Long
Splash Damage	No**	Yes
Combo Ability	Yes	Yes
Starting Ammo	20	20
Maximum Ammo	50	50
Ammo Depletion Time	12	11
Rate of Fire	Very Fast	Fast
Trajectory Affected by Gravity	No	No

* Combo damage varies between 160 (caught by edge of splash damage) to 245 (direct hit).

** Yes if fired as part of a combo attack

Tournament Official Info-tag

ASMD Shock Rifle Mk.1 Classic

ASMD Shock Rifle Mk.2

Ammunition: Shock Core (10)

The ASMD Shock Rifle has changed little since its incorporation into the tournaments. The ASMD sports two firing modes capable of acting in concert to neutralize opponents in a devastating shockwave. This combination attack is achieved when the weapon operator utilizes the secondary fire mode to deliver a charge of seeded plasma to the target. Once the slow-moving plasma charge is within range of the target, the weapon operator may fire the photon beam into the plasma core, releasing the explosive energy of the anti-photons contained within the plasma's EM field.

Ordnance Tactics

Whether you're using the classic Mk.1 model or the newly redesigned version, this weapon can hit a fleeing or distant enemy almost instantaneously (with primary fire), waylay nearby enemies (with secondary fire), or clear a room and bounce an enemy around (with a combo shot that fires a primary bolt that connects with a secondary ball to explode). Weigh these advantages against the weapon's lack of instant killing and the lack of a knockdown punch in closer quarters. If you go against a flak cannon firer, dodge about and make sure your blasts connect.

The straight bolt (known as a shock beam) fire can travel an infinite distance. Although you can't zoom in and accurately aim at extreme distances, this functions like the lightning gun's primary blast, but reloads faster and delivers far less damage. Use this to harass long-range foes, especially as the weapon outfires the rocket launcher, giving you the edge if you can hit your foe constantly.

The secondary fire not only inflicts damage, but shoves the foe slightly from their route. The slower balls are easier to dodge the farther away you are and the larger the area. Use this attack at closer range to bounce an enemy away from an item or off a cliff. Two balls hitting each other from different rifles dissipate without exploding.

Some shock combos have become instant classics. When firing a shock ball, fire a second one and combo that instead of the first, as the enemy always thinks you're going to connect the first time. If you see another player using a shock rifle, try to connect with your own rifle to surprise them with a combo (this is good if you're working with a teammate and can fire off combos together using each other's secondary fire).

Dueling shock rifles mean you can wait for a foe to fire, and instantly combo the ball in his face! Finally, use it for enemies hiding around corners. Fire a ball at the corner, and explode it in a combo just as the ball passes the victim. Tournament players regularly call a player who overuses this technique a "shock whore" or "combo whore."

For this reason, use the shock rifle on a team Scorpion to give it some extra push. For enemy vehicles, their size makes the weapon's primary fire exceptional to inflict damage; even flying Raptors can be downed with the instant-hit capacity. Know when to use the primary fire (wide open spaces), secondary fire (tight corridors), and the combo. Defend against the combo by keeping either extremely far away or near your shock rifle user to minimize the risk. Master the combo, and you can win every match.

InstaGib Shock Rifle

	Primary Fire	Secondary Fire
Damage	Death (50)	Death (50)*
Head Special	Yes	Yes
Instant Hit	Yes	Yes
Ranged Fire	No	No
Range	Infinite	Infinite
Splash Damage	No	No
Combo Ability	No	No
Starting Ammo	N/A	N/A
Maximum Ammo	N/A	N/A
Ammo Depletion Time	N/A	N/A
Rate of Fire	Very Fast	Very Fast
Trajectory Affected by Gravity	No	No

* Instant kill on infantry, 50 damage to vehicles

Tournament Official Info-tag

InstaGib Shock Rifle (ST 115 Modified)

Ammunition: Ammunition not available

The ST 115: Modified InstaGib Shock Rifle has had the power of its electromagnetic field increase considerably, focusing all available power to the main shock beam technology. In order to increase power bandwidth to such a devastating extent, secondary fire functionality was removed, and an additional photon beam maximizer was implemented.

Ordnance Tactics

The "gib" part of this weapon's name refers to the mess of body parts the rifle inflicts as an instant-kill hit. Otherwise, this weapon offers the same capabilities as the shock rifle's primary fire—refer to the shock rifle for additional tactics. No shock balls are fired though. This weapon is available only when the "instaGib" mutator is selected. If you select the "zoom instaGib" mutator, the weapon's secondary fire becomes a range finder, and the weapon acts as a fast-firing lightning gun with instant kills. Aim for your foe's torso, the biggest surface area.

Link Gun

	Primary Fire	Secondary Fire		Primary Fire	Secondary Fire
Damage*	22	90**	Maximum Ammo	120	120
Head Special	No	No	Ammo Depletion Time	7	7
Instant Hit	No	Yes	Rate of Fire	Fast	Very Fast
Ranged Fire	Yes	Yes	Trajectory Affected by Gravity	No	No
Range	Medium	Medium			
Splash Damage	No	No			
Combo Ability	No	No			
Starting Ammo	40	40			

* Secondary fire heals teammates, PowerNodes, and vehicles at rate of 33 points per second.

** Damage per second for secondary fire; triple this per person in link chain

Tournament Official Info-tag

Riordan Dynamic Weapon Systems combines the best of weapon design in the Advanced Plasma Rifle v23, commonly known as the link gun. While the primary firing mode of the link remains the same as

Riodan Dynamic Advanced Plasma Rifle v22 Classic (Link Gun)

Riordan Dynamic Advanced Plasma Rifle v23 (Link Gun)

Ammunition: Link Charge (50)

its plasma-firing predecessor, the secondary cutting torch has been replaced with a switchable energy matrix. Upon contacting a teammate, it converts to a harmless carrier stream, offloading energy from the onboard cells to boost the output of any targeted player also using the link. It should be noted that while players are boosting a teammate, they are unable to defend themselves from attack.

Ordnance Tactics

One of the best choices for firing across multi-level environments, in close melee combat, or even in open areas, the link gun is a versatile weapon with both offensive and defensive capabilities. It is perhaps the most well-rounded weapon available. It doesn't have the stopping power of other weapons, and the primary fire is slower than the minigun's, but it's still deadly. Make sure you can dive into cover, as the bright green signature makes you a prime target.

The primary pulses cause damage with a single strike and don't lose effectiveness over range (as does the flak cannon). Use this attack with enemies at very close range (when you know you can't miss) or at extreme range (so that any strikes hit with the same punch). Constantly hitting a person with primary pulses inflicts more damage than the secondary stream.

The secondary stream is deadly, but a little unpredictable. You must keep a bead on your target because the attack damage is for a constant second of striking fire. Usually a foe receives a hit for only a moment before dodging away. The closer you are to your foe, the more effective this attack.

But the secondary fire's real power comes when you fire at a teammate, who then fires his weapon. This blast (which changes color the more teammates are added to the chain) inflicts triple damage and fires faster. Run through a level cutting foes down with this excellent technique. A logo in the screen's bottom right signifies when you are chaining attacks. You can attack only one person at a time, so larger groups should split into pairs. You won't stand a chance if hit by a chain trio, so always fire at the middle of the chain to break it, not the firer.

Try using this weapon to surprise an enemy, but the range is only 30 feet, so get close. Fire this at mid-range, and follow the fleeing foe.

In Assault and Onslaught maps, link guns are even more practical, as they allow chained groups to assault objectives. Secondary link gun fire can heal vehicles and PowerNodes (but not cores). A teammate's name appears in green if you can link to him. The yellow and red HUD tells you how many people can link to you. Chain link at nodes, as this uses less ammo and the firer can look around for more. The stream changes to a straight line when healing or building. The link gun is the best weapon to destroy objectives in Assault and Onslaught. Commandeer as much ammunition as possible.

Minigun

	Primary Fire	Secondary Fire
Damage	4–8*	8–10**
Head Special	No	No
Instant Hit	Yes	Yes
Ranged Fire	No	No
Range	Medium	Medium***
Splash Damage	No	No
Combo Ability	No	No
Starting Ammo	150	150
Maximum Ammo	300	300
Ammo Depletion Time	9	27
Rate of Fire	Fast	Fast
Trajectory Affected by Gravity	No	No

Damage per bullet. Primary fire inflicts around 75 damage per constant second of hitting.

** *Secondary fire damage rates apply to vehicles only. Otherwise, same as primary against infantry.*

*** *Accuracy becomes impaired the farther away you are.*

Tournament Official Info-tag

Schultz-Metzger T23-A 23m rotary cannon (Minigun)

Ammunition: 50 Bullets (50)

The Schultz-Metzger T23-A 23mm rotary cannon is capable of firing both high-velocity caseless ammunition and cased rounds. With an unloaded weight of only 8 kilograms, the T23 is portable and maneuverable, easily worn across the back when employing the optional carrying strap. The T23-A is the rotary cannon of choice for the discerning soldier.

Ordnance Tactics

Choose the minigun to quickly inflict a lot of damage to many enemies. The amazing fire rate makes it excellent for close-quarter melee combat. It's good against enemies between 10 and 30 feet away but not very accurate at mid-range or longer. Avoid the half-second build-up time by tapping the Fire button, then press to attack.

New this season is the secondary fire function. It's slightly slower but is more accurate than the primary fire, so use it at a slightly longer range. Its exploding rounds do more damage to vehicles, PowerNodes, and cores in Onslaught and Assault modes (and if the minigun is your only weapon, use it to take out objectives).

This formidable weapon quickly chews through ammunition. The bullets leave a tracer pattern that reveals the firer's location. Step into a room with the minigun blazing and clear it of two or three enemies in as many seconds. The good line of sight and instant hits make it useful outside, but the lack of splash damage means you must follow the enemy.

Grenade Launcher

	Primary Fire	Secondary Fire
Damage	100	N/A
Head Special	No	N/A
Instant Hit	No	N/A
Ranged Fire	Yes	N/A
Range	Medium	N/A
Splash Damage	Yes	N/A
Combo Ability	Yes	N/A
Starting Ammo	10	N/A
Maximum Ammo	50	N/A
Ammo Depletion Time	9*	N/A
Rate of Fire	Medium	N/A
Trajectory Affected by Gravity	Yes	N/A

* Up to eight grenades can be launched before they must be exploded

Tournament Official Info-tag

MGG Grenade Launcher

Ammunition: Grenades (5)

The MGG Grenade Launcher fires magnetic sticky grenades, which will attach to enemy players and vehicles.

Ordnance Tactics

This classic weapon has one important difference from the mine layer: the grenades are magnetic. They attach to vehicles, other players, nodes, and turrets, making them *the* requisite close-range anti-vehicle weapon in Onslaught and Assault matches (the only ones where this weapon is present). Primary fire shoots the grenades and secondary fire detonates them. This means you can drop a grenade at your feet without fear. You can fire up to eight grenades; then they must be detonated before more are launched. When you press secondary fire, all grenades explode.

Leap down by an enemy vehicle, run behind it, and stick a batch of grenades to it. You can even fire grenades, change weapons, and return to the grenade launcher to finish the job. Plaster an enemy attacking you because if you die, all the grenades explode!

Shoot up to eight grenades in a location, wait for enemy forces to arrive, and then detonate. The grenades merge into shadows on the gloomier maps.

To take out grenades laid near you, approach the grenades and dodge jump at the last second to fake the enemy into detonating them. Or shoot rockets to destroy them (gunfire destroys grenades, so use a weapon with splash damage). Play with the firing angle: a 50 or 60 degree angle upward for far shots, or vertically if you want them to land on your head! Customize grenades to various combat situations.

NOTE

See the spider mine section for some interesting tactics to try with both grenades and mines in linked attacks.

Unreal TOURNAMENT 2004

Flak Cannon

	Primary Fire	Secondary Fire
Damage	117*	142
Head Special	No	No
Instant Hit	No	No
Ranged Fire	Yes	Yes
Range	Medium	Medium**
Splash Damage	Yes	Yes
Combo Ability	No	No
Starting Ammo	15	15
Maximum Ammo	35	35
Ammo Depletion Time	11	14
Rate of Fire	Fast	Medium
Trajectory Affected by Gravity	Yes	Yes

Primary weapon number is maximum damage if all flak shards hit victim. Each primary attack splits into 9 shards inflicting 13 damage. The number of shards hitting the target diminishes with range.

**Accuracy becomes impaired the farther away you are.*

Tournament Official Info-tag

Trident Defensive Technologies Series 7 Flechette Cannon Mk3 "Negotiator" (Flak Cannon)

Ammunition: 10 Flak Shells (10)

Trident Defensive Technologies Series 7 Flechette Cannon has been taken to the next step in evolution with the production of the Mk3 "Negotiator." The ionized flechettes are capable of delivering second- and third-degree burns to organic tissue, cauterizing the wound instantly. Payload delivery is achieved via one of two methods: ionized flechettes launched in a spread pattern directly from the barrel, or via fragmentation grenades that explode on impact, radiating flechettes in all directions.

Ordnance Tactics

Behold the deadliest short-range combat weapon. Its one-hit kill, close-quarter damage is exceptional in melees, and the equally deadly secondary fire grenade is just as potent at mid-ranges. However, it's pretty useless at long range. Use it with extreme care in tight corridors, as the primary fire ricochets and can kill its user.

The primary ammo strike is like a shotgun blast. A cone of shards from the weapon's barrel spreads out over range. At ranges within 10 feet, most of the shards connect, and you'll cut an enemy into chunks.

The secondary fire is an arcing grenade that explodes with a small splash damage and it usually results in a one-shot kill. Use this attack when the enemy is too far away to be hurt by the primary fire, but aim at the head or torso.

Use this in small enclosed areas, and put it away in larger maps with open areas. Wait and watch a firefight, then fire shards that strike multiple enemies to mop up. It's difficult to hit foes above you, and the splash damage is minimal even when fired from above. Sneak up or run into your enemies, firing at the last second to really rip them to shreds. Ricochet the primary fire around corners to tear open enemies you can't see, or ricochet up to the ceiling as you're being chased. Try charging right at your enemy from mid-range, firing a grenade and finishing the job with a primary load.

AVRiL

	Primary Fire	Secondary Fire
Damage	200	200
Head Special	No	No
Instant Hit	No	No
Ranged Fire	Yes	Yes
Range	Long	Long
Splash Damage	Yes	Yes
Combo Ability	No	No
Starting Ammo	5	5
Maximum Ammo	25	25
Ammo Depletion Time	20	N/A
Rate of Fire	Slow	N/A
Trajectory Affected by Gravity	Yes	N/A

Tournament Official Info-tag

Anti-Vehicle Rocket Launcher

Ammunition: Anti-Vehicle Rockets (5)

The AVRiL, or Anti-Vehicle Rocket Launcher, is a bulky rocket launcher variant that shoots slow-moving homing missiles that pack quite a devastating punch on enemy vehicles. Not suitable for taking down infantry, the AVRiL is the mainstay of Onslaught matches, the friend of pedestrian soldiers, and the bane of drivers and pilots.

Ordnance Tactics

The AVRiL has a very specific purpose: to cripple and destroy vehicles. Do not use against people, as the fired rockets are easily dodged. Many disregard the AVRiL as overly cumbersome—not so. The primary fire shoots the rocket in a straight line. When you reach long range and have an enemy vehicle in your crosshairs, a red target appears. Hold down the secondary fire button. The AVRiL guidance system locks on and follows the vehicle, even through the sharpest maneuvers. Give this system aiming control (although you can override it). Fire the rocket and it's guided to the vehicle—an almost guaranteed hit! Keep aiming until the rocket connects.

There are some ways to dodge the rockets. Listen for the lock-on warning. If you're in a Raptor, fly behind a hill so the rocket slams into it instead of your vehicle. Or exit your vehicle and fire on the AVRiL wielder. Be wary of this if you're using this weapon—keep a teammate nearby for supporting fire. Finally, the rockets do have a finite fuel supply, so with enough outrageous air dodging you can escape.

Other strategies to attempt: Try firing AVRiL rockets blindly into the air when running toward a combat area. AVRiL rockets gain acceleration over time, so when a valid vehicle target comes into view, you can target it and the AVRiL rocket will streak down from the sky at tremendous velocity and destroy the target. Sometimes you may even have two rockets in the air with enough timing to bring them both down onto an enemy target.

If tanks and turrets have located your position and have pinned you behind a rock or obstacle (with constant fire), you may not have enough time to jump out, aim, and fire a rocket before you are killed. Try firing an AVRiL rocket into the air and jump out long enough to put the AVRiL crosshair on the enemy and then duck back down again. If the AVRiL is traveling fast enough, targeting the enemy for even a split second is enough to perfectly re-target the AVRiL at your enemy.

Rocket Launcher

	Primary Fire	Secondary Fire
Damage	90	270*
Head Special	No	No
Instant Hit	No	No
Ranged Fire	Yes	Yes
Range	Long	Long
Splash Damage	Yes	Yes
Combo Ability	No	Yes
Starting Ammo	12	12
Maximum Ammo	30	30
Ammo Depletion Time	9	11
Rate of Fire	Medium	Slow
Trajectory Affected by Gravity	Yes	Yes

* Secondary fire if all three rockets connect. 180 if two connect.

Tournament Official Info-tag

Trident Tri-barrel Rocket Launcher

Ammunition: Rocket Pack (9)

The Trident Tri-barrel Rocket Launcher is extremely popular among competitors who enjoy more bang for their buck. The rotating rear-loading barrel design allows for both single- and multi-warhead launches, letting you place up to three dumb-fire rockets on target. The warheads are designed to deliver maximum concussive force to the target and surrounding area upon detonation.

Ordnance Tactics

A mainstay of multiplayer mayhem, the rocket launcher fires missiles that will slay an enemy with a single direct hit. Follow an enemy in your crosshairs for a couple of seconds and you hear a beep; the rockets now home in on the target (although sharp moves and diving behind cover cause the rockets to miss). Watch the splash damage—you can badly wound yourself if your shot hits a nearby wall or enemy. Be sure you're more than 10 feet away from the blast radius.

The primary rocket attack fires a single missile. Always fire at the enemy's feet so the explosion strikes a dodging foe. The secondary fire function lets you launch one, two, or three rockets simultaneously, depending on how long you hold the Fire button down. Try building up the rocket salvo before you enter a room, and release it as you round a corner.

While you're building up secondary fire, hold the primary fire button also, and the launched rockets spiral in a tight formation. Use the tight trio to take down vehicles and slower enemies in narrower areas. Use the spread to tackle dodging, fast-moving foes, or in larger settings such as the city streets of AS-FALLENCITY. To dodge an incoming rocket, leap over them or dodge jump to the side.

Use the rocket launcher in all but the more restrictive fighting zones. The lock-on feature makes the weapon hugely popular in open fields or courtyards, but use it in multi-level zones and high-traffic areas too. In narrow hallways, switch to another weapon to avoid wounding yourself.

Predict where the enemy will be, and land a rocket there. Inflict splash damage around corners by aiming the rocket so it detonates near a hiding enemy. Use this on punk campers. Finally, if you face dozens of veteran players in a tight environment, continuously fire at a coveted object to eventually hit someone trying to grab it.

Lightning Gun

	Primary Fire	Secondary Fire
Damage*	70	70
Head Special	Yes	Yes
Instant Hit	Yes	Yes
Ranged Fire	No	No
Range	Infinite	Infinite
Splash Damage	No	No
Combo Ability	No	No
Starting Ammo	15	15
Maximum Ammo	40	40
Ammo Depletion Time	21	21
Rate of Fire	Very Fast	Fast
Trajectory Affected by Gravity	No	No

* Damage is doubled if head is struck.

Tournament Official Info-tag

Lightning Gun

Ammunition: Lightning Ammo (10)

The lightning gun is a high-power energy rifle capable of ablating even the heaviest carapace armor. Acquisition of a target at long range requires a steady hand, but the anti-jitter effect of the optical system reduces the weapon's learning curve significantly. Once the target has been acquired, the operator depresses the trigger, painting a proton "patch" on the target. Milliseconds later, the rifle emits a high voltage arc of electricity, which seeks out the charge differential and annihilates the target.

Ordnance Tactics

This weapon delivers a great one-shot kill if you can hit the victim's head. However, it takes a couple of seconds to recharge the weapon for a second shot. Don't fire indiscriminately; a single shot to the head is better than three improperly aimed blasts to the torso.

The secondary fire function zooms the view toward your target (the longer you hold the button, the tighter the zoom). Hit it again to zoom out. You have no peripheral vision while zoomed up, so make sure you're safe before trying this function.

The lightning gun becomes more popular the larger the map (it's also excellent for maps with long corridors). Locate a safe sniping spot and aim at high-trafficked areas; exceptional huntsmanship can allow you to control large areas. Don't snipe if there's nowhere to hide or in short sharp corners unless you're incredibly skilled. Try strafing left and right, holding the Fire button down, and line the crosshairs up with a dodging opponent just as the weapon is ready to fire again.

You'll be surprised how much ammo this weapon uses, so snipe near extra ammo packs. Both this and the sniper rifle have infinite range, but the lightning gun's vision isn't clouded when you fire. The shot is much more visible, so move after you fire. Head shots are a little easier with this weapon than the sniper rifle.

Sniper Rifle

	Primary Fire	Secondary Fire
Damage	38	38*
Head Special	Yes	Yes
Instant Hit	Yes	Yes
Ranged Fire	No	No
Range	Infinite	Infinite
Splash Damage	No	No
Combo Ability	No	No
Starting Ammo	15	15
Maximum Ammo	35	35
Ammo Depletion Time	17	17
Rate of Fire	Very Fast	Fast
Trajectory Affected by Gravity	No	No

* Damage is doubled if head is struck. Smoke appears after each shot.

Tournament Official Info-tag

High Muzzle Velocity Sniper Rifle

Ammunition: Sniper Ammo (10)

This high muzzle velocity sniper rifle with a 10x scope is a lethal weapon at any range, especially if you can land a head-shot. Veterans from earlier tournaments protested the lack of sniper rifles in the previous season's matches, and their remonstrations were duly noted. However, this sniper rifle (which in all other regards, is exactly the same as the weapon utilized to great effect in *Unreal Tournament*) has a slight difference in the form of a puff of smoke from the spent cartridge, which can partially obscure the view and show the location of the sniper. The secondary fire function targets (press the button longer to zoom in further).

Ordnance Tactics

Be warned that the enemy (and every other player witnessing the shot) can see a long flash of light that impacts the target, so they can learn your location (a plume of smoke rises from your weapon, too). Direct body shots tend to inflict more damage (around 60 points), while a head shot can defeat a foe with a single round.

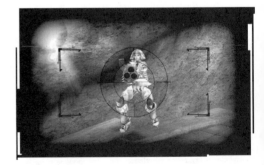

The range is the same as the lightning gun—infinite. Despite the smoke problem, the sniper rifle's scope is cleaner than the lightning gun's viewfinder, making targets slightly easier to get a bead on. Sit up in a crow's nest or some other high, protected spot, and offer supporting offensive fire.

Avoid the smoke clouding your vision by taking the shot, then strafing a little past the smoke. Can't move from your sniping spot? Then stand up, shoot, then duck down for the next round so the smoke's either above or below you. The smoke and slow rate of fire hinder an otherwise lethal weapon.

Redeemer

	Primary Fire	Secondary Fire
Damage	Death (1,500)	Death (1,500)*
Head Special	No	No
Instant Hit	No	No
Ranged Fire	Yes	Yes
Range	Infinite	Infinite
Splash Damage	Yes	Yes
Combo Ability	No	No
Starting Ammo	1	1
Maximum Ammo	1	1
Ammo Depletion Time	1	1
Rate of Fire	Very Slow	Very Slow
Trajectory Affected by Gravity	No	Yes

* 1,500 points of damage for a direct hit on vehicle.

Tournament Official Info-tag

Redeemer Mk.2 Miniature Nuclear Device

Ammunition: Redeemer Miniature Nuclear Rocket shown

The first time you witness this miniature nuclear device in action, you'll agree it is the most powerful weapon in the tournament. Launch a slow-moving but utterly devastating missile with the primary fire; but make sure you're out of the redeemer's impressive blast radius before it impacts. The secondary fire allows you to guide the nuke with a rocket's-eye view. Keep in mind, however, that you are vulnerable to attack when steering the redeemer's projectile. Due to the extreme bulkiness of its ammo, the redeemer is exhausted after a single shot.

Ordnance Tactics

You can carry only one ammo for this weapon (if you somehow pick up a second redeemer, it is wasted). Unlike the ion painter, however, the redeemer can be fired immediately. Also known as the "big dumb rocket," the redeemer's rocket can be easily shot out of the air with any instant-hit weapons (such as the minigun). The rocket does not detonate if it's shot out of the air. You're vulnerable when firing the rocket with secondary fire, and the rocket is notoriously difficult to fly. The walk button slows the rocket enough to turn corners, but this makes it easier to fire at.

Many maps (such as Deck17) become a constant battle to reach the redeemer just as it respawns. Shoot it into a heavily trafficked area, and run. You'll be destroyed if you're caught in the mushrooming splash damage area. Put a physical object between you and the blast or translocate away. Avoid the secondary fire function in small, tight spaces.

Shield packs don't protect you against this blast. You may survive if you're wearing armor and at the edges of the explosion. The explosion comes in three waves, with the first one pushing you up and away from the center the most. If you jump as the wave hits, you can be pushed away (although you'll still be incredibly damaged).

Ion Painter

	Primary Fire	Secondary Fire
Damage	Death (900)*	N/A
Head Special	No	N/A
Instant Hit	No	N/A
Ranged Fire	Yes	N/A
Range	Medium	N/A
Splash Damage	Yes	N/A
Combo Ability	No	N/A
Starting Ammo	N/A	N/A
Maximum Ammo	1**	N/A
Ammo Depletion Time	4–8	N/A
Rate of Fire	Very Slow	N/A
Trajectory Affected by Gravity	No	N/A

* 900 points of damage to direct hit on vehicle

** One strike per pick-up

Tournament Official Info-tag

Multi-gigawatt VAPOR Orbital Targeter (Ion Cannon)

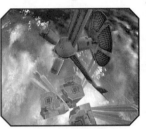

Ammunition: Orbital Cannon shown

Sometimes known as the TAG Rifle (Target Acquisition and Guidance), the ion painter seems innocuous enough at first glance, emitting a harmless low-power laser beam when the primary firing mode is engaged. Several seconds later a multi-gigawatt orbital ion cannon fires on the target, neutralizing any combatants in the vicinity. The ion painter is a remote targeting device used to orient and fire the VAPOR Ion Cannon. The ion painter offers increased targeting accuracy via its telescopic sight, easily activated by the secondary fire mode of the weapon. Once the ion painter has been used to designate a target, it is highly recommended that the user put considerable distance between themselves and the weapon's area of effect. Note that the force of the blast leaves only a charred skeleton.

Ordnance Tactics

This single-shot weapon (meaning you can't pick up more than one) fires a weak red laser into the ground. You must be at mid-range or closer and have a clear line of sight to your target. The orbital cannon must have clear line of sight to your laser point too; it won't work inside buildings, for example. Hold still for three seconds to allow the laser to build in brightness and create enough of a signal for the orbital cannon to strike. The secondary attack zooms in on the target, but it isn't really necessary.

Veteran players can run about while targeting, but it's extremely difficult. If you move while aiming, the laser begins to build up again. To check if a map may contain an ion painter, look for the tiny orbital cannon floating in space.

An impressive purple ray emits from the cannon and explodes in a huge area of effect, killing anyone in the radius. If you're caught in a laser, flee immediately. If you see the ion painter user, retaliate so they move the laser, then finish them off.

Target Painter

	Primary Fire	Secondary Fire
Damage	Death (4 x 1,500)*	N/A
Head Special	No	N/A
Instant Hit	No	N/A
Ranged Fire	Yes	N/A
Range	Medium	N/A
Splash Damage	Yes	N/A
Combo Ability	No	N/A
Starting Ammo	N/A	N/A
Maximum Ammo	1**	N/A
Ammo Depletion Time	8–10 secs. for strike	
Rate of Fire	Very Slow	N/A
Trajectory Affected by Gravity	No	N/A

* 1,500 points of damage to direct hit on vehicle. Four redeemer rockets are dropped.

** One strike per pick-up

Tournament Official Info-tag

Redeemer Mk.2 Miniature Nuclear Device Multi-launch targeter

Ammunition: No Ammunition available (nuclear rocket quartet shown)

During certain Onslaught matches, even the most heavyweight of vehicles may not be enough to halt a charging squadron of enemy units intent on taking over your PowerNode or core. As a last-ditch effort, the Liandri Corporation introduces the target painter, a tactical nuclear strike launched with a stroke of a laser pointer weapon which is identical to the ion painter, but features a large targeting rangefinder. Eight to ten seconds after the ground the laser points to has been chosen, a dropship warps into the skies overhead, drops four redeemer-class missiles vertically, and teleports away.

Ordnance Tactics

Order this classic airstrike on Onslaught maps. The effects are like four redeemers exploding in one long line. Although the ensuing maelstrom can wipe out entire teams, it takes 8–10 seconds to order a strike, meaning enemies can get out of the way. The secondary fire function simply zooms in the view.

Find a high point before you fire, ideally behind cover. Your target painter has a huge range—it can fire about a third of a mile away. Don't aim directly in front of or on top of a vehicle; you don't want the enemies to see the laser. Instead, fire just behind the team, or to the side before they pass through a ravine. Bombard the team with regular ordnance while the enemy is preoccupied with the missile strike.

The redeemer missiles are dropped in a line, depending on the way you're facing. Try to be in front of or behind an enemy convoy or concentrate on a well-guarded PowerNode. A great time to use this weapon is at a node the enemy is advancing on.

To avoid this airstrike, bring out any instant-hit weapon (the minigun is best) and fire at the dropping missiles. They explode harmlessly if you hit them with only a couple of shots.

75

Ball Launcher

	Primary Fire	Secondary Fire
Damage	N/A	N/A
Head Special	N/A	N/A
Instant Hit	No	N/A
Ranged Fire	Yes	N/A
Range	Long	N/A
Splash Damage	N/A	N/A
Combo Ability	N/A	N/A
Starting Ammo	1	N/A
Maximum Ammo	1	N/A
Ammo Depletion Time	N/A	N/A
Rate of Fire	Fast	N/A
Trajectory Affected by Gravity	Yes	N/A

Tournament Official Info-tag

DT06-H Ball Launcher

Ammunition: Ball

The DT06-H Ball Launcher is automatically equipped to tournament players, and activates as soon as the ball itself, a floating metallic sphere designed to withstand extreme ionization and nuclear attack, is picked up. The ball launcher overrides all other weapons systems you may be using, and the ball is carried in the nozzle. It can then be manually passed or automatically sent to a teammate within your vicinity.

Ordnance Tactics

This ordnance has no offensive capabilities and is only used in Bombing Run matches. The weapon's primary fire launches the ball in the direction you're facing. Pitch up to fire a long distance, or down to fire at your feet. The secondary fire automatically seeks out the nearest teammate within a line of sight from you in any direction, and the ball is flung unless you or your teammate moves to block this line.

As you cannot equip any weapons when using the ball launcher, it automatically disappears when you rid yourself of the ball, and reappears when you grab it again. However, you regenerate around four health points per second while holding the ball, up to a maximum of 100. You cannot instantly switch from ball launcher to translocator as you could last season.

Learn some techniques to help your team score. Lob the ball from long range so it arcs into the goal; know where to run in every match so you can score from long range. Shoot the ball at the enemy so he picks it up, then blast the foe, pick up the ball, and score. These tricks (along with excellent teamwork) help you reach the goal.

Weapon Lockers

Thoroughly familiarize yourself with this new object. The weapons you get are what you see hooked to the locker. Once you pick them up, you can't return and reload. Some weapons contain maximum ammunition, others have starting ammo. You can run through a locker.

Vehicle and Turret Inspections

This chapter walks you through the vehicles available in the Onslaught (and to a lesser extent, the Assault) matches. The machine's armor, weapon capabilities, and recommended tactics are all listed.

General Vehicle Tactics

Before you fire up an extremely heavy, difficult-to-maneuver vehicle, be sure you understand the following:

- You can shoot the enemy out of Scorpions, Mantas, or Hellbenders.
- If you take a bank or ravine at too sharp an angle, you may overturn your Scorpion or Hellbender. Flip it back with the Use key (the default Use key is "E"). If it's near a wall, it flips, then lands back on you. Prevent flipping by accelerating hard to launch yourself.
- If your Raptor receives a lock-on, jump out rather than suffer your vehicle's fate; deploy your shield as you hit the ground.
- When manning turrets, the next or previous weapon cycles any turrets once you're at a turret terminal. Learn the location of each turret terminal on the map.
- Unless you trust your driver not to make amateur mistakes, use the number keys to flick between seats in a vehicle.
- Try using the first-person camera view while in the Raptor.
- If you secure a Leviathan, let a single team member loose with it while the rest pillage the remaining opposition.
- If you're going down in a blazing Raptor, try to steer it into a PowerNode or enemy.
- Energy turrets do a great deal of damage to vehicles. They can push enemies and small vehicles against walls, wounding them and impeding their progress.
- Park two (or more) Hellbenders and shoot a large number of sky mines, then combo each other's mines for a greater threading and damaging effect.

Sentry Guns and Turret Terminals

 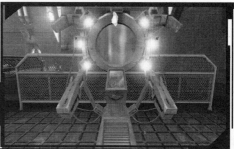

Usually encased in a mustard-colored armor cone, sentry guns placed at spawn points prevent spawn camping. They are automatically triggered when an enemy approaches within 25 feet.

Link and mothership turrets are accessed via a turret terminal. These stations allow you to personally fire turrets, and with link turrets, allow teammates to heal the turret you're controlling.

Scorpion

	Primary Fire	Secondary Fire
Damage	145–455*	Death
Head Special	No	No
Instant Hit	No	No
Ranged Fire	Yes	No
Range	Medium	Close
Splash Damage	Yes	No
Combo Ability	Yes	No
Starting Ammo	Infinite	2**
Maximum Ammo	Infinite	2**
Ammo Depletion Time	N/A	N/A
Rate of Fire	Fast	Very Fast
Trajectory Affected by Gravity	Yes	N/A

*Primary fire depends on number of connecting energy balls:
3 = 195, 4 = 260, 6 = 349, 7 = 455

** Manta secondary fire is side razor pincers. Damage is
random depending on strength of hit. Pincers can snap if hit
hard against rock.

General Tactics

Armor: 300

This fast, four-wheel-drive vehicle carries a single player and has a primary fire of linked energy balls. This is by far the best way to take out an enemy Manta (the rotating lift fans on the Manta actually attract the balls). The longer you hold down the fire, the more linked balls are created.

The secondary fire consists of two scythe-like blades whipping horizontally out of the sides. These pack a major sting; if used on a foe, expect an instant kill. The force of the springing blades cutting through a foe is what kills, not the blades themselves. Less damage is inflicted if the blades are constantly out, and you run the risk of breaking them if you scrape a wall or flip over.

Tap primary fire once to release three linked balls, and charge to fire up to seven. While this inflicts reasonable damage to a node, it's better to step out and use link gun fire. The Scorpion is a great way to get to and from nodes, and is also the finest vehicle for launching off ramps and spinning around, doing tricks. It's easy to lose control, but you can use a handbrake on tight corners or as you leap a ramp. Bullfight this if you're defending against a Scorpion, as you can leap over it as it charges, turn and fire a shock rifle or rockets.

Manta

	Primary Fire	Secondary Fire
Damage	30	N/A
Head Special	No	N/A
Instant Hit	No	N/A
Ranged Fire	Yes	N/A
Range	Medium	N/A
Splash Damage	No	N/A
Combo Ability	No	N/A
Starting Ammo	Infinite	N/A
Maximum Ammo	Infinite	N/A
Ammo Depletion Time	N/A	N/A
Rate of Fire	Fast	N/A
Trajectory Affected by Gravity	No	N/A

General Tactics

Armor: 200

The airborne equivalent of a Scorpion, the Manta is a quick hovering vehicle. Hold down Jump to boost, or jump around, giving you more flexibility to maneuver. Aside from the Raptor, this is the fastest vehicle. Use it immediately to grab as many nodes as possible. Primary fire are plasma bolts with a reasonably good damage and great rate of fire. If you're careful with your strafing, and learn evasive moves such as leaping out of gunfire and circling around a foe, you can take out a Goliath with this!

It's excellent for patrolling nodes, and even better for squishing pedestrians (the secondary fire inverts the fans and slams the Manta onto the ground). You can wall climb and jump cliffs with this machine. However, they become premier targets for tanks, so stay away or extremely close to them. Use the Manta as an impromptu troop transporter. Stand teammates on the wings and carry them where you want!

Hellbender

Passenger Turret

	Primary Fire	Secondary Fire		Primary Fire	Secondary Fire
Damage	25*	25**	Maximum Ammo	Infinite	Infinite
Head Special	No	No	Ammo Depletion Time	N/A	N/A
Instant Hit	No	Yes	Rate of Fire	Fast	Very Fast
Ranged Fire	Yes	No	Trajectory Affected by Gravity	No	No
Range	Long	Infinite			
Splash Damage	Yes	Yes***			
Combo Ability	Yes	Yes			
Starting Ammo	Infinite	Infinite			

* Damage is per sky mine.

** Secondary fire combo attack varies between 80 (caught at edge of splash damage) to 120 (direct hit).

*** If fired as part of a combo attack

79

Main Turret

	Primary Fire	Secondary Fire		Primary Fire	Secondary Fire
Damage	200*	N/A	Maximum Ammo	Infinite	N/A
Head Special	No	N/A	Ammo Depletion Time	N/A	N/A
Instant Hit	Yes	N/A	Rate of Fire	Very Fast	N/A
Ranged Fire	No	N/A	Trajectory Affected by Gravity	No	N/A
Range	Long	N/A			
Splash Damage	No	N/A			
Combo Ability	No	N/A			
Starting Ammo	Infinite	N/A			

* Turret can be powered up between a tap and three seconds, and held for more than three seconds. Damage (approx) depends on build-up time: tap = 30, 1 second = 100, 2 seconds = 160, 3 seconds = 200.

General Tactics

Armor: 600

Armor (in AS-JUNKYARD): 1,400–1,600 (dependent on number of players)

This heavyweight equivalent of the Scorpion is the mainstay of your Onslaught force. It's faster and more maneuverable than a Goliath, with less armor. One person drives, a second takes a passenger turret, and a third stands atop the main back turret. Shoot nodes and infantry using these turrets. Good communication is the key. If you are solo, drive until you reach an enemy, then change position with the number keys and fire, then switch back to the driver to continue. The driver's Fire button sounds the horn.

The passenger turret fires a sky mine—a slower-moving shock ball. The passenger secondary fire is an instant-hit blast that doesn't do much damage when fired alone, but links all the sky mines in an awesome mass explosion that's useful for clearing entire nodes. Fire at your sky mines within three seconds of launching the last one.

The main turret's primary fire is a charged energy twin-beam; hold it down longer for more power. Secondary fire on the main turret is a range finder, allowing you to use this main turret from great distances. The force of the blast can knock a Manta or Scorpion off course as well as damage it. With all this firepower, the Hellbender is as versatile and deadly, but use it primarily for node sniping.

Raptor

	Primary Fire	Secondary Fire
Damage	25	150
Head Special	No	No
Instant Hit	No	No
Ranged Fire	Yes	Yes
Range	Long	Long
Splash Damage	No	Yes
Combo Ability	No	No
Starting Ammo	Infinite	Infinite
Maximum Ammo	Infinite	Infinite
Ammo Depletion Time	N/A	N/A
Rate of Fire	Fast	Slow
Trajectory Affected by Gravity	No	Yes

General Tactics

Armor: 300

Use this nimble but badly armored flier to set up recon stations or to take out-of-the-way superweapons. This is the only vehicle that actually flies (use the Jump button with crouch to descend). Primary fire consists of energy bolts with a range and destructive capabilities similar to the Manta's. The secondary fire is a lone rocket that's effective against enemy Raptors and Mantas, and should be employed against them exclusively.

When piloting the Raptor, keep moving quickly and stay airborne. Raptors are the fastest vehicle but the most fragile. Don't scrape against anything—your armor is low enough as it is! They are excellent for taking out Goliaths (especially from above), as the tank's only defense from this angle is the machine gun, which the Raptor can easily dodge.

A Raptor's main menace comes from the AVRiL. Break the enemy line of sight when fleeing one, ideally by scooting behind a mountain. Use the vehicle to quickly reach the next PowerNode or to run interference against the enemy by swooping at them.

Goliath

Top Turret .50 Caliber Machine Gun

	Primary Fire	Secondary Fire		Primary Fire	Secondary Fire
Damage	3*	N/A	Starting Ammo	Infinite	N/A
Head Special	No	N/A	Maximum Ammo	Infinite	N/A
Instant Hit	Yes	N/A	Ammo Depletion Time	N/A	N/A
Ranged Fire	No	N/A	Rate of Fire	Very Fast	N/A
Range	Long**	N/A	Trajectory Affected by Gravity	No	N/A
Splash Damage	No	N/A			
Combo Ability	No	N/A			

* Per bullet, fired 25 per second = 75 damage a second.

** Accuracy becomes impaired the longer the range.

Main Turret

	Primary Fire	Secondary Fire		Primary Fire	Secondary Fire
Damage	300	N/A	Starting Ammo	Infinite	N/A
Head Special	No	N/A	Maximum Ammo	Infinite	N/A
Instant Hit	No	N/A	Ammo Depletion Time	N/A*	N/A
Ranged Fire	Yes	N/A	Rate of Fire	Slow	N/A
Range	Long	N/A	Trajectory Affected by Gravity	No	N/A
Splash Damage	Yes	N/A			
Combo Ability	No	N/A			

* Ammo doesn't deplete but has a one-second delay between shots.

General Tactics

Armor: 800

This two-man, lumbering tank is fully armored and features a driver's seat with a main turret and a secondary top turret with a .50 caliber machine gun. Use the machine gun for tagging flying Raptors, hover vehicles, or troops. It whips around far faster than the main turret, so use it to offer covering fire. The secondary fire on the main turret is a range finder.

Use the huge main turret's primary fire to take out Mantas, Scorpions, and Raptors in one well-aimed shot (the secondary fire zooms). The weapon takes a split-second to connect with its target, which can lead to missing (especially against airborne opponents who can also fly higher than your main tank cannon can aim).

Try using Goliath tanks to encroach on a PowerNode, blasting from the top of a ridge and then retreating to avoid retaliation. This is the main firepower to bring to an Onslaught battle. Although it's not the best troop transport, if you have a bunch of teammates healing this tank, it can devastate.

Watch out for circle-strafing enemy Mantas, as the main turret can't keep up. Instead, swing 180 degrees and wait for the turret to catch up with the target. You can fire off a round while the turret is swinging. Finally, work as a team; hide behind the superstructure and then ambush.

Leviathan

Turrets

	Primary Fire	Secondary Fire		Primary Fire	Secondary Fire
Damage	25	25*	Starting Ammo	Infinite	Infinite
Head Special	No	No	Maximum Ammo	Infinite	Infinite
Instant Hit	No	No	Ammo Depletion Time	N/A	N/A
Ranged Fire	Yes	Yes	Rate of Fire	Fast	Fast
Range	Medium	Medium	Trajectory Affected by Gravity	No	No
Splash Damage	No	No			
Combo Ability	No	No	*Primary and secondary fire are both the same.		

Main Weapon

	Primary Fire	Secondary Fire		Primary Fire	Secondary Fire
Damage	50 or 800*	N/A	Maximum Ammo	Infinite	N/A
Head Special	No and No*	N/A	Ammo Depletion Time	N/A	N/A
Instant Hit	No and Yes	N/A	Rate of Fire	Fast	Very Slow
Ranged Fire	Yes and No	N/A	Trajectory Affected by Gravity	No	N/A
Range	Medium	Infinite			
Splash Damage	No and Yes	N/A	*50 is the damage per pulse with vehicle moving. 800 is the damage per shot with vehicle clamped. First and second information refers to both types of primary fire.		
Combo Ability	No and No	N/A			
Starting Ammo	Infinite	N/A			

General Tactics

Armor: 5,000

Make the Leviathan your primary goal in the Onslaught maps, and expect to lose numerous lives when attacking it. Raptors can hover above, and an ace Manta driver could circle-strafe the beast until it explodes, but the bristling turrets make this unlikely.

Too slow to be an effective troop transporter, this vehicle is a moveable battle base with a driver and four turret gunners (the turret gunners have an energy pulse fire like the Manta and zoom in for secondary fire). Move to defend a choke point or push back advancing forces.

The driver's primary fire consists of guided rockets that can continuously arc toward an enemy if you keep your crosshairs on them. However, if the driver uses the secondary fire function, the behemoth stops and pins itself to the ground, and the driver's second weapon emerges—a giant turret with capabilities similar to the ion cannon! Press secondary fire again to return to the mobile mode. Use this to decimate large forces, nodes, and bases. Be sure to hold the node that spawns this vehicle.

Park at a strategic location (such as a PowerNode), then link heal as a team and bombard the enemy. Focus all four passenger turrets on a single enemy to completely destroy them. You can even take out a Goliath tank.

Ion Tank (and Ion Cannon)

	Primary Fire	Secondary Fire
Damage	Death (900)*	N/A
Head Special	No	N/A
Instant Hit	Yes	N/A
Ranged Fire	No	N/A
Range	Infinite	N/A
Splash Damage	Yes	N/A
Combo Ability	No	N/A
Starting Ammo	Infinite	N/A
Maximum Ammo	Infinite	N/A
Ammo Depletion Time	N/A	N/A
Rate of Fire	Slow	N/A
Trajectory Affected by Gravity	No	N/A

900 points of damage to direct hit on vehicle

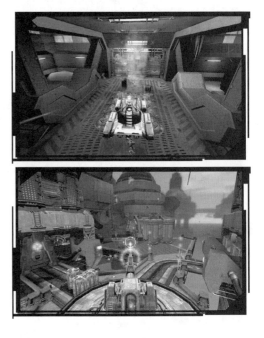

General Tactics

The ion tank (available in AS-GLACIER) and the ion cannon (available in AS-ROBOTFACTORY) have the same weapon effects; the tank is mobile and fires faster, but the turret is near indestructible (it can be destroyed after withstanding massive amounts of damage). Otherwise, the ion tank is identical to Goliath, so refer to that vehicle for more information. These machines shoot an ion blast like an ion painter.

**Armor (Tank):
1,400–1,600 (depends on number of players)**

**Armor (Ion Cannon):
Infinite**

The tank's secondary fire function is a seismic shove. This doesn't cause damage, but it pushes enemies away. Hold down the Fire button to launch the primary attack—you can continue to hold to fire again; each charge takes around two seconds. Shoot frequently!

Space Fighter (Type I and II)

	Primary Fire	Secondary Fire
Damage	70	200
Head Special	No	No
Instant Hit	Yes	No
Ranged Fire	No	Yes
Range	Long	Long
Splash Damage	No	No
Combo Ability	No	No
Starting Ammo	Infinite	Infinite
Maximum Ammo	Infinite	Infinite
Ammo Depletion Time	N/A	N/A
Rate of Fire	Fast	Slow
Trajectory Affected by Gravity	No	No

General Tactics

These space fighters, which appear only on the Assault level AS-Mothership are available to both the attackers and defenders. They have slight differences in shape but their effectiveness is the same. Their primary fire consists of moderately powerful instant-hit plasma bursts. The secondary fire is a homing missile similar to the Raptor's. Wait for a lock-on beep and a green square target to appear before you fire.

Armor: 300

85

"Next weapon/previous weapon" cycles through visible targets (default setting is mousewheel up/mousewheel down). Press forward to speed up, backward to slow down, and left and right to strafe. Crouch centers and right-sides you if you're upside down. "E" cycles through visible targets. Hold jump, then left or right to barrel roll; this looks impressive and gives slightly better protection when you're zooming down a tight corridor, avoiding turret fire.

Try strafing the turrets instead of flying straight at them because it takes only six shots to destroy your craft. If it is disintegrating, steer it into an enemy turret. When defending, take out as many of these fighters as possible.

Minigun Turret

	Primary Fire	Secondary Fire
Damage	15*	N/A
Head Special	No	N/A
Instant Hit	Yes	N/A
Ranged Fire	No	N/A
Range	Medium	Medium**
Splash Damage	No	N/A
Combo Ability	No	N/A
Starting Ammo	Infinite	N/A
Maximum Ammo	Infinite	N/A
Ammo Depletion Time	N/A	N/A
Rate of Fire	Fast	N/A
Trajectory Affected by Gravity	No	N/A

15 damage per shot, at 12 shots per second = 180 damage per second.

** *Accuracy is impaired the farther from the target you are.*

General Tactics

Armor: 500

These turrets, which appear throughout Assault maps, are like a slightly more powerful minigun with infinite ammunition. However, you can be shot out of them and your head is an easy target (especially from the side), so retaliate quickly at snipers. The primary fire is a rapid-shot unloading, while secondary fire zooms in and out.

If you're taking out these turrets, learn their locations, check for a gunner's head, and snipe. These turrets are loud, so you know when one is in operation. It takes a fair amount to destroy one, so band together.

Energy Turret

	Primary Fire	Secondary Fire
Damage	30	N/A
Head Special	No	N/A
Instant Hit	No	N/A
Ranged Fire	Yes	N/A
Range	Long	N/A
Splash Damage	No	N/A
Combo Ability	No	N/A
Starting Ammo	Infinite	N/A
Maximum Ammo	Infinite	N/A
Ammo Depletion Time	N/A	N/A
Rate of Fire	Fast	N/A
Trajectory Affected by Gravity	No	N/A

General Tactics

Armor: 350

A human-shaped turret with two refitted custom shock rifles in each suit, these are also known as manual base guns and are found on Onslaught maps, often near nodes or bases. The primary fire consists of nasty shock bolts. They can knock over Hellbenders or push enemies against walls and keep them there until they explode. The secondary fire function zooms in and out, allowing you to target advancing forces.

The energy turret can swivel 360 degrees and point straight up to tackle Raptors. Jump in and man these defensive weapons when the immediate area is under attack. Energy turrets have weak armor—Goliaths can tear a turret apart in one or two shots, and infantry with a few rockets. Quick damage drops them more easily, and your aim is thrown off when you're under attack.

Link Turret

	Primary Fire	Secondary Fire		Primary Fire	Secondary Fire
Damage*	35	260**	Maximum Ammo	Infinite	Infinite
Head Special	No	No	Ammo Depletion Time	N/A	N/A
Instant Hit	No	Yes	Rate of Fire	Fast	Very Fast
Ranged Fire	Yes	Yes	Trajectory Affected by Gravity	No	No
Range	Long	Long			
Splash Damage	Yes	No			
Combo Ability	No	No			
Starting Ammo	Infinite	Infinite			

* Secondary fire heals other turrets at rate of 33 points per second.

** Damage per second for secondary fire. Double this per turret in link chain. Can be linked to via infantry with link gun.

87

General Tactics

Armor: 400

Appearing in AS-MOTHERSHIP and ROBOTFACTORY, these turrets are very similar to the link gun with their primary damage (which also causes small splash damage). The very fast-firing secondary stream isn't as effective as the primary fire and is used for linking. Chain link guns to turrets for even more power, which is exceptional in ROBOTFACTORY. Also try turret-to-turret linking.

The front and side shields make turrets difficult to destroy from these angles. Shoot from behind to bypass the shields. Forward and reverse keys zoom the turret in and out. Although it has limited ammo, this does recharge infinitely, and it takes minutes of constant firing to run low on energy (keep this in mind for larger matches). The turret auto-fires if not manned.

Mothership Energy Turret

	Primary Fire	Secondary Fire
Damage	45	N/A
Head Special	N/A	N/A
Instant Hit	No	N/A
Ranged Fire	Yes	N/A
Range	Long	N/A
Splash Damage	No	N/A
Combo Ability	No	N/A
Starting Ammo	Infinite	N/A
Maximum Ammo	Infinite	N/A
Ammo Depletion Time	N/A	5*
Rate of Fire	Fast	N/A
Trajectory Affected by Gravity	No	N/A

* Secondary shield lasts for up to five seconds.

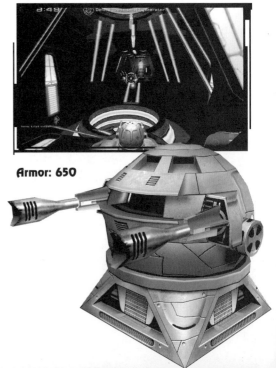

Armor: 650

General Tactics

Also known as ball turrets, these are positioned around the mothership in the Assault level. They fire energy plasma. The secondary fire is a small shield, used only when an enemy space fighter strikes you (shield yourself just before impact). It auto-fires if not manned, usually doing a better job.

PowerNode and PowerCore

General Tactics

The PowerNode is attached to other nodes and/or the core by links. Stand on the node's pulsing middle to change it to your team's color. It takes 30 seconds of unassisted pulsing (15 with the link gun) to power up the node and link it to previously taken areas. To take an enemy node, make sure it is one link away from your nearest node (it should be glowing yellow), then bombard the top or base of the node with gunfire until it is destroyed and turns neutral. Then activate it as normal.

The PowerCore is a large solid structure pulsing with your team's color in your base. An enemy core can be attacked only when your team owns the node linking to it.

Single-Player Strategies

The Liandri Corporation's Unreal Tournament enters its 12th year as a legally sanctioned competition. This year's tournament is the most highly anticipated yet, with teams captained by highly regarded former champions Malcolm, Gorge, and the long absent Xan Kriegor, as well as a dangerous team from the Skaarj Empire. Before you can enter the tournament proper, you must first defeat other hopefuls in the qualifying rounds.

Creating a Profile

Single-player mode allows a rookie to earn stripes before jumping into multiplayer. It's much less embarrassing to get beaten by a bunch of Bots than to chew lead online with 30 strangers. Single-player mode begins with a short tutorial, goes into a series of single-player Deathmatch games, and ends with you assembling a team of battle-hardened warriors ready to claw up the competitive ladder of *Unreal Tournament*.

In the main menu, six tabs detail the following:

Profile: where you load or create your character

Tutorials: showing you the basics of playing Deathmatch, Capture the Flag, Double Domination, and Bombing Run

Qualification: the Deathmatches you go through before you're deemed worthy to captain your own team

Team Qualification: four team games to prove you're hiring the best mercenary scum around

Ladder: where you play four event series before challenging the most experienced veterans

Team Management: where you heal, fire, and hire your assortment of clinically insane killing machines

All the submenus have a Play button that you click to resume your struggles, and a Back button that returns you to the main menu. After you become a champion, you receive a Details button showing how you matched up against your opposition.

Single-player mode begins as a one-on-one experience. First, create a profile to record your progress. From the Profile submenu, you can delete, load, create a profile, and view your player's high scores. The Details box lists your character, your team, the game's difficulty level, and your character's kills, deaths, and goals, as well as the number of times certain accolades have been bestowed on him/her/it (such as "Godlike").

If you don't have an existing profile, click New Profile to create one. You choose a character and team symbol by clicking the arrows under the pictures. Enter your name in the Player Name field and the name of your team in the Team Name field, and adjust the difficulty of the game via the Difficulty field. Default is Experienced—if you're unsure, tweak the Bot difficulty levels in an Instant Action game, then come back here. When all is ready, click Create Profile.

Qualification

Next, you must qualify for the tournament. With your profile loaded, click the Qualification tab. A short video explains the basic controls and goals of Deathmatch. The next step is a One-on-One (1-on-1) Deathmatch against some chump you should have little problem defeating. The match plays out on one of two compact maps, chosen randomly. Step 3 is another Deathmatch against two opponents. The fourth rung on the qualification ladder is another Deathmatch, but now you face two enemies. Fortunately, they're both out for themselves. Catch them while they're fighting each other.

   Step 5 is a Five-Way Deathmatch—a quintuple free-for-all. Step 6 is Draft Your Team, Then Defeat Them. Assemble your team and take on the characters you choose in an every-man-for-himself Deathmatch. Check the Cartographical Evidence section for specific Deathmatch map tactics, and the Training section for overviews on hunting down your opponents.

> **NOTE**
>
> A few of the matches in this season's tournament take place on older maps. This guide provides comprehensive strategy for only the new maps appearing in *Unreal Tournament 2004*. Consult *Prima's Official Unreal Tournament 2003 Strategy Guide* for information on many previous maps. All older maps are marked with an asterisk (*).

Qualification Maps

> **NOTE**
>
> Depending on the profile you create, the initial maps available for each ladder can vary. If you have more than three map selections (such as Team Deathmatch #1), you can choose either the selectable map (for zero cost) or one of the other maps (for additional credit expenditure). New tournament stages specifically crafted for *Unreal Tournament 2004* are usually the default.

Step 1: Tutorial	Step 3: One on One	Step 5: Five-Way Deathmatch
DM-Tutorial	DM-1on1-Spirit	
Step 2: One on One	DM-1on1-Trite	DM-1on1-Desolation
DM-1on1-Idoma	**Step 4: Cutthroat Deathmatch**	**Step 6: Draft Your Team, Then Defeat Them**
	DM-1on1-Albatross	
	DM-1on1-Roughinery	DM-1on1-Irondust

Drafting Your Team

Each potential team member has five important attributes:

Accuracy: Skill with a weapon

Aggression: Tendency to fight or flee

Agility: Ability to dodge bullets

Team Tactics: Ability to play with others

Salary: Cost of the character

Maximize the first four statistics and keep the fifth as low as possible. It would be phenomenally advantageous to have a team of characters with Accuracy, Aggression, Agility, and Team Tactics skills in the 90s, but you could never afford them. When new freelancers approach you (which occurs randomly throughout the single-player game), or you wish to hire and fire your own team (accessed at the Team Management screen at any time), you can view their statistics and decide whether they're worth their asking price. Remember you need extra money for entering challenges, subsequent matches, and healing wounded teammates. If you're low on credits, replay previous matches.

> **NOTE**
>
> When hiring your team, be aware that Species Statistics are not employed in single-player competitions; therefore teammates with identical attribute levels really are identical.

When you've selected your team, you must train them in their roles. Use the pull-down menu under their thumbnail portraits to assign them tasks. Your choices are as follows:

Auto: The computer automatically determines the best place for the character.

Defense: The character defends your team's base or goal.

Offense: The character leads the charge on the opposing turf.

Roam: The character floats between defense and offense.

Support: The character plays neither offense nor defense but specifically helps the player achieve match goals (moves the ball down the arena, picks off opponents in pursuit of their flag, and so forth).

Assign them tasks based on two important criteria: the attributes of your opposing team, and the type of match you're about to play. Assigning teammates to certain roles affects your tactics. Play around with the settings if you're constantly suffering embarrassing defeats, and follow these general rules for deciding who is responsible for in-game objectives.

Auto Bots

Leaving a teammate to act alone has him taking various elements from the other Bot roles and reacting to events, usually slower than those with specific orders. Choose this during Deathmatches, when you're first starting out or when you want to quickly get on with a match.

Defense Bots

Defense is useful when playing Capture the Flag, Bombing Run, and Assault, but isn't used in matches lacking a defined "base." Weigh your propensity of offensive combat; can you overwhelm the opponents without using defenders? The answer is sometimes, on smaller maps. For larger maps, or areas you haven't studied, keep at least one teammate on base patrol. Defenders should have high Team Tactics and Accuracy ratings.

Offense Bots

These killing machines are a constant thorn in your enemies' side. Great for attacking objectives in Assault, but lacking the finesse and cranial capacity to operate under squad-based conditions, these loners simply find the enemy and attack. Good on Deathmatch and Assault levels, and possibilities on Team Deathmatch modes, they don't play well with others; choose them if you already have a core of helpers or think you can handle the enemy without Bot help. Offense Bots do well with high Aggression, and to a lesser extent, Agility and Accuracy. Team Tactics isn't a factor, so choose a friend with low social skills.

Roaming Bots

The roaming Bot is useful to bridge gaps in larger levels, if you're competing against a team you know little about, or if there's a specific zone outside the base you want the Bot to guard. Roaming Bots are a little more intelligent than those with one-track offensive or defensive minds, and they can cope with tide-turning situations. They are more willing to break off an attack to defend a flag base, for example. Roaming Bots should be well rounded statistically, with high Team Tactics.

Support Bots

This is the most useful Bot type, although a balanced team won't have more than two. Support Bots stick by you. They are incredibly useful in Team Deathmatches when you can overrun enemies or pick up stragglers by forming a close squad and rampaging through the level. Take at least one support Bot during Assault, CTF, DD, and BR games to provide covering fire and soak up the enemy fire. Great Team Tactics helps your Bot stay with you and understand your objectives.

Team Qualification

Once you've drafted your team, the tournament moves on to the Team Qualification. You've proved your worth, but your socially irresponsible killing machines must strut their stuff. Remember that of the additional maps available on the matches with more than two map choices, only one can be selected.

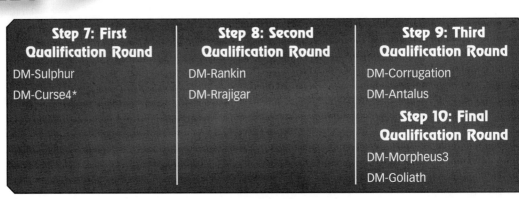

Step 7: First Qualification Round	Step 8: Second Qualification Round	Step 9: Third Qualification Round
DM-Sulphur	DM-Rankin	DM-Corrugation
DM-Curse4*	DM-Rrajigar	DM-Antalus

Step 10: Final Qualification Round

DM-Morpheus3

DM-Goliath

Ladder

After you make it through the 10 tournament qualification steps, take the show on the road and start climbing the *Unreal Tournament 2004* ladder. The four brackets are Bombing Run, Capture the Flag, Double Domination, and Assault.

You start in Double Domination, and the competition gets progressively tougher. Once you're partway through the Domination bracket, you can opt to proceed to the Capture the Flag, Bombing Run, and finally the Assault brackets. Conquer them all, and you can challenge the most incredible Tournament players and seek the ultimate prize of becoming the undisputed champion! Here's how the different match types are unlocked:

Tournament Unlocking Chart

Match Type	Unlocked at Completion
Team Qualification	The last Qualification match
Double Domination	The last Team Qualification match
Capture the Flag	The second Double Domination match
Bombing Run	The second CTF match
Assault	The second Bombing Run match
Championship	All previous ladders

Here are the level maps available for each ladder match.

Double Domination

DOM Match 1
DOM-Atlantis
DOM-ScorchedEarth*

DOM Match 2
DOM-Renascent
DOM-Junkyard*

DOM Match 3
DOM-Access
DOM-Outrigger*

DOM Match 4
DOM-Ruination*
DOM-Suntemple*

DOM Match 5
DOM-Conduit
DOM-Core*

DOM Match 6

DOM-Aswan

DOM-SepukkuGorge*

Capture the Flag

CTF Match 1

CTF-FaceClassic

CTF-Maul*

CTF-Citadel*

CTF Match 2

CTF-Grendelkeep

CTF-Magma*

CTF-Geothermal*

CTF Match 3

CTF-Smote

CTF-DE-TwinTombs *

CTF Match 4

CTF-Grassyknoll

CTF-Avaris*

CTF Match 5

CTF-January

CTF-Lostfaith*

CTF Match 6

CTF-MoonDragon

CTF-Orbital2*

CTF Match 7

CTF-BridgeOfFate

CTF-DE-LavaGiant2*

CTF Match 8

CTF-AbsoluteZero

CTF-DoubleDamage*

Bombing Run

BR Match 1

BR-Serenity

BR Match 2

BR-Bifrost*

BR-Anubis*

BR Match 3

BR-Canyon*

BR-DE-ElecFields*

BR Match 4

BR-Disclosure*

BR Match 5

BR-TwinTombs*

BR Match 6

BR-IceFields*

BR Match 7

BR-Skyline*

BR-BridgeOfFate*

BR Match 8

BR-Colossus

Assault

AS Match 1

AS-FallenCity

AS Match 2

AS-RobotFactory

AS Match 3

AS-Convoy

AS Match 4

AS-Glacier

AS Match 5

AS-Junkyard

AS Match 6

AS-MotherShip

Championship Matches

Championship Match 1

DM-Deck17

DM-DE-Osiris2*

Championship Match 2

DM-HyperBlast2

Challenge Accepted

Once you've reached the Team Deathmatch portion, the individuals and teams challenging you throughout the single-player tournament are pretty much predefined for each match. The various teams are arranged in four groups, based on how impressive they are. With some special calculation, the type of team challenging you comes from within these types:

Team Ability	Team Names
Easy	Sun Blade, Super Nova, Goliath
Weak	Firestorm, Black Legion, Bloodfist
Medium	Hellions, IronGuard, Juggernauts
Strong	Thundercrash, Iron Skull, Corrupt

95

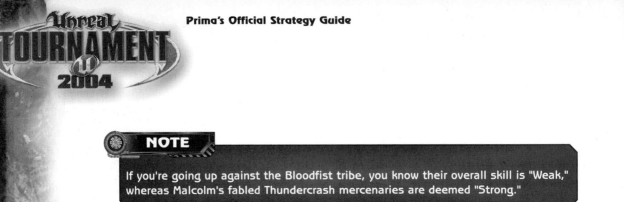

NOTE

If you're going up against the Bloodfist tribe, you know their overall skill is "Weak," whereas Malcolm's fabled Thundercrash mercenaries are deemed "Strong."

For Team Deathmatch and all Ladder matches, the least-played-against team from the Easy group is used. For the last Team Deathmatch challenge, the best team from the Easy group is used. The best team is selected on the basis of the team's rating. All teams start with a rating of 0. If the team beats your team, their rating increases by +1 for every point received, minus any points your team received. So if you were beaten 10 to 5 by Thundercrash, they instantly gain five points (+10 for score, -5 for your score = 5). If you beat Thundercrash by the same amount, they would lose 5 points. The team with the highest rating is deemed the best.

For the Capture the Flag, Bombing Run, Double Domination, and Assault ladders, the following teams are used:

Weak Group (least played)	Medium Group (least played)	Strong Group (least played)
CTF Matches 1–3	CTF Matches 4–6	CTF Matches 7–8
BR Matches 1–3	BR Matches 4–6	BR Matches 7–8
DOM Matches 1–2	DOM Matches 3–5	DOM Matches 6
AS Matches 1–2	AS Matches 3–5	AS Matches 6

When the Championship match is unlocked, the best team from the Strong group is used as the opposing team. This team is then locked in your profile.

Over time, the layout of the teams can change when you challenge the team for a Bloodrite. In a Bloodrite challenge, you fight an opposing team for one of their members (except the team leader). If you win, you receive the player, and the enemy team loses them. If you already have a full team, you must remove (or "fire") one of your teammates to make way for the new blood. This ex-member of your squad then becomes a free agent. Should you lose a match in the same manner, a member of your squad is removed by the opposing force.

After you play a game against a team, they might challenge you. The chance that they challenge you depends on how well the team did against you, but also on the difficulty you chose when you created your player. Higher difficulty means a higher chance to be challenged. The team-rating change that the team earned in the last match controls if the chance increases or decreases.

All Eyes on the Prize

The ultimate prize is unlocking the team leader of the Strong team that was your championship opponent. These character skins are available only once you defeat their team in this mode.

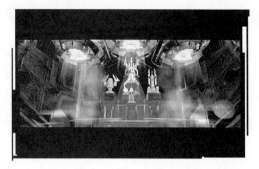

Championship Team to Beat	Unlocks Specific Skin
Thundercrash	Malcolm
Iron Skull	Clan Lord
Corrupt	Xan

For more information on these veteran tournament stars, refer to the Players' Club chapter. One note of warning: enabling cheating in single-player prevents you from unlocking the particular player skin. However, if you're having constant trouble battling through the upper echelons of the single-player mode, quit out and start an Instant Action game. Then slow down the time with the "slomo" command prompt ("slomo 0.5" is good). Now you can pick up instant-hit weapons (particularly the minigun) and consistently hit your opponents before they can react (even during the final championship match)!

NOTE

Multiplayer and Instant Action Games are covered in the Training section.

UNREAL TOURNAMENT 2004

Assault Maps

NOTE

Please note! As with the other game types, basic information and strategy on playing this particular match style has been thoroughly detailed in the Training section of this tome.

AS-CONVOY

Recommended Players: 6–14

Main Legend*

(#) - Object visible

(#) - Object obscured

[#] - Objective

[BO] - Bonus Objective

* This legend applies to all maps.

Legend

1   50 Shield Pack (Attackers' initial spawn point)

2   Weapons Locker (Attackers' initial spawn point)

3   50 Shield Pack (Attackers' initial spawn point)

4   50 Shield Pack (either side of crane transport front end)

5   50 Health Pack (rear of front transport)

6   Attackers' Weapons Locker and 50 Shield Pack x2 (bonus transport)

7   Shock Rifle +2 Ammo Packs (forward transport)

8   50 Health Pack (alcove on Juggernaut)

9   Defenders' Weapons Lockers (inside Juggernaut)

10   Weapons Locker (inside Juggernaut)

11   Link, mini, shock ammo (both ledges)

12   50 Health Pack (both ledges)

13   Defenders' Weapons Lockers (spawn point)

14   Weapons Locker (left exterior entrance)

15   50 Health Pack x2 (cylinder transport)

16   Shock Rifle

17   Rocket Launcher

18   50 Health Pack x2 (between mesh and metal arches)

19   50 Health Pack (bottom of O5)

20   Weapons Locker (inside)

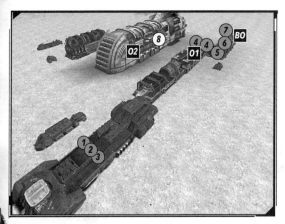

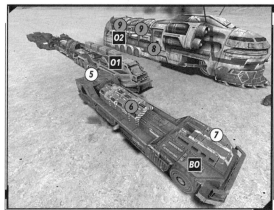

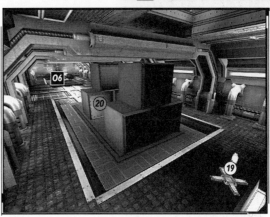

Overview

The Attackers have hatched a manic high-speed robbery plan! From their armored spawning truck, they move along a maintenance wagon train and attempt to operate a platform that will swing toward a central Juggernaut brimming with Defenders. Attackers can also dash to the front vehicle and commandeer this to create a spawn point nearer the first objective. Once the platform is extended, the Attackers must quickly dash and place explosives on a door leading inside the Juggernaut. Once inside, pull a lever opening the back of the Juggernaut to summon a repair truck and a new spawn point. Then press a lever at the far end of the Juggernaut's interior to open up the Juggernaut's left side. This leads to the more important vehicles in the train, including a vehicle carrying N.E.X.U.S. missiles in its cargo bay. Breach the bay by jumping and entering it, and pull a lever next to the missiles to winch the stack of missiles out of the vehicle bay and onto a waiting transporter.

Attackers' Objectives	Defenders' Objectives

1. Extend the boarding platform
  * Open the panel
	1. Defend the boarding platform
	  * Defend the panel

2. Place explosives on the door	2. Defend the door
3. Open rear door	3. Defend rear door
4. Open the side doors	4. Defend side door switch
5. Reach the N.E.X.U.S. missile trailer	5. Defend the N.E.X.U.S. missile trailer
6. Retrieve the N.E.X.U.S. missiles	6. Defend the N.E.X.U.S. missiles
* bonus objective	** bonus objective*

Attacking Objective 1: Extend the Boarding Platform

You begin inside the main Attackers' vehicle, and your first objective is ahead, across a series of linked vehicles. You see two objective markers: the one ahead is the boarding platform; the one to the right is a hatchway at the vehicle caravan's far end. This is the optional objective; send at least two of your team to secure this. Your Attackers begin by grabbing a 50 shield pack (one on either side of the locker) and taking four extra weapons from the locker.

Attackers' Weapon Locker 1*

Assault Rifle (additional)

Minigun

Rocket Launcher

Sniper Rifle

*Inside Attackers' vehicle

Have your team stream out of the left and right exit doors, which are always open. Select the more battle-hardened (or foolish) of your team to take the left hatch, as you come under enemy fire from the largest, central vehicle in the convoy (which is where the defenders are incoming from). Retaliate by hopping into the minigun turret at the end of the Attackers' vehicle on the left side and zoom in on the main vehicle. Shoot any Defenders in their shadowy sniping holes, or pepper the minigun to occupy the gunner while the rest of your team assaults the boarding platform vehicle. The minigun used as covering fire for teammates streaming up the train isn't as useful—the shots bounce off the arched gantry.

Once a minigunner is covering the boarding party with rapid-fire ordnance, have the rest of the team board the back end of the boarding platform via the arched cargo area. The two sentry guns prevent this from becoming a spawn-camping bloodbath. There are two main ways to run through this area: either underneath, stopping at the crates on the left, or leaping through the gap near the oil drums on the right (the right route offers more protection). Tackle any foes before you reach the main boarding platform.

There's a farther, sneakier way across the arched cargo vehicle. When you emerge from your boarding vehicle, head up the ramp, double back and jump onto the roof of your vehicle, then run to the edge of the vehicle and continually dodge jump to the top of the arches. Run across the arches and double jump to the huge cylinder's top. You're completely exposed, so attempt this only if you can shrug off attacks or know where your enemy is.

NOTE

Mind the gap! You must jump the area between the initial Attackers' vehicle and the cargo trailer, as there are sliding surfaces and deadly drops. Dropping down onto the sand beneath the giant vehicles' tracks results in instant and embarrassing death (if translocators are allowed, you can quickly save yourself).

Once your team is at the giant cylinder (ideally on its right side to avoid almost constant sniping from the larger central vehicle), leap across and onto the main boarding platform swivel mechanism. From here, an expert shield jump lands you atop the entrance to the boarding platform, which stretches along the vehicle, above the main mesh floor. If you've dashed over the top of the arches and over the giant cylinder, then double jump atop the boarding platform's end and into the relative safety of the partially covered platform.

When you reach this point, attackers may be stationed on the larger left-side vehicle, or the forward weapons vehicle on the right with the minigun turret. If no enemies are present to the right, run in and secure the forward weapons cache; even if you meet resistance, send at least two of your team to secure this optional objective.

The other, more standard ways to reach the boarding platform all involve a run through a nasty choke point underneath the platform. Run directly to the end of the underside of the platform, toward the health pack, then double back around and up one of two ramps (take the one farthest from the main Defenders' vehicle). When you reach the top of this ramp (and the 50 shield pack), you have two entrance options: you can continue forward and leap to the orange exterior square platform, doubling back on yourself. From here, double jump onto the giant cylinder, turn around, and jump onto the platform. Do this from the orange platform or the wire fence along the side of the vehicle. You can then move out and use the platform lever between gunfire shots, ideally with the shield gun lessening the damage you're taking.

If you want to throw off the Defenders' attack patterns, when you reach the top of the ramp, make a rapid 180-degree turn, leap across the gap from which you just came, over the wire fence, and run for the boarding platform entrance—one of two double-ramped areas on either side of the main platform. Alternately, the main route is to reach the ramp and shield pack, run under the platform, and then choose a ramp side to jog up and into the platform.

TIP

Want an even crazier entrance to the boarding platform? Flummox the enemy, especially those tightly defending the platform, by running past the ramp to the objective point (you can even run up and down it, inches from the objective!), dodge jump toward the end of the platform exterior, and land on the front of the vehicle. Or run around and leap up the front of the vehicle to the roof. Clamber onto the roof, then double jump onto the top of the boarding platform, and drop to the objective; or run to the platform's far end, drop in and double back!

When you're inside the platform, repel any threat, switch to your shield gun, and stand on the objective to swing the boarding platform around toward the central enemy Juggernaut. If you move off the objective point, the rotating platform moves back to its original position. It takes three long seconds to move that platform, so back up a teammate trying this. If necessary, sacrifice yourself by standing in front of him; your well-being is secondary to meeting the objective. Once the platform is in position, your objective is complete.

103

CAUTION

Whether you're an Attacker or a Defender, don't be in the way of the boarding platform when it rotates! Stand near the 50 shield pack nearest the central vehicle, and you'll be violently shoved to your death!

TIP

The shock rifle is a tremendous asset to both sides during this match, because you can easily knock an incoming foe from their route and off the vehicles to their deaths. This is classic strategy at closer quarters if the Attackers are leaping for an objective, and it allows last-minute objective saves. Feeling left out, Mr. Attacker? Then pick up a shock rifle at the forward vehicle cache (or the top rear of the bonus vehicle); you'll be glad you did!

Defending Objective 1: Defend the Boarding Platform

Defenders begin their match with a height advantage, starting inside an upper corridor on the main Juggernaut vehicle. Once out of the spawning point, pick up all the weapons at either of the two lockers, and depending on your location, run left or right along the interior corridor to one of three exits. The one to the right leads to a sniping point. This sniping point offers nearer views of the Attackers' starting point but with limited visibility of the boarding platform. Deploy a sniper in this position, while the rest of the team

storms through the final exit (the two doors in the corridor's middle). Don't forget your full complement of weapons from either of the two lockers before you leave!

Defenders' Weapon Lockers 1 and 2*

Biorifle

Shock Rifle

Link Gun

Minigun

Sniper Rifle

*Inside Defenders' Juggernaut

These doors (with the white and red arrow signs above them) lead to a minigun turret on a small ledge and two jump pads. Someone should hop into the turret and zoom in and strafe the Attackers as they wind through the boarding vehicle. Begin by targeting the right side of the arena, perhaps taking out the minigun turret on the Attackers' entrance vehicle. Have an eagle-eyed colleague snipe Attackers attempting to damage the turret while the turret tears through the Attackers before they can reach the orange boarding area. Meanwhile have the rest of the team (ideally about half) use either of the jump pads to leap onto the boarding vehicle.

This becomes important as the Attackers have two objectives, and you must keep them from obtaining both. First, if you double jump off the right-side jump pad, you can fly over and land on the end of boarding platform! This allows you to defend from either end of the platform almost immediately—meaning the Defenders can fend off the Attackers before they reach this area. Then run to the objective, or stay inside the boarding platform and quickly look for incoming enemies, and demolish them when they attempt to reach the objective. You have a greater chance if cohorts on the outside blast incoming Attackers.

Alternately, you can throw caution to the wind, and from the end of the boarding platform, stand and blast at the Attackers running along either side of the cylinder. As you have shock rifles and biorifles, well-placed shots can cause real havoc and annoyance! Feeling reckless? Then double jump on the cylinder's top and run to the edge of the arched cargo area; don't leap on top of the arches or the two sentry guns will mow you down. If your foes are less than professional, you can use the cylinder area to shock combo any of the hapless punks that dare to appear from their spawn point. You won't last long, but it'll be fun!

Otherwise, the Defenders should quickly learn this match's first main choke point: the platform at either end of the cylinder. Set up at least two Defenders anywhere on the end of the boarding vehicle, and begin some fearsome ordnance deployment! Optionally stay on the middle "bolt" linking the boarding vehicle to the cylinder cargo vehicle so you aren't struck by incoming fire, or keep moving and lay down both goo and shock combos; this results in a fearsome firestorm guaranteed to hamper Attacking progress!

When Attackers break through, set up a nasty choke point under the boarding platform; adept Defenders can keep Attackers at bay for minutes if they focus all firepower here. If the Attackers break through, grab the two 50 shield packs, and retreat to the ramp leading to the boarding platform objective. With a Defender on either side (one inside the boarding platform and the rest sniping or on the bonus objective vehicle), there's plenty of room to move and defend.

TIP

Crack sharpshooters fed up of being struck down by Attackers can locate new sniping spots instead of the regular nests near the minigun turret. Drop down near the objective #2 door for a good view of the boarding platform, or use the red-lit shadows near the health pack at the opposite end for cover. You can even use the jump pad to leap to the Attackers' objective; perfect if you're attempting to stop the platform at all costs!

Attacking Bonus Objective: Open the Panel

Why go for the forward vehicle weapons cache? You spawn inside the vehicle, and don't have to run the gauntlet from your initial starting position; you control both minigun turrets once the vehicle is yours; you are in partial cover until you board the platform; and the weapons you retrieve from the locker are much more impressive. There are two 50 shield packs inside here as well. Note that the spawning area inside the forward vehicle only unlocks (and can be moved into) once the bonus objective is complete.

Attackers' Weapon Locker 2*

Link Gun

Shock Rifle

Flak Cannon

Rocket Launcher

Sniper Rifle

*Inside forward vehicle

While the rest of your team secures the boarding position, and splits the Defenders' time and energy, take a couple of your trusted comrades, and force yourself onto the forward vehicle. Instead of heading directly to the boarding platform, leap off and to the right, onto the minigun turret area. If you can position a teammate at a sniping point to annoy the minigunner (ideally hiding to the right side of the giant cylinder, with another on the minigun turret on your own vehicle roof by your starting point), you can create a diversion. Attack the turret with your biorifle for a quick and unpleasant death, or blast some rockets at the base of the turret. Either incapacitate the gunner or destroy the turret entirely.

Ignore the turret at the far end of the vehicle, unless you're after the shock rifle and ammo pack. If it is manned, attack the turret. When the turret is out of commission, run down the vehicle's right side, up the ramp, and stand on the hatch that opens the forward weapons cache. It takes three seconds to open, so use the shield gun and throw yourself in front of the teammate who's attempting to finish this objective. The minigun can't hit you from here, so run behind and destroy the gunner if you wish, but only after the objective is complete!

Defending Bonus Objective: Defend the Panel

With two obvious objectives, and no way of knowing which one the Attackers will attempt to reach, Defenders must prepare for every eventuality. Until the Attackers breach the orange metal structure of the boarding vehicle, you can use the many choke points detailed above. However, should Attackers begin to break through your defenses, or you want extra firepower, station at least one Defender on the minigun turret near the platform on the forward vehicle. Here you can blast the Attackers' turret far away on their initial vehicle, or anyone running down the outside platforms near the cylinder and cargo areas. Mow them down with vigor, and have a couple of helpers nearby to tackle stragglers as the Attackers near your turret.

It is in the Attackers' best interest to reach the bonus objective, as they will spawn from inside this vehicle if they commandeer it. If they don't, they must run all the way from their initial start, even when the boarding platform is moved; this means you can continue to hold the choke points previously mentioned. Should you get an Attacker or two attempting the bonus objective, set up an ambush with one of your team hiding near the front of the orange vehicle to step out and blast them, and others guarding the objective point. The turret near the objective is of limited use; you're better off using shock combos to knock opponents off the sides of the vehicle.

NOTE

Even if the bonus objective is completed, the lack of sentry guns in this area means that you can spawn camp over the top of the now-open bonus weapons locker, raining down biorifle goop and creating havoc while the rest of the team prepares to prevent the Attackers from boarding the main Juggernaut.

TIP

Is your Attacking enemy about to claim an objective? Coat the objective pad or switch with nasty biorifle goo just before the Attacker arrives so he has to contend with these nasty leftovers, plus your ordnance pummeling!

Defenders can rush into the forward vehicle spawn point to collect the Attackers' weapons locker ordnance, but expect fierce resistance.

Attacking Objective 2: Place Explosives on the Door

It usually takes a crack team of Attackers only moments to complete this objective, simply because the narrow balcony along the main central Juggernaut is so difficult to defend. Assuming you've taken the bonus objective (for the link gun and shock rifle availability), immediately head across the boarding platform, ideally as a group. You'll encounter heavy fire at the platform's end before you drop down to the balcony. Send one or two crack shots to either side of the platform to tag the Defenders from their hidey-holes. Clamber around the front of the platform vehicle to get a good sniping spot.

Employ necessary restraint in this close balcony (ricocheting your pal into the ground with an accidental shock combo won't go over well). Either combo your link guns to create a deadly wave to repel all Defenders, or scatter and let two of your team charge to the balcony's end, while the others pick off any Defenders dropping in. The minigun cannot reach you from here. Also try running along the wire fence or leaping the giant mud-guard wheel protectors. When you reach the door, just stand there to lay the three explosive bombs and wait three seconds for them to detonate. Stand away from the blast, ideally in the alcove farther along the balcony (you'll receive a tiny blast; use your shield gun and power it up for the dash to come). It only takes a tap of the Use button to place and start the explosives, so keep plugging away until it happens.

Defending Objective 2: Defend the Door

You still spawn from the same position, so make the Attackers' short route to the door as difficult as possible. First, know your Attackers spawn location. If they haven't yet obtained the bonus objective, stay on the upper balconies or create choke points until the Attackers reach the boarding platform. Once the Attackers overrun your defenses, train all your fire on the platform's open far end, as the Attackers must maneuver through this choke point.

Try launching shock combos straight through the platform from the lower balcony while teammates pepper the exit platform with biorifle effluent and the minigunner blasts the gaps between the platform walls. Station a couple of your best shots at the far end of the lower balcony near the door and combo their link guns to devastate any Attackers still standing. As soon as the Attackers blast through and lay the explosive charges on the door, suicide and immediately move into the Juggernaut's interior corridor to ambush the incoming Attackers—there's nothing you can do about the door now!

Attacking Objective 3: Open Rear Door

This is another quick challenge, as the lever to open the doors is in front of you, on the far left corner of the Juggernaut's interior. However, any Defenders worth their salt will have set up a horrific welcome committee in this chamber—usually primed shock rifles or a series of comboed link guns. The main Defender entrance lies at the far end. They only drop in from the side balconies once the next objective is breached and the rear left door has opened.

Perform your duty and make a shield gun dash for the lever, shrugging off attacks with the shield, perhaps avoiding the lever at the last moment to fake the Defenders out while another teammate attempts the objective. Either approach this objective as a group, wiping out all Defenders with chained link gun attacks, or try to push the Defenders back while a prechosen Attacker automatically rushes for the lever every time.

You spawn from the forward vehicle, so it's imperative that you attack as a team, waiting for Defenders to peer out from the blasted door (the main choke point for this objective) and then taking them down so they don't push you back too far. The best chance you have is right after exploding the door. Note that when you stand on the objective icon, the lever automatically descends (taking three seconds). If you are killed or move off the target during this time, only the remaining time is needed for the objective to complete—a particularly worrisome fact for the Defenders.

Defending Objective 3: Defend Rear Door

As soon as the Attackers plant their explosive charges on the door, retreat into the Juggernaut and quickly take up an effective defensive position by dropping through the open trapdoor at the far end of your spawning corridor. When the door explodes, your spawn point moves to the far end of the interior Juggernaut corridor, where you find additional weapon lockers (although they lack shock or biorifles). Speed to the exploding door and cover the ground in goo if possible—it's imperative to stop a quick rush to the rear door switch. One way is to place teammates between the door and the switch to mow down incoming Attackers. Lay biorifle goo all over the switch, and continue to blast anyone entering through the door.

Defenders' Weapon Lockers 3 and 4*

Link Gun

Minigun

Sniper Rifle

*Inside Defenders' Juggernaut

Set up your team to severely frustrate the Attackers by chaining your link guns and training the powerful blast on anyone venturing through the smoldering doorway. Or, if you grabbed a shock rifle from the initial weapons lockers, combo or shoot the Attackers so they bounce away from the corner switch; combat testing has proved this to be an incredibly annoying tactic if you're an Attacker, so use it!

Stand on top of the mesh ledge above the exploded door to make yourself difficult to hit, while others dot themselves around the far end of the interior near the switch (using the three crates or fuel truck as cover). The Attackers' spawn point hasn't changed from the previous objective—they must still charge over the boarding platform—so you can continue to push them back or stay at the exploded door and snipe at them before sidestepping to cover.

Expert Defenders can hem in the Attackers by attacking them from the doorway or the interior while sneaky comrades drop down from the upper balcony and swarm them from behind. But don't overstretch your team; consider concentrating your firepower on the rear door lever so no one stands a chance pulling it. Out of ammo? Then dash up to the upper mesh platform to objective #4's switch; the side ledges have health packs and ammo (minigun, sniper rifle, and link gun ordnance on each side).

Attacking Objective 4: Open the Side Doors

The Attackers now gain an advantage as they spawn inside the main Juggernaut, on either side of a repair vehicle that trundles in once you meet objective #3 and docks with the main vehicle. This raises a mesh cage up to the balconies. Stand on these as they rise, defending yourself as best you can. Leap to either side by dodge jumping to the mesh balconies on either side of the interior, in the same area as the fuel truck.

Step to the back of the rising cage so the Defenders in front and below cannot blast you, and watch for Defenders dropping in from the roof. Continue leaping as you strive for the next objective: to open the side doors by flicking the switch, which is on a mesh balcony directly ahead. Reach this via jumping or blasting your way up the side ramps.

109

Assuming you made the ascension and leapt to the side balconies (a very precise dodge jump to either balcony, or a double jump to the fuel truck, and another to the left side balcony), execute a jump to a wall dodge onto the side wall, then off again and onto the mesh platform with the switch on it. Leap and hit the wall above the crates without touching them, and finish by landing on the mesh balcony. Yes, this is possible!

Mix up your action, or if you fail to execute this difficult maneuver, drop down and run through the obstacles below. Also make sure your team approaches the switch from both the wall ledges, the crates down below, or simply runs up the ramps and behind the switch. Mix up the charge so the Defenders don't know who to aim at!

If you're on the ground, notice some important strategic factors. The door you blew up (objective #2) is now filled with mangled piping, so don't worry about Defenders entering from there. Two sentry turrets are under each balcony adjacent to the repair vehicle. These activate if the Defenders swarm your spawning location—use their powerful ordnance to your advantage.

Try keeping your group's sharpshooter inside the dark shadows of the repair truck with a sniper rifle trained down the corridor; you have a clear line of sight to the switch (objective #4). Provide back-up fire to your charging comrades from this point or from a crouching position behind the stack of crates in front of the repair truck. Because the Defenders have a nasty habit of targeting splash-damage weapons (such as the rocket launcher) between the spaces in the middle of the crate stack, stay behind the crates for only a moment. From here, charge or dive into the side locker bays that open up when the repair vehicle docks. Find an identical locker on each side, along with two 50 shield packs.

Attackers' Weapon Lockers 3 and 4*

Link Gun

Minigun

Flak Cannon

Sniper Rifle

Inside main Juggernaut

Assaulting the objective along the lower ground means more cover, but easier pickings for the Defenders. You can leap atop the crates in front of the repair vehicle, then jump atop the front of the repair truck (if you want extra height to provide covering fire), or else double jump onto the fuel truck in the middle of the interior corridor (this is most useful for jumping to the side upper ledges as mentioned previously). Those on fire support can also flit between cover from the weapons lockers to the support strut and back again.

Those at the forefront, meanwhile, need to worry about Defenders dropping in from front and behind. Run around one side of the fuel truck. This truck can be destroyed (and Defenders often do so). It takes around 12 rockets to detonate the truck (weapons with splash damage only), and afterward, the two main burning pieces of truck wreckage force you to speed through the middle, or risk 20 damage dashing through the burning right or left edges of the interior. Of course, you can just light the puddle of fuel beneath the truck to demolish it instantly—a key tactic to try from a safe distance on a hapless foe.

Split your team to befuddle the Defenders, and have some leap up the small crate stack on either wall (don't hang around or seek cover for too long, as Defenders can drop in from the wall ledge behind and above you), and then double jump to the objective switch. Meanwhile, run interference by splitting other teammates and having them run under the mesh platform and switch, and up one of the two ramps at the interior's far end. You can side jump onto the final mesh platform instead of moving all the way round.

Alternately, move into the stack of crates at the far end, hide in the shadows, and face the repair truck, using a sniper rifle to tag any Defenders following your Attackers toward the objective. Or, leap to the space in the corners above the crates, double jump to the ramp's top, and dash for the switch.

When you reach the final mesh platform, ledges on either side house two minigun bullet ammo cases, two sniper rifle bullet cases, two link gun charges, and a health pack—all of which the Defenders will have grabbed. Bring out the shield gun, dash for the switch, and stand next to it to complete your objective. The main Defender exit is behind the switch, and enemies may be pouring out of here—lay down suppressing fire to assist your objective seeker.

Defending Objective 4: Defend the Side Door Switch

Once the rear door lever has been breached and pulled, have your entire team retreat to the far end of the Juggernaut's interior. The repair truck is docked at the back of the vehicle and the two sentry gun turrets prevent you from spawn killing, so position yourself behind the fuel truck or you'll be mown down.

With the fuel truck intact, the Attackers have two main paths through the corridor, with a wide gap to the left of the fuel truck (assuming you're facing the repair vehicle). Or, concentrate your fire on the fuel truck with chained link guns and explode it, forcing your foes to maneuver in the middle area only (the two wall routes are narrow and Attackers take fire damage as they pass through).

Attackers stream through this corridor, so hold fast, placing a couple of sharpshooters in the corners of the crates under the mesh platform, while others guard the mesh's edge from the crate clusters on either side of the corridor. Keep dodge jumping to minimize advancing forces striking you. Have a teammate blast enemies that run up to holes located where the two ramps connect to the mesh. When all else fails, try coating the ramps and switch with biorifle goo.

Attacking Objective 5: Reach the N.E.X.U.S. Missile Trailer

As soon as the switch is pressed (objective #4), two bay doors on the left wall open (this takes 3–5 seconds). The doors are under the mesh platform's left side at the interior's far end, and a second side passage with a weapon locker opens to the repair truck's left. This is easy to miss, as it's near the left side weapon locker (#3), by the sentry gun. You're likely to use this entrance the most when you respawn (as you start by the repair vehicle), but vary your exit strategy as the Defenders keep their guns trained on this entrance.

111

Your Defenders' positions are similar to those at the beginning of the match. They have an additional area from which to start: a passage above you, leading to a balcony with two jump pads and a minigun turret. The Defenders will probably take up position on the far trailers near your objective, as well as sniping from spots on the balcony, effectively creating a convergence of fire. Avoid this by having most of your team wait for the side doors to open, just before objective #4 is complete, and then rush out before the Defenders can take position.

If you're working well as a team, join a couple of link guns, stay at weapon locker #5, and blast at the turret atop the balcony. It can't hit you, and destroying it simplifies the final part.

Attackers' Weapon Locker 5*

Link Gun

Minigun

Flak Cannon

Sniper Rifle

*Left exit of main Juggernaut

While this is happening, your nimblest teammate should zip across to the trailer. The trailer is the red rear of the towing vehicle. Leap across a cylinder-carrying vehicle, and then head left, to the roof gap and into the trailer. The entrance to the missile bay is a trap door at the trailer's far end.

One of the most important areas to breach and claim is the last minigun turret at the trailer entrance. If the Defenders grab this, they can train it on the entrances and demoralize your team. Dash to the minigun early (especially as the armor on it makes you incredibly difficult to hit). With a big enough team, have two to three move to the trailer while a couple stay on the cylinder-carrying vehicle to act as fire support, digging out Defenders from their hiding positions on all three of the vehicles. Have another couple train weapons at the sniping points and jump pads, and perhaps a madman can leap the Bulldog (landing on the small armored truck following the cylinder-carrying vehicle, and wait for the missile trailer doors to open).

Assuming you aren't taking the Bulldog, the choke point comes at the lower balcony's far end, as your team leaps to the cylinder-carrying vehicle and then onto the trailer vehicle. Minimize your hang time by dodge jumping onto the cylinders. There are two sets of giant cylinders on this vehicle, and enemies are usually positioned to deal with you if you leap straight across. Sometimes leap atop the cylinder nearest the truck end, and dodge jump across to the trailer, but split your forces so other teammates move to the two health packs between the cylinder sets; or move directly to the vehicle's front, leap

to the trailer's front, and proceed back along the trailer, tackling Defenders as you go. Set up a sniper on the front of either the trailer or the cylinder-carrying vehicle to fire at the Defenders swarming out of the Juggernaut upper balcony, or those already on the trailer.

Those moving forward should do so on the far side of the trailer; don't underestimate the cover that the trailer's middle part allows. Use the shock rifle on the trailer's right side platform to take out a minigunner or Defenders holed up in sniping positions.

Grab the rocket launcher atop the trailer's middle and immediately drop down to avoid incoming fire. Vary your maneuvering by zigzagging along the trailer's sides, heading under a mesh platform just behind and below the rocket launcher. Your goal is to destroy the final turret (if you haven't commandeered it), and enter the relative safety of the trailer top. There is a health pack on either side of the cylinder as you enter. Stay to the right to avoid unnecessary gunfire from the left.

TIP

If Attackers commandeer the minigun turret, and then lose it to the Defenders, it becomes incredibly difficult to storm the trailer; you may wish to destroy it as soon as possible. Also beware when sidestepping off the cylinders (especially on the trailer near the shock rifle), as a quick step right can send you off the railing and onto the ground.

The final part of the objective is to enter the trailer. Achieve this by dropping through the trap door (onto a health pack) at the trailer's far end. There may be Defenders inside the trailer, or waiting as you maneuver along the trailer's top. However, once you're down the hole, two huge side doors lower, allowing three separate entrances to the final objective. This makes it easier to reach the trailer, so leap for the trapdoor without regard for your safety.

Defending Objective 5: Defend the N.E.X.U.S. Missile Trailer

As the side doors open, the grating to the second spawn point closes, and the upper corridor on the opposite side of the Juggernaut opens. This set up is identical to the initial spawning point, except there is only one weapons locker. However, there are three exits (the middle one has two doors), and both the extreme left and right exits lead to a sniping balcony. Have one team member stay here and tag enemies who infiltrate the trailer vehicle, but most of the team should go to the minigun turret (which should mow down anyone entering the trailer as a second line of defense) and use either of the jump pads.

Defenders' Weapon Locker 5*

Biorifle

Link Gun

Minigun

Sniper Rifle

*Inside Defenders' Juggernaut

From now to the end of the match, you must successfully watch and react to what your Attacking opponents are doing, even after they secure the entrance to the missile trailer. You have a couple of seconds' advantage over the Attackers and their slow-opening side doors; exploit this by leaping across from the jump pad or dodge jumping from the right side sniping balcony, and land on the trailer. From here, secure the rocket launcher and the shock rifle while a couple of teammates train weapons on the lower balcony from which the Attackers will soon stream. It's imperative to keep the Attackers from even making it from the lower balcony, so work as a team and train your fire!

Pick a Defender to jump into the turret on the trailer. Set up a teammate on either sniper balcony to constantly drop biorifle ooze onto the lower balcony, while snipers position themselves to cover both side entrances. Try placing snipers near the minigun turret on the trailer, or inside the trailer archway area next to the health pack, looking over the fence (you can't fire through the mesh wall). These snipers cover the left side entrance, tagging those coming out of the right side entrance, from positions where you can see almost to the Attackers' spawning point, at the front of the cylinder-carrying vehicle, or on the front of the trailer. Finally, if you have enough competitors, stick a final guy on the minigun turret on the Juggernaut near the jump pads, and train that weapon on the choke point where the Attackers leap onto the cylinder vehicle.

A well-disciplined team of Defenders can hold off Attackers for minutes using the defense points detailed above. Should Attackers break through, they are likely to head toward the shock rifle and rocket launcher (which you should by now have appropriated), or quickly maneuver into the arched trailer end to the missile bay entrance.

Over at the rocket launcher, place a Defender inside the partially enclosed alcove under and slightly ahead of the rocket launcher to blast those wounded Attackers who make the leap over the cylinders (you have an excellent view of them and the Attackers attempting to bag the shock rifle). Once the enemies are on the trailer, try the shock rifle to bounce them away from the archway area, and train both miniguns on those attempting to reach the rocket launcher.

> **TIP**
>
> Try the more insane sniping spots, such as between the front grating and the trailer engine's giant front wheel (either side), giving you a long view down toward the arches and both preferred weapons. Drop next to the wheel to avoid being hit.

If the intruders entered into the arched cargo area, form a protective barrier around the area, keep three Defenders at the far end, waiting for the Attacker to reach them, and another inside the missile bay to coat the ground with biorifle goo as the objective falls. Bring your team onto the trailer now, as the mesh walls and arches mean the sniping and minigun turret positions on the Juggernaut aren't much use.

Roam the trailer's deck, staying at the shock rifle and rocket launcher and try to combo your enemies into the ground. Finally, there's a cunning sniping ambush point behind the fence at the trailer's far end, behind the objective. Leap over the fence (don't fall from the edge you land on), then crouch and pop up to fire on advancing foes.

Attacking Objective 6: Retrieve the N.E.X.U.S. Missiles

The final, most vicious firefight of all now plays out as your Attackers swarm the trailer, and the Defenders hold it from a variety of positions (either inside the trailer or on sniping roof points on the main Juggernaut). However, the doors on the trailer sides have lowered, creating two platforms for you to reach, so split your team into four different groups. Have group #1 reach the trailer by the regular trapdoor method. Group #2 should ride the Bulldog, leaping from the Juggernaut wheel cover to the Bulldog, using its turret and crouching for cover, and then leaping onto the open red platform. Alternately, group #2 can board the trailer's top, then go left along the left side to the health pack, and leap over the open fence and drop onto the red platform. Meanwhile, group #3 maneuvers to the trailer top and leaps across to the far red platform where the missiles will be loaded. Either dodge jump from the trailer entrance or drop down from the right health pack fence area. Finally, group #4 should attempt to guard the runners from incoming fire, or roam the trailer and cylinder-carrying vehicle for Defenders to plug.

TIP

Although it's difficult, a dodge jump from atop the minigun turret on the trailer allows you to reach the arched structure and run across it, after which you can drop down to either of the open side platforms. Or jump off the far end onto the back of the trailer, and hop over a fence to the trapdoor.

Once inside the trailer, Attackers (usually those being pursued) run directly to the final objective. Mix this up a little by pivoting around as you land, then dash to the jump pad behind the trapdoor, and bounce back up onto the trailer's top, "dogfighting" your opponents until you're behind them—become the hunter! Bring them down, and then dash past the final weapons locker (#6) and toward the final lever. The jump pad bounces you up through an auto-opening trapdoor that closes immediately, meaning there is still only one trapdoor down to the inside of the trailer.

Attackers' and Defenders' Weapon Locker 1*

Biorifle

Link Gun

Minigun

*Inside trailer

The final battle rages inside the trailer until the Attacking team successfully steals the missiles or time runs out. Keep most of your team at the doorways, pouring biorifle goo on the ground (and the trapdoor ground) to repel incoming foes, but leave one or two assaulters to run directly to the switch that moves the missiles along and out of the far side of the trailer to a waiting Bulldog.

You can leap over and onto the missiles and off onto the switch instead of running around. The entire process to steal the missiles takes eight seconds, but fortunately for the Attackers, the missile tray cannot be reset, and it remains at the place it was before the Attacker stepped away (or was forcibly removed) from the objective point. Crouch to begin with so the missiles shield you from incoming attacks, then use your shield gun or step in front of the objective holder to ensure victory!

NOTE

You know the three locations from which enemies will stream. Both Attackers and Defenders should secure these three points with a mixture of weaponry (the biorifle or shock combos on incoming foes), positioning (watch the trapdoor and blast those dropping in, or stand near or on the crates by the jump pad for extra protection), and skill (know your limits and the job you're suited for, and prepare to sacrifice yourself for the good of the team).

Defending Objective 6: Defend the N.E.X.U.S. Missiles

Should the fifth objective fall, saving the missiles becomes harder, as there are now three different entrances to choose when entering the missile bay. Learn some of the techniques detailed above that the Attackers use (such as using the jump pad to get behind a chasing enemy), and employ them. Coat the entrances of the bay with goo.

Have half your team outside the bay, continuing to batter incoming Attackers, and have a foolhardy helper on the Bulldog to waylay enemies attempting this crazy shortcut; keep those punks away from the shock rifle and rocket launcher. The shock rifle is most useful for tagging enemies dropping onto the side entrances; see if you can knock them onto the desert ground! Coat the final objective switch with goo, and guard it with at least two of your team, while another prowls inside and outside the trailer for incoming foes, using the crates as cover.

TIP

The interior crates make good ambush points! Stand on the three nearest the final weapons locker for an unobstructed view of the left side entrance and area where all the Attackers jump to the cylinder-carrying vehicle. Plug away! Or, step onto the second set of crates and fire at this area. Finally, you can step on the crates or onto the top crate above the jump pad, and catch enemies using the pad, or drop down from the open trapdoor. Gotcha!

AS-FALLENCITY

Legend

1 Attackers' Weapons Locker (either side of space fighter)

2 Weapons Locker (end of tunnel)

3 50 Shield Pack (in rubble)

4 Defenders' Weapons Locker (in building)

5 Link and flak ammo packs (under defenders' walkway)

6 Shock Rifle +1 ammo pack

7 Flak, rocket ammo packs

8 Defenders' Weapons Locker (inside corridor)

9 Rocket Launcher +3 ammo packs (Defender balcony)

10 50 Health Pack (in dark corner)

11 Attackers Weapon Locker (in crates)

12 50 Health Pack (near street entrance)

13 50 Shield Pack

14 50 Health Pack (near lamppost)

15 Shock x2, sniper x2 ammo (near concrete wall)

16 Rocket x2, minigun ammo (under lamppost)

17 Weapons Locker

18 50 Shield Pack

19 Sniper, rocket, minigun ammo (between entrances)

20 Defenders' Weapons Locker (on roof)

21 50 Health Pack (on roof)

22 Sniper x2, rocket x2, minigun ammo (on roof)

23 50 Health Pack x2 (inside entrance)

24 Rocket x2 and Shock x2 ammo (dark corner opposite stairs)

25 50 Health Pack x2 (top of stairs)

26 Minigun x2 and sniper x2 ammo (on station platform)

27 Defenders' Weapons Locker (on station platform)

28 Defenders' Weapons Locker (above hole)

Overview

A few city blocks await the Attackers as they plan to devastate a Defender stronghold! From their space fighter landing location, Attackers scale a rise, then drop down and engage Defenders in a fierce battle to open a barricade by destroying a piece of explosive junk. Once through, the Attackers must locate a forward outpost beacon and activate it while Defenders pop out of cover and buildings to intercept them.

Once the outpost and new spawn point is secured, the Attackers must gain entrance to the Defenders' bunker; no easy task since two minigun turrets and a fortification block their path! After choosing a disused monorail line or the ground to attempt their attack, and once they've opened two doorways to the bunker, the Attackers must battle to a subway platform where the Defenders are holed up, and lay explosives on a support pillar and inside a train carriage to thoroughly destroy the bunker and win the match.

Attackers' Objectives	Defenders' Objectives
1. Destroy Barricade	1. Defend Barricade
2. Secure Forward Outpost	2. Defend Forward Outpost
3. Infiltrate the Bunker	3. Defend Bunker
4. Destroy the Command Center	4. Defend Command Center

Attacking Objective 1: Destroy Barricade

When you spawn near your landed space fighter, you are not in visual contact with your objective or the enemy. You are at the foot of a large ramp whose top is a drop down to the initial combat area. The Defenders begin from the balcony opposite on the building in front of you.

Once at the top of the snow bank and steps, beware of multiple snipers from different directions. The drop prevents you from retracing your steps to your starting point; this prevents Defenders from spawn camping. Before you reach the steps, however, claim weapons from the lockers on either side of the space fighter.

Attackers' Weapon Lockers 1 and 2*

Assault Rifle (second)

Minigun

Rocket Launcher

Sniper Rifle

*Alongside the Space Fighter

At the top of the snow bank and steps, four white concrete columns provide minimal protection to your advancing forces; the enemy is now in sight and has begun sniping your location. If you have some premier sharpshooters, station one or two behind each front column to decapitate Defenders firing from their far balcony or on the ground. Destroy the barrels near the rear column to avoid being caught in the blast if they explode. You must destroy the blockade (tons of masonry near explosive junk) by firing at the junk.

Of the two ways around the initial junk pile, the left path is slightly easier because the minigun turret on the far balcony can hit you only sporadically due to debris in its trajectory path. Don't hang around, however, as Defenders attempt to seal off the entire arena and take out your team. Prevent this by storming around this left corner, learning the locations of key Defenders, and tagging them with preferred weapons (clear larger areas with rockets, and single campers with sniper rounds).

The Defenders fill this preferred route with ordnance and team members, so split your crew into two strike forces. Have half your team head left, traveling to the wreckage tunnel and concrete near the explosive pile. The other force runs around the right side of the initial junk pile to tackle the Defenders up in the balcony while dodge jumping toward the 50 shield pack near the strewn concrete blocks.

Tackling the explosive pile is a little easier than you might suspect. Head around the left side of the initial junk and find the main route (and choke point) toward the explosive pile; then go to the weapon locker accessible by both teams, and then into the corrugated iron tunnel and out the other side. Expect a fearsome defense here. While at least two team members defend this position, have two or three Attackers try various ways to strike the explosive pile.

The first is to run through the tunnel and let rip with the flak cannon (collected at the previous locker) while disregarding your own life and pummeling the explosive pile. Those wanting to be a little sneakier can leap onto the left side of the tunnel's roof, and deftly dive over the tunnel to tag the explosive pile. Those with pure cunning will stay to the tunnel's left side and either crouch at the small gap in the concrete with the steel bars, or jump up at the far left gap with steel support bars protruding out of the fallen concrete, and fire their flak cannon from these partially covered locations.

Attackers' and Defenders' Weapon Locker 1*

Assault Rifle (second)

Minigun

Flak Cannon

Rocket Launcher

Sniper Rifle

*Entrance to corrugated tunnel

You can return to the first gigantic pile of junk, run around the left side (if you're facing the Defenders' turret), double jump onto a steel pole poking out of the left side, and then double jump up the pile of junk to a flatter area near the top. You can even reach the top with continued jumping, and then to the top of a nearby lamppost; from there, you can execute a difficult dodge jump to the freeway sign pole (but you're likely to be cut down before you can reach this area), run along the pole, and drop into the Defenders' spawn point. This affords extra height and a clear shot of both the explosive pile and any Defenders inside the balcony or down below; however, you are subject to enemy attack from up here.

Alternately, you can run past the tunnel entrance, around the exploding barrels, and then left along the main flat roadway toward the explosive pile. This is the easiest way to get shot, so attempt it only if the Defenders are off their game.

121

Attackers can circumvent the minigun turret by dodge jumping across from the tunnel (or around the right side of the initial junk pile) toward the shield pack area just beyond the shield pack (where the minigun turret can't harm you), and then press themselves against the Defenders' wall. The turret's mounting doesn't allow it to fire at enemies that are under it, so sneak along the wall and lob flak cannon bombs up into the turret to finish it, or blast the explosive pile from this area, preparing one of your team to blast Defenders dropping in from above.

Finally, you can run behind the explosive pile or leap over it and blast it from point-blank range, if team objectives are more important to you than your safety—which they should be!

TIP

Grab the flak cannon from the locker in the middle of this zone, as this weapon's shrapnel or bombs tear apart the explosive pile in record time and are much more effective than rockets (the second-best weapon to use). Also remember that the wall behind the explosive pile doesn't take damage, so aim only for the pile.

Defending Objective 1: Defend Barricade

Your entire team begins on a balcony overlooking a street, with a minigun turret and a drop to where you meet the Attackers. Begin by grabbing the ordnance in the weapons locker; you can get rockets from the dual weapons locker outside the corrugated tunnel ahead and below the turret.

Your enemy approaches from the snow and concrete bank ahead of you. Do not attempt to traverse this area—it's inaccessible to prevent spawn camping. Instead, set a couple of arch snipers near the turret, ideally behind a window giving you wall cover, and plug anyone that peers over the rise. Pay close attention to the pillars, the only real cover. The minigun turret threatens the Attackers, but trajectory difficulties prevent it from firing in much of the area. Use it as fire support rather than the central part of your defenses.

Defenders' Weapon Locker 1*

Assault Rifle (second)

Minigun

Flak Cannon

Sniper Rifle

*Inside building balcony

A better plan may be to drop to the left, near the shield pack, and set up a sniping squad that flits between the different massive concrete blocks. Concentrate your firepower on the two routes around the junk pile closest to the Attackers' spawning position. Dash to the base of the snow and concrete bank and wait, ambushing Attackers as they drop down. Keep the Attackers away from the corrugated tunnel and main weapons locker with judicious fire, keeping your team in cover and blasting incoming enemies.

Jump around the rusting junk to the tunnel's right, or run up the concrete slab near the explosive pile and dodge jump around, pushing the Attackers back. However, the main choke point is around either side of the far junk heap; keep sniping from the shield pack area to the heap's right, and use the remaining force to take care of enemies venturing out in the open to the left side (this is where the turret comes in handy).

Finally, once the explosive pile starts to receive damage, discover where the fire's coming from and retaliate quickly; you can consistently destroy the enemy if you stay near the locker, blasting, then quickly trot in to refill on weapons (throw away used ones).

Attacking Objective 2: Secure Forward Outpost

As soon as the explosive pile detonates, your team spawns from the weapons locker near the tunnel, while the Defenders appear in a long set of corridors above and ahead of the destroyed barricade. The most dangerous area is directly above and right of you. The overpass window has a minigun turret facing your spawn point, and it can devastate your advancing team.

Have two of your team zigzag the area with rockets firing at the turret while a third teammate moves quickly around the pile of junk (right of where the explosive pile was), under the turret. Then destroy it with flak grenade bombs or rockets. Once the remaining team is under the overpass, get ready for another minigun turret!

Also, enemies may leap down from the two overpass entrances or from a building near the next objective. Claim the flak shells and link cartridges on the underpass' left side, then check the area near the shock rifle; that's going to be useful!

The temptation is to run straight for the shock rifle, but prepared Defenders will have positioned a minigunner on a second turret and a couple of others firing from the hole or among the wreckage farther into this courtyard. As before, destroy the turret by staying under its firing arch and blasting upward with rockets, flak, or shock combos. The two barrels next to the minigun turret damage it when detonated, making the turret easier to destroy.

123

If you're receiving sizable defensive fire, continue to blast at this hole. If there's little defense, it means the Defenders are positioning themselves at the other spawn point exit around the corner. Therefore split into two teams as you near the shock rifle.

With a few of your team tackling the turret, send a few good men along the underpass's right side, picking up the sniper ammo, rockets, grenades, bullets, and minigun rounds. Turn the corner, and split your team up to make them more difficult to pin down. Have one teammate run around the left of the wreckage, to the right of the cylinder, and dash to the objective. Have a second teammate head right of the concrete fence, then leap into the mangled wreckage, jump onto the two protruding metal girders pointing to the objective, and run across.

Meanwhile the remainder of your team can stick to the walls or leap onto the series of narrow concrete fences leading around the objective's right side. Double jump the gaps and foil any Defenders, then sweep around and tackle the objective from behind, overwhelming any stragglers. Finally, station a man below the Defenders' exit position (the openings in the building to the right) so he can blast those dropping down.

Back at the shock rifle, you could traverse around the left side of the L-shaped corner, supporting your advance party. Grab the flak and rocket ammo behind the cylinder stack to the left, and watch for snipers in the shadows near the health pack (which Defenders sometimes use to lure you into a firefight). Look for Defenders in the wreckage, in dark corners, and on the building to your right.

Dash to the left of the cylinder, destroy the barrels, and clear the area of remaining Defenders—this choke point shouldn't be used all the time—and dive behind the concrete wall to the objective's right. It only takes two seconds of standing time to complete the objective. Be sure you detonate the barrels partially hiding the objective first.

Defending Objective 2: Defend Forward Outpost

Your defensive spawn point has three main exits, two of which come with a minigun turret. All the Attackers spawn by the weapons locker near the corrugated tunnel, so place two or three Defenders by the turret overlooking the pile explosion zone, one in the turret, and the others with rocket launchers. The rest of the team can block that tunnel choke point with shock rifle blasts and more rockets.

Stay either in this balcony or on the ground near the flak cannon ammo and let the enemy come to you. Choke them out at the tunnel's end or on the road to the tunnel's left. Use the shock combo to blast those firing at you in the gaps between the concrete structure.

Defenders' Weapon Locker 2*

Assault Rifle (second)

Minigun

Rocket Launcher

Sniper Rifle

*Inside building corridor

When the Attackers move under the underpass, blast them in the second turret, but watch for the barrels nearby; they damage you and your machine. The Attackers attempt to secure the shock rifle and split their team up, so keep them at the underpass entrance as long as possible. Then send the rest of your team (leave a couple to waylay the Attackers at the second turret) out to grab the weapons locker inside the corridors, and then out into the L-shaped courtyard near the objective.

Position one Defender on top of the boxes by the open windows, overlooking the courtyard. From here, you have a view of the barrels and cylinder (a choke point) and the wall in front of the objective. This covered sniping point has limited visibility.

Station a quick team member in cunning cover (in the shadows near the courtyard's far end), waiting to attack the incoming enemy. Or, climb up the flaming junk heap, on the same side as the objective, near the cylinder, and leap to the top. Smoke partially obscures your form and gunfire!

Situate the rest of your team in various excellent positions. Drop from the spawn building onto the awning and use that for extra height and partial cover to spot enemies near the concrete fence and cylinder choke point; keep a sharpshooter at the windows, too. Place a player with rockets near the end of the concrete fences and Attackers' weapon locker crates just in case they sneak around the back. Then have two or three troops mill around the objective point, staying close to the wall for partial cover, and blast enemies coming in from the choke point; there's a large open expanse to cover before they reach the outpost objective!

TIP

Flak cannon aficionados can fire under the long vertical wall in the courtyard's middle, partially obscuring the objective. There's a narrow gap in the concrete, and flak cannon blasts can quickly demolish anyone standing near the objective, without you taking time to run around the corner!

Attacking Objective 3: Infiltrate the Bunker

With the outpost secured, the Defenders may still be lurking behind you, so watch your backs. However, when they die, they respawn at the bunker entrance, at the far end the street. The concrete wall that previously blocked your path has fallen into separate pieces, the largest of which has formed a ramp to a raised train track. The Defenders will take up sniping and blasting positions around the corner, but you have two incoming options: to pass through the entrance and up the ramp to the train tracks, or via street level. Load up at either weapons locker inside the crates near the outpost.

Unreal TOURNAMENT 2004

Attackers' Weapon Lockers 3 and 4*

Shock Rifle

Flak Cannon

Rocket Launcher

Sniper Rifle

In crates in front of Objective #2

Your Defenders are holed up well, and they have two minigun turrets to defend those doors. You must blast the door access panels before the doors open (behind the main entrance, on either side of the lower minigunner). This is problematic.

Split two teams and have one third take the upper tracks and the rest move through the streets. Those on the ground should get the 50 shield pack in the dead-end near the street entrance. Then enter the street, using the large train track support girder as cover. Unless the Defenders overextended themselves, they haven't ventured this far, so dodge jump left or right, splitting your team up and training your weapons at the distant bunker. Expect no attacks from above.

Your plan is to deal with the minigun turrets and then snipers. You have the benefit of range over the turrets, so plant rockets into the turret until it explodes. Use your sniper rifle zoom to hone your aim, then switch to rockets and let rip from extreme range.

The Defenders attempt to snipe you, so split up your crew. Venture down the road's right side (if you can nimbly avoid enemy fire) and stop at the small barricade and side wall before you're destroyed. Optionally pick up the minigun and rocket ammo. Quickly dodge jump to the junk pile in the street's middle, before charging for the objective. Take out as many enemies as your rockets allow, and remove both those turrets!

If you want a safer role, stay behind charging teammates, find where the firing is coming from, and blast the snipers. Follow along the right wall, checking the gap in the roof wall where the upper turret is, and use the tree, lampposts, and train supports as cover. The bunker's right side lacks many hiding spots (the Defenders are likely to be behind the bunker entrance), so plant rockets at the corner of the bunker wall entrance, letting the splash damage annoy your adversaries.

Meanwhile over on the street's left side, quickly reach the concrete wall, peek around the right side, then run to the junk heap or charge the left concrete barrier along the left wall. If you reach it, use it as cover.

Gradually push the enemies back behind the bunker entrance, then destroy them or blast them as they drop from their rooftop spawning platform. The weapons locker in front of the bunker contains weapons you already own. Instead, check the shock and sniper ammo in front of the junk pile, and the 50 shield pack to the right, in front of the bunker entrance. There are also two barrels here; explode them before you pass near them.

Attackers' and Defenders' Weapon Locker 2*

Shock Rifle

Minigun

Rocket Launcher

Sniper Rifle

*Entrance to bunker

NOTE

You can jump over and land on the junk pile near the bunker entrance. This draws the enemy's fire while your teammates skulk around the sides.

TIP

Don't underestimate the value of the shock combo! If you're facing an enemy behind a barricade, detonate a combo on the other side of the barricade and it will pass through and bounce (and damage) your foe!

If you've taken the train track route to the bunker, you have less room to maneuver left and right, but a better overall targeting area. Before you turn the left corner, double jump off the platform, onto the narrow concrete wall with the shield pack behind it. This leaves you prone, but offers a great view of the upper bunker area; plug away!

On the track, turn and double jump to any of the lampposts, then turn and let rip with sniper fire. Again, you're prone up here, so leap on the lamppost on the left, just at the corrugated tunnel, then leap atop the shop awning. This sniping spot offers a partially obscured view of the top balcony and turret; perfect for taking out it and befuddled enemies who can't see where the gunfire is coming from!

As you advance down the track, zoom in on the turret, and blast it often before you reach the tunnel. You are exposed, so crouch to prevent being shot from the ground, and finish the upper turret. Your task is complete! Drop down at any time or onto the top of the junk pile, and make a final dash for the objective. To achieve this objective, battle to the bunker entrance, sidestep around, and blast the two door-opening devices at the back of the entrance wall. Flak cannon shells or rockets can take out a device in around eight shots. Once both devices are destroyed, you're ready for the final firefight!

Defending Objective 3: Defend the Bunker

You have the benefit of two turrets at this location, and you spawn on the bunker's roof, giving you extra height to view the enemy incursions. There are two Defenders' weapons lockers on the roof, along with health packs, sniper rounds, minigun bullets, and rockets. Guard the bunker, and train all weapons on the raised train tracks and the street below.

The first plan of defense is to remain on the roof where you're harder to hit and it is easier to spot incoming Attackers. Double jump on top of the turret, then single jump onto the wall's top. You can drop down when you're fired upon and really blast the enemies from this vantage point. Once you drop from the roof, you cannot return here.

Defenders' Weapon Lockers 3 and 4*

Shock Rifle

Minigun

Rocket Launcher

Sniper Rifle

On top of bunker roof

Down on the ground, the main defense is the turret. If it comes under fire, have one or two Defenders shoot at the Attackers while the turret concentrates on the main attacking force. The Attackers will move behind the concrete wall, the barricade on the left, and the lampposts or steel support girders; have a rocket or sniper bullet waiting for them at these points.

Stay on the move and have a couple of Defenders run interference (shock combo Attackers off the train track, and leap to the junk pile's top to view and blast) while others repel the force. If the Attackers aren't storming en masse, they probably won't reach the objective.

Stand your ground until you're overwhelmed, then use the walls with the objective devices as cover. The enemies must attack the devices from the interior side, under the roof, and the close proximity to the spawn point means they are difficult to take out in one attack; use the walls as cover and shoot anything that sprints across the open ground!

Attacking Objective 4: Destroy the Command Center

When the doors open, additional doors open above, letting the Defenders down two sets of stairs that are almost immediately visible when you enter either bunker entrance. Finish off the remnants of the Defending force or try to bolt to the objective for a quick finish, before the Defenders have time to regroup.

Taking a more methodical approach, however, grab your weapons from the locker at the entrance, take the shield pack, and move past the health pack into the bunker. Your first choke point is at the two ramps leading to the narrow door. Work as a team, firing rockets and shock combos through this door, then dash in, make a swift right attack with a minigun at anyone hiding near the benches, and claim this antechamber for the Attackers!

NOTE

To restock your weapons, move up the ramps to the Defenders' previous spawning point, and grab the ammo and health packs.

The second choke point is at the exit to the benched antechamber. Using the pillars as partial cover, push into the upper floor of the subway station, blast into the right corner, and leave some ordnance behind the crates in front of you. The remnants of the Defenders will attempt to keep this room or set up a nasty barricade at the objective.

Count the Defenders in this upper room, and wait for reinforcements before taking them out. After you push the Defenders down the escalator stairs to the platform, destroy the barrels and prepare for a final firefight. Keep at least two veterans at the top of the steps to blast the Defenders back down into their platform, allowing you to keep the rooms you infiltrated.

TIP

For an amusing sniping position, stand atop the crates in the room above the final platform, face the platform, and jump up and down to view the platform's right side and the barrels. You can tag both (damaging the Defenders) or shoot any of them with ordnance of your choice.

Now for the final push! Dance down the steps, zigzagging through the pillars to either side of the path, and prepare to meet some powerful gunfire! Try a mass rush with three or four players; split your team at the platform's beginning. Have half your team leap through the doorway, onto the train carriage, while the others dive for the central pillar (there's sniper and minigun ammo).

Flit around the pillar, dodge jumping and clearing a path; while one player shields himself and stands on the objective pillar, the others rout the Defenders from the partial cover of boxes near the pillar. Mix up your routine; split your forces and attempt to claim both objectives, or force everyone to move to a single objective.

Dodge jump sideways through the carriage window, then fire rockets at the Defenders behind the small barricade. Have some of your team pass to the carriage's left, double back over the plank and into the far entrance, and clear the way for others. Push the enemy back to the hole in the platform's far left corner where they spawn, and pick them off as they appear. Stand on the objective briefly to lay one bomb; lay three at each location for victory. With deft maneuvers, teamwork, and a little luck, the final objective is yours.

TIP

You only need to face the objective (either the pillar or train wall) and pass through the objective circle to lay an explosive, so keep moving!

Defending Objective 4: Defend the Command Center

As soon as objective #3 falls, suicide or dash to the connecting rooms before the enemy does to avoid being overrun. If you're caught on the stair ramp leading to the two chambers, you'll be ignored or picked off, and your team will be in disarray. Instead, retreat to the first chamber and blast with rockets and shock combos to bounce the enemy back from the choke point entrance. When this falls, stay in the second room, using the crates and the dark corner to the door's left side and repeat the plan.

Once a breakthrough here is imminent, focus all your forces on the platform. Your new spawn point is a hole in the ceiling at the platform's far end. A weapons locker is in one corner, with another on the platform. Run directly for the platform locker unless the enemy is fighting in this area.

Defenders' Weapon Lockers 5 and 6*

Shock Rifle

Minigun

Rocket Launcher

Sniper Rifle

On platform and inside spawn roof

Defending the pillar is slightly problematic unless your team is working cohesively. Train all your fire at the ramped stairwell, as this is the choke point for the remainder of the match. Fire all the rockets possible, drop the launcher, grab another from the locker, and continue to fire. With at least three to four teammates launching rockets, the base of the ramp becomes a firestorm!

Once the enemies breach this, have a separate teammate tackle any foes leaping through, ideally with rockets or the minigun, while the rest of the team keeps focus on the base of the stairwell. Prevent any foes from encroaching on the pillar—use any means necessary (a shock combo is great here if you're quick). Shock combos also work well from behind the crates to the pillar's right; you can fire them through the hole in the middle.

Defending the train tests your team's mettle. There are a variety of entrances to the train: via the door at the far end, through any of the windows, or around the back, over the plank, and through the back entrance. It's fairly enclosed, and dodge jumping through the windows is a risky proposition, so train your fire on the door, popping up from cover to watch any foes run by the windows.

If the other objective has fallen, keep teammates out on the platform to slow the enemies down. You can even attempt a shield stance at the objective, although this is a last resort. Otherwise, shock combos through the windows from the platform work well, as do flak bombs lobbed up through the back entrance from the tracks below.

AS-GLACIER

Recommended Players: 8–16

Legend

1 50 Shield Pack x2 (Attackers' spawn point)

2 Weapons Locker (Attackers' spawn point)

3 Big Keg-O-Health (inside crate)

4 Bio Rifle +2 ammo packs (near bonus objective)

5 Weapons Locker (Defenders' spawn point)

6 50 Shield Pack x2 (Defenders' spawn point)

7 50 Health Pack (inside each base entrance)

8 Defenders' Weapon Locker (each room)

9 Weapons Locker (tunnel junction)

10 50 Shield Pack x2 (tunnel junction)

11 Double Damage (inside crate)

12 Weapons Locker (near tank park)

13 50 Shield Pack (near tank park)

14 50 Health Pack (inside base door)

15 50 Shield Pack x2 (Defender's base spawn point)

16 Weapons Locker (each side of Defenders' base spawn point)

17 100 Shield Pack (inside crate)

18 50 Health Pack (near entrance)

19 Shock Rifle +2 ammo packs (inside entrance)

20 50 Health Pack x2 (above shutoff room)

21 50 Shield Pack (three, near drop hole)

22 Defenders' Weapons Locker (above shutoff room)

23 Grenade Launcher +2 ammo packs (roof overhang)

24 50 Shield Pack x2 (Attackers' spawn point)

25 Weapons Locker (Attackers' spawn point)

26 Grenade Launcher +2 ammo packs (roof overhang)

27 50 Shield Pack (three, near drop hole)

28 Defenders' Weapons Locker (above shutoff room)

29 50 Health Pack x2 (above shutoff room)

30 Weapons Locker

31 50 Shield Pack x2

32 50 Health Pack (near entrance)

33 Flak Cannon +2 ammo packs (inside entrance)

34 Link ammo packs x2 (base of antenna)

35 50 Health Pack x2 (on balcony)

36 Link ammo packs x2 (base of antenna)

37 50 Health Pack x2 (on balcony)

38 50 Shield Pack (two in each Defenders' spawn point)

39 Weapons Locker (one in each defenders' spawn point)

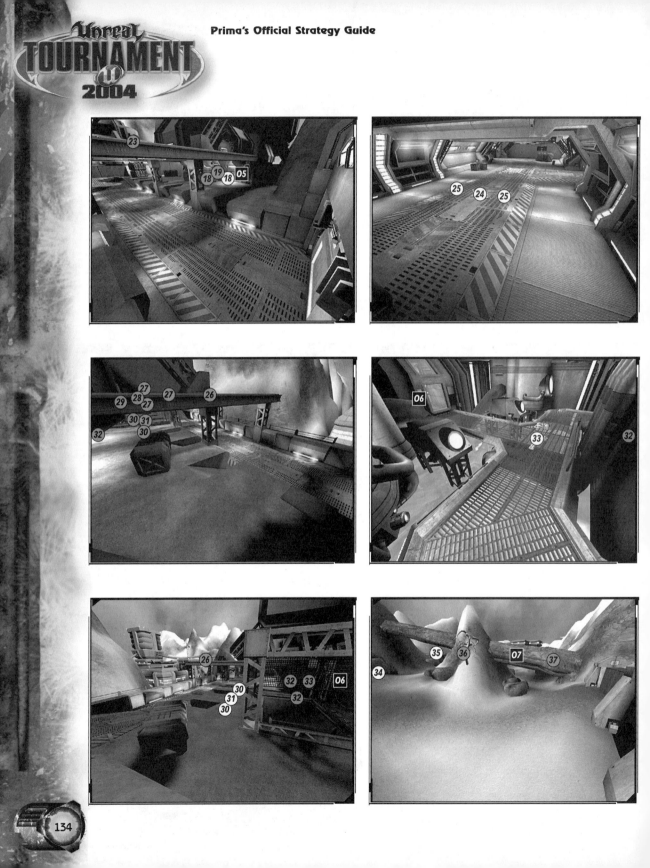

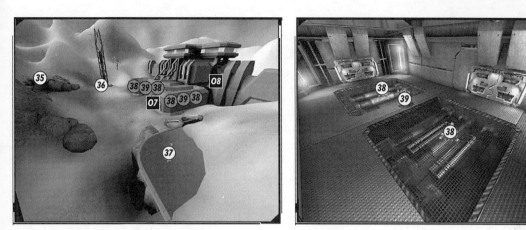

Overview

The Attackers have a base infiltration, then a tank hijacking, and finally a joyride out of the base to complete! From their spawning point across a river, they need to get across and through the base doors. They can run to an alcove on the right side of the base entrance to flick a switch that raises a central bridge, making subsequent base assaults easier.

Once inside the base, the Attackers quickly flick two switches on either side of an ion core, raising a door that leads to a tank bay. The Attackers must use the tank's prototype ion cannon to demolish an exit door, then trundle up to a power station.

Inside the station, a switch is flicked and a security gate lowers, enabling the Attackers to enter a road near a primary dam. Inside the dam entrance is a shutoff room that, when demolished, the power to a depot door fails. This allows the tank to blast it open, enter another roadway near a secondary dam, and destroy another shutoff chamber. When complete, the attacking team needs to drive the tank toward an exit building, demolish a blast door, and maneuver the tank out of the base.

Attackers' Objectives	Defenders' Objectives
1. Infiltrate the Base *Raise the Bridge	1. Defend the Base *Defend the Bridge Control
2. Activate the Ion Core	2. Defend the Ion Core
3. Capture the Tank	3. Defend the Tank
4. Destroy Access Tunnel Doors	4. Protect Access Tunnel Doors
5. Open Security Gate	5. Defend Power Station
6. Shut Down Primary Dam	6. Defend Primary Dam
7. Destroy the Depot Door	7. Defend the Depot Door
8. Shut Down Secondary Dam	8. Defend Secondary Dam
9. Destroy Blast Door	9. Defend Blast Door
10. Escape the Base	10. Prevent the Tank from Escaping
* bonus objective	* bonus objective

135

Attacking Objective 1 (and Bonus Objective): Infiltrate the Base (and Raise the Bridge)

The Defenders will take up positions on the other side of the bridge in the shadows, behind giant container crates, and along a set of open windows in the main base. Snipers can set up in numerous areas. Defenders must prevent infiltration at three separate areas, meaning your team can react to the highest concentration of enemies.

You start at the other side of a raised bridge over a turbulent river. Saunter over to your weapons locker, secure your four guns, grab one of the two 50 shield packs, and split your forces up.

Attackers' Weapon Lockers 1 and 2*
Shock Rifle
Link Gun
Minigun
Sniper Rifle
*Inside Attackers' initial base

Because the bridge control switch (bonus objective) and one of the doors are on the base's right side, there are likely to be more Defenders there. This isn't always the case, so try various charging tactics. The first is an en masse charge across the icy platforms to the side of the river. If all your team members dodge jump together, the enemy may be overrun before they can bring in reinforcements, and you can quickly secure the bridge and enter the base while the Defenders are caught running to aid their overrun colleagues. This means a high mortality rate for your team, but the speed in which you can swarm overcompensates for this.

It is very important to secure the bridge, as it makes it a lot easier to swarm the base for the second objective, and provides yet another route to try if you're splitting your forces, creating extra havoc for the Defenders.

If the en masse charge along the right bank isn't working, try a leap along the left icy platforms near the river. Move to the lone gate on the base's left side if you think the Defenders expect you to charge the bridge switch.

Splitting up the team is the third viable option. Have snipers provide covering fire. Place a couple underneath the bridge at river level, in the shadows (as they have a great view of the base windows). Put another on the bridge entrance using the crates as cover, and have more cover advancing troops behind either of the large rocks to the right of the spawn point. The rest of your team leaps across the river.

Finally, diving into the river is also an option; dodge jump across the left ice platforms, then dive into the river, swim underwater (and out of sight) to the other side, and climb up.

Across the river, expect fierce resistance from the Defenders, who can use the nearby crates to their advantage. If the big keg-o-health has appeared inside the left side container, grab it! Enemies, unless they appear from the doors you must open, have to drop down from a ceiling gap above the central entrance. Train your rockets there!

Those wishing to run interference can leap on the sloped concrete blocks at the base of the bridge scaffold, and run up the bridge support, zipping over the bridge structure to the other side (and changing supports using the chains linking each side). The enemy won't be expecting this, and although you're a visible target, this is a great way to get the enemy focused on you, and not the rest of the team infiltrating the base!

TIP

If you land in the water and attempt to clamber onto an icy platform, you may become stuck and completely prone. Avoid this, and instead head to the stairs at the base entrance which are easier to ascend.

Power up your shield gun, and defend yourself from attack with it when you reach the doors or the bridge switch (press Use to complete this objective).

NOTE

Raising the bridge (the bonus objective) is an excellent plan. It increases the number of routes to the base and offers quick access from the spawn point when attempting later objectives. Two giant containers also offer increased protection—hide behind them and vary the side you exit from when charging from this cover.

TIP

Flummox your foe by using the steps up onto the base courtyard from the river. Head up the stairs, then retreat if you come under fire, step to the small ledge to one side of the steps at the water's edge, and use this as cover before ambushing the curious Defenders.

Defending Objective 1 (and Bonus Objective): Defend the Base (and Defend the Bridge Control)

From your interior starting position, you have several options. After grabbing the prerequisite weapons from the locker and snagging one of the two 50 shield packs near the front of the base room, you and your team can drop through the hole in front of the weapons, and peer down at the ion core. Or, skip up the steps on either side of the hole, and stay at the horizontal open window slits and attempt to get a bead on the advancing Attackers with sniper fire.

137

You're likely to be shot yourself, as the relatively small surface area of this position means that enemies will be looking for movement up here. Prevent this with constant movement, and step back a few feet from the window while still looking down at the river and Attackers' spawn point below.

Defenders' Weapon Locker 1*
Link Gun
Minigun
Rocket Launcher
Sniper Rifle
Inside initial base/spawn point

This sniping point is suitable for only one or two of your team, as it allows limited views. Most of your team should drop down the hole and secure the perimeter and the three objectives, which is the main problem for the Defenders. Stay above the ion core or drop down into the ion core room only if the Attackers are about to breach the base and secure the objective.

What's even more embarrassing is that you can head out from inside the base, and open either objective door! The enemies still have to reach these doors, but don't need to wait for them to open. Don't accidentally activate the doors you're meant to be defending!

Spend most of the time guarding the three objectives. With three sensitive areas, you must pull together as a team and really watch what the Attackers are doing. Are they attempting to rush one door? Move your team to that location, with one or two teammates hanging back in case of a double bluff. If the enemies don't have a concrete plan, split your team into thirds. Have one squad immediately grab the big keg-o-health in the container near the right door. Have the second squad patrol the center of the container yard and left door, while the rest

stay with rocket launchers poised to blast anyone dashing for the bonus objective bridge switch!

The bridge is important to the Attackers as it allows them to cross the river without precariously leaping across icy blocks, but don't overstretch your forces; protecting the doors takes precedence over guarding the bridge switch. Continue this patrol until the enemy breaches one of the doors, and then immediately fall back to the ion core and guard objective #2.

TIP

The enemy emerges in one of two places on either set of steps from the water. The torrent of water and the narrow area make this an excellent choke point—fill it with rocket launcher fire and other choice ordnance. Leap on the bridge support bridge, then to the top of the containers, to overlook the area and keep the pressure up.

Here's a classic and annoying gameplan for the mavericks on your team: Leap on the bridge span support, and leap across it, over the gap, to the other side. Then let rip with rockets at the Attackers spawning! Crouch on the right-side support, making sure the sentry gun on the ground to the left, inside the spawning area, shoots and hits the nearby container and not you!  You're a sitting duck up here, so use the chains to dash across to the other side. If you can wound six or a dozen enemies with rocket splash damage, you make it a lot easier for the rest of your team to finish them off!

Attacking Objective 2: Activate the Ion Core

Don't think the attacking gets any easier once the base doors are opened! When you enter either base door, both doors open wide, but any Attacker casualties respawn at the original area, meaning that the Defenders still can guard the doors. Inside the base, grab a health pack from behind each door. If you head through the left base door, the corridor is to your right and slightly longer. If you head through the right base door, the corridor is to your left and slightly shorter. No matter which way you head, expect severe enemy retaliation, especially in the core room.

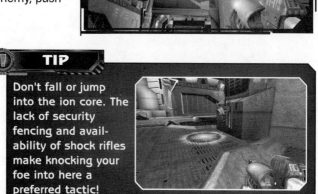

Attackers can use the shock combo and point it upward at any Defenders gathering at their spawn point, which is directly above the two ion core switches. Knock them back, allowing the switch runner to reach the core and complete the objective. You can also bombard the Defenders on the corridor, or launch rockets and link rounds in a fracas designed to destroy the enemy, push them back, or push past them.

Although the Defenders have a spawn point advantage, the Attackers can choose whether to secure one core switch, or both at the same time. Mixing up this strategy allows you to conclude this objective in record time. Blast up into the balcony above the core with shock combos from both sides and quickly press the switches. Don't forget to push the Defenders back into the core; you'll never rid the entire area of enemies, so

TIP

Don't fall or jump into the ion core. The lack of security fencing and availability of shock rifles make knocking your foe into here a preferred tactic!

continuously push them back instead. Finally, be wary of Defenders who use the former exit down to the main entrance and then fire on your forces coming in from the spawn point, or who follow behind your Attackers as they enter the base and sandwich them.

NOTE

It takes around two seconds of standing near the switch for it to activate. If you're removed from the switch during this time, the switch remains in the position it was when you last touched it, meaning it becomes increasingly easier to finish the task.

Defending Objective 2: Defend the Ion Core

The enemy now heads for two levers attached to the ion core, behind and below your starting point. Your job is to waylay them for as long as possible. Accomplish this by correctly determining where most Attackers are coming in and being prepared for them, whether they storm in from the left or right door. Fight them every step of the way as they attempt to gain entrance.

139

Because the Attackers spawn from the initial location, keep half your team positioned where they were for objective #1 (outside in the loading bay near the river) to damage the advancing hordes, and steal the rocket ammunition and keg-o-health. Retreat back into the base as the enemies close, whittling down their health as you move back to the core. Have the rest of the team fall back inside the core room before blasting anyone coming near either switch.

Careful preparation in rocket aiming means you can destroy them before they arrive. Consider using the balcony directly above the core as partial cover when firing down at Attackers below. If you can knock the enemies into the core, or through the gaps around the edge of the core, so much the better!

> ### TIP
>
> Aim downward from the ion core balcony near the spawn point. Whenever the objective icon turns yellow (signifying that the enemy is close), unload on the objective point to create a zone of terror.
>
>
>
> Drop down to the narrow ledge on the core, and down again onto the spikes protruding around the core. You gain the extra height needed to shoot down on your foe, and you can drop onto the core and block it with your body; this suicidal strategy can save your team precious seconds!
>
> Remember that even though the enemy has breached your base defenses, they still spawn from across the river, and thus are susceptible to gunfire as they cross the bridge or icy platforms. They may enter the other door if too many Defenders guard the area behind the initial breach.
>
>
>
> Discover your adversary's location by peering through the weapon-proof windows overlooking the initial loading bay. You can see enemies running for a particular door and create an ambush for them as they enter.

Attacking Objective 3: Capture the Tank

Capturing the tank can take an instant, or a teeth-grinding couple of minutes to achieve, depending on how familiar both teams are with its location, and the costs to both sides if the tank is entered. It's unlikely that the Defenders can stop your team if you know what they're doing. As soon as the second switch is pressed, a large gate lowers from top to bottom, adjacent to the core. Ignore or dodge any incoming fire, and leap over this door. You and your team must immediately change to the link gun. Whoever reaches the tank first should press Use and enter it to complete the objective. Meanwhile, have half your squad deal with the Defenders pouring through the doorway, while the others link-heal the tank. Do not let the tank be destroyed during this and the next objective!

TIP

Those pesky Defenders can't harm the tank until you enter it, so they will fire at you until you reach the tank. The problem is the spawn point; you begin in your initial position, so take the tank the instant the core is activated.

Defending Objective 3: Defend the Tank

Your next task is simple. When both core levers are pressed, the large garage doors on either side of the ion core open, allowing the Attackers another way into the base (through the main doors), and a way out and into the prototype tank your team is guarding!

The Attackers will use the confusion and close-quarter fighting of the previous objective to attempt a quick tank hijack, so make sure your entire team dashes for the tank courtyard door the moment objective #2 falls. Create a wall of enemies using the cover of the cabinets and the tank to form a large choke point, while some of your team stand by the core and weaken the Attackers by aiming at them as they advance—once again—from their initial starting point.

It's extremely hard to hold the choke point, as an Attacker can take a quick zigzagging run through your defenses to reach the tank and accomplish the objective. Use the ion core room to dodge around, blasting the incoming foes while the remainder of your force stays by the tank to blast anything that moves. Even a wall of your teammates can halt the Attackers for a moment!

TIP

It's imperative for your team to be a cohesive unit for objective #4. As soon as someone is about to enter the tank, have all your team train a chained link gun at the tank to demolish it immediately!

A locker behind and right of the tank holds a shock rifle and other weapons, but this is a spawning zone for the Attackers once objective #4 has been breached. Don't enter here unless you really want the shock rifle and can withstand a sentry gun.

Attacking Objective 4: Destroy Access Tunnel Doors

The tank driver must precisely know the plan of action, as this objective is over in seconds with a cunning team. While the rest of your squad link heals the tank, use its anti-personnel wave (secondary attack) to bounce any crawling Defenders off its superstructure. To complete this objective in record time, keep the tank stationary, hold the fire button to power the ion cannon turret, and release it at full power, aiming at the door's top left. Trundle your tank around the corner and blast the door. Do this before your team is overpowered, because once the door is destroyed (which only takes one ion cannon hit), your team spawns at the base to the right of the tank and doesn't have the long walk from the start any more.

141

NOTE

As soon as the tank is captured, the Defenders start to spawn at the power station, meaning you encounter less of them. The longer you take blasting this door, the more holed up and ready the Defenders will be!

TIP

If you're not driving the tank, you should be healing it. Change weapons and guard the doorway you just entered as the Defenders gradually dwindle in number; they're readying themselves up ahead. If there are enough healers, leap in the minigun turret and let rip!

NOTE

The tank's ion cannon is the only weapon that can damage the door and the other access doors in this match!

Defending Objective 4: Protect Access Tunnel Doors

Although the enemies respawn from the starting point, your team respawns to the power station near the switch to the security gate (objective #5). So your last hurrah is at the tank. Blast this vehicle and anyone nearby with all your ordnance before dying in this zone and reappearing at the station.

Don't wander up the tunnel after the Attackers or you'll be no use on base defense during the next objective! Instead, wait until one of the Attackers enters the tank (as the vehicle is invincible until then), and chain link gun the entire vehicle; you can demolish it in seconds! When you run out of link gun ammo, switch to rockets, and plug away at the sides of the tank, taking care not to step too close to it or you'll be forced back with its anti-personnel wave attack.

Damage the machine as much as you can, making yourself as much of a nuisance as possible. Use all your ordnance on the tank to try to prevent it from blasting the door. It won't do much good though; that door blows apart with one ion blast! Retreat!

Attacking Objective 5: Open the Security Gate

Once the access door is smashed, you have a moment to regroup. All your team now spawns from the building to the right of the tank's starting location, so wait for key members of your team before engaging on the security gate assault. Your plan isn't to reach the security gate; instead, maneuver your

Attackers' Weapon Lockers 3 and 4*

Shock Rifle

Minigun

Rocket Launcher

Inside Attackers' tank depot

tank to the tank spawning plate at the tunnel's far end, up the ramp, and at the entrance to the power station. Once you reach this point, even if your tank is destroyed, it reappears halfway through the tunnel, while the rest of the infantry appear behind it at the next set of weapons lockers. For now though, move the tank through the access doorway you just destroyed, plugging an ion charge at the ramp ahead, and another at the right side of the junction at the ramp's top as you reach the next spawning area, and turn right.

When you emerge from this tank depot, if the tank is waiting for you, leap aboard and ride the tank up the tunnel ramp without having to walk. The weapons lockers here contain no link guns; find these attached to the lockers at the top of the first ramp, on the left. When you reach the top of the first ramp, have the tank driver wait a moment for the rest of the team to grab link guns, and then begin the assault.

Attackers' Weapon Lockers 5 and 6*

Shock Rifle

Link Gun

Minigun

Rocket Launcher

Inside tunnel

When the tank turns right, have half your team ready to heal it, while the others run alongside it, shooting any Defenders holed up behind or inside the crates scattered about the ramp leading to the power station. Your infantry should use the crates as cover, dodge jumping to the next crate area on both the left and right sides of the ramp, or staying behind the tanks for cover. Rockets work well here. Have a second gunner in the tank's turret, as there's much to strafe when you reach the top of the ramp.

When the tank maneuvers up to the tunnel exit, take careful aim with the ion cannon, and blast the minigun turret in the far distance ahead with one shot. Don't power out of the tunnel, as you'll lose your cover and get caught in the crossfire with a second minigun turret. If the enemy enters the tunnel to destroy you, retaliate with all troops, using the crates and tunnel entrance as cover.

When the coast is clear, point your turret at 11 o'clock, and drive over the tank spawning plate (ensuring all your team start at weapons lockers #5 and #6, with options to grab one of two 50 shield packs). Charge and fire your ion cannon at the second minigun turret on the station's left balcony. Back up your shot with the tank minigun turret. Have the infantry concentrate on the forces within or scattered around the building.

The tank driver's final act is to drive toward the building's nearest corner, to the ground plate with the flashing yellow lights, and park the tank here. As soon as the tank reaches the plate, the blast door in front of you opens, creating an excellent entry point to the power station and freaking the Defenders out! Once the blast doors are down, they stay down, so you can suffer a tank destruction and still continue to the objective.

Charge the entire team in at once, with three link gun healers using the tank as cover and keeping the machine intact while the rest of the team storms the facility. Watch for the crate just to the left of the tunnel exit, as a double damage rests in there, and you need to destroy the owner of this power-up before he or she can do some real harm.

NOTE

If the tank is unoccupied and out of visual range for more than 20 seconds, it becomes unstable and self-destructs. It'll reappear at its nearest spawn point. Keep a driver handy at all times!

TIP

When you've parked your tank at the opening blast doors, horrify the enemy by firing straight through into the building! You can blast ion charges at the weapons locker and objective, forcing the Defenders out of their most secure area!

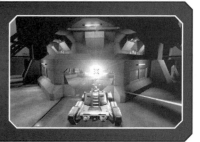

When the tank is parked up at the open blast doors, and your team has successfully used the tank to heal against and shield themselves from enemy attacks, the assault on the power station can begin! The enemy is holed up inside here, so expect major retaliation. However, the base is difficult to defend, as there are five entrances! The first is the entrance the tank just created: this is quick, you can use the tank as cover, the tank's awesome power allows you free access inside, and the objective is directly ahead. However, this is a straight shot through and you easily can be ambushed from the sides.

So why not try entrances two and three? These are on either side of the building, under the balcony leading to where the minigun turrets were. You can storm in there. This offers a health pack, but the enemy is likely to be here, away from the tank blasting.

So try entrances four and five. Run toward entrance two or three, then turn just prior to the entrance and double jump onto the support strut and run up, then double jump to the upper balcony (either near the turrets, or above the blast doors). Then run around the top floor, shooting stragglers, enter the Defenders' spawn point, collect shield packs and weapons, and drop down the central hole to the mesh floor next to the objective. Mix up the number of troops going for each different entrance to allow a quick objective capture. Split your team into groups, or take one huge force and storm that switch!

TIP

Stand by the switch (with a shield gun if enemies are near) for two seconds to open the security gate. Continue from the point you left off if you're removed during the switch opening. Once the gate opens, the Attackers spawn from this building, the tank spawns at the plate outside, and the Defenders appear at the first dam.

Defending Objective 5: Defend Power Station

Defenders' Weapon Lockers 3 and 4*

Shock Rifle

Link Gun

Rocket Launcher

Sniper Rifle

Inside power station

Defenders' Weapon Locker 5*

Shock Rifle

Link Gun

Minigun

Rocket Launcher

Sniper Rifle

Inside power station

Keep the Attackers away from the power station lever. Recognize where your spawning point is: You're on the top floor of the power station with the objective switch under you, two weapon lockers of equipment, and two 50 shield packs. Drop through the hole in the floor to the building's base where there's a third weapons locker opposite the dead end with the switch in it. This locker contains an additional minigun and two more shield packs.

Two health packs lie near the two ground doorway exits, with identical doors above them that lead to a balcony with a minigun turret at the far end. Reach this balcony from the ground by double jumping onto the nearby support and leaping up the metal structure. However, your first goal is to prevent the tank from reaching the tunnel's exterior. As soon as your team spawns at this new location, grab what you can and head outside.

The enemy must reach the tank plate outside the power station, near the transmitter tower to make the ion tank spawn at the tunnel. Note that enemy Attackers also spawn at this point, at the far end of the ramps. A number of stalling tactics can prevent the tank from ever reaching the station.

Rush down the ramp to the spawning location at the end of the middle tunnel. You can save your team critical seconds if you and a couple of teammates chain your link guns to destroy the tank before it reaches this area (throw the link guns away and claim more from the enemy locker as needed). Of course, the link gunners don't have to peek out from the corner of the tunnel junction, making this a reasonable plan if your foes are slow on the uptake. Remember! Your enemies respawn at the initial tank parking spot until the tank reaches the plate, so hold them off for as long as possible and pick any stragglers off with sniper fire!

If the tank turns the corner and starts up the latter part of the tunnel, fall back to the cover halfway up and at the top of the tunnel exit. Crouch behind the lip of the tunnel ramp and snipe the incoming forces, or hide behind either of the crate stacks (you can leap atop either). You can pass around the edge of each crate stack, too. However, you can't aim at enemies actually heading up the ramp, just those on the flat ground before and after it.

A chain of link guns starting behind the crates can prevent the enemy from blasting everyone and is devastating for the tank. All of your team should run to the tunnel exit and plug away at either troops or the tank itself (use around three or four to take the tank out, with sharpshooters blasting the stragglers and a rocket launcher or two for enemies running near the tank).

145

The minigun turret directly behind the tank plate with a full view of the tunnel will be the tank's first target, so use it as early as possible to add to the blasting needed to stop the advancing hordes. When the tank is destroyed, dash back to the lower weapons locker and replenish your weapons before returning to your positions. You get pushed back as the tank exits the tunnel, but keep pounding on it.

TIP

It's possible to take out a tank in five seconds with a minigun that's powered with the double damage icon! The double damage is in the large oblong crate at the tunnel exit. Use it primarily on the tank as it appears. Don't waste it!

When the tank reaches the plate, all hell breaks loose as the Attackers now begin their romp from the end of the tunnel. Plus, the tank can park in front of the power station, opening the garage door adjacent to the ground weapons locker, and fire straight into the facility to clear anyone guarding the objective! Want the worse news? Five separate entrances make this building almost impossible to guard!

Remember these important points: Always secure the double damage. Don't let the tank driver get out, grab it, and hop back in the vehicle. Attempt to contain the Attackers at the tunnel exit. Have the second minigun turret operational as soon as the tank exits the tunnel, and pepper the vehicle with crossfire. Keep the turrets operational for as long as possible. Have the rest of the team set up positions around the courtyard and blast the enemy before they enter the facility. Snipers on the upper balcony are a great way to stop incoming Attackers as they attempt to run into the base with little or no cover—the balcony is near your spawning point.

TIP

The ground level also provides some interesting ambush points. Stand to the left of the tunnel exit, behind the transmitter mast that is sometimes overlooked. Leap out and butcher those hijackers!

You also can use the dark shadows of the right side of the tunnel exit and courtyard for some sniping. Even more cunning is to leap on top of the minigun turret, double jumping to the top of the crates (and even to the edge of the wall right of the tunnel) and on top of the crates containing the double damage!

If the Attackers manage to burst through the tunnel exit choke point, they're likely to be wounded. Follow any that succeed in breaking free into the base to cut them down before they reach the objective. When the tank opens the garage door, this is the likely spot for the enemy to gain entrance, so concentrate your fire on here and on the tank so it can't send a nasty ion burst into the base. Have one or two of your team milling about the ground floor to cut down enemies running into the objective room, but follow them in. Don't wait inside the room as you're easily blasted.

Attacking Objective 6: Shut Down Primary Dam

Objectives six and eight are almost identical, so learn the strategies from objective #6 and apply them later. You have to shut down the primary dam by blasting the central dam switch. This is in a small chamber sealed with glass, near a walkway overlooking a deadly vat, with two small choke point entrances and the Defenders' spawn point overhead! This makes destruction of the dam difficult (and almost impossible in one try).

While the rest of the team runs toward the dam shutoff room, the tank driver should trundle toward the now-open gates, either via the path, or between the support cable and the pipeline support. As you reach the road toward the sealed door, train your ion cannon on the top of the deck structure ahead, and let rip! Keep the minigunner so he can strafe the area and rid the tank of Defenders.

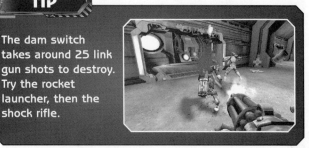

TIP

The dam switch takes around 25 link gun shots to destroy. Try the rocket launcher, then the shock rifle.

Meanwhile, use your ion cannon and infantry to clear the exterior of all enemies, allowing you to take the 100 shield pack from inside the second crate. You don't need to heal the tank either, as the spawn point is close enough to keep the tank trundling in for more mop-up duties. Or move your tank under the balcony, in the middle of the road, and park it so the turret is facing a ramp and has a clear line of sight into the shutoff room. Then clear the area continuously with ion charges. This requires a good aim, but it really annoys the enemy!

The Attacking troops push the enemy inside the building and claim the initial crate-filled area left of the road. Attempt to muscle into the room, avoid the drop off the mesh floor below, and begin to pummel the shutoff switch. Use the link gun and begin to fire, smashing the main panel with your first shot. Dodge jump to avoid gunfire. Have a couple of teammates blast the ceiling (where the enemy can shoot you from), and even leap into the shutoff booth, ideally with another team player guarding the door. Vary the entrance your team uses, try shock combos on the enemy as you head inside (hit them off into the vat below), and after a few bloody bouts, you'll eventually blast the objective.

147

Defending Objective 6: Defend the Primary Dam

The security detail moves from a large facility with many entrances to a small chamber with two adjacent entrances and a partially covered chamber with the shutoff switch. With a variety of excellent defensive points both here and in the almost identical secondary dam (objective #8), try the following strategies in both locations (allowing for different item placements).

Defenders' Weapon Locker 6*

Biorifle

Link Gun

Minigun

Rocket Launcher

Sniper Rifle

Inside primary dam

Grab the contents of your weapons locker and decide whether you're on grenades detail or not. Around half of the team should stay inside the dam shutoff room (both on the ground and above it) to seal it from advancing foes. The rest of the team takes potshots at enemies as they venture into this area. Head to the balcony area above the road and grab the two health packs on one outcrop and a grenade launcher (plus two grenade packs) on the other. One should annoy the tank (it isn't vital, but it helps for the subsequent objectives). Without the tank's help, the playing fields are leveled.

The teammate running interference drops down onto the ground with grenades as soon as possible to cause the maximum amount of annoyance, and also to grab the 100 shield pack hidden inside the large crates to the left of the dam entrance. Fifteen grenades can take down an entire tank. The road where the tank is moving is narrow, meaning you can get close to the tank without being blasted, and even when you die, your grenades explode!

Snipers move camping spots on top of the building, both near the grenade launcher, firing at the enemies as they attempt to move from the power station, and also from the far balcony where you can get a clear shot at the road below. Another option is the lip of the balcony around the upper dam exterior, where you can scurry into the shadows along the near side, above where the shield pack is located (or leap onto that crate).

Meanwhile, the rest of the team should keep the doorways to the dam shutoff room as watertight as possible. If you're on the ground and you can see enemies charging in, leave a load of biorifle goop at the entrance to damage intruders. Bounce grenades off walls so they land at the doorway, and detonate them at your leisure. The shock rifle, just inside the entrance, provides a great way to bounce

TIP

Set up a great sniping viewpoint by leaping onto the sloping scaffold support and running even farther up the building, then stop in the shadows at the top.

enemies away from the entrance, or off the walkway inside. Use the spawn point to run to the hole above and aim downward at the enemy. Turn around from the weapons locker, grab the six health vials, and fire a sniper rifle through the mesh at anyone who nears the shutoff room. Finally, the most cunning plan involves standing in the entrance to the shutoff cubbyhole, presenting yourself as a target to thwart the enemies even more, and making sure shots hit you, not the objective. Keep this up until the shutoff finally occurs.

TIP

With the left entrance being predominantly used, "run away" from the enemy as they enter the entrance, then around and out the right side entrance. Circle around to blast them from behind, using the same entrance they did!

Attacking Objective 7: Destroy the Depot Door

The tank driver should power up an ion cannon shot and be ready to send it directly to the gate at the end of the road the instant the primary dam falls. Whatever the Attacker team's skill level, the door falls quickly. Bring your tank under the balcony, have the rest of the team link heal it as you take the three shots necessary to destroy the gate. Any remaining Attackers should plug incoming Defenders (along with the turret gunner) that drop from the roof or head out of the shutoff doorway. Choke the doorway with rocket and shock fire to prevent Defenders from reaching you. Three shots later, the door is destroyed, and you can trundle toward your next objective.

Defending Objective 7: Defend the Depot Door

The tank can easily blast the door from any distance. As soon as the shutoff switch is about to go, pile your entire team onto the outer balconies or onto the road below, and aim everything you have at the tank. The teammates outside should have continuously lobbed grenades at it; ideally the vehicle is at the tank plate outside the power station and can be waylaid with a mixture of ordnance throwing and suicidal running techniques. Charge at the tank, attempting to throw off the driver's aim if you can; anything to gain a few more seconds. After three strikes, the door explodes, so don't lose hope after one strike; continuously attack the tank, retaliating against enemy infantry only if the need arises.

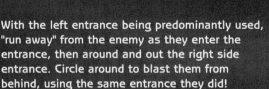

Attacking Objective 8: Shut Down the Secondary Dam

As soon as the doors are destroyed, both teams' spawn points move. The Defenders appear atop the secondary dam, in a room identical to the primary one. The Attackers meanwhile, appear inside a hangar. The tank needs to turn right, then left at the exit to appear at the secondary dam. The spawn point offers two weapons lockers and two 50 shield packs.

Charge as one, out through the hangar exit choke point and into the secondary dam road. Once on the road, climb onto and double jump off the tank to the upper balcony and shutoff room entrance, using the crates as cover. The tank driver should try to land a couple of ion cannon blasts on top of the facility's roof, and then drive under the upper balcony, park on the right side of the road, and fire ion cannon bursts into the shutoff room! Your infantry should heal the tank or enter the shutoff room and destroy the secondary dam in exactly the same way as for objective #6. The only difference is that a flak cannon inside the shutoff room makes taking this objective easier; use it to bombard the room and the switch.

Attackers' Weapon Lockers 7 and 8*
Shock Rifle
Link Gun
Minigun
Rocket Launcher
Sniper Rifle
*Inside hangar

NOTE

The tank can really destroy the scenery, such as the hangar exit. Push this superstructure with the tank, and infantry can use it to leap on and over, gaining a new method of entering the shutoff room.

TIP

Throw away your empty weapons and grab more from the two weapons lockers at the spawn point for objective #9.

Defending Objective 8: Defend Secondary Dam

Defenders' Weapon Locker 7*
Biorifle
Link Gun
Minigun
Rocket Launcher
Sniper Rifle
*Inside secondary dam

As soon as the enemy destroys the gate (objective #7), they spawn inside a second L-shaped small tunnel, while your team appears in a second, almost identical dam. The rules for objective #6 apply here; so use the strategy mentioned there. The weapons locker holds identical ordnance, but the left balcony holds the grenade launcher and ammo this time, not the right one (which holds two health packs).

Initially throw everything you've got at the tunnel exit choke point, then while a couple of ground infantry try to stop the tank from reaching the tank plate, the rest of your forces should seal that second shutoff area using identical techniques as before. The excellent flak cannon is perfect for tearing open incoming enemies from close quarters; aim it at both exits. If you crave a shock rifle, run out to the two weapons lockers to the left of the dam, used mainly by the Attackers for objective #9, and grab one from there.

Attacking Objective 9: Destroy Blast Door

Attackers' Weapon Lockers 9 and 10*

Shock Rifle

Link Gun

Minigun

Rocket Launcher

Sniper Rifle

*Outside secondary dam

As soon as objective #8 is met, the Defenders spawn at their last point—the base exit area and blast doors—while the Attackers appear behind the last two weapons lockers, to the right of the opened door leading to the final blast doors. Make sure your tank has reached the spawn plate at the base of the shallow ramp leading to the opened doors or you have to trundle in from the hangar again. Pick up your weapons, grab one of the two 50 shield packs, and move toward the final area. Those with shield jumping skill can move away from the team and shield jump to the right of the gate entrance, up and onto the wall to the right of the gate, overlooking the right side roadway.

Once on the roadway, you can turn right, to the shorter path to the blast doors, or left, past two flaming towers. Don't fire the ion cannon as you enter the road and turn right, shooting through the rock arch and taking out the blast doors from extreme range. The reason is that a pair of side entrances open and enemies can pour out instead of simply having the front entrances (where they can be contained with ion, turret, and regular gun fire).

Either route to the blast doors is usable, but the longer route has health packs and three link charges at the base of each of the two towers. Continue to link heal the tank, and keep your team close together, checking the rocks around the path for snipers or Defenders hiding out, then bring all your weapons to bear. Once at the blast doors, allow your team to blast anyone exiting the front doors (you can shoot an ion charge in, although enemies continue to spawn, meaning you're better off firing at the blast doors). Time your three ion shots so that the final one destroys the door just as the tank reaches it, allowing you to escape without any major retaliation.

Attacking Objective 10: Escape the Base

Once the blast doors are out of commission, make sure the tank survives to the far end of the tunnel behind the blast door wreckage. The side entrances near the Defenders' spawn points are now open, so train all your fire on these two areas. Just drive on through here, with the rest of the team link healing, and you'll have few problems.

Defending Objectives 9 and 10: Defend Blast Door, and Prevent the Tank from Escaping

You begin both objectives #9 and #10 in the same area, with pretty much the same battle plan, so similar strategies apply to both attempts to keep the tank from exiting the base. As soon as the second dam is shut down, you appear inside a base check-point exit, in one of two identical spawning rooms. Grab the plentiful weapons from either locker (there's one in each room), and immediately exit. You're making your last stand outside. But fortunately, you have spider mines to make your job a little easier.

First of all, wait until you spot the tank trundling out to the rocky ground, and note which direction it's moving. Scatter so your team isn't caught by any incoming blasts, and quickly attack the tank. Throw everything you can at it, such as chained link gun fire (move to the two towers with three link gun ammo packs for an extra punch). Crouch behind the rocks lining the roads and launch spider mines as the tanks pass; eight mines completely destroy the tank. Focus some firepower on the tank (especially from distance—keep at least two teammates at the exit), while the rest try to break up the chain link gunners on the attacking team.

Defenders' Weapon Locker 7*

Shock Rifle

Link Gun

Minigun

Mine Layer

Rocket Launcher

Sniper Rifle

*Inside checkpoint exit

> **TIP**
>
> Use the sniping points from the upper ground and rocks to the left and right of the checkpoint exit. Show no mercy!
>
> ---
>
> The interior of the inside hill, opposite the final doors the tank attempts to shoot, is a great ambush spot; leap out from a direction the enemy won't expect!

Nothing works better than spider mines to stop the tank! Place a load at the entrance to the exit corridor, and once the exit is breached, pour out of the side entrances throwing spider mines; this is the best way to halt an Attacker's break for freedom!

AS-JUNKYARD

Recommended Players: 8–16

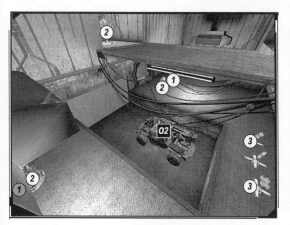

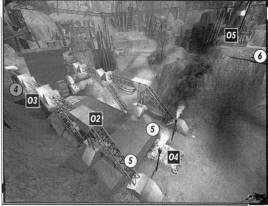

Legend

1. 50 Shield Pack (each side of Attackers' spawn point)
2. Weapons Locker (three in spawn point)
3. 50 Health Pack x2 (four total in spawn point)
4. 50 Health Pack x2 (near minigun turret, front of bridge)
5. Weapons Locker (far side of bridge)
6. AVRiL (metal roof section)
7. Weapons Locker (Defenders' spawn point near exit)
8. 50 Health Pack (minigun turret hill near exit)
9. 50 Health Pack (front hill near exit)
10. Shock, link, mini, flak, sniper ammo packs (two each, on hill over junkyard)
11. 50 Health Pack (on hill overlooking junkyard)
12. 50 Health Pack (each side of jump pad, Defenders' initial spawn point)
13. Weapons Locker x3 (on Defenders' initial spawn point)
14. 50 Health Pack (edge of hill near turret)
15. Shock x2, bio x3, sniper x2, link x3, mini x2, flak x2 ammo packs (on hill)
16. Weapons Locker x6 (inside ironworks)
17. Mine Layer (lower balcony of ironworks)
18. Redeemer (on steps near door)
19. Weapons Locker (Defenders' spawn point)
20. 50 health Pack (behind Defenders' spawn point)
21. Link x3, mini x2, flak x2 ammo (behind Defenders' spawn point)
22. Shock Rifle +3 ammo packs (above crusher)
23. Bio x3, sniper x2 ammo packs (above crusher)
24. 50 Health Pack (above crusher)
25. Grenade Launcher +2 ammo packs (above crusher)

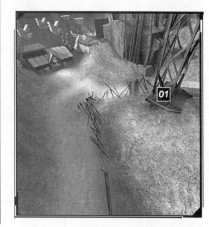

155

Overview

It's time for one wild ride, courtesy of a Hellbender and multiple pathways through a gigantic and initially confusing junkyard! The Attackers steam out of a shed, running to a nearby junk hill to secure an energy core and bring it back to their base. This activates the Hellbender, which they drive over to a bridge, while the rest of the team defends it or reaches the bridge by other means.

Flick a switch to lower the bridge, enabling the Hellbender to cross and drive to a junction. At the junction, the Hellbender can drive left up to a giant magnet that picks up the vehicle and deposits it at a bridge on the other side of the map. Or the Hellbender can steer right, along a road marked with obstacles (such as a crusher), and over to an ironworks where the Defenders are assembling en masse. With the ironworks taken over, the Attackers can drive the Hellbender toward the main gates for a final fracas with the remaining Defenders attempting to keep the jeep from escaping.

Attackers' Objectives	Defenders' Objectives
1. Find the Energy Core	1. Protect the Energy Core
2. Return the Core to the Vehicle	2. Prevent the Attackers from Returning the Core
3. Lower the Bridge	3. Prevent the Attackers from Lowering the Bridge
4. Cross the Bridge	4. Prevent the Attackers from Crossing the Bridge
5. Open the Checkpoint Gate	5. Prevent the Attackers from Using the Switch
6. Secure the Checkpoint	6. Protect the Checkpoint
7. Proceed to the Main Gates	7. Protect the Main Gates

Attacking Objectives 1 and 2:
Find the Energy Core and Return the Core to the Vehicle

Your team starts inside a large shed with a Hellbender (the giant jeeplike vehicle) parked inside. Your opponents begin on the nearest hill, in front of your base, although they can use jump pads to leap to anywhere in the yard, including tall buildings and hills to the right and behind your shed. It's easiest to make a mad rush for the metal tower on the hilltop, which holds the engine-shaped energy core designed to fit inside the Hellbender engine bay.

Dodge jump and zigzag across the ground outside your base, having already taken all of the weapons from either locker (or the one on the shed's top floor where some teammates spawn after objective #2 is complete), and hopefully one of the two 50 shield packs. Separate your team to maximize the targets the enemy can shoot at. Optionally keep a couple of snipers inside the shed to shoot the main defenses on the hill.

Attackers' Weapon Lockers 1, 2, and 3*

Assault Rifle (second)

Link Gun

Minigun

Flak Cannon

Sniper Rifle

*Inside Attackers' shed

The Defenders may be too spread out to effectively battle, so send most of your team in a straight charge through the metal posts at the hill's base, then around either the objective's left or right side. Expect a nasty choke point in this area, all the way to the opposite flat area, which is the only entrance to this platform under the tower. Enter from either the left or right, dashing into the middle or around one side (between the tower legs), and grab that energy core!

Return by leaping from the tower platform, zip through the posts, and dash back to the shed. If you're shot, you drop the core where you die. Another team member can grab it but not the enemy. When you return, have the rest of the team cover you. You can still use weapons, but don't pause to fight with someone; the objective is too important! When you return to the shed, the Hellbender automatically roars into life and the main garage door opens.

TIP

When you're retrieving the energy core from the tower platform, vary your entrance and exit. For example, approach from either side, run toward the platform supports under the objective as if you're circling left, then double back and move right to confuse your foes. When you finally grab the core, vary your route back by dodge jumping off the sides or front of the platform.

157

Unreal Tournament 2004

Defending Objectives 1 and 2: Protect the Core and Prevent the Attackers from Returning the Core

The Defenders have the advantage at the beginning of this match-up, with a preferable height, weapon, and location. Obtain the excellent array of weaponry from the three lockers, then set most of your team on the hillside, away from the jump pads. Create a hazardous hill by firing all of your spider mines so they stick to the hill's side and entrance to the platform holding the core—if there's six on your team, that's 24 mines! Then switch to your biorifle, and plaster the Attackers as they're waylaid by the mines. Covering the objective with goo makes it improbable to grab that core! Some of your team can set up sniping spots and take potshots at the enemy while they run out in the open; keep moving so you're not on the receiving end of a bullet, and grab the two health packs behind your spawn point.

Defenders' Weapon Lockers 1, 2, and 3*

Assault Rifle (second)

Biorifle

Link Gun

Mine Layer

Minigun

Flak Cannon

Sniper Rifle

*On hill/spawn point

TIP

When using the jump pad, continuously tap the jump key while you're flying to add an extra leap. Do this only when the landing spot is safe and don't overshoot!

To really annoy your Attackers, take the jump pad across the right Hellbender path, then another to the giant magnet. Anywhere along this cliff top is a great place for sniping or dropping mines. Continue past the magnet to a minigun turret (on a lower cliff overlooking the bridge), and strafe anyone running up the hill. You can't get a full view of the ground, but you can blast anyone shooting at you, and your height means arcing weapons can't reach you.

Continue around the Attackers' spawn point, using a jump pad to leap the drawbridge, and land on the corrugated building above the Attackers' shed. From here you can rain sniper fire down on the enemies as they run out, or double jump to the bridge scaffolding and drop onto the shed roof. You can even drop flak cannon bombs on the upper exit, which becomes functional once objective #2 is achieved. Continue taking shots at the enemy until they finally bring that core back.

TIP

Concentrate all your firepower on the enemies seeking the core, and the area around the core once it has been taken—delay your foes as long as possible!

Have a couple teammates keep an eye on wayward Attackers. If one or two stragglers leaves the group or tries to reach the bridge before you, split off and guard the minigun turrets using your jump pads to reach these key locations and hold them!

Attacking Objective 3: Lower the Bridge

The third objective becomes available when the Hellbender is functional. Forward-thinking teams should already know the location of the switch to lower the bridge. The bridge is above the shed, and you must drive your Hellbender to it for objective #4. However, for this objective, send a crack two- or three-man team across from the start to the Defender's hill, and then the jump pad heading left to the minigun hill near the giant flaming furnace outlet. Do this while the rest of the team attempts to complete objective #1.

Once at the minigun, it's a short couple of jump pad hops to the switch at the start of the bridge (jump pad to the platform, then the building balcony with the Defenders' weapons lockers, and drop onto the bridge structure). Time your team leaping so a member arrives just as objective #2 completes and the switch becomes functional. Then stand on the marker for three seconds to lower the lever, and the drawbridge descends. If you're shot or move from the marker, another can take your place and continue the objective—the lever doesn't reset. Finally, if you didn't plan ahead, the route to the bridge lever is just the same, except you should expect much more enemy fire.

Attacking Objective 4: Cross the Bridge

When the bridge is lowered, a new objective point appears at the bridge's far end. The Hellbender must reach this point, not an infantryman, for the objective to be complete. With this in mind, make sure your Hellbender has a full complement of crew: a veteran driver, a passenger with turret skills, and an eagle-eyed teammate on the larger back turret. The multiple paths to the bridge present better or worse choices depending on where the enemy is (they usually spawn from the building balcony over the bridge, so train your weapons there and follow them as they move).

Once out of the shed, zoom to the first junction at the base of the initial hill. Take a left, or cut across the ground on the left, and drive around the hill's left side, optionally using the trench on the left as extra cover before driving over a ramped area of fence and rejoining the main road. Make a left here. Otherwise, you can head right, around the hill's right side, where you take less enemy gunfire before the road joins near the next junction.

TIP

Train your biggest guns on the minigun turrets, as they're the most problematic defenses to overcome. Also try to chain your shock combos from your passenger turret, and use this turret to shoot incoming AVRiL rockets—this is possible if you're skilled enough!

When you reach the next junction, the road leading to the left is shorter than the right. Both maneuver around a hill with a bridge, which is part of objective #6 (depending on the route you take). Watch for the minigun turret atop this hill, and another as you reach a steep-walled entrance to the bridge. Your team should be link healing your Hellbender and dealing with the enemies on all sides, especially those on the minigun turrets.

The left road leads to a ramp. Zoom up the ramp after the black smoke stops moving. A furnace outlet can destroy the vehicle if you drop onto it while the flames are burning; keep your speed up! On the right road, zoom around and rejoin the road, charge into the bridge entrance, and have one of your passengers complete objective #3. Drive to the other side, claiming a new spawn point for both your vehicle and team.

TIP

Don't be a sitting target in the Hellbender; snake left and right in a serpentine pattern to avoid enemy fire and become less predictable. Vary your routes too.

Defending Objectives 3 and 4:
Prevent the Attackers from Lowering and Crossing the Bridge

Defenders' Weapon Lockers 4 and 5*

Assault Rifle (second)

Biorifle

Link Gun

Mine Layer

Minigun

Flak Cannon

Sniper Rifle

*On corrugated building ledge/spawn point

You spawn on a ledge on the corrugated building above the bridge and Attackers' shed as soon as objective #2 has been completed. This area is easy to reach from the initial spawn point, too. This means you probably will beat the Attackers to the bridge. Get a good vantage point on the Hellbender, and try shooting it with minigun turrets from the bridge's far side and the first hill near the ramp; the crossfire is incredible!

Meanwhile, keep the Attackers in check by posting a couple of guards on the turret near the ramp, mount the minigun turret at the road's end where the bridge lever is, and have a couple guard the lever while the rest bombard the Hellbender with any ordnance you can muster from the weapon lockers near your spawn point. The vehicle is easier to hit if it heads left at the first junction, but don't all race toward it—wait until it is near the first mesh ramp and the second junction, and then devastate it!

Continue the barrage until someone reaches the bridge lever (which should be coated with ooze or mines). Then focus all resources into destroying the Hellbender before it reaches the bridge's far side, as this is when the Attackers' spawn point changes.

TIP

We recommend against playing chicken with the Hellbender. However, if you want a close-combat attempt, dodge jump just before your face hits the Hellbender's front grill. Don't expect to last long, but do expect to annoy the enemy with this plan!

A good tactic is to formulate a place, such as the road before a junction or halfway across the bridge, where all the Defenders can lay their mines on their way to their chosen positions. Twenty exploding spider mines will put a serious dent in the Hellbender's armor.

161

Remember that the enemies can also use the jump pads by your spawn point to reach you, and you have no extra defenses to help you. Make sure you aren't blasted from a sniping point and overrun; stay mainly at the minigun turret areas.

If the Attackers are link gun healing the Hellbender, arm the shock rifle (near the crusher, behind spawn point #2) or the grenade launcher (farther along the crusher) and bounce the enemies away from the vehicle!

Another vantage point from which to rain fiery death down on the Hellbender is the mesh overhang opposite the Attackers' shed, near an ammo dump and the level exit. Reach this area by jump padding to the gap near the exit, then leaping left. Rain down flak bombs or spider mines from this area. There's a great view too, so you can check where other enemies are heading and inform your team.

Double jump from pads heading toward the corrugated building where you spawn, and then land on the roof, gaining extra height and a good sniping spot.

Attacking Objectives 5 and 6: Open the Checkpoint Gate and Secure the Checkpoint

You can accomplish this objective via two different routes: the shorter (and more dangerous) "magnet" route, or the longer "ironworks" route. Once you cross the bridge, the next target is the minigun turret atop the hill on your left. The recon team on your side should have moved and destroyed (or commandeered) this point, and the rest of your infantry should be either link healing the Hellbender, or atop the left hill shooting at the enemy as they leap in from the ironworks (which is initially on the bridge's other side).

Drive the Hellbender up the road, making sure the enemy hasn't grabbed the AVRiL above you on the metal roofing sheets; at the end of the road, turn left (drive up the incline and left again to save time), or turn right depending on which path you wish to pursue. Skilled Hellbender turret gunners can blast an incoming AVRiL rocket out of the air.

Attackers' Weapon Lockers 4 and 5*

Assault Rifle (second)

Shock Rifle

Minigun

Flak Cannon

Sniper Rifle

*Far end of bridge

 NOTE

It takes three direct shots from the larger Hellbender turret to take out a minigun turret, so make sure your gunner aims with skill!

Turning Left (The "Magnet" Route)

This route works only if your Attackers have secured all available minigun turrets (that is, they are in your hands or destroyed) and you don't have any enemies with shock rifles or AVRiLs to blast the Hellbender when it becomes prone. Drive left, up the ramp, and park underneath the huge magnet. Your teammates should have cleared the area of enemies or should be battling them.

Then wait for the magnet to grip the vehicle, transport it to the junkyard's other side, and drop it on top of a hill with a bridge. Heavy enemy fire dislodges your Hellbender, as does moving the larger turret, so be aware of the risk. If you fall, you return to the starting road. Should you succeed in the magnet maneuver, both objectives at the ironworks (the switch and the exit) are completed, and you can move to objective #7. Trundle across the bridge (park your Hellbender facing right at the magnet so you can drive straight off—you can drive up to this point earlier in the match, but two mesh fences bar access to the bridge), climb the ramp, and turn left onto the road just right of the ironworks. Make a right.

Turning Right (The "Ironworks" Route)

Should you take the long route, skid right, and then power down the road; you can be attacked only from the right or on the road. Zoom straight by the stack of concrete tubes on the left, unless the Defenders are firing at the barrels near them. If they destroy the coupling or the barrels near the tubes, they spill onto the ground and force you into a scrap metal tunnel, where you are more open to attack. Keep moving!

If you drive through the gap in the right wall halfway along the tunnel, you fall back to your spawn point. You could move out of the tunnel on your left, but this involves stopping, reversing, and repositioning, which usually results in severe damage. When you reach the two red and black arrow points, choose your route.

One option is to head left and enter an outdoor drive-in parking lot. Enemies jump in from the large shack to your right and the crusher. You can't knock over the posts dotted throughout the area, so don't ram them. When you drive over the shallow mesh ramp into the flat area, you cannot retreat, so skid right, and head slightly left to the only exit; there's another shallow mesh ramp to the right. Unfortunately, there's more than just small-arms fire to worry about here; the far left corner of the parking lot area (the doorway and small steps) houses a redeemer! Make sure your recon team reaches this first and guards it, or you'll have constant gigantic missiles from which to drive away—this almost always results in Hellbender explosions!

The other option, heading right, is the route the Defenders want you to take, and you must negotiate the crusher. If the crushing walls on either side are receding, accelerate through the crusher. If you see yellow energy sparks, you have three seconds to stop or drive to the middle area before the crusher starts and destroys anything it touches. There's also a constant stream of enemy fire from above, so have most of your team blasting these reprobates, while the turret gunners do their job, and have a couple ride on the Hellbender with

healing link guns. At the end of the crusher, make a sharp right, rejoining the road.

When the roads merge, stop when you see the ironworks in the distance, which is where the enemies are spawning. If your vehicle gets destroyed now, you respawn back at the bridge, so make these tactics count! Have half your team use jump pads to annoy the Defenders, ideally running in front of the Hellbender, or attacking from the other side of the ironworks. Park the Hellbender at extreme range and blast the minigun turret apart at the ironworks entrance. Then follow your troops in, checking behind you for enemies, and have one of your turreteers or infantry flick the objective #5 lever while the passenger turret shock combos the inside of the base. The lever takes three seconds to pull, and stays in position if you're removed from the objective halfway through.

Now comes the assault on the ironworks! Continue to push forward, as you'll spawn from the bridge until you power through the ironworks and reach the checkpoint at the other end and open the gate. As soon as this occurs, you can begin your final objective run, and spawn from the ironworks.

Defending Objectives 5 and 6: Prevent the Attackers from Using the Switch and Protect the Checkpoint

When the Attackers reach the bridge's other side (objective #4), you appear inside the ironworks. Quickly work out where the Hellbender is going—for the magnet or the long route through the ironworks. Pick up ordnance from one of the many lockers inside the ironworks, and dash to the area overlooking the route the Hellbender will take. Keep around half your team inside the base, looking out at the hill and minigun turret below. The quick-dash team should learn to dodge jump quickly to nearby jump pads and leap either across the junkyard to the initial spawn point and continue across, or to the bridge and second spawn point and around.

Defenders' Weapon Lockers 6, 7, 8, 9, and 10*

Assault Rifle (second)

Link Gun

Minigun

Flak Cannon

Sniper Rifle

Inside ironworks/spawn point

When the Hellbender makes its turn, radio the position to the rest of the team, and then stay around to blast the vehicle, just so you know the direction it has chosen. Then have your team react accordingly.

If the Hellbender Turns Left

If the vehicle goes left up the road to the magnet, have some of your team stay at the spawn point, with sniper rifles, the AVRiL (bound around the level to grab it), or the shock rifle (behind the crusher, near spawn point #2), and then continuously shoot the vehicle from the time it appears to the moment you dislodge it from the magnet!

The rest of the team, meanwhile, keeps the Attackers from using the jump pads at the hill where the Hellbender is likely to end up, and collects all the ammunition to prevent the enemies from grabbing any. When (or if, as the shock combo is a great way to dislodge the Hellbender from the magnet) the vehicle finally drops down at the hillside, make sure your team has left spider mines. Place more on the bridge as the vehicle tries to make a getaway to the final objective.

If the Hellbender Turns Right

If the Hellbender turns right, you have much more opportunity to blast it in an enclosed area! Have a team member at the large tunnel structure and shoot out the metal clamp or the barrels near a stack of concrete tubes, releasing them to tumble into the road. These will crush you if you stand by them (which can be a plan if you want to retreat back to the ironworks). This forces the Hellbender down the tunnel, where you can blast the vehicle from the sides or top. In fact, you can double jump from the jump pad next to the Attackers' spawn

point and lodge yourself in the side of the tunnel and let rip with weaponry. Meanwhile the rest of your team, except two, should be by the crusher, shooting shock combos at the left turn so that the Hellbender is coaxed into the crusher. If it moves this way, drop whatever you have onto it from the sides (flak is an excellent choice, but watch out for Attackers attempting to clear the way).

If the Hellbender drives toward the open air parking lot, have the two team members run and grab the redeemer and fire at the Hellbender as it hits the ramp into the open area. Don't fire at it when the vehicle is near any of your team! Keep this up and the enemy may change routes or mount an infantry assault, so don't overuse this weapon or let it fall into enemy hands.

Drop mines at the junction where the crusher and parking lot paths meet, and then retreat your entire team to the ironworks (even using suicides to quicken the pace). Have a minigunner blasting away on the turret, a sniper holed up in the dark corner to the left of the balcony containing the turret, and the rest blasting from the balcony or leaping around and behind the vehicle. Continue this until the lever is pulled (shock combo enemies away from it, and keep this target in your sights), and the Hellbender accelerates to the far end of the ironworks. Now retreat to your final spawn point!

TIP

Crave more Hellbender blasting? Then stand on one of the metal platforms near the route the vehicle is taking, thus ensuring you aren't shot at from below. Then drop onto the vehicle and blast it with flak, link gun fire, or grenades until one or both of you are smoldering heaps.

Attacking Objective 7: Proceed to the Main Gates

For the remainder of this match, Attackers spawn at the ironworks and can use the weapons used by the Defenders during the fight for objectives #5 and #6. When you begin your final assault and maneuver out of the junkyard, you encounter the remaining resistance at the final area. There is a minigun turret on the right bank as you emerge from the ironworks (avoided if you take the magnet route), so pour your available offensive ordnance at it, or have a recon unit head out in front to claim or destroy it for your team. Pass the emplacement and the

flat plateau covered in ammunition, pass the junction where you emerged if you used the magnet, and head to the opposing force's final base area.

As you pass right, watch out for enemies on the upper part of the hill shooting down at you. The road then splits into two, heading left and right around a hill with a final minigun turret at the top, near your team. If you can get a recon team here early enough, use the jump pads that litter the area, and have them dismantle this minigun turret (which makes the final area easier to drive through). With both of your Hellbender's turrets blazing, tackle the turret and any other foes in the immediate area, then have your infantry team help heal the Hellbender while two or three of your best shots tackle individual Defenders with classic combat routines and jump pad leaping. When you reach the junction, watch out for a trap!

There's a giant metal tower with a gas canister underneath it, and any worthy Defenders will have blasted it so the tower falls, forcing you to the right. If the tower is standing, try to zoom under it before it falls, or risk exploding the vehicle if the tower lands on it. The tactics are simple:

gun the engine, shrug off the gunfire, have all remaining infantry link heal your vehicle (to the detriment of their lives), and charge straight for the open exit and victory! Whatever the enemies throw at you, your Hellbender and some veteran infantry can cope. Gun the engine and go for it, and don't turn too early and snag yourself on the mesh fencing.

Defending Objective 7: Protect the Main Gates

Fall back to the main gates once the Hellbender reaches the far end of the ironworks or reaches the bridge via the magnet. If the Hellbender is coming via the ironworks, jump pad over to the ammo dump and the minigun turret, and slow the vehicle down from this rarely used position. Ignore this area if the vehicle is heading to the exit via the bridge.

Defenders' Weapon Lockers 11 and 12*
Assault Rifle (second)
Biorifle
Link Gun
Mine Layer
Minigun
Flak Cannon
Sniper Rifle
*On ridge near exit/spawn point

When you begin to spawn from your final point, pick up all the weapons, have the team lay one final huge set of spider mines along an area of road you know the Hellbender will drive over, and then head for the area with a minigun turret. Defend this turret, crouching to avoid fire below, then blanket the area in front of the vehicle, and the vehicle, with gunfire.

When you first spot the vehicle, have your entire team available to fire at it, and anyone foolish enough to venture forward from the Hellbender. Bounce back across the two main hills, and watch for anyone jump padding in from afar. Blast the gas cylinder under the metal tower with three flak bombs, so one more bomb will collapse the tower. Time it so the collapse destroys

the Hellbender (or blocks it inside the tower). Fool the attackers (blanket the other route with gunfire) into taking the route nearest the metal tower, then demolish the tower at the last moment, ideally landing the tower on the enemy Hellbender, or at the very least, forcing it to back up while you pepper it with gunfire. The next time the Hellbender appears, it must drive to the right, around the blocked route. Lay more spider mines here and back to the final exit area. Concentrate all your fire on the choke point: the entrance to the small courtyard before the ramp and the exit.

Ammunition Dumps

This map contains a number of ammunition dumps, and most of them can be grabbed (or defended) by either side. One of the biggest is on the hill where the minigun turret and ramp over the furnace outlet is located. Here you'll find two each of sniper, mini, and flak ammo, and three each of shock rifle, biorifle, and link gun ammo.

Three bio and two sniper packs are on the far side of the shock rifle pick-up (which is surrounded by four ammo packs too). On the near side are three link and two each of minigun and flak ammo near spawn point #2. Don't forget the grenades and two ammo packs farther along, overlooking the crusher, and the health pack. All of this is behind the Defenders' second spawn point.

Find two sniper, flak, link, minigun, and shock ammo packs on the rarely used overlook on the junkyard's far side, along the final stretch of road past the ironworks and near the exit. Reach it from the Defender's first spawn point, using the jump pad heading to the exit.

AS-MOTHERSHIP

Legend

1. 50 Shield Pack (near elevator)
2. Weapons Locker (near each lower entrance)
3. Weapons Locker (upper bridge entrance)
4. Weapons Locker (Defenders' spawn point)
5. Flak ammo packs x3 (each upper ledge)
6. 50 Health Pack (on upper balcony)
7. 50 Health Pack (Attackers' entrance corridor, each side)
8. 50 Health Pack (entrance to elevator)
9. Health Pack (Defenders' spawn point between sentry gun #1 and #2)
10. Defenders' Weapons Locker (between sentry gun #1 and #2)
11. Rocket and mingun ammo pack (between sentry gun #2 and #3)
12. Rocket and minigun ammo (near third sentry gun)
13. Weapons Locker (near third sentry gun)
14. 50 Health Pack (each side of exit corridor)
15. 50 Health Pack x2 (entrance to curved corridors)
16. 50 Shield Pack (entrance to curved corridors)
17. Weapon Locker (two total, each entrance to curved corridors)
18. Shock ammo pack (near crate)
19. Link gun cannon (near Defender's final spawn point)
20. Link ammo packs x2 (near Defenders' final spawn point)
21. Weapons Locker (Defenders' spawn point, two in total)
22. 50 Health Pack (base of each junction room)
23. Lightning, shock, rocket ammo (base of each junction room)

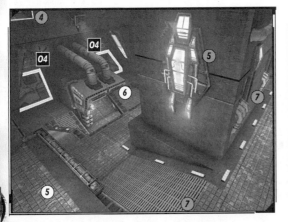

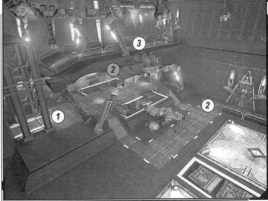

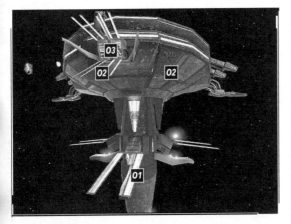

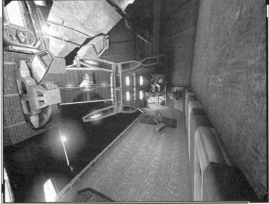

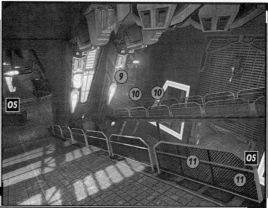

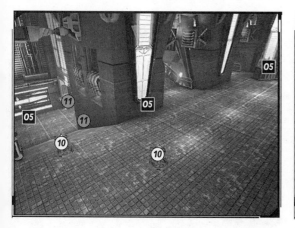

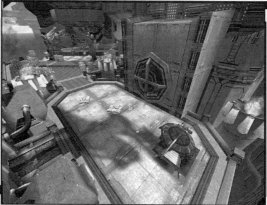

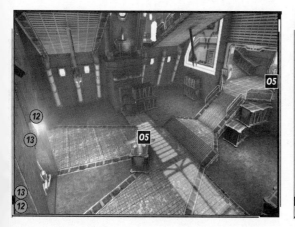

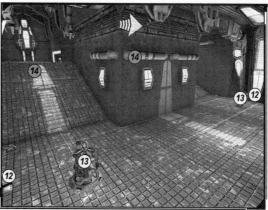

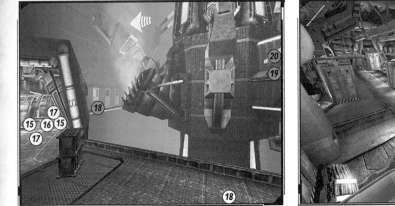

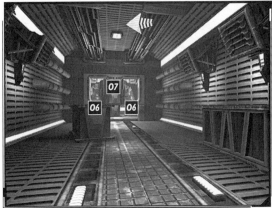

Overview

Starting off near a gigantic spiraled space station (the Mothership), Attackers must breach the structure's lower part, flying in space fighters, and destroy a thin generator while Defenders attack them with a mixture of implanted Mothership turrets and their own space fighters. After this, the entire inner tube of the Mothership opens up, allowing multiple places for the Attackers to fly into the upper interior and demolish two more generators while the Defenders do their best to thwart this action.

The Attackers fly into one of two adjacent hangar entrances, after which the action changes to an on-foot fracas. From the landing bay, the Attackers stride into a bypass room and blast two power bypasses, opening an entrance between them. Then it's a romp down into a ramped entrance way and a firefight to take out three mobile gun emplacements called sentinels. The Defenders are keen to prevent this action. Finally, the Attackers must run across and around a circular outer path, enter a junction room, and finally battle to an inner core, remove both the hatches, and destroy the core.

Attackers' Objectives	**Defenders' Objectives**
1. Destroy Lower Shield Generator	1. Defend Lower Shield Generator
2. Destroy Upper Shield Generators	2. Defend Upper Shield Generator
3. Proceed to Landing Bay	3. Stop the Enemy from Entering the Landing Bay
4. Destroy Energy Bypass	4. Defend Energy Bypass
5. Destroy Sentinels	5. Defend Sentinels
6. Use Panel to Unlock Core Hatch	6. Stop Any Usage of the Core Panels
7. Destroy the Conductor	7. Defend the Conductor

Attacking Objective 1: Destroy the Lower Shield Generator

Your team members pilot small, nimble, and lightly armored space fighters (detailed in the Vehicles chapter) with a couple of different weapons: the main repeating laser bolts and the lock-on missile launcher (secondary fire). It takes only six enemy turret shots to destroy your fighter, so your team must approach the storming of this Mothership with seriousness and planning, or you'll never make it inside!

Assign half the team to take the objective while the others target the enemy turrets on the superstructure's lower portions. The enemy sends space fighters at you, so fly a couple of Attackers to the Mothership's top to wait for these to launch from the landing bay (the area you enter on your third objective) and intercept them. That way the Defenders concentrate on your interference while the rest of the team tackles the objectives below!

With a couple of your ace dogfighters blasting the enemy as they appear, the rest of the team can ignore any flying foes until they close in. Have some team members clear a path for a couple of fighters to consistently blast the objective. In this case, the objective is a shield generator inside the bottom part of the space station, in the tubelike interior.

This generator takes around 60 laser bolts to destroy, so you need a few passes to strike it, or a long run-up and a clear flight path. Two or three of your team should go for the objective, heading below the flashing arrows pointing to the Mothership's bottom entrance. Meanwhile, have at least three or four of your comrades blast the Defender turrets.

There are eight Defender turrets, and five entrances to the base of the Mothership. The easiest way to blast the shield generator is to come straight up from the main entrance where the arrows are pointing; four duct entrances are above this area, each with a turret mounted to the exterior. Fly in a circular pattern around these turrets, staying outside of the Mothership, and destroy all four turrets if possible. Then enter one of the ducts, and take care of the four turrets mounted on the edge of the inner tube passage above the shield generator.

There are different ways to approach these turret takedowns. One way is to skim around the exterior in a circle, blasting the turrets on the outer edge, and then turning to the inside turrets. The second is for four teammates to each take a lower entrance and focus firing on it, blasting the outer and inner turrets in that order. Or, confuse any Defender inside a turret by having two (or more) teammates approach a turret from different directions so that the turret can't target both at the same time.

Once this is finished, or while the turrets are being bombarded and are otherwise occupied, have the team members responsible for the objective destruction attempt their fly-by. Again, you can vary the entrances you fly into, but the four duct entrances have turrets inside, and it's difficult to gain more than a few direct shots on the generator. You cannot get a good line-of-sight shot until you're inside the ducts and under turret fire.

Inside, complete the first objective by flying down past the base entrance, and stop at the flashing arrow sign. Position your ship at the lowest arrow, turn it toward the entrance, and slow to minimum speed before beginning a constant stream of blasting at the target. If you go down to the last pulsing arrow, then make your shooting run, you can take out the generator in one pass. Multiple ships attacking make this easier to pull off, so enter the base entrance earlier if the objective is already damaged.

TIP

You can easily distinguish between the enemy and friendly space fighters as the contrails are color-coded (blue or red).

Change your perspective and camera with F4 (default). You lose the "behind ship" camera view, allowing you to see in front and below you (where the ship blocked your vision in the regular view). However, you cannot as accurately judge narrow spaces to fly through if you can't see your ship, but many prefer the cockpit view.

Attacking Objective 2: Destroy Upper Shield Generators

If you're inside the Mothership during the destruction of the lower shield generators, you can use the continuation of the inner tube, and head to the ship's top end, where two more identical shield generators are ready to be totaled. If you're outside of the Mothership, five new entrances provide access. Many of these are shown by a series of blue arrows pointing at the entrance. Your team should decide which entrances to zoom into, who is targeting what, and how many of your team should go on turret-hunting missions while others focus on the two generators.

The first two entrances are on opposite sides of the circular bulbous area of the Mothership, flanked by spiked guidance markers (flashing green lights sealed onto metal prongs of the superstructure). These markers are above the entrance, while there is a protrusion under the entrance that contains a turret. Focus on the turret and let your fellow fliers inside the ship with less enemy bombardment.

Over on the opposite side of the Mothership is a second, identical entrance with a turret. Don't confuse these two entrances with the hangar entrances (currently sealed), which are 90 degrees to the left and right of each generator entrance. The hangar entrances don't have entrance arrows, are smaller in size, have two turrets and a link turret (causing you problems), and two narrow vertical entrances. Fly into here, and you'll destroy your craft in a dead end!

TIP

Eagle-eyed sharpshooters should be aware that the Defenders' ships can exit from these hangars, so fly around these, picking off foes before they can find you; approach from above and behind the exits.

If you're approaching the two upper generators from the lower destroyed one, you can fly up the Mothership's central tube. However, once you reach the upper generators, you must quickly change direction, or four turrets will strike you. Use the upper entrances for easier flying and less dying.

With the two main entrances covered, there are three more to find (not including the lower five entrances). All three are available at the superstructure's top. Fly to the Mothership's middle, directly above it, and then dive down into the large central tube. Make your trajectory extremely steep, slow down when you're above the tube hole, and then fly into it. This gives you more time to adjust your position, and hopefully avoid the damaging link gun turret fire.

There are two turrets behind each of the two massive "fins" on opposite sides of the entrance hole; if you reach higher altitudes you may be targeted by them, so keep between the fins and them. If you come in at a lower angle, you can view two regular turrets inside the tube, guarding one of the cylinders. Try to take both out before you head inside the ship.

The final two entrances are on top of the Mothership. From the arrows pointing to the entrance, fly up and over the ship, and you'll likely be bombarded with link gun fire from two turrets ahead of you. These are extremely damaging if the enemy is using them (instead of the computer), as these turrets can be linked and healed!

If you dive into the duct below and in front of the link turrets, you fly very close to two regular turrets inside the Mothership (these could be the same ones you saw if you flew toward the vertical tube entrance). You fly into the Mothership in front of one of the cylinders, between it and the turrets. There's little time to react to the turrets, and these two entrances (one opposite the other with identical turrets) are the most difficult to infiltrate. Either ignore them, or use them only after the turrets have been destroyed.

Now that you know all the entrances, it's time to come up with a game plan. First determine whether the two sets of two link gun turrets are worth bothering with. You can avoid them completely by using the lower, two main, or vertical tube entrances, so pit your space fighters against them only if you have teammates to spare.

You must efficiently take out the two sets of two regular turrets inside the Mothership, both in front of an upper generator. You have the most time to blast them if you attack from vertically above. Focus all your firepower on one turret at a time. If you use the main entrances with the arrows pointing into them, move to one side (to avoid the central columns), and then blast a single turret until one of you is destroyed. Keep this up until all four interior turrets fall. Then launch 60 space fighter energy bolts to detonate each of the two upper generators. The longest route you can take is via the main two entrances with the arrows. You can ignore the turrets, but the enclosed position makes it very difficult not to be struck by them as you pass.

TIP

Attack the same two turrets from two different directions to maximize confusion and minimize being struck yourself. If you can coordinate a firing run with a cohort, you can easily take out a turret or two if both ships aim at the same one, while two more of your team blast another turret.

Once inside the duct with the two generators in it, fire your shots and pass it. Instead of exiting through the opposite area, or heading up the exit chute to face the two link gun turrets, swing your craft around a pillar inside the passage and begin another run. This is possible if you whip your mouse around quickly!

If you're wandering the Mothership's top exterior, use the interior trenches etched into the superstructure, plus the curve of the ship, as cover. The mushroom sides of the upper area are also excellent for providing partial cover.

Attacking Objective 3: Proceed to the Landing Bay

Once both the upper shield generators fall, land in the bay. As soon as the first space fighter makes it into the bay, the spawn point changes and subsequent starting points occur inside the bay. Anyone still flying around after you secure this objective may wish to suicide and start the interior objectives instead of wasting time docking.

The two hangar entrances are opposite each other and guarded by two regular and one link turret. With this heavy concentration of enemy firepower, this is one of the few times where you don't want to split your team. All available ships should converge on one of the two entrances (ideally from all directions) and attack the link turret first (from all directions), then the other turrets while a couple of craft attempt to sneak in during the confusion and explosions. If you're consistently failing to enter either of the vertical entrance holes, turn all available firepower to these turrets and race into the bay.

Defending Objectives 1, 2, and 3: Defend Lower Shield Generator, Defend Upper Shield Generator, Stop the Enemy from Entering the Landing Bay

We've grouped these three specific defense objectives together as they all involve repelling an attack using space fighters and turret areas. Your entire team spawns at the landing bay every time. Four space fighters are ready to launch, and five turret terminals are labeled with the group of turrets you control when you use them.

As soon as the action starts, pick four senior team members to each dash to a space fighter (choose which fighter each is taking before the action starts, so two players don't run for the same ship), and then have the rest of the team concentrate on turret-to-ship combat. Learn the layout of the landing bay so your most experienced turret operator runs to the set of turrets to see combat first. No weapons lockers exist, only turret terminals or space fighters, until the enemy breaches the Mothership.

> **TIP**
>
> Because your turrets automatically turn and fire at incoming enemies with or without an operator, those teams with fewer than nine players should opt to pilot all the space fighters first (to add extra firepower to the space combat). Accessible space ships and terminals are signified by red arrows pointing down at them.

> **NOTE**
>
> Although it's not much of a plan and may earn the wrath of your team, those stuck inside the landing bay can practice double and dodge jumps inside the hangar. It's a great way to perfect your leaping, and all the pipes and the top of the hangar exit scaffolding (which is sealed, opposite the landing bay turret terminal) can be reached.

Objective 1 Plan

Those brave pilots in the space fighters have to run a protective ring around the lower exterior portions of the Mothership while turret gunners back you up. As the second objective is also inside the Mothership's main central tube, and the only way to enter the Mothership is via the four lower horizontal ducts or the vertical hole in the base, travel directly to this area. As soon as you jet out of your landing bay chute, accelerate and head down to the lower section of the superstructure. If you spot an enemy fighter, engage it, especially if it is attacking your turrets. Follow the laser fire to find a battle.

TIP

During patrols, avoid an embarrassing collision with a fellow pilot by having all fighter pilots to agree to fly left (or right) if they are on a head-on course. Do this before the match starts, otherwise you could smash into a wall, or explode if friendly fire is on. This is an especially cunning plan if you're executing circuits through the central tube.

Don't be duped into heading out into deep space for a dogfight, and don't head for the Attackers' exploding battle cruiser. It's more effective to provide an additional barrier and fire support to the turrets on the Mothership. If enemies are on an attack pattern, by all means fly to intercept them, softening them up for the turrets or taking care of them yourself. But execute real dogfighting plans (such as dropping down or above and arcing round behind them before letting rip with all ordnance) only if the enemy is heading for the Mothership. That way, your foe will be preoccupied with Mothership destruction, knowing full well that breaking off from this plan will waste considerable time. Although there are more enemies than friendly fighters, their mission will most likely overrule their desire to live, and make target allocation easier!

TIP

Did you spot an enemy fighter heading up to the top of the Mothership exterior? Let the players in the upper turrets deal with him; he's most likely lost and doesn't present a threat compared to the force heading for the generator.

If you're not patrolling the space around the base of the Mothership, try zipping your craft through one of the four lower duct entrances (each armed with two turrets) in a circular path. This way you can create an extra obstacle or distract the incoming fighters. If they're firing, crashing into, or dodging you, then they're spending less time firing at the objective. Keep these patrols up until the objective fails.

TIP

Man two relevant turret terminals during this objective defense. The first activates the lower outer turrets (accessed to the right, next to the sealed bay door). These are the four turrets on the ledge leading to the four ducts. Defend with the turret shield if the enemy attacks are too numerous, and flick between all four turrets to judge the best place to attack. Always manually aim at craft that have passed over or to the side of you. Also maintain excellent radio contact with the inner gunner and fighters so they can let you know which turret to man or whether one is coming under attack.

The second terminal runs the lower outer turrets (accessed to the left, next to the sealed bay door). Know the enemy's location. Flick between turrets and aim outward to begin with, following a craft as it attempts to zoom into a duct, and continue to follow it until you've demolished it.

Objective 2 Plan

When the first objective fails, there is still more than enough work for the lower turret gunners; their plans of attack (shoot everything flying that isn't on your team) are unchanged. The difference is that the Mothership is almost impossible to defend as all the entrances are now opened to the main inside tube. The battle becomes much more hectic, with the Attackers flying in all directions.

Make sure your team is ready inside the top inner turrets (the terminal is ahead and slightly left of the main sealed doors) and the top outer turrets (the terminal is ahead and slightly right of the main sealed doors). These turrets are the most important, especially as the gunner inside has four turrets to man at once. They are all visible at the same time, meaning you don't really need to worry about which one you man.

If you're manning the outside turrets, you have an insane number of turrets to worry about (eight). These include four link turrets, which you can link to blast the adjacent turret with a line of fire and let it aim at incoming fighters. Keep flicking back to a turret under fire, or when a large concentration of crafts appears.

Space fighters should zip in and out of the superstructure; have half the team remaining below, while the others patrol the upper areas. Don't forget to have at least one fighter inside the main tube to block incoming fire and fighters. Keep your patrols and your trigger-fingers twitchy until both generators fall.

TIP

Bring your space fighter patrols up to the top of the Mothership, and create cunning patrol patterns to follow. One such example is to fly out of the exit vent just after one of the two generators, swoop upside down over the main hole in the top of the Mothership, and dive into the opposite duct on the other side and repeat the route. Shoot anything that moves!

177

Unreal TOURNAMENT 2004

Objective 3 Plan

When the only thing stopping your Attackers from descending into the on-foot portions of this match is the landing bay entrance, immediately send all your fighters to this location. Remember that there is only one entrance to the landing bay (the other side is blocked and is where the Defenders' fighters scrambled from). As the enemy attempts to navigate into either of the two landing bay entrances, bring your full squadron of fighters into this area and fly them straight at the incoming forces. When you launch from your opposite bay exit, quickly accelerate around the side of the Mothership or over the top, and engage any enemy craft on their way to the other bay entrances.

If you're manning the turrets anywhere other than the landing bay, just attempt to blast any enemies you see. If you're blasting from the landing bay turrets, remember there are three (two regular and one link), and all are important and devastating. Aim at the enemy craft closest to completing the objective; you are the last line of defense before the final outdoor objective is complete!

Attacking Objective 4: Destroy Energy Bypass

Once your team is assembled inside the landing bay, you have a moment to get your bearings (there are two bays separated by a central raised area with an elevator) and attack the energy bypass. You reach the bypass via either of the two doors at the far end of the bay, next to the weapons lockers. Load up on weapons before you emerge through one of the doors. Consider using the third entrance inside the base, which is accessed via the elevator (look for the 50 shield pack at the foot of the elevator) and a gangplank leading to an upper door on the same wall as the lower two entrances. A third weapons locker up on this entrance gangplank contains the same weapons. Find extra minigun ammunition near a support post on the raised area of the bay opposite the elevator.

Attackers' Weapon Lockers 1, 2, and 3*

Biorifle

Link Gun

Shock Rifle

Minigun

*At each hangar bay exit

The enemy spawning point is above the objectives, making combat quick and inevitable. However, compared to other objectives, the Attackers have the advantage, given the sheer number of entrances the Defenders have to guard, the open area near the two bypasses that must be shot, and the speed at which fallen teammates can re-enter the action. Your team tactics can follow one of two main plans—to spread out and swarm the objective from all three entrances, or to approach from one entrance and continue to battle your way through. React to the enemy before contemplating either tactic.

When you have decided which entrance to rush, step through the self-opening door. If you're on the bottom passages, there may be a health pack as you enter. A short corner leads to a force field blocking a passage to the main core ramps (ignore this until the objective is met), and the two bypasses up on the far wall, on either side of a couple of main conduit pipes.

Expect resistance from everywhere—a ramp ahead turns and leads to an upper balcony (also reached by the upper door) where the enemy can stand, or they can blast you from in front, or high above the bypasses from a square opening (the entrance to their spawn point, which cannot be accessed). If you have a Defender lobbing ordnance down from this point, use a shock combo to knock him from his perch or make him lose aim, while a second teammate attempts to bombard a bypass with link gun fire. It takes around 50 link gun shots to destroy each bypass.

If you have a coherent team, chain your link guns together, creating three- to four-man teams that can cut a swath through to the objective with powerful waves of link gun energy. If your team enters via the top door, you can swarm a little more effectively (running left or right), jumping along the outer ramp area and grabbing up to three flak ammo packs (three either side) before launching for a central upper overhang with a health pack. You don't have a flak cannon, but steal the ammo anyway so the Defenders run out. If a Defender discards the weapon, grab it; it takes around nine shots from the flak cannon to destroy the bypass, and it's the weapon of choice for close-range assaulting.

Gaining the height advantage means that many of your team may choose the upper entrance as their best bet for objective-taking. If you're on the upper balcony, test some dodge jumping and other leaping antics to create a distraction for your other team or to reach areas you normally can't. You can leap from the three flak packs across to the two central pipes above the force field, or jump across after collecting the health pack, and then move behind the pipes to blast the objectives while under partial cover and in the shadows. This is a great tactic for a quick objective takedown.

You can also shield jump on top of the pipes, then stand and blast the objectives or enemies as they drop out of their spawn point windows above you. The flak cannon can still tear you apart, so don't overuse this tactic. Finally, it is easier to blast the spawn point windows from the corners of the upper path near the entrance door (darting back behind cover if applicable), or shooting the bypasses from this position instead of rushing in and incurring damage.

TIP

Members of either team can clamber on the lower three pipe areas to the outer side of the ground ramp and force field, crawl to the shadows at the back, and blast incoming enemies.

Defending Objective 4: Defend Energy Bypass

Once the Attackers are entering from the opposite landing bay, your team appears in a large spawn alcove with a weapons locker in front of you. There are only two weapons to pick, so grab them both, run to the alcove openings, and attempt to defend the two energy bypasses underneath. Split your team into two, depending on the actions of the Attackers. Half your team should guard the top floor and single entrance, while the rest leap downstairs and blast the incoming foes trotting in from either of the two lower doorways.

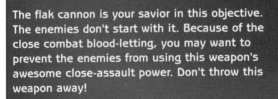

Defenders' Weapon Locker 1*

Flak Cannon

Rocket Launcher

Defenders' spawn alcove, near bypasses

There are some upper areas to leap to, but those guarding the ground floor should stay on either of the ramps, halfway up as the ramp turns, directly under a bypass. Sidestep back and forth, watching both entrances, and pump rockets into any enemies you see—and hope your teammates on the other ramp do the same. If there are enough teammates, position two secondary guards on the upper ramp (one each side) who can aim directly across the lower junction to the opposite Attacker entrance, and bombard this area with flak bombs and rockets.

With this concentrated firepower, the enemies are likely to be pushed into taking alternate routes. Keep the flak cannon ammo coming by grabbing some from the three packs on each side of the upper area.

TIP

The flak cannon is your savior in this objective. The enemies don't start with it. Because of the close combat blood-letting, you may want to prevent the enemies from using this weapon's awesome close-assault power. Don't throw this weapon away!

Don't be greedy! You've got comrades holding both the lower entrances and those up above, and only six flak cannon ammo packs to go around. Grab a maximum of two at a time so your entire team has enough ordnance to go around!

Take time out before the match to work out where the lower level Attackers need to stand to strike the bypass. You'll find out it's a couple of feet to the side of the lower corner where you're firing, in front of the first green strip light. Aim your bombs to land here for extra annoyance!

A good lower-level tip (and one that can be applied to the area above) is to have one or two close-assault kamikaze teammates prowling the area near the Attackers' doorways, wounding as many as possible with flak. Die, respawn, and repeat this classic "interference" strategy.

While the lower teammates create an explosive entrance choke point at each entrance, the rest of your team can defend the upper level, and drop ordnance on the lower levels. The premier spot to throw down flak is from the green-lit alcove on either side of your spawn point. The enemy can't reach you here, and you have a commanding view of one of the upper corridors (where you can lay down suppressing fire). Peer out to the lower level, to the health pack on the ledge above it, add support fire to the lower-level teammates, or shoot any Attacker who manages to evade the rest of your team. You're visible to incoming Attackers, so prepare for incoming fire. You don't have to stand next to the edge of the alcove; you can annoy enemies coming in from the top exit by standing on any of the protruding wall struts (the angled edges in front of the pulsing green horizontal lights) and firing off rockets or flak bombs at the top corner from where enemies appear. There are multiple struts to stand on, although your aim won't be too impressive from this distance.

Man the upper corridor. Although the doors to the landing bay open only for Attackers, you can reach the upper one before your enemy does (this isn't such a good idea for the bottom doors; stay in partial cover at the ramp). Dash and aim flak cannons at the door and blast anything. A couple of teammates, on each side of the door to avoid being struck at the same time, can completely demolish a force of Attackers before they can react if you reach the corner fast enough (and you can use the corner for cover, too). This waylaying tactic can cause the Attackers to

rethink the entrance they're moving in from, which is great for the rest of your team on basement detail!

TIP

You don't have to stand on the edge of the alcove to fire; you can double jump to the narrow ledge on the outer wall, between the alcove and the flak ammo below and ahead of you, and hang out here. That way you can drop down and engage in combat on the upper or lower levels and be in an unexpected position.

Other tactics include walking around the ledge on the central structure so you're standing opposite the health pack on the ledge, facing it, and ambushing enemies coming around the corner. Double-jump to the pipes in the middle, adjacent to either bypass, and shoot out from the shadows either under or on top of the pipes, especially as the Attackers love to use this to quickly demolish the bypass. Finally, keep an eye open on both bypasses, locating the source of any gunfire that's damaging a bypass, and react accordingly. When one bypass is demolished, continue with the same basic strategy as before, but the enemy will concentrate on this bypass, so reinforce it.

TIP

If you're feeling a little malicious, and you know the Attackers are going to head through the upper entrance, move to it and shield jump onto the three pipes on either side of the door, then double jump up onto the jutting partial arch above the doorway entrance, and wait here. Fire on the enemies when they arrive! It's a full-on delivery of flak!

181

Attacking Objective 5: Destroy Sentinels

Attacking the three sentinels is a serious and brutal undertaking. Rush through the doorway under the blown bypasses (near the force field), pausing to grab a health pack, and then choose one of three routes (an elevator in front of you, and two side entrances to the downward ramps). Check the left and right exits first; both lead to a long ramp sloping down to the Defenders spawn point.

At the far end of the left ramp is the first sentinel, which automatically starts to fire when it spots enemy movement. This cuts down your forces in seconds, along with the Defenders who attempt to blast you before you can charge. Once you defeat the first sentinel, you must run to the lower area, turn right, turn right again, blast the second sentinel, and then battle to the ground below where a final sentinel guards two force fields leading to the final two objectives. However, some cunning strategies can throw off your foes.

Use flak or link gun ammunition to take care of the sentinels in the fastest time possible. It's possible to sidestep out onto the left ramp, walk down it a couple of steps, aim your secondary flak cannon fire up at the square green pulsing ceiling panel, and shoot out a flak bomb that arcs toward the panel, misses it and lands on the sentinel below. You can get two of these attacks out (cutting the sentinel's health down by half) before you're struck by its fire.

Not handy with trajectory weapons? Then chain your link guns and battle down each ramp in two teams. Focus on the sentinel. Fire a stream of link gun fire at it from the top of the left ramp, or across from the top of the right ramp. Alternately, use the minigun (or especially the shock rifle) from a few steps down from the top of the left ramp. Shoot out a combo while standing near the fence. The fence absorbs the sentinel energy bolts (meaning you're unharmed) while you blast the sentinel with three or four combos, which destroy it! You don't have to run down to the sentinel and come under heavy fire.

Prevent the enemies from attacking those chosen to destroy the sentinels by guarding them. Have three of your team on sentinel destruction duty, while the rest guard them, annoy the enemy, and run interference. Blast a sentinel from at least two different directions.

It's easier to destroy the third sentinel before the second one! Bring out your biorifle (or use the shock rifle, flak cannon, or link gun), and head for the top of the left ramp. Leap up onto the right side fence at the top of the ramp. Maneuver so you can see the sentinel down below you. It begins to fire at you, so back up along the fence until you reach the crack between the underside of the ramp and the structure to your right. The sentinel continues to fire, but the shots dissipate off the scenery. Shoot carefully aimed ordnance through the gap, onto the

sentinel, or look down from the fence below (you come under more fire here). Spread a load of bio ooze on the sentinel and take it out in seconds! Back up your colleagues if you're on the right ramp by aiming at the lower sentinel too. With two or three different shots, and the entire ramp and balcony to aim from, the last sentinel falls in no time. This leaves sentinel #2.

Although the elevator at the start of this new section leads to the third sentinel (jump on the lift to activate it), you're subject to sentinel fire. If you must use the elevator, when you reach the bottom, double jump to the right, over the boxes, and then take cover behind them and the crates underneath the ramp to the right. From here you can bear the brunt of the damage while cohorts above batter the sentinel, leaving only the second one left. Travel down here, then maneuver up the ramp and attack the sentinel and the enemies from behind as they attempt to secure the ramps. With this final sentinel, use arcing flak cannon shots or carefully fired shock combos (with a wide splash damage).

If you're running down from the ramps, pass between the two Defenders' weapons lockers, staying away from the lip of the lower short ramp leading to the sentinel, so it fires at the lip but can't hit you. Then fire a secondary flak cannon bomb, aiming your reticule between the first and second wall lamps behind the sentinel. The bomb lands on the sentinel without it even scratching you! From the elevator and lowest short ramp, walk up and get a clear line of sight on the sentinel and bombard it with any ordnance you like. It doesn't have the height to hit you (it blasts the lip of the lower ramp instead).

If you're gung-ho, run to the bottom of the right ramp, make an instant 180 right, then double-jump over the tiny gap and land on the top of the lowest ramp and kamikaze your way to destruction—hopefully taking the sentinel with you! This is also a great route if you want to lap around the Defenders' spawn point and tackle them from behind. Once the sentinels fall, your spawn point moves to this lower area with the removed force field doorways, while the Defenders appear at the core. This occurs for the rest of the match.

Defending Objective 5: Defend Sentinels

Defenders' Weapons Locker 2*
Assault Rifle (second)
Biorifle
Link Gun
Minigun
*On ramp between sentinel #1 and #2, spawn point

The bad news is that the Attackers have the height advantage, while you have three sentinels to defend, all in different areas, and two of them can be simultaneously attacked. They can't be link healed. The good news is that the enemy still spawns at the landing bay. Split into three different teams, each with a different area to defend, and meet your foes with killer gunfire before you're overrun. Start from your spawning point, near the ramp down to sentinel #2 and across from sentinel #1.

Run up to the top end of either ramp, and shoot incoming enemies as they move from the opened bypass area, up a short ramp, and choose one of the three entrances. Don't move through the doorways at the top end of the ramps, as this activates a sentry gun preventing you from spawn camping. However, a couple of chained link gun waves and a biorifle floor ooze can really annoy those rushing in from the hangar. Position the first two groups of your team with one covering the far ramp and the other covering the closer one.

If the enemy pushes in, they're likely to strike out at the sentinels, causing them to return fire; don't get in the way! Use the tactics presented above to learn just how and where the Attackers will be and react accordingly. Stave them off at the doorways, and if you're overrun, make sure the Attackers aren't throwing ordnance off the ramps' edges to destroy sentinel #3; shoot them before they can accurately fire. Brace for enemies streaming down the ramp by holding the far end and pushing upward, usually with chained link guns.

183

The third group of your team should be stationed next to sentinel #2. Their job is to listen for notification that the ramps have been breached, so they can run back to the spawn point to dish out some damage, and defend sentinel #2 while reinforcements respawn. Note that sentinels #2 and #3 can be shot at from the ramp, or gaps in the ramp (see the Attackers' strategy), so prepare defenses accordingly.

This group also halts Attackers from using the elevator, effectively pushing them down either of the two ramps and into your main forces. The elevator platform makes noise, alerting you to power up your minigun to strafe anyone making the trip—usually no more than two enemies descend at a time. Attempt to blast enemies dropping fire from above or dropping down themselves, as they may try to land near sentinel #3 and take it out; the last third of the team needs to make sure this doesn't happen. As the sentinels fall, move nearer to the remaining sentinels and defend them vigorously until the objective falls.

Attacking Objective 6: Use Panel to Unlock Core Hatch

Attackers' Weapon Lockers 4 and 5*

Link Gun

Minigun

Rocket Launcher

Behind doorway, lower level

Attackers' Weapon Lockers 6 and 7*

Biorifle

Shock Rifle

Link Gun

Minigun

Lightning Gun

Entrance to core corridor

> **NOTE**
>
> Actually reaching the core room requires a gauntlet-run relevant to both objectives #6 and #7, presented below.

Your spawn point has finally changed. Run across to the next weapons locker behind one of the doorways that was locked with a force field earlier and find a rocket launcher. Find rocket launcher and minigun ammo to the side of each locker, and two more ammo packs for each near where the second sentinel stood. Run along one of the two straight humped corridors to the exit, and another set of weapons lockers (#6 and #7).

Once someone from your team has entered the main core area, the passage you just ran through seals, and your final spawn point is at weapon lockers #6 and #7, on the central core ring corridor. There is a health pack and a 50 shield pack in this area, and two Attacker sentinels to guard the spawn point (only after the core has been entered). This means you cannot obtain the rocket launcher for the last part of your match, but you can grab the bio, shock, and lightning weapons at any time.

Agree on the best use of your team. Two essentially identical routes lead to the core, one to the left of the last spawn point and one to the right. A giant link gun turret guards each path. Consider heading down only one route, giving the turret less time to attack all your forces, and maneuvering past Defenders with all your team and overpowering them quickly (especially as they don't know which direction you'll choose).

> **TIP**
>
> Humans naturally take the right hand path at a junction if they have to make a split decision, so choose the right path if your team is unruly (as you're likely to see more of your team), or the left path if you're trying to out-fox your enemy!

There's still the link turret to worry about. If it's firing bolts, it's probably computer controlled, and you can dodge jump (or even strafe) around the circular path without being hit (don't stop!). If the link gun is firing a constant beam, it's player controlled. Either head in the other direction, or take down the turret. The enemy can heal the turret! Either chain your link guns and fire, or shoot out shock combos as you sidestep (have one or two shoot while the rest protect the turret-shooters).

Keep plugging away until the turret falls, or if this is proving impossible, ignore it and don't stop moving, using the crates as cover, shooting out lightning shots at incoming enemies on the ground. Eventually, you'll reach the connecting junction to the core room and Defenders' spawn point. Use shock combos because there's shock ammo by the middle crate.

> **TIP**
>
> Are Defenders swarming out of the connecting junction and around the curved outer corridor, hoping to push you back? Post a sniper with a lightning gun at the last set of weapons lockers, or move to the outer edge of the connecting room entrance. Then crouch in the shadows and plug anyone emerging from the connecting room doorway.
>
>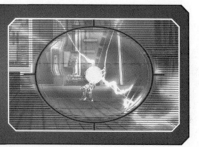

The two connecting junctions are symmetrical. If you head left, you turn right to head up into the core corridor, and vice versa. Inside this junction is a small alcove (where you can provide covering fire), a health pack, and three ammo pieces on the ground corridor under the ramp. Don't go down this corridor. Instead, shield jump or run up onto the upper area, and flee straight into the core corridor, continuously dodge jumping and using the two crates inside the core corridor as cover.

The ramp heading up, opposite the entrance to the core corridor, leads to the Defenders' spawn point and an invincible sentry gun, so ignore this area except to blast Defenders. Minimize the time spent in this connecting junction choke point. When you reach the core room, head to either of the objective switches and press Use. You cannot stand on either side of the switch to use it; you must be facing inward, looking at

> **TIP**
>
> You trigger the final spawn point and "enter the core" when you head up the ramp from the connecting junction, into the start of the core corridor.
>
>

the core. Plan to send a couple of guys in to shield themselves and execute the objective while the rest of the team blasts Defenders. The other side of the core room has an exit leading to the other connecting junction. Once both switches have been pressed, you can attempt the final objective.

185

NOTE

The Defenders' only exits are the two connecting junctions, so bombard these exits with rapid gunfire while others scoot under and up into the core corridor.

TIP

Ready for a charge? Group your team by having them sneak to a connecting corridor, and then out of the opposite side to the curved outer corridor. The Defenders don't usually come out this way, so you can wait for a couple of reinforcements, and then all charge up to the core corridor!

Attacking Objective 7: Destroy the Conductor

Appearing in the same spawn point, you must continue to battle to the core room, but now with a final purpose: to destroy both core conductors to devastate the Mothership! It takes 25 flak bombs or 95 link energy bolts to explode each conductor. Save your flak for the conductors, or come in with a chained link gun plan. If you can survive long enough to have one teammate on crowd control (blasting Defenders as they enter from either core corridor), and one teammate on conductor control (strafing around using dodge jumping while aiming directly at the conductor), you'll eventually win the match.

TIP

Use the crates around the room to your advantage; hide behind one and peek out to fire at the conductor, then watch to the left for enemies coming from a core corridor, while the crates protect you from fire from the right (although enemies can sneak around behind you).

Vary your acrobatics by launching from the top of the two stacked crates on either side of the core, onto the core ledge above the core switch, and pummel the core from close quarters. Double jump onto the core lip at the base of it, then again to the ledge, although you are a very prone target!

If you're working well as a team, have one player watch each core corridor for advancing troops and hold them off as long as possible. You'll run out of ammunition, but the Defenders have the same problem.

Defending Objectives 6 and 7:
Stop Any Usage of the Core Panels and Defend the Conductor

The last two objectives have been paired, because your team starts in the same place for the remainder of the match. You randomly appear in one of two corridors with a terminal at one end to operate a link turret, with a weapons locker at the other. These are followed by a set of ramps leading to two lower doorways and a corridor entrance beneath the weapons locker that leads to the final core.

The bad news is that you have a massive area to defend. The good news is that you have a powerful link turret on each side of the gigantic circular pathway. First waylay your opponents for as long as possible; keep them out of the corridors leading to the main core.

Defenders' Weapons Lockers 3 and 4*

Link Gun

Minigun

Rocket Launcher

Lightning Gun

*End of spawn point corridor, top of each junction

Do this through strategic placement of your team. Discover which end of the core you randomly spawned at by checking where your link turret is located. If you're facing away from the turret terminal, and the exit to the balcony and the turret is on the right side, then the enemies will enter the junction via the right doorway; head down to this area immediately. Obviously, the reverse is true on the other side. Aim to have half your team on each side of the core (which is difficult based on the respawning, and don't waste time running through the core room to reach the other side); when the enemy pokes out from the entrance at the far end of the circular platform, begin your attack.

> **TIP**
>
>
>
> The enemy won't be sure where the largest concentration of Defenders are, so they may run in from both sides. More cunning Attackers may simply choose a side and attempt to overwhelm you. Radio your team if this is happening, and do it fast!
>
> Don't move from the junction room toward the spawning point or you'll be overrun by Attackers. However, if you're overconfident, send in a maniac with a minigun to strafe and tear up the enemies, softening them for the rest of the team, and acting as a scout to let you know which way most Attackers are moving.

Ready your team at the junction entrance with lightning guns, and blast at the incoming foes (usually train your weapons on the weapon lockers you can see). Advance to the crates if you wish, but make sure the Attackers are cut down before they can reach the junction. If the enemies are hiding at the entrance to this area, don't attempt to flush them out; they have to come to you.

When the damaged enemy reaches the junction, make sure there's a welcoming committee. With two or three good players constantly grabbing extra rocket and lightning gun ammo from the ground below the center ramp, you can hold off a squad of enemies!

Meanwhile, have at least one turret gunner using the link gun cannon turret as soon as possible. Strafe the area below and don't worry about incoming fire; it takes a lot to damage your turret. Strafe and cut down as many advancing foes as you can. It's better to wound a larger number of enemies rather than concentrating on a few; teammates at the junction can finish them off! Also be sure you grab some link gun ammunition from behind the cannon on the ledge where it rests. Teammates should take this, and either link heal from this point, or chain link the turret's attacks by flowing their link gun into the turret operator at the spawn point. Mass enemy destruction is almost certainly guaranteed!

TIP

If you're having fun cutting down the enemy with the turret, double the trouble by shield jumping and standing on top of the turret, then bring out the lightning gun and start taking potshots at the foes below!

If the Attackers break through one of the two junction rooms, then your team isn't doing its job properly. You need at least one of your team inside the main core room, patrolling the corridor and ordering the team to fall back if the enemies are consistently overrunning this area and dashing into the core room. However, the plan to defend both the junctions should work for the rest of the match.

If you're concerned that your team can't work well in this large area of defense, or the enemy has quickly completed objective #6 and released the hatch locks, retreat into the core room for a last stand. Here you have the advantage (aside from a lack of available weapons) because the enemy must charge down the long core corridors, so post Defenders at the end leading to the core to waylay them. Place the remainder of your team in various areas to blast them when they enter. Hole up in here until the last objective falls.

TIP

The nearest extra ammo is in the junction room, so venture here only if the coast is clear. Elongate your survival time by grabbing the link gun ammo packs next to the link turret when you spawn, and the rocket and lightning ammo from the base of the junction room before you sprint for the core area. Use your respawn as an advantage: drop quickly down, follow enemies into the core corridor, and mow them down from behind—particularly useful if they're hiding behind the corridor crates.

Otherwise, set up a good defensive position from inside the core. Leap up the protruding pipe ducts on the core, then double jump to the double crates overlooking the core corridor and stand on them. You can also stand around or behind the crates in the core (as described in the Attackers' section).

Once the hatches have been activated, and the final objective is being attempted, stand on the hatch after it has been activated, and next to the core. From the core, you have a partial view of both corridors and excellent lightning gun sniping positions. When the enemy reaches the core, you can use your body to absorb incoming fire—hey, whatever helps the core stay intact, right?

189

AS-ROBOTFACTORY

Recommended Players: 12–20

Legend

1 Weapons Locker x3 (Attackers' spawn point)
2 Lightning gun ammo packs x2 (behind crates)
3 50 Shield Pack (behind crates)
4 Flak Cannon +2 ammo packs (between crates)
5 Health Vials x4 (near crates)
6 Minigun ammo packs x2 (near crates)
7 Rocket Launcher +2 ammo packs (middle of dip)
8 Double Damage (near support)
9 Flak ammo packs x2 (near crates)
10 Minigun +2 ammo packs (between crates)
11 Lightning, rocket ammo packs (behind crates)
12 50 Health Pack x2 (communications area)
13 Weapons Locker (communications area)
14 Health Vials x4 (side road entrance)
15 Defenders' Weapon Lockers x3 (inside spawn point, upper level)
16 50 Shield Pack (on ledge near Defenders' spawn point)
17 Minigun ammo packs x2 (near crates)

18 Flak Cannon +2 ammo packs (next to support)
19 Rocket Launcher +2 ammo packs (next to support)
20 Lightning Gun +2 ammo (middle of dip)
21 Flak cannon +2 ammo (next to support)
22 Minigun ammo x2 (next to support)
23 50 Health Pack x2 (on moveable crate)
24 Health Vial x4 (edge of walkway either side of cannon base)
25 Weapons Locker x2 (Defenders' spawn point)
26 50 Shield Pack (corner of road)
27 Rocket Launcher (on mesh, right entrance to crate chamber)
28 Weapons Locker (entrance to crate chamber)
29 50 Health Pack (left entrance to crate chamber)
30 50 Shield Pack (top of crate)
31 Flak Cannon +1 ammo pack (crate chamber)

32 50 Health Pack x2 (crate chamber)
33 Weapons Locker
34 Double Damage (in tunnel)
35 Lightning Gun +2 ammo packs (top of tunnel entrance)
36 Weapons Locker
37 50 Shield Pack (upper ledge)
38 50 Shield Pack (ground floor)
39 Rocket Launcher +2 ammo packs (upper balcony)
40 Health Vial x4 (data cable room)
41 Weapons Locker (data cable room)
42 Weapons Locker (generator room)
43 Weapons Locker (generator room)
44 50 Health Pack (Defenders' spawn point)
45 Weapons Lockers (Defenders' spawn point)
46 Health Vials x4 (under Defenders' spawn balcony)
47 50 Shield Pack (end of corridor)
48 Weapons Lockers (Defenders' spawn point)

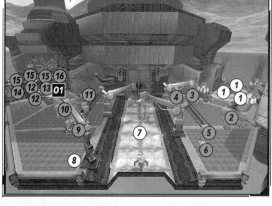

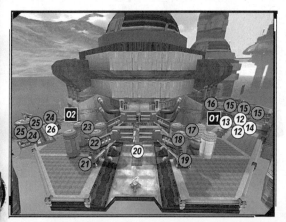

Overview

This full-scale skirmish has the Attackers attempting to destroy a robot factory; and they press two Goliath tanks into service at the beginning of hostilities. Using the power of the tanks to punch through the enemy link cannon turrets, the Attackers must reach a communications building across a giant courtyard, and press a switch to align the satellites. After this, they must make a second charge toward a giant ion cannon and a base door to breach the gate and enter the base.

Then the action switches from outdoor space to tight interior corridor fighting. Attackers must blast data cables inside a room after negotiating a series of corridors, and then take apart three shield generators inside a heavily fortified room. Finally, they must reach and destroy the artificial intelligence generator, deep in the factory.

Attackers' Objectives	Defenders' Objectives
1. Activate the Satellite Dish Switch	1. Defend the Satellite Dish Switch
2. Destroy the Gate	2. Defend the Gate
3. Cut the Data Cables	3. Protect the Data Cables
4. Destroy Shield Component	4. Protect the Shield Nexus
5. Destroy the AI Generator	5. Protect the AI Generator

Attacking Objective 1: Activate the Satellite Dish

The epic battle to the interior of the robot factory requires two Goliath-class tanks. From your starting courtyard, go to the weapons locker nearest you and load up. Then (with pre-fight strategy in mind) assault on foot, riding on (or in) the gun turret or driving the tank. Your biggest hurdle is the three link gun turrets that can easily pick off your tanks. You must demolish these before you can achieve your goal.

Attackers' Weapon Lockers 1, 2, and 3*

Biorifle

Shock Rifle

Link Gun

Minigun

*Attacker's spawn point, near tanks

Concentrate your firepower on each link gun turret, even if you lose a tank or two (the tanks respawn). Drive your tank over the initial bridge, turning the turret right, and aim at the farthest of the three turrets—it takes only three well-placed shots to detonate each link gun turret. Then trundle a bit forward, blast the far left turret before link gun bolts blows apart your tank, and then deal with the nearest turret. This method prevents your tank from absorbing the most damage and is a lot easier if the turrets are bot-controlled (although the tactics remain the same).

With both tanks moving, the enemy turrets can't target both, leaving you free to blow at least one of the turrets apart before a tank is destroyed. Have your tank turret gunner attack the same turrets as the main gun.

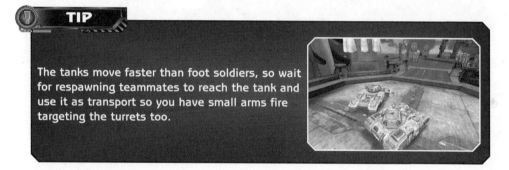

TIP

The tanks move faster than foot soldiers, so wait for respawning teammates to reach the tank and use it as transport so you have small arms fire targeting the turrets too.

While the tanks tear apart the three link gun turrets, foot troops can try a couple of crate-hiding escapades. Split the rest of your team in two. The first half offers supporting fire. Use the cover of the tanks to dash across the main area to the stack of boxes on the courtyard's left side, grabbing the lightning gun (and three ammo clusters) as you go. Fire at the turrets. If the enemy swarms in from the satellite viewing area (the objective), position snipers to creep forward after the turret threat is gone. Move your sub-team to the crates nearer the left turret; there's a minigun, three packs of bullets, and four health vials.

Meanwhile, the second infantry squad moves close to the objective, running interference and attacking turrets from close quarters (the two turrets ahead and to the right). Run across the bridge, then turn right. Race around the stack of crates to the 50 shield pack, then to the second set of crates with the flak cannon and three ammo packs. From here, take out the initial right turret, dropping to the crate stack and ricocheting flak ordnance into the turret while dodge jumping around it. After this, either run to the two crates or dodge jump to the larger cluster of crates. Enemies may be patrolling, so expect combat.

193

> ### TIP
>
> From the starting bridge, you can double jump onto the bridge's side (watch out for the bottomless drop to your right), and then onto the various bridge parts, gaining height and a shortcut when dashing for the shield pack.
>
>
>
> Have infantry back up the tanks. Get behind each turret, as they have no shielding on their rear. Two seconds' worth of minigun fire destroys a turret from behind!
>
> Attack the far left turret from the crates next to the front right turret. Stand with the lightning gun between the front two crates, facing the left turret. A tiny gap offers a shot at the turret with a zoomed-in lightning gun. Take it out with seven shots, and you're in cover!

After you destroy the left turret, have your sniping team dash across the courtyard, secure the double damage, or fight if the enemy is pushing you back in this area. The next tactical spot is the central cluster of crates near the final turret. Find a minigun and three ammo packs at the far end. Over on the right side are two more crates with a lightning gun (plus three ammo packs).

Push your team to this area, backed up by the two tanks, and demolish any enemy troops. Finish off the turret from here if necessary, then move to the objective: the communications building. Resistance is fierce.

Stay near the third turret support and wait for your forces to arrive (watch for gunfire from the balconies inside the comm building and the ground). A large link gun turret past the communications building can cut down advancing infantry! We recommend a three-pronged approach. Take fully healed tanks up the left and right ramps (grabbing the four health vials on the left ramp), go out the other side, and blast apart the fourth turret. Then back the left tank out of the reach of the subsequent turret.

Meanwhile, send a few infantry from under the third turret support and around the crates, blasting inside the communications area (choose the left crate entrances and grab two health packs along the left wall). Back them up with the right tank. If resistance is too strong, jog alongside either tank, swing around, and blast the communications area from behind. Wait for your team, especially if you're attempting to flush the enemy out with chained link gun fire. Wait at the objective switch (on the comm building's interior right wall) with your shield gun raised for two seconds to complete the objective.

TIP

Is the enemy refusing to die? Jog to the double damage enroute to the first objective and tear the enemy apart with flak cannon fire.

During the confusion, dash into the communications building and use the turret control area (on the wall opposite the objective) to command one of the four remaining turrets. Point the turret toward the enemies or take fire from an enemy turret in the next area.

If the situation is hopeless, dodge jump past the objective to the ion cannon, coaxing as many Defenders as possible into following you while your team storms the building. You can even return with rockets from a pick-up point!

You can attack the fourth turret from inside a tank without meeting it head-on. Maneuver back and forth in front of the third turret's support struts, aim through the gap in the crates to the left, and fire with quick precision.

Defending Objective 1: Defend the Satellite Dish Switch

The Attackers have two Goliath tanks to punch a hole through your defenses, but you have the link gun turrets. Quickly drop into the middle section of the communications building after claiming the minigun from one of the lockers above. Find a 50 shield pack on the balcony, with a drop onto four health vials at the other end. However, you're better off dropping down into the well-barricaded central area of the building containing the objective switch. The third weapons locker offers a biorifle and a grenade launcher—both of which are invaluable as the enemy closes in.

Defenders' Weapon Lockers 1 and 2*

Shock Rifle

Link Gun

Minigun

Defender's spawn point, inside communications building

Your main defenses are the giant link gun turrets. Move into the computer terminal that controls the turrets. The first terminal enables a team member to switch between four different link gun turrets: the two in the loading bay dip, the one in front of the communications building, and the one behind it. Use the front turrets first, strafing infantry only when you can't see the tanks. If you can't view your target from one turret, flick to another. Similarly, if a foe is blasting a turret, manually operate it to increase its productivity. Turrets work independently if uncontrolled.

Defenders' Weapon Locker 3*

Biorifle

Shock Rifle

Link Gun

Grenade Launcher

Under defender's spawn point, inside communications building

TIP

Manually link a stream attack from one turret to another, considerably increasing its power. Use this to destroy the enemy quickly when you can trust the computer turret to accurately fire at the enemy.

Heal the turrets by standing near the computer terminal from which the team member is working, and fire at him. This heals the turret.

When the enemy advances, back up the link gun turrets for as long as possible. Split your team into three roughly equal sides. The first is a turret gunner and chain link gun healers. The second group stays atop the balcony overlooking the incoming enemies, preventing them from taking the left bridge sides and running straight to objective #2. Also prevent them from running around or through the containers in front of the switch.

The third group comprises those who excel at using the more menacing weapons. Have them run to the third link gun turret in front of the containers, grab the lightning gun and ammo packs, and then spread across the near side of the dip in the courtyard. Do this quickly before the enemies reach this area. Back up the two front link gun turrets with supporting fire. Creep or dodge jump across the containers, picking up the lightning gun again and the minigun and the flak cannon. Most importantly, dash to the double damage and grab this before the enemy ventures across.

From here you have obstacles to hide behind, and from the double damage, an almost unobstructed view of the enemy spawn point; let those lightning guns rip! Continue the barrage until the enemy breaks through to the ramp nearest you and heads toward the third turret. When this happens, back up for a final stand inside the communications building.

When the enemies reach the building, make sure your fourth turret is blasting any tanks that move to the left and right roadways to take out the turret. Two- or three-man crews of infantry with chained link guns are a great way to take out a tank; destroy one tank at a time, channeling both turret and infantry fire at it before moving to the other. Blasting shock combos from the balcony and the tops of the containers in front of the base is also an option. However, if you can guard the left and right roadways, the enemy must push through the gaps between the large containers. Push them back from here.

TIP

It takes your enemy a long time to return from the spawn point, so move to the third turret and blast with lightning guns if the Attackers fail to approach you as a team. Darting behind cover and pushing the enemy back and retreating to finish off stragglers can lead to stalemate and eventual defensive victory!

Lay eight grenades on one end of the roadway ramp as a present for an incoming tank. As each team member can lay eight grenades, and a tank only takes 15 grenade hits to explode, this is a great ambush tactic!

Once the Attackers begin storming the containers, repel boarders with a shock combo aimed through the gap in the containers! If they dodge that, then lay biorifle goop as they enter the building at either of the two choke points. Grenades also are extremely helpful in destroying an enemy charge. Don't commit so many troops to the inside of the building that you get surrounded from the two side roads; keep infantry and the gunner trained on these side areas, and also use shock rifle combos, biorifle goop, and grenades on any enemy. Continue pushing back the enemy until you're swamped, which usually happens only after a concentrated attack.

TIP

Attempt an indefinite holdout by dropping to the objective switch, grabbing health packs so the enemy can't get them, and taking all ordnance. Stragglers are easily dealt with. The entire attacking force is more difficult, but if the Attackers are waiting to roll in one large formation, meet them halfway, wound some, then respawn at the building to finish them off!

197

Attacking Objective 2: Destroy the Gate

When you finish the first objective, your entire team spawns above the communications building, where the Defenders spawned at the match's start. Take advantage of the two weapons lockers before dropping down, either from the holes adjacent to the lockers, or from the two balcony openings facing the ion cannon. Now dash to the gate: a door to the ion cannon's right leads into the robot factory. Before you leave the communications building, move to the weapons locker (#6) on the ground, near objective #1. This locker holds an additional grenade launcher, which can prove invaluable for this objective. Concentrate all your weapons on the ion cannon (the tanks should make it the primary target) until it is destroyed, or you pass under its aiming trajectory.

Attackers' Weapon Lockers 4 and 5*

Shock Rifle

Link Gun

Minigun

*Attacker's spawn point, above communications area

Attackers' Weapon Locker 6*

Biorifle

Shock Rifle

Link Gun

Minigun

*Under Attacker's spawn point, below communications area

TIP

During your assault on the gate, the enemy may try to blast you with the powerful, but unwieldy, ion cannon. If the ground turns purple, you're doomed; check for the laser sight and sprint away from the epicenter before you're struck.

Now your team, either riding tanks or on foot sprinting for the gate, can employ the previous turret takedown tactics. This time, however, keep on the move to avoid ion cannon fire and stay in cover (those tanks should be consistently firing at it to weaken and destroy it). You also have only two turrets to worry about. Trundle toward the set of giant fuel cylinders (which are impervious to damage), firing at the right turret while the rest of your team uses small arms fire to finish off the turret.

Meanwhile, move the second tank left around the side of the first set of cylinders, and deal with the final link gun turret (after the ion cannon is no longer a threat). With both tanks hidden from the ion cannon, and the respawn point for the tanks so close by, you shouldn't have too much trouble. Focus all your venom on the enemy guarding the gate, or the one sauntering into view from the bridge. This is the final, bloody choke point until the interior of the robot factory is finally breached.

TIP

For more cover (but limited defensive maneuvering), drive your Goliath tank between the quartet of giant cylinders, over the rocket launcher, and down the ramp to the dip. Repeat the plan on the other side. This lessens your chances of the ion cannon striking you.

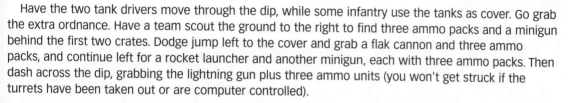

Have the two tank drivers move through the dip, while some infantry use the tanks as cover. Go grab the extra ordnance. Have a team scout the ground to the right to find three ammo packs and a minigun behind the first two crates. Dodge jump left to the cover and grab a flak cannon and three ammo packs, and continue left for a rocket launcher and another minigun, each with three ammo packs. Then dash across the dip, grabbing the lightning gun plus three ammo units (you won't get struck if the turrets have been taken out or are computer controlled).

On the other side, grab another flak cannon, rocket launcher, and minigun, each with three more ammo units. Your team should zip about, attracting the turrets while the tanks blast at them, and attempt to sneak around behind the turrets to deal more damage. Then you can breach the gate area.

Dive toward the right side and a crate with two health packs, where the Defenders may really give you grief. With your team pushing forward, weather the incoming ordnance and employ precision dodge jumping, taking out enemies and blasting the gate with flak if you get close or rockets from farther away. Try to fire off three close rockets into the gate before you're cut to pieces.

You can also lay up to eight grenades, which detonate when you die (probably a split second later because the Defenders' spawn point is on the ion cannon platform's lower part. Watch for sniping from this platform; use the jump pad by the cannon, on the right corner near the door and shield pack, to leap up and strafe the area with gunfire. If your tanks can get close, have them destroy the gate in two turret shots. Now the building is yours!

TIP

If you can, move to the left doorway opposite the gate, look down at the Defenders' spawning area, and lay waste to the right side of it by aiming rockets through the gaps in the pipes and wall.

Remember to jump! Avoid enemy gunfire by charging en masse, but have the more proficient team members come from the right side by the two crates, double jumping across the right wall, and landing on the jump pad. Air dodge onto the crates facing the gate, then blast away!

Know your role: Take a couple of lightning gun snipers and tackle any Defenders you can spot from the giant cylinders, or use the lower outer walls as cover. If you're on gate demolition, use rockets, almost from the beginning of the L-shaped bridge, aiming right, at the door. You don't have to be near to damage it!

TIP

One of the craziest plans involves a special ops mission: From the game's beginning, have a couple team members dash along the far right side of the walls, hugging the crates and ignoring turrets. Ignore objective #1, dodge to the gate (which isn't defended; the main firefight occurs as you near objective #1), pepper the gate with grenades, and then wait to destroy objective #2—objective #1 must fall first. You'll save an incredible amount of time. Don't detonate the gate too early, as it won't be damaged until objective #1 is taken.

Defending Objective 2: Defend the Gate

Defenders' Weapon Lockers 4 and 5*
Biorifle
Shock Rifle
Link Gun
Minigun
Rocket Launcher
Lightning Gun
*On spawning platform, under ion cannon

When the objective falls, your team retreats to the lower platform underneath a large and invincible ion cannon—the next objective for the Attackers. Pick up your weapons from either side of the spawn point, and go up the ramp to ground level; or better yet, use the two main jump pads to quickly bounce to the top (use air dodging to prevent the enemy from tagging you).

From here, grab the health vials on the outer wall (four on either side), and then a 50 shield pack in the middle of the roadway. To the left are containers and the gate. The roadway to the right leads to another small courtyard with two sets of massive cylinders, two link gun turrets, and the incoming enemy. Choose your location based on team tactics and prepare for incoming!

TIP

If the enemy didn't destroy the fourth turret in the first set of controllable link gun turrets, it can be used against you! Train your own turret on this before the enemy gets a chance to use it!

Regardless of whether the tanks made it to objective #1 or not, they respawn at the communications building when it is taken. If you are still battling a tank in the initial bay areas, pull back and ignore it, leaving it to trundle toward the building at a slower rate than killing it and a respawning would have taken.

The first defensive plan involves the larger turrets; the two link gun turrets and the bigger ion cannon. Stop the enemy at their spawn position by leaping to the turret controls at the ion cannon's base and pelting the Attackers with bolts from the left turret. Have a teammate or two chain link you.

While you blast the enemy, have a comrade use the jump pad at the spawning platform's edge to bounce up to the ion cannon. Press Use at the cannon's left ladder to take control of this cannon (but it can take more punishment than you, so make sure you're covered or can move to cover when the enemy nears). Bring both turrets to bear on the advancing tanks, concentrating your firepower on the front of the Attackers' new spawn point.

TIP

The ion cannon can zoom in its attack with the secondary fire, but either way, it traces a large laser beam at its target. Use it to your advantage: Aim at an area the enemy can't see (such as behind the giant cylinders), then at the last second change the aiming point to the tank or cluster of infantry and fire! Or, aim at the ground where the enemy can see, thus shepherding them away from this point and into an ambush.

If you're finished with the ion cannon (when you're being overrun or it has been destroyed), you appear at the ladder's top and can double jump onto the cannon's left side. This is a great sniping point—if you're not spotted!

Those without turrets to attack should split into two teams (aside from those link healing the turret operator). The first set of infantry should run toward the enemy and hold them at bay at the dip in the courtyard for as long as possible. If you can, race to the minigun, rocket launcher, and flak cannon ammo and weapons and use them on the advancing foes, backing up the turrets. Don't let the enemy snag either of the two health packs on the left side, and watch for enemies double jumping across the left wall edges.

As the enemy closes in (don't attack them from behind, or your forces will be spread too thinly), fall back to the ion cannon. You can hide behind the container near the doorway on the right and attack passing enemies. However, the main stand occurs near the gate. Use all available ordnance (such as rockets) to ensure no tanks can aim at the gate; blast them before they reach this point.

The remainder of your team (or all of them if you don't want to back up your turrets) should ready their lightning guns. Use the jump pad to reach the top ion cannon platform, and fire from up here, using the cannon's structure as cover; this is a great place to camp! Otherwise, air dodge or double jump to the containers' top to gain height; aim at the enemy from here. Make sure that the jump pad near the shield pack isn't used by the enemy to reach either the gate or the ion cannon. Cunning enemies fire at the gate from afar, so be prepared for lightning gun blasts from a distance (on both sides). Continue blasting until the Attackers breach the gate.

Attacking Objective 3: Cut the Data Cables

When the gate is destroyed, you respawn (without the tanks) at the Defenders' previous spawning point, and you can grab their weapon lockers (listed previously). Jump pad up to the bridge, grab the 50 shield pack if it's there, and nab the rocket launcher or flak cannon ammo before running through the door. A ramp ahead leads to a winding corridor to a data cable room with a central objective.

Attackers' Weapon Locker 7*

Biorifle

Shock Rifle

Link Gun

Minigun

Start of container crate room

Although there's one main route, you can clamber over areas or traverse upper or lower walkways to keep your opponents guessing. The first plan is to reach the weapons locker at the container crate room (pass it above or below), and run through the doorway in the far left corner of the container room; you'll respawn at the base of the ramp when you reach this point.

Halfway down the central ramp, find two side passages that lead to an upper mesh walkway. At the edge of these are crates that you can either double or dodge jump across, or drop down and move around as cover. You might want half your team to leap across the crates (which can be attempted from either mesh platform). A rocket launcher and three boxes of ammunition on the right balcony make it the preferred area to move to.

Dodge jump to the single crate near the exit in the left corner, and then to the double container with the shield pack. Set up some blasting points, aiming at this doorway. Grab the flak cannon and three ammo packs from the ground behind the two containers, and the two health packs in the room's far right corner before your foes do. Your team's main task is to hold the choke point at this room's exit and force the Defenders back to the subsequent corridor and finally the to cable chamber.

TIP

From the double container crates with the shield pack, vary your camping spot by double jumping to the narrow far ledge (giving you a good view of the doorway ahead); or leap over the two health packs to the pipe in the corner, and then double jump to the two crates opposite the doorway. This is another prime spot.

If you're in this chamber at ground level, locate two health packs to the weapon locker's left. There's also a good sniping spot between the container crate and the left wall, near a health pack. Otherwise, sidestep right around two containers and blast incoming enemies at the doorway.

Once through the door, grab weapons as you clamber over or run down a ramped corridor junction with robots dangling from the ceiling. Split your team up and have some jump across the chamber's left side and remain up here to annoy the enemy. Some of your team can run down the ramp to the weapons locker, and up the other side to a second weapons locker (with identical ordnance). A third team leaps across the right side of the junction, picking up the lightning gun and two ammo packs.

But your initial teammates should rush across the junction and then drop into the underground passage at the ramp's base (either by jumping down from the right or by running down the ramp). They should then zoom through the corridor, and grab the double damage halfway along the route. Expect fierce resistance here, but push the enemy back by streaming past them and varying your route; both the ramp and the double damage corridor end in a final chamber with the data cable room to your left. The ramp leads to a mesh walkway above the corridor exit, and you can drop from the walkway to the ground at any time.

Attackers' and Defenders' Weapon Lockers 1 and 2*

Biorifle

Minigun

Flak Cannon

Rocket Launcher

*In corridor junction, near data cable room

At the final room, if you're on the ramp, double jump to the right side wall for a 50 shield pack, or continue along the ground for another shield pack at the room's far end. The walkway surrounds the entire room, and leads to a small set of steps with a rocket launcher and two sets of ammo at an upper entrance to the data cable room. In the middle of the room is a jump pad.

This setup benefits the Attackers because the jump pad means you can consistently drop and leap up from the walkway and ground to avoid gunfire and randomize your maneuvering. There are two stacked entrances through which you can enter the data cable room. The rocket launcher, meanwhile, means you can forgo grabbing other weapons and head straight for it, again giving your enemy less time to react or learn your strategies.

The data cable room is the main spawn point for the Defenders, so shoot from outside the room, but with a clear line of sight to the objective. You don't need to see the energy bar of the data cables to damage it. After six rockets, the data cables explode, and the door on the opposite side of the connecting room opens, leading you deeper into the factory.

TIP

When you reach the data cable room, you can dash inside but expect heavy fire. If you're entering via the top floor balcony, you can leap onto the adjacent support and double jump to the pulsing energy cables and scaffolding pieces surrounding the structure.

If the data cable core is about to blow, wait at the right side of the connecting room for the doors to open (on the ground and balcony above), and make a quick charge to the next objective!

Defending Objective 3: Protect the Data Cables

At the ramped connecting junction area, tool up at the central weapons locker (the list of weapons is shown in "Attackers' and Defenders' Weapon Lockers #1 and #2"). Optionally leap above the corridor to the double damage, and grab the lightning gun and ammo, and then run for the choke point: the doorway leading from the container room to this area. You have an advantage because the enemy must now come to you; so don't all charge toward the ramp leading to objective #2 or you'll lose the ability to adequately protect this area. Holding the doorway at the end of the container room is an absolute priority.

This doesn't mean, however, that you should wait for the Attackers to charge into this area. Take some of your team, and when you spawn, run up the ramp to the container room, taking cover behind the container with the shield pack on top of it, and grab the flak cannon. Switch to the lightning gun if you can, and then hunt around this room's far end for enemies coming around the sides of the containers (especially the wall edges), or leaping across the overhead containers. You can take them down easily because they're concentrating on landing on the next container. If there are too many enemies, retreat to the doorway, where the remainder of the team should set up the usual choke point trap: crossfire!

At the doorway, have teammates dotted around the room, including some on the far walls near the second weapons locker, looking through the hanging robot parts and aiming with a lightning gun. Have a flak cannon ready with double damage taken from the corridor, but train all weapons on the doorway. Then continuously cover the ground

TIP

When an enemy makes it through the doorway into the junction room, your spawn point changes to inside the container room, so blast the enemies before they make it through.

with bio goop, flak ammo, and lightning gun shots. Throw in a charging teammate with shield and double damage and a flak cannon blazing to temporarily hold the Attackers off before they dash into this room. Once they do, your spawn point changes and you appear inside the core data cable room, inside a steaming pipe. Exit the pipe, grab six health vials surrounding the central data cable structure, and prevent the enemies from taking a shot at this structure.

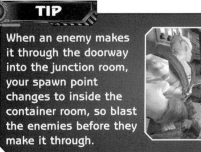

Defenders' Weapon Locker 6*

Biorifle

Shock Rifle

Minigun

Flak Cannon

Rocket Launcher

*Inside data cable room

In the data cable room, you see that the enemy is shooting from the exposed data cable pipe in the middle of this chamber; they get a good aiming spot from anywhere inside the room, or near the jump pad in the connecting chamber outside the room. They will likely enter the room from the lower or upper entrances and will appear from the weapon locker ramp area (right of your spawn room point or the double damage tunnel).

TIP

The jump pad located below the rocket launcher ledge and two doorways is the only cunning method of guarding both entrances to the room at once; keep moving about and engage the enemy when you spot them.

The enemies must still negotiate the container room and junction area with the ramps, so position teammates to cut them down in the doorway. Three or four of your team should take both shield packs in the adjacent room; have a shock rifle ready to combo anyone coming out of the DD tunnel (stand to the right of the wall support on the room's opposite side). Position a couple of your team on the mesh walkway to gain a better height and employ another "choke point plan" by the second weapons locker. Finally, have one teammate patrol the lower mesh area for enemies who break through and attempt to tag the target from outside, or who break into the data cable chamber.

Attacking Objective 4: Destroy Shield Component

Once the two large doors slide open, you spawn at the damaged data cable room (access the weapons locker the Defenders had in objective #3), then move into a similar connecting chamber. Run across either the ground or on a catwalk above, and look to the left doorways, which lead to the shield component room. This has three components to blast, from either of the two choke points, which are the doorways. These are both on the left wall, but the ground entrance is farther along the wall. Expect enemies milling about and ordnance hitting this zone.

Taking out the three shield component generator targets is difficult. Use the flak cannon or rocket at the upper entrance to take a couple of well-placed shots at one of the two front generators without even stepping into the room! Sidestep onto the lower ground, and then charge into the room afterward to vary your path. This can happen on the ground too, to a lesser extent. Otherwise, keep a constant barrage into the room, with most of your team attempting suicide runs.

Flummox your foe by attempting to blast the back generator first, which is usually the hardest to hit due to its grating. You're likely to be blasted after completing a single run, so try strafing around the back of the rear generator armed with the biorifle and pepper the generator with ooze—you can take it out with one pass if you're quick and precise!

TIP

If your team is about to take out the final generator, position the rest of the team near the doorway with the force field that dissipates after the objective is completed. Then dash through to the final objective.

205

Defending Objective 4: Protect the Shield Nexus

Defenders' Weapon Lockers 7 and 8*	Defenders' Weapon Lockers 9 and 10*
Shock Rifle	Shock Rifle
Link Gun	Link Gun
Minigun	Minigun
Rocket Launcher	Rocket Launcher
*In crushing room, spawn point	*Base of shield nexus room

Starting in a chamber with two large pieces of machinery, zip through, pausing at a weapons locker, and exit via either doorway onto a balcony overlooking the three shield generators in the room. The two nearest the two entrances where the enemies stream in are where the foes are likely to strike first, so guard the three pillars with covering fire. However, the nearest, third pillar is encased in protective mesh. It can't be shot from the front, so enemies must move behind it (and under your walkway). This gives you ample time to create some major disturbances and protect this last generator.

Guard the two entrances solidly. Have around half of your team on the ground, grabbing weapons from the other two lockers. The enemies can fire only at the two closest pillars from the behind the doorway with limited cover, so launch a few rockets or dash to the top doorway. A constant stream of shock combos from both the ground troops and those up on the walkway makes it impossible to enter the chamber!

When the enemy breaks through, have a carpet of bio goo waiting for them at the doorway, and then knock them with more shock combos. Have a team of three strike down incoming enemies with a chained link gun; the stream is easy to lock on to a target.

When an enemy makes a break for the back generator, cake him in goo and destroy him before he turns the corner and fires at this well-defended choke point. Set up a mixture of your favorite weapons at either side of the generator.

TIP

The enemy must blast both the shield generators and your team, while you must concentrate only on the Attackers, giving you the advantage.

Attacking Objective 5: Destroy the AI Generator

There's only one route to the final objective. From your spawn point at the shield generator room (where you tool up with the Defender's weapon lockers from objective #4), run toward the final generator room. The enemy spawns from the generator, so the main choke point is probably the doorway before the final right turn. Head left before the Defenders and claim a 50 shield pack. Station a teammate or two on top of the grinding wheel for a nasty surprise. Push the enemy back so you're constantly in charge of this area—which is easier to manage because you have a clear line of sight from your starting point.

For the final push, dash through the enemy to the main circular generator chamber. Enemies are all over this place. The top of the ramp's lit part is the place farthest from the objective where you can fire at it, so there's no chance to stay away from the action and take down the generator. Run toward the mesh ramp, choosing the main route or run through either of the small tunnel-like constructions (although you may find enemies waiting at the far end).

Once on the main ledge, throw everything you have at the generator, ignoring the enemy fire. Try to circle-strafe and jump around the generator, changing direction randomly to throw off the enemies, and constantly stream your gunfire on the generator. If necessary, have a couple of your team distract the enemy by shooting them, but focus almost all firepower on destroying the last objective. It falls after around 35 rockets.

TIP

Double jump off the circular ledge, onto the pipes at the generator's base, and then back onto the ledge to avoid the enemy. Even if you fall, get one or two final rockets or shots off at the generator before you die.

If you're defending or attacking the doorway choke point before the final right turn and ramp, you can camp out by leaping over the fence opposite the grinding wheel and standing on a pipe. Crouch and take potshots from this rarely visited location.

Dodge jump onto the right "tunnel," and then onto a large dangling robot. You can't shoot the generator, but you can harass the enemy while your team attempts to complete the goal.

Finally, when you're halfway down the mesh ramp to the generator room, double jump diagonally left or right, around a vertical pipe, and land on the circular generator ledge. Don't mess this up or it's a bottomless plummet! This prevents you from being struck by the barrage of fire at the ledge entrance.

Defending Objective 5: Protect the AI Generator

Your last chance at saving your factory comes from the defense of a giant circular chamber with an AI generator in the middle of it. The room is vast, and the enemy will throw themselves in there to whittle down the generator's energy; fortunately, you have a couple of choke points.

207

Unreal TOURNAMENT 2004

Defenders' Weapon Lockers 11 and 12*

Biorifle

Shock Rifle

Link Gun

Minigun

Flak Cannon

Rocket Launcher

Balcony of AI generator room; spawn point

From your spawn point above the circular walkway, some of your team can stand guard and launch shock combos on the incoming enemy, bouncing them off the walkway. Don't fall off the walkway's sides! When you're finished on the walkway, or at the start of this part of the match, drop down either side onto the lower walkway.

The enemy can fire on the generator only from halfway down the ramp leading to the room, so move as a cohesive unit to the entrance ramp. At the top, create a choke point at the doorway on the left, past the two "container tunnels." Stay in the passage and blast anyone coming round the corner with shock combos, goop, rockets, or flak cannon ordnance. Head to the far end of this area before the Attackers arrive and grab a 50 shield pack.

If the choke point is holding, keep this up until the match finishes, optionally leaping atop a tunnel, or hiding around one of the containers to vary the area from which your shots come. Once the enemies get through this point though, annihilate the entrance ramp, aiming everything you have at the top of the ramp's lighted part.

If anyone breaks through this choke point, have one or two of your team bounce the enemy off the walkway with shock combos or rocket fire. Vary the firing locations; have some of your team on the balcony, others on the pipes below the central generator, and the rest on the walkway. The ramp entrance must hold!

Onslaught Maps

NOTE

Each Onslaught map features scenery, PowerNodes, and identical bases, joined in the middle (usually by a central PowerNode). Strategy and descriptions apply to both "sides" of the map (usually north and south), and work for both teams. Minor differences are mentioned where necessary. PowerNodes and bases are relevant only to their specific side of the map, unless otherwise stated.

ONS-ARCTICSTRONGHOLD

Recommended Players: 10–18

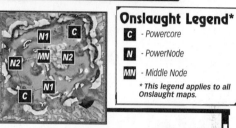

Onslaught Legend*

C - Powercore

N - PowerNode

MN - Middle Node

* This legend applies to all Onslaught maps.

Legend

1   Health Vials x3 (each side)
2   Mine Layer +2 ammo packs
3   Weapons Locker
4   50 Health Pack
5   50 Shield Pack
6   Biorifle +2 ammo packs
7   Sniper Rifle +2 ammo packs

8   Grenade Launcher +1 ammo (blue base)
9   Sniper Rifle +2 ammo packs
10 Weapons Locker (and 50 Shield Pack at one end)
11 Redeemer
12 50 Shield Pack
13 50 Health Pack
14 Weapons Locker and 50 Health Pack at one end

15 Grenade Launcher +1 ammo pack (red base)
16 50 Shield Pack (and 50 Health Pack at one end)
17 Mine Layer (+ 50 Health Pack at one end)
18 Big Keg-O-Health (one end only)
19 Weapons Locker
20 50 Health Pack
21 50 Health Pack

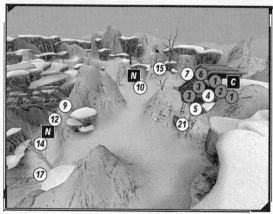

Overview

Welcome to Arctic Stronghold, a map filled with moguls and hills. Starting at either base, find your first PowerNode on a hill to the right. Either follow the ravine to the middle node and hold the bridge, or head around the outside to PowerNode #2, then to enemy PowerNode #1 and a base assault. Also check the areas between the PowerNodes for shield and health packs, and always pack an AVRiL to avoid enemy bombardment.

Hard-Fought Onslaught: Level Check

Home Base

Links to: PowerNode #1

Vehicles Spawned: Goliath, Hellbender, Manta (x2), Raptor (upper floor), Scorpion

Other Defenses: Energy Turret (x4)

Available Weapons

Biorifle (right upper area, corner behind energy turret)

Sniper Rifle (right upper area, next to energy turret)

Mine Layer (under central ramp, near core)

Weapon Lockers (x2—middle lower base, middle upper walkway)

Link Gun, Minigun, AVRiL, Rocket Launcher

Each base has four entrances (two on the ground, two in the air), along with two turrets on top, and two below. A 50 shield pack is at one end of the lower entrance, with a health pack at the other. This well-placed base can be attacked only from the front, and the core is behind impenetrable glass and a ramp, making sniping impossible. Hold the enemy at the four entrances (mainly the ground) and you'll be fine, especially as this links only to PowerNode #1.

PowerNode 1

Links to: Home Base, Middle PowerNode

Vehicles Spawned: Manta, Scorpion

Other Defenses: Energy Turret (red), Energy Turret (x2 blue)

Available Weapons

Grenade Launcher (between PowerNode)

Sniper Rifle (blue only, north of PowerNode next to energy turret)

Weapon Locker (next to PowerNode)

Link Gun, Mine Layer, Flak Cannon, AVRiL

Located on a hill and featuring a turret linked to the PowerNode (available once the PowerNode is linked), this node is essential for attacking or defending a base. The lack of larger vehicles means you must snipe or use the turrets. Th height is an advantage. The node links to both #2 nodes and the middle node. Note the grenade launcher (and ammo pack) near each mogul and base, which is useful for both offensive and defensive combat.

PowerNode 2

Links to: PowerNode #1 (north), PowerNode #1 (south)

Vehicles Spawned: Hellbender, Manta

Other Defenses: Energy Turret (red), Energy Turret (blue)

Available Weapons

Sniper Rifle (blue only: next to energy turret over hill from blue base)

Weapon Locker (next to PowerNode)

Shock Rifle, Link Gun, AvRiL, Sniper Rifle

Both PowerNode #2s link to a PowerNode #1, and the rest of the node is exposed except for a nearby turret. Use the visibility to launch attacks from below or set up spider mines. Go for either the bridge or the opposing PowerNode #1 before attacking the enemy base.

Middle PowerNode

Links to: PowerNode #1 (north), PowerNode #1 (south)

Vehicles Spawned: Goliath (on bridge), Manta, Raptor, Scorpion

Other Defenses: Energy Turret (x4)

Available Weapons

Sniper Rifle (behind sand bags, north end of bridge)

Redeemer (on snow ledge next to jump pad under bridge)

Weapon Locker (next to PowerNode)

Link Gun, Minigun, Grenade Launcher, AvRiL, Sniper Rifle

The key to a decisive victory is holding the middle PowerNode and the bridge above it. Use the Goliath tank and four turrets. The ravine contains two health packs, a 50 shield pack, a big keg-o-health, and a mine layer. The jump pad next to the PowerNode is the quickest way to the tank and the redeemer.

Other Weapons

Mine Layer (x2)

PowerNode to Joy: Planning Victory

The first part of your plan is to take PowerNode #1. Then send a Raptor pilot zipping to the middle node. He should land on the ledge, pick up the redeemer, and then either wait for the bridge PowerNode to come online, or fly into the enemy units at their PowerNode #1 and deal out a redeemer. Fly to a plateau accessible only by the Raptor, then fire off a redeemer into a huge mass of foes.

211

Have the rest of your team descend on the bridge and hold it while a splinter group heads to PowerNode #2. You can take the enemy PowerNode #1 instead of taking the bridge or PowerNode #2, depending on the enemy reaction. When you head to the enemy base, split your forces, use the Goliath tank, and send in a couple teammates while other vehicles get into range.

Use the big guns from the Goliath and Hellbender main turrets. Peek over a hill, blast a PowerNode, and retreat. The Hellbender turret has exceptional range, so blast targets from afar. When the enemy moves toward you, gun them down!

ONS-CROSSFIRE

Recommended Players: 10–18

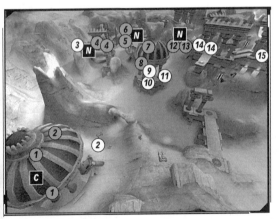

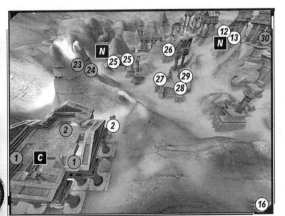

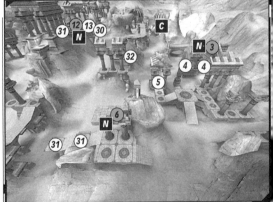

Legend

1	50 Health Pack	12	Double Damage	22	50 Health Pack	
2	Weapons Locker	13	Weapons Locker and Grenade ammo pack x2	23	Mine ammo packs x2	
3	Weapons Locker	14	50 Health Pack and Mine Layer +2 ammo packs	24	Weapons Locker	
4	50 Health Pack	15	Lightning Gun +2 ammo packs	25	50 Health Pack	
5	50 Health Pack	16	Redeemer	26	Big Keg-O-Health	
6	Weapons Locker	17	50 Health Pack	27	50 Health Pack	
7	Big Keg-O-Health	18	Weapons Locker	28	50 Shield Pack	
8	50 Shield Pack	19	100 Shield Pack	29	Weapons Locker	
9	Weapons Locker	20	Weapons Locker	30	Grenade Launcher	
10	Mine x2 and Grenade x2 ammo packs	21	50 Health Pack	31	50 Health Pack and 50 Shield Pack	
11	50 Health Pack			32	100 Shield Pack	

Overview

Crossfire is perhaps the most complicated map, despite the scarcity of PowerNodes. The central PowerNode *doesn't* link to the outside PowerNode areas. Flying is the way to get around due to the high number of Raptors, so have ground troops bring out an AVRiL!

Hard-Fought Onslaught: Level Check

Home Base

Links to: PowerNode #1

Vehicles Spawned: Hellbender, Manta, Scorpion

Other Defenses: Energy Turrets (x2)

Available Weapons
Weapon Locker (left side of base)

Link Gun, Minigun, Flak Cannon, AVRiL

Weapon Locker (middle exterior of base)

Shock Rifle, Link Gun, Flak Cannon, AVRiL

The home base is in a corner, so you face attack from only two sides. Although vehicles can drive up the rocky walls, most ground attacks come from the left path or the arch. Concentrate your firepower on these choke points. PowerNode #1 is more important to defend, so have most of your forces facing the left outer pathway. Get the health packs on either side of the temple.

PowerNode 1

Links to: Home Base, PowerNode #2, Middle PowerNode

Vehicles Spawned: Hellbender, Manta, Scorpion

Other Defenses: None

Available Weapons
Weapon Locker (next to PowerNode)

Link Gun, Minigun, Mine Layer, AVRiL

Holding this PowerNode is a constant battle. With it you can claim either PowerNode #2 or the middle PowerNode; it offers little else besides a pair of health packs. Hold it with a small team.

PowerNode 2

Links to: Home Base, PowerNode #1, Middle PowerNode

Vehicles Spawned: Goliath, Manta, Raptor

Other Defenses: None

Available Weapons

Weapon Locker (next to PowerNode)

Link Gun, Rocket Launcher, Lightning Gun

This section offers a Raptor and a Goliath and power-ups surrounding the PowerNode (nearby ruins contain 100 and 50 shield packs and various health packs). Capture this so your vehicles can trundle to the enemy base, which is almost visible from the upper area near the PowerNode. Stay atop the ruins to defend this area. This PowerNode connects only to PowerNode #2 (as well as your PowerNode #1).

Middle PowerNode

Links to: PowerNode #1 (east and west)

Vehicles Spawned: Manta, Raptor, Scorpion

Other Defenses: None

Available Weapons

Ion Painter (north of PowerNode, on edge of ruined temple)

Weapon Locker (next to PowerNode)

Link Gun, AVRiL, Grenade Launcher, Rocket Launcher, Lightning Gun

The ruins surrounding the upper plateau offer powerful weapons, accessible from the PowerNode. However, it connects only to the opposing PowerNode #1 (and your own PowerNode #1). In addition to the weapons and items (including the double damage near the PowerNode), find another Raptor.

Other Weapons

Mine Layer

Lightning Gun

Redeemer

Weapons Locker

Link Gun, Rocket Launcher, Lightning Gun

Weapons Locker

Link Gun, Mine Layer, Rocket Launcher

PowerNode to Joy: Planning Victory

Air superiority is the name of the game, because this map contains more Raptors than any other. Start by locating and staying at PowerNode #1. Raptor pilots can zip off to PowerNode #2 or the middle PowerNode, or they can locate the redeemer at the ruins. Mantas can reach both PowerNodes in time. Then use the redeemer on the enemy at PowerNode #1 (for example).

If the enemy is decimated at a particular PowerNode, use the Raptors from PowerNodes #2 and the middle to swarm or even attack in formation. Send a Goliath (spawned at PowerNode #2) to your foe's base. When PowerNode #1 in the enemy area falls, take out turrets while the rest of the team attacks from the opposite side.

Bring out your Hellbender and blast at PowerNodes from long range. For example, attack the west PowerNode from the northwest corner. From the ruins with the redeemer there's a straight shot into the core.

ONS-DAWN

Recommended Players: 8–16

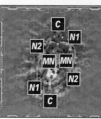

Legend

#	Item	#	Item	#	Item
1	Weapons Locker and Shock, link, flak ammo x2	11	Grenade Launcher +2 ammo packs	19	Grenade Launcher +2 ammo packs
2	50 Health Pack	12	Weapons Locker and shock, link and flak ammo x2	20	Weapons Locker and shock, link and flak ammo x2
3	Grenade Launcher +2 ammo packs	13	Grenade Launcher +2 ammo packs	21	50 Health Pack
4	50 Health Pack	14	Rocket Launcher +1 ammo pack	22	Grenade Launcher +2 ammo packs
5	50 Health Pack	15	Big Keg-O-Health	23	50 Health Pack
6	Weapons Locker and shock, link, flak ammo x2	16	50 Health Pack	24	Weapons Locker and shock, link and flak ammo x2
7	Grenade Launcher +2 ammo packs	17	50 Health Pack	25	Grenade Launcher +2 ammo packs
8	100 Shield Pack	18	Weapons Locker and shock, link and flak ammo x2	26	50 Health Pack
9	Sniper Rifle +2 ammo packs				
10	Weapons Locker and shock, link, flak ammo x2				

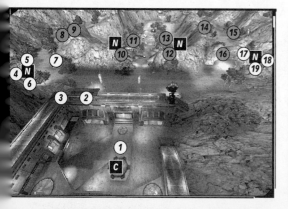

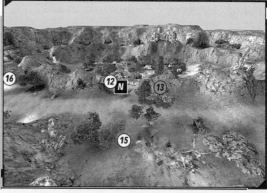

Overview

Dawn's tranquility is soon to be replaced with carnage. Opposing teams face off from secure initial bases. A perimeter road contains PowerNodes. Use the middle glade area for stealthy exploration or shortcuts.

Hard-Fought Onslaught: Level Check

Home Base

Links to: PowerNode #1, PowerNode #2

Vehicles Spawned: Goliath, Hellbender (outside), Manta (outside), Raptor

Other Defenses: Energy Turret (x4)

Available Weapons

AVRiL (top left side of base, on parapet corner)

Weapons Locker (middle of base interior

Shock Rifle, Link Gun, Flak Cannon

The bases on this small map are difficult to breach. Outside are two turrets, with another on the balcony next to the satellite dish (near the only health pack on the walkway). A fourth turret inside devastates anyone who reaches the base interior. The base must be ready for action, as PowerNodes #1 or #2 can expose the core. Brace for an attack from either direction, or even the glade entrance ahead.

PowerNode 1

Links to: Base, Middle East PowerNode (red), Middle West PowerNode (blue)

Vehicles Spawned: Manta, Scorpion

Other Defenses: Energy Turret

Available Weapons

AVRiL (next to energy turret)

Weapons Locker (next to PowerNode)

Shock Rifle, Link Gun, Flak Cannon

PowerNode #1, near the base, connects the base and the middle east/west PowerNode. Two health packs are nearby, and it spawns a couple of small vehicles. This is an important area to hold, and sometimes a weak link if you're spread too thinly. Bring in defenses from your base to guard this.

PowerNode 2

Links to: Base, Middle West PowerNode (red), Middle East PowerNode (blue)

Vehicles Spawned: Goliath, Raptor

Other Defenses: Energy Turret

Available Weapons

AVRiL (in front of Goliath on north side, to side of Raptor on south side)

Weapons Locker (next to PowerNode)

Shock Rifle, Link Gun, Flak Cannon

The second PowerNode is farther from the base but offers a Goliath. The PowerNode can be sniped from a distance, so watch your incoming fire and defenses. Find two health packs here. The PowerNode links to the base and the east/west middle PowerNode (the opposite PowerNode to PowerNode #1's link).

Middle East and West PowerNodes

Links to: PowerNode #1 (north and south), PowerNode #2 (north and south), Middle East (middle west), Middle West (middle east)

Vehicles Spawned: Hellbender, Manta

Other Defenses: Energy Turret

Available Weapons

Weapons Locker

Shock Rifle, Link Gun, Flak Cannon

The middle PowerNodes both access a PowerNode #1 and #2 on different sides. Find a big keg-o-health near a burning space fighter to the west, and a 100 shield pack and sniper rifle near a satellite dish to the east. The rock wall offers some protection. The opposite middle PowerNode can be attacked when the first is taken. This is the last vital link to destroying a base.

217

Other Weapons

> ### Available Weapons
>
> **Grenade Launcher** (south of middle west PowerNode, right of turret at junction)
>
> **AVRiL** (south of the middle east PowerNode, near sparkling pool)
>
> **Rocket Launcher** (x2, north of southern PowerNode #1, south of northern PowerNode #1)
>
> **Sniper Rifle** (next to satellite dish on middle east edge)

PowerNode to Joy: Planning Victory

Either zoom to the initial PowerNode #1, or head a little farther to PowerNode #2, where better vehicles spawn. Then choose either PowerNode #2 or one of the middle PowerNodes (we recommend PowerNode #2 for the Goliath spawn).

The action depends on which middle PowerNode your opponents take—the one nearer the PowerNode #2 lets you use your tank. Then continue to the opposite PowerNode near your enemies' base. Attack this tough base with Goliaths and Hellbenders.

Use your Raptor to check your opponents' PowerNodes. If any are poorly defended, guide your team there. It's easier to defend the base and PowerNode #1, so you head up this side, using the Raptor to land at the middle east/west PowerNode while your team secures PowerNode #1. When this happens, your enemy will react defensively. This lets you head to the PowerNode opposite the one your enemy is approaching.

For example, blue team takes PowerNode #1, then heads north to the middle west PowerNode. Your opponents see that PowerNode disappear, and defend their PowerNode #2 in the northwest. Your Raptor take the middle east PowerNode, and you press on into the base. To blast the base, have your Raptor take care of the balcony turret, while your Hellbender and tanks deal with the ground ones.

The enchanted glade is a good shortcut to the opposite outer pathway (to cut off a tank, for example). The Manta or Scorpion are excellent for driving over a rise to attack from above. Use the tank in your base to cover PowerNode #1. Break out the Hellbender's turret to destroy the middle PowerNodes from behind the giant mushrooms.

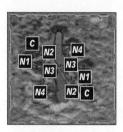

ONS-DRIA

Recommended Players: 12–24

Legend

1 Grenade ammo x2	**16** Weapons Locker
2 Weapons Locker	**17** Grenade ammo x2
3 Weapons Locker	**18** Sniper Rifle +2 ammo packs
4 Grenade ammo x2	**19** 100 Shield Pack
5 50 Health Packs x2	**20** Weapons Locker
6 Sniper Rifle +2 ammo packs	**21** Grenade ammo x2
7 Weapons Locker	**22** Weapons Locker
8 Grenade ammo x2	**23** 100 Shield Pack
9 50 Health Packs x2	**24** Target Painter
10 Weapons Locker	**25** Weapons Locker
11 100 Shield Pack	**26** 50 Health Pack x2
12 Sniper Rifle +2 ammo packs	**27** Target Painter
13 Sniper Rifle +2 ammo packs	**28** 50 Health Packs x2
14 50 Health Packs x2	**29** Weapons Locker
15 Weapons Locker	

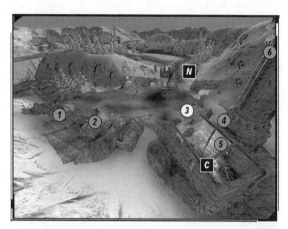

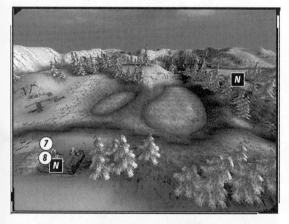

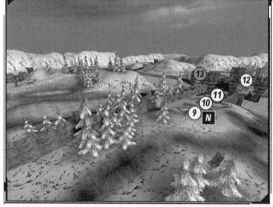

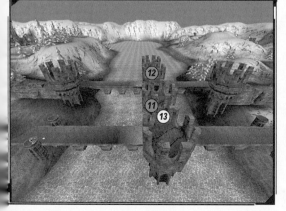

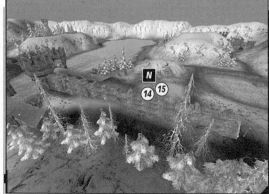

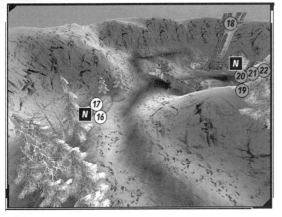

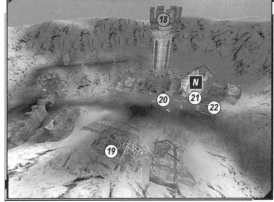

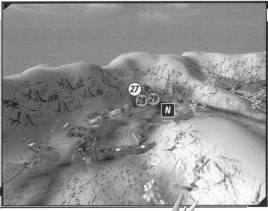

Overview

A massive and relatively flat area of arctic tundra, Dria is extremely accessible from the air. The four PowerNodes on each side present a number of pathways to the other side. Although the main battles often occur on a bridge, the frozen lake allows anyone to quickly travel anywhere. This allows greater opportunities for domino-style PowerNode-linking of empty or enemy PowerNodes.

Hard-Fought Onslaught: Level Check

Home Base

Links to: PowerNode #1, PowerNode #2

Vehicles Spawned: Hellbender, Manta (x2), Raptor, Scorpion (x2)

Other Defenses: Energy Turrets (x4)

Available Weapons

Sniper Rifle (on top of massive tower, teleport to grab it)

Weapons Locker (x2, either side of core building)

Shock Rifle, Link Gun, Minigun, AVRiL

Your base has a core inside a building to the right of a huge tower. A teleport at the tower's base allows you to reach a sniper rifle. This base offers vehicles, a 50 shield pack in an outbuilding near one of the exits, and some fine turrets. The base's core can be breached only if PowerNode #1 is taken. Keep a sizable force at PowerNode #1, then retreat into the base if that falls.

PowerNode 1

Links to: Base, PowerNode #2, PowerNode #3

Vehicles Spawned: Manta, Raptor, Scorpion

Other Defenses: Energy Turret (side of PowerNode)

Available Weapons

Weapons Locker (front of PowerNode and building)

Link Gun, AVRiL, Flak Cannon, Sniper Rifle

Claim and keep this important PowerNode. It allows access to the base core, PowerNode #2 near the frozen lake (allowing easy access to the opponents' PowerNode #4), and PowerNode #3 near the bridge (charge across the bridge or over the lake to the opponents' PowerNode #3). Keep a skeletal patrol over here in case of attack; otherwise, press on.

PowerNode 2

Links to: PowerNode #1, PowerNode #2 (opposite side)

Vehicles Spawned: Manta, Raptor, Scorpion

Other Defenses: Energy Turret

Available Weapons

Weapons Locker (front of PowerNode and building)

Link Gun, AVRiL, Flak Cannon, Sniper Rifle

Take PowerNode #2, which links to the opposing team's PowerNode #2. After claiming this, push your foes to PowerNode #1 and then the base. It's easy to reach and links to PowerNode #1. Take this only if you're planning on a shorter attempt to tear through your opponents' PowerNodes.

PowerNode 3

Links to: PowerNode #1, PowerNode #3 (opposite side), PowerNode #4

Vehicles Spawned: Goliath, Hellbender, Manta

Other Defenses: Energy Turret (x2)

Available Weapons

Weapons Locker (behind wall from core)

Shock Rifle, Link Gun, AVRiL, Rocket Launcher

PowerNode #3, each on one side of the frozen lake, offers the biggest vehicles and firepower. If you want an all-out war, start your construction here. It links to the opposite PowerNode #3, PowerNode #4, and PowerNode #1. Grab two health packs if the combat is incessant. Once you own the area, man two turrets on your side of the river, and blast the opposing turrets (turrets don't respawn). This is the quickest way to a Goliath tank and the 100 shield pack.

PowerNode 4

Links to: PowerNode #3

Vehicles Spawned: Goliath, Manta, Scorpion

Other Defenses: Energy Turret (x2)

Available Weapons

Target Painter (top of tower, accessed with ground teleport)

Weapons Locker (front of PowerNode and building)

Link Gun, Minigun, AVRiL, Sniper Rifle

The final PowerNode, accessed via PowerNode #3, offers another tank and a couple more vehicles to bolster your troops at PowerNode #3. For example, force the Goliath at PowerNode #3 over the bridge or across the lake while bringing the tank at PowerNode #4 forward to guard PowerNode #3. The PowerNode is huge (don't mistake it for your base). Find a target painter on a tower accessed via Raptor or teleport (the teleport is at the tower's base near two health packs).

Other Weapons

Sniper Rifle (x2)

PowerNode to Joy: Planning Victory

Multiple PowerNodes and an open environment spells multiple tactics for the team leader. Start by taking PowerNode #1, but first decide whether to attack from PowerNode #3 (a longer match but with more firepower), or PowerNode #2 (a quick resolution but less offensive force). Either way, send out a Raptor pilot.

Take a Manta, Raptor, or Scorpion to PowerNode #2 while the rest of the team links PowerNode #1. Quickly build #2 and cross to the opposite PowerNode #2 for a quick claim and a push to victory. A safer plan is to push most of your force at PowerNode #1. Have the Raptor pilot zoom to PowerNode #3 or #4 to claim the target painter, and then back to start PowerNode linking, and then fly a final mission to use the target painter.

Don't underestimate PowerNode #4 either; it's easy to access and provides an extra tank that's handy for battling at the bridge. As soon as PowerNode #3 is taken, place two teammates on the turrets and destroy the opposite turrets.

Finally, the frozen lake provides several "interference run" opportunities using a Scorpion, Manta, or even a sizeable force. Head only toward areas that link to your PowerNodes to avoid spreading your forces too thin. Drive along the hillsides in Scorpions or Hellbenders to ease your journey through wooded areas. Breach your opponents' base by driving a Hellbender around the side of the entrance and behind the core building; shoot through the windows or from the hill opposite the tower. This provides a useful distraction.

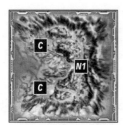

ONS-FROSTBITE

Recommended Players: 6–10

Legend

1	Big Keg-O-Health	**9**	Double Damage
2	Sniper Rifle	**10**	Lightning Gun +2 ammo packs
3	Weapons Locker	**11**	Lightning Gun +2 ammo packs
4	Health Vials x2 (in each alcove)	**12**	100 Shield Pack
5	100 Shield Pack	**13**	Weapons Locker
6	Weapons Locker	**14**	Weapons Locker
7	Weapons Locker	**15**	Health Vial x2 (in each alcove)
8	Big Keg-O-Health		

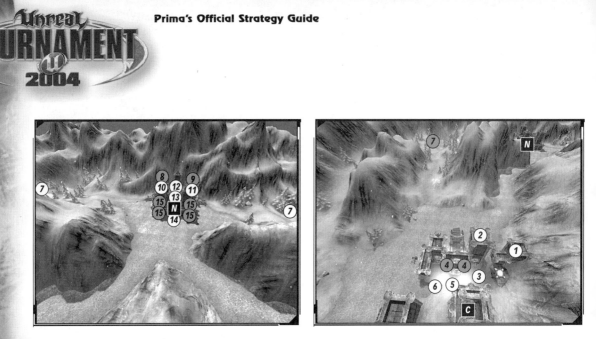

Overview

Frostbite is a perfect introduction to the Onslaught game match. The two bases are nearby, and claiming a single PowerNode makes the cores vulnerable. Claim the core, or fight at the core so your enemy doesn't claim it. Most of the action takes place at the PowerNode, so send all your troops here unless you can spare one or two to run interference. Press the PowerNode attack until it's yours or you reach a stalemate.

Hard-Fought Onslaught: Level Check

Home Base

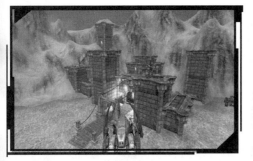

Links to: PowerNode #1

Vehicles Spawned: Goliath, Manta, Raptor, Scorpion (x2)

Other Defenses: Energy Turret

Available Weapons

Lightning Gun (on top of front middle tower)

Weapons Locker (x2, inside left and right sides of base)

Shock Rifle, Link Gun, Minigun, AVRiL

The base's tightness and many turrets make attacking the core problematic. You must get in close and not hit the stone tower surrounding it. Grab the big keg-o-health atop the turret nearest the snow wall and the 100 shield pack near the core tower. Then expect close combat and vehicular madness. Use the Goliath to tear into the middle Node and the opposition's tank.

PowerNode 1

Links to: Base (red), Base (blue)

Vehicles Spawned: Hellbender, Manta, Scorpion (x2)

Other Defenses: Energy Turret

Available Weapons

Lightning Gun (x2, top of both the front towers)

Weapons Locker (x2, inside front and rear of base)

Link Gun, AVRiL, Flak Cannon, Rocket Launcher

The single PowerNode links to both bases, and the team that captures the PowerNode can blast the core. However, with both teams so close, this PowerNode constantly changes hands. If you claim the PowerNode, climb into the Hellbender that spawns. Four paths reach this PowerNode (two usually accessed by the other team, and two by your own). Grab the big keg-o-health from a turret at the rear and the double damage on the opposite turret. Use the energy turret and snipe incoming forces or battle at close quarters near the PowerNode. A 100 shield pack is on either side of an archway with four health vials inside.

Other Weapons

Weapons Locker (x2)

Link Gun, Rocket Launcher, Lightning Gun

The weapons lockers are on a rise between the base and PowerNode. Snipe at the PowerNode or at enemies taking the long route from their base.

PowerNode to Joy: Planning Victory

Station most of your force at the PowerNode. You must hold the PowerNode (to stop your opponents from linking). Flit from sniping on the roof to using the energy turrets (if possible) to fighting inside vehicles.

Take advantage of the Hellbender's extreme range by having teammates blast enemies leaving their base. Try attacking the enemy base at the start. Have one teammate lead a few enemies on a wild goose chase while the rest of the team claims the PowerNode. When the PowerNode is yours, dish out turret blasts and keep a strong presence; the PowerNode must not be lost once taken!

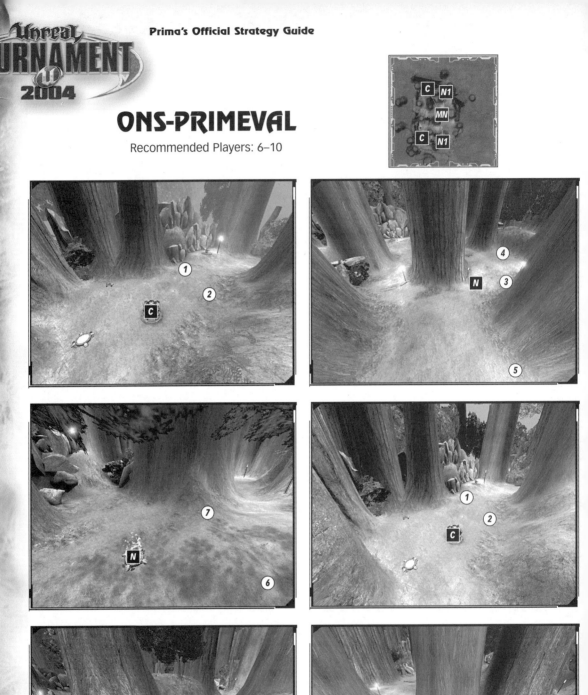

ONS-PRIMEVAL

Recommended Players: 6–10

Legend

1	Weapons Locker	7	Weapons Locker
2	Weapons Locker	8	Weapons Locker
3	Weapons Locker	9	Weapons Locker
4	50 Health Pack x2	10	Weapons Locker
5	50 Health Pack x2	11	Weapons Locker
6	Weapons Locker		

Overview

This small practice map is the key to winning victories on larger zones. Choke points do exist. You can't fly over hills, there are no Raptors, and the paths are flat. Split your forces to gain extra firepower (and closer spawning points) by taking and holding your PowerNode #1, without being overrun in the middle, where a base-blasting Goliath tank is the reward.

Hard-Fought Onslaught: Level Check

Home Base

Links to: PowerNode #1, Middle PowerNode

Vehicles Spawned: Hellbender, Scorpion

Other Defenses: Energy Turret

Available Weapons

Weapons Locker (x2, left and right sides of path)

Link Gun, Mine Layer, Grenade Launcher, Flak Cannon

At the dead end of a clearing, the home base can be attacked only from the energy turret. Push forward all the way (or to the weapons lockers if you're on foot) and use your vehicles as a barrier. Man the turret to prevent the enemy overrunning your base. Your opponent can claim either your PowerNode #1 or the middle PowerNode and then attack.

PowerNode 1

Links to: Base, Middle PowerNode

Vehicles Spawned: Manta, Scorpion

Other Defenses: None

Available Weapons

Weapon Lockers (x2, left and right side of path)

Shock Rifle, Link Gun, AVRiL

Although the route to this point is confusing (particularly to the blue team), you head through the middle PowerNode to reach this forest clearing by only one path—the way you came in. This PowerNode offers some quick-moving vehicles, but don't take it until the middle PowerNode is yours.

TOURNAMENT 2004

Middle PowerNode

Links to: Bases (red and blue), PowerNode #1 (red and blue)

Vehicles Spawned: Goliath

Other Defenses: None

Available Weapons

Weapons Locker (north side of PowerNode)

Link Gun, Rocket Launcher

Most of the fighting starts here, as both teams vie for the Goliath. Find the two health packs near the PowerNode, and use the trees as cover as you defend this PowerNode.

Other Weapons None

PowerNode to Joy: Planning Victory

This small level provides hours of enjoyment for novice tacticians. Each base has only one entrance, but you can blast a base if any PowerNodes are linked. Most combat occurs in the middle.

You risk being overrun (or shot) if you advance to PowerNode #1 while most of your force attempts the middle PowerNode. If you leave a player at your PowerNode #1 and get all respawning teammates to appear here, they can reach the middle faster. Use your Hellbender to wreak havoc in the middle, then claim the Goliath and add a turret operator to prevent foes from advancing on your base.

ONS-REDPLANET

Recommended Players: 12–16

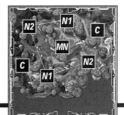

Legend

1 Mine Layer +2 ammo packs	11 Link ammo x2	22 Shock ammo x2	34 Weapons Locker
2 50 Health Pack	12 Rocket ammo x2	23 Grenade ammo x2	35 100 Shield Pack
3 50 Health Pack	13 Weapons Locker	24 Double Damage	36 Link ammo x4
4 Grenade ammo x2 (or Rocket ammo x2)	14 Health Vials x2	25 Sniper ammo x2	37 Flak ammo x2
5 Weapons Locker	15 Grenade ammo x2	26 100 Shield Pack	38 Weapons Locker x2
6 Weapons Locker	16 Health Vials x2	27 Link ammo x2	39 Health Vials x2
7 Grenade Launcher +2 ammo packs	17 Mini ammo x2	28 Flak ammo x2	40 Mine ammo x2
8 Shock ammo x2	18 Weapons Locker	29 Weapons Locker	41 Health Vials x2
9 Sniper ammo x2	19 Big Keg-O-Health	30 Health Vials x2	42 Sniper ammo x2
10 Bio ammo packs x2	20 Mine ammo x2	31 Grenade ammo x2	43 Shock ammo x2
	21 Weapons Locker x2, Link ammo x4, and Health Vials x4	32 Health Vials x2	44 100 Shield Pack
		33 Sniper ammo x2	45 Redeemer

Overview

Although Redplanet is a large level, the PowerNodes are few and spaced apart. Three different linked routes lead to your opponents' base. The Raptor is vital for patrolling and claiming distant PowerNodes before Scorpion and Manta backup can arrive. Employ a nasty Hellbender or two to fire along the vast canyons at distant PowerNodes and enemy vehicles.

Hard-Fought Onslaught: Level Check

Home Base

Links to: PowerNode #1

Vehicles Spawned: Goliath, Hellbender, Manta (x2), Raptor, Scorpion

Other Defenses: Energy Turrets (x3)

Available Weapons

Mine Layer (left side of base, near turret)

Grenade Launcher (right side of base, near turret)

Weapons Locker (left side of core, looking outward)

    Shock Rifle, Link Gun, AVRiL

Weapons Locker (right side of core, looking outward)

    Link Gun, Rocket Launcher, Sniper Rifle

Both bases are surrounded by roadways and rocks, so be extra vigilant. The main attack usually comes from PowerNode #1, across from your base, but be ready for surprise attacks from the rear. Find three health packs inside the base. Amateur attackers charge in from the "tusks" on three sides, while others sneak up the rocks on either side of the entrances.

PowerNode 1

Links to: PowerNode #2

Vehicles Spawned: Hellbender, Manta, Raptor, Scorpion

Other Defenses: Energy Turrets (x4)

Available Weapons

Weapons Locker (x2, either side of PowerNode, below structure)

    Link Gun, Minigun, AVRiL, Rocket Launcher

Don't forget the big keg-o-health at the base's rear and the two health vials by the PowerNode. Because three PowerNodes link here, this node is important to maintain. Keep a small defensive force here. There are only two main paths, so check both ways and stay alert.

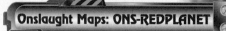

PowerNode 2

Links to: PowerNode #1

Vehicles Spawned: Manta (x2), Raptor, Scorpion

Other Defenses: Energy Turrets (x4)

Available Weapons

Weapons Locker (x2, either side of PowerNode, below structure)

Link Gun, AVRiL, Flak Cannon, Sniper Rifle

Similar to PowerNode #1 (but with a 100 shield pack behind the base), PowerNode #2 has more areas from which to attack. Combat usually begins here as you can reach either PowerNode #2 from your own side's PowerNode #2. The middle PowerNode isn't connected from here, but it is still an important strategic area to hold as you can quickly launch an attack on the enemy PowerNodes within seconds of claiming this.

Middle PowerNode

Links to: PowerNode #1

Vehicles Spawned: Goliath, Hellbender, Manta (x2), Scorpion

Other Defenses: Energy Turrets (x4)

Available Weapons

Weapons Locker (x2, either side of PowerNode, below structure)

Shock Rifle, Link Gun, Grenade Launcher, AVRiL

This node, with a turret at each corner, a double damage, and a 100 shield pack, is difficult to hold. Capture it, at least briefly, for the exceptional vehicles (including the Goliath and Hellbender).

Other Weapons

Redeemer

PowerNode to Joy: Planning Victory

Ready your Raptor for recon! While the rest of the team heads off to hold PowerNode #1, land at the middle PowerNode or by the redeemer. If you grab the redeemer, land on an upper rock ledge (or any safe spot), then pilot the rocket into the main concentration of foes.

Or drop in on the central PowerNode, and wait for the rest of your team to nab PowerNodes #1 and #2. Unless you're attacked by a load of enemies, you can hold off foes with the double damage and extra armor. Pick up the DD only when an enemy is near.

Don't underestimate the power of the Hellbender's turret. From far away at a path junction, or almost at an adjacent PowerNode, drive around until you spot a crack between the tusked columns of a PowerNode, and then blast it down in seconds from extreme range.

As there are three PowerNode-linking paths to victory, you can go almost an entire game without enemy incursions, and attack each other's bases simultaneously. Avoid this by sending out a Raptor while Scorpions or Mantas reach adjacent PowerNodes to link as soon as PowerNode #1 is done. Throw off your foes momentarily, then link up and attack the base, using the rocks as cover.

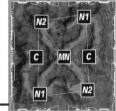

ONS-SEVERANCE

Recommended Players: 10–20

Legend

#	Item	#	Item	#	Item	#	Item
1	Weapons Locker	15	50 Health Pack	28	Weapons Locker	42	50 Health Pack x2
2	50 Health Pack x2	16	Weapons Locker	29	50 Shield Pack	43	50 Health Pack
3	50 Health Pack	17	50 Health Pack x2	30	50 Health Pack x4	44	Weapons Locker
4	50 Health Pack	18	Big Keg-O-Health	31	Weapons Locker	45	50 Health Pack x3
5	Double Damage	19	Weapons Locker and 50 Health Pack	32	Target Painter	46	Big Keg-O-Health (100 Shield Pack on opposite ruin)
6	Weapons Locker			33	50 Health Pack		
7	50 Health Pack x2	20	Weapons Locker	34	50 Health Pack	47	50 Health Pack
8	50 Health Pack x2	21	50 Health Pack	35	50 Health Pack	48	Weapons Locker
9	Weapons Locker	22	Double Damage	36	Weapons Locker	49	Weapons Locker
10	50 Health Pack x2	23	Weapons Locker	37	50 Health Pack	50	50 Health Pack
11	Weapons Locker	24	50 Health Pack	38	50 Health Pack	51	Weapons Locker
12	50 Health Pack	25	Weapons Locker	39	Weapons Locker	52	50 Health Pack
13	50 Health Pack	26	50 Health Pack x2	40	50 Health Pack x2	53	50 Health Pack
14	50 Health Pack	27	50 Health Pack	41	Weapons Locker	54	Weapons Locker

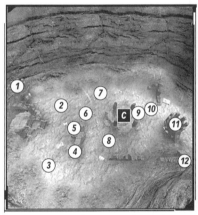

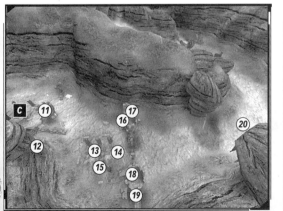

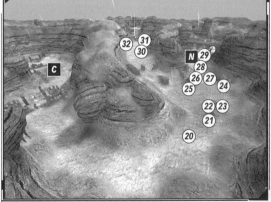

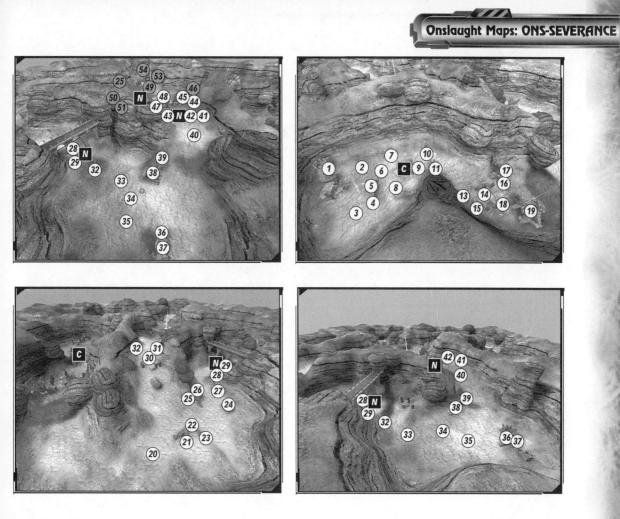

Overview

This base is surrounded by hills with one narrow pathway through the level to a PowerNode under a bridge. PowerNode #1 is extremely important because it links to either PowerNode #2. Don't forget the target painter! Scouts can camp out at various turrets. PowerNode #2 is on a plateau; perfect for long-range fire, while the middle PowerNode must be claimed for the mighty Leviathan!

Hard-Fought Onslaught: Level Check

Home Base

Links to: PowerNode #1

Vehicles Spawned: Goliath, Hellbender, Manta, Raptor, Scorpion (x2)

Other Defenses: Energy Turrets (x5)

233

Available Weapons

Weapons Locker (rear of base, left turret)
    Lightning Gun

Weapons Locker (rear of base, near Scorpion
   spawn and double damage)
    Grenade Launcher

Weapons Locker (behind the core)
    Link Gun, Mine Layer, AVRiL, Sniper Rifle

Weapons Locker (in front of the core)
    **Shock Rifle, Link Gun, AVRiL,
    Rocket Launcher**

Weapons Locker (top of turret in front of core)
    Flak Cannon

Weapons Locker (top of left turret at front
   of base)
    AVRiL

Weapons Locker (top of right turret at front
   of base)
    Shock Rifle, Mine Layer

The elongated home base has outer and inner tower defenses around the core, half-hidden inside a turret. Find seven health packs, plus single-weapon lockers in every turret. The double damage is in an arch near the main spawn point, but save it for when your base is being attacked. At the front of the base's inner part are two health packs plus five more by the twin turrets at the base's front, and a big keg-o-health. Defend from here and then fall back. Only one path leads out of the base.

PowerNode 1

Links to: Base, PowerNode #2 (both sides)

Vehicles Spawned: Hellbender, Manta (x2), Raptor

Other Defenses: None

Available Weapons

Target Painter (on ruined raised area next to
   PowerNode)

Weapons Locker (under bridge)
    Link Gun, Minigun, Flak Cannon

Find a double damage in an arch of a ruined building at the junction between the base and the PowerNode #1, the four health packs en route from the base to PowerNode #1, and the two health packs near the lone tower. The PowerNode lies under a tall arched bridge. Fly and land atop the bridge for a great sniping spot. Otherwise, this PowerNode is simply a link in the outer pathway. It is vital to take the target painter, as it is an ideal defensive weapon; use it or carry it to the next cluster of enemies. Push forward to the two turrets en route to PowerNode #2 to get six health packs. Stand your ground here, retreating to the PowerNode if you're overrun.

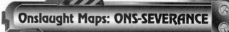

PowerNode 2

Links to: PowerNode #1 (both sides), Middle PowerNode

Vehicles Spawned: Goliath, Hellbender, Manta, Scorpion (x2)

Other Defenses: None

Available Weapons

Weapons Locker (x2, either side of PowerNode)

    Shock Rifle, Link Gun, Grenade Launcher, AVRiL

Weapons Locker (top of left turret, facing middle of map)

    AVRiL

Weapons Locker (top of left turret, facing middle of map)

    Shock Rifle, Mine Layer

PowerNode #2 overlooks the map's center and offers 10 health packs. Once you claim PowerNode #1, your team can link to either of the PowerNode #2s. This quickly shuts off your opposition so you can reach the all-important middle. One path runs straight through this area.

Middle PowerNode

Links to: PowerNode #2 (both sides)

Vehicles Spawned: Leviathan

Other Defenses: None

Available Weapons

Weapons Locker (next to PowerNode)

    Link Gun, Mine Layer , Rocket Launcher

The PowerNode is next to a pulsing purple light. Standing or riding over this destroys you. On either side of the PowerNode are temple ruins with a big keg-o-health or a 100 shield pack under them. Guard this higher ground and watch for incoming forces. The Leviathan that spawns once you own the PowerNode spells doom for your foes.

Other Weapons

Weapons Locker (x2)
  Grenade Launcher (one locker only),
  AVRiL (one locker only)
 	
Weapons Locker
  Mine Layer
	Weapons Locker
	  Grenade Launcher, AVRiL
	
	Weapons Locker
	  Mine Layer
	
	Weapons Locker
	  Lightning Gun
		Weapons Locker
		  Grenade Launcher, AVRiL
		
		Weapons Locker
		  Mine Layer

235

PowerNode to Joy: Planning Victory

All of the turrets contain a single weapon. Grab an AVRiL or grenade launcher in a turret overlooking an enemy PowerNode and try an interference run (ideally near PowerNode #2 or the middle) while the rest of your team conquers PowerNode #1 easily.

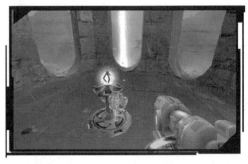

Have a teammate fly over a concentration of enemy forces and drop the target painter over their PowerNode #1. Keep a couple of friends at PowerNode #1 while the rest of the team marches on PowerNode #2. Either PowerNode #2 can be reached from PowerNode #1, so have your maverick tell you where the enemy is heading, and split your main forces to meet them at the opposing PowerNode, while a small force claims your PowerNode #2.

Claim the critical middle of the map and you can march on your opponents' base with the Leviathan, or at least decimate their PowerNodes en route. The enemy is too preoccupied with taking down this vehicle to cohesively destroy the middle PowerNode.

Drive the Hellbender to a junction, hide behind a large rock, and blast away from extreme range. From any of the four plateaus, park near cover and decimate enemies coming over the opposite brow. Or drive atop the crags. From the plateau, accelerate up the rock wall to the top; drive around the base perimeter blasting the core while your main force goes through the main entrance. Park three Scorpions around your opponents' base, then have a few vehicles attack from below to get the enemy away from the core. Move over the brow and decimate that base (this is possibly the only strategy to snatch victory if your opponent has the Leviathan).

ONS-TORLAN

Recommended Players: 8–16

Legend

1	Grenade Launcher +2 ammo packs	6	Lightning Gun +2 ammo packs	13	Double Damage
2	Mine Layer +2 ammo packs	7	50 Health Pack	14	Weapons Locker
3	50 Shield Pack	8	Weapons Locker	15	Weapons Locker
4	Weapons Locker	9	50 Health Pack	16	Big Keg-O-Health
5	Big Keg-O-Health (and Weapons Locker)	10	100 Shield Pack	17	50 Shield Pack
		11	Weapons Locker	18	Target Painter (top of tower)
		12	50 Health Pack		

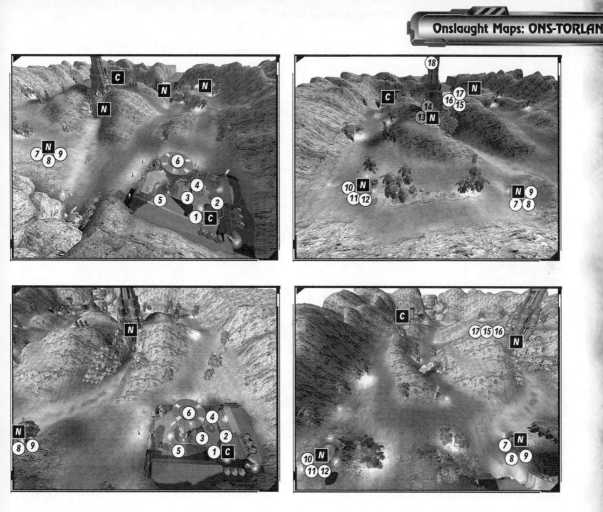

Overview

This medium-sized map has two PowerNodes on each side and a central PowerNode with a large tower above it. The level is open, meaning the Raptor and the Hellbender's turrets are more devastating. Carefully check how the PowerNodes link—both PowerNode #2s are linked, making a quick victory possible.

Hard-Fought Onslaught: Level Check

Home Base

Links to: PowerNode #1

Vehicles Spawned: Hellbender, Manta, Raptor

Other Defenses: Energy Turrets (x3)

Expect enemy attacks from the three main pathways converging on this area. Find a 50 shield pack and big keg-o-health on the raised platform near the base tower. Teleport to the top for a lightning gun and a commanding view. The covered and lowered core area is somewhat easier to defend because the enemy can't shoot it from far away.

Available Weapons

Grenade Launcher (small walkway next to and above the core)

AVRiL (small walkway next to and above the core)

Lightning Gun (on roof of tall central base tower)

Weapons Locker (x2, near either ground exit to base)

Shock Rifle, Link Gun, Flak Cannon

PowerNode 1

Links to: Base, PowerNode #2, Middle PowerNode

Vehicles Spawned: Manta, Scorpion

Other Defenses: Energy Turret

Available Weapons

Weapons Locker (next to PowerNode)

Minigun, Mine Layer, Link Gun

PowerNode #1 is to the west (red) or east (blue) of the main base. It offers two health packs on either side of the weapons locker, but no defenses aside from the turret. Holding this PowerNode is critical, so patrol with a force that can withstand enemy bombardment (or at least radio in for quick help). The enemy approaches on two main paths.

PowerNode 2

Links to: PowerNode #1, PowerNode #2 (opposite)

Vehicles Spawned: Goliath, Manta

Other Defenses: Energy Turret

Available Weapons

Weapons Locker (next to PowerNode)

Link Gun, Grenade Launcher, Lightning Gun

This PowerNode, with a 100 shield pack and health pack, is hugely strategic. It links to the PowerNode #2 at the opposite side, and if you can capture both, you can quickly swarm the enemy (the vehicles spawn on the enemy's side). The monumental Goliath battle tank appears only at this location. Trundle it to the enemy PowerNode #1, blast everything, then march to the base and victory!

Middle PowerNode

Links to: PowerNode #1

Vehicles Spawned: Hellbender, Manta, Raptor, Scorpion

Other Defenses: None

Available Weapons

Target Painter (top of tower, center of map)

Weapons Locker (x2, one next to PowerNode, one at structure on upper level, next to tower)

Shock Rifle, Link Gun, AVRiL

The main strength to this site is its easy defense (block the ravine and check the sides for enemies). It spawns vehicles above, inside, and to the side of the PowerNode. To the side is a triple-pod platform with 50 shield pack and a big keg-o-health where the rest of the vehicles spawn. Use the central tower as a landmark, and fly the Raptor to the top for a 100 shield pack and the target painter.

Other Weapons

> **None**

PowerNode to Joy: Planning Victory

Immediately fly the Raptor to the central tower's top and grab the target painter. Now decimate the opposition moving toward PowerNode #1; drop those bombs while your team treks to its first PowerNode. With the enemy in disarray, claim either the center PowerNode or PowerNode #2.

A parked Hellbender's turret gun can demolish PowerNode #2's energy turret from halfway across the map. Get a clean shot from the north-south path at the maps' edge. Defend PowerNode #1 constantly, and react to the enemy. If they head to the center PowerNode, build up PowerNode #2 and use the tank to maximum effect. Link PowerNodes directly from the north and south PowerNode #2s. Send a force to claim the enemy's PowerNode #2 just as your PowerNode #2 comes online.

To attack the base you should own at least one of the PowerNode #2 areas. If you take the opposition's, the tank can strike down PowerNode #1 quickly, then aim at enemies rushing out of the main base. The Hellbender and the Goliath's main guns can take out turrets and vehicles inside the base from PowerNode #2! Attack from across and below at the enemy base. Get your Raptor pilot in on the fun because the base's core is easier to shoot from above (you can even land on your opponent's tower and blast the core!).

Unreal TOURNAMENT 2004

Deathmatch Maps

NOTE

Deathmatch maps are also used in Invasion, Last Man Standing, Mutant, and Team Deathmatch game modes. Although this strategy focuses on Deathmatch play, elements work in other submodes.

DM-1on1-ALBATROSS

Recommended Players: 2–2

Legend

1	Health Vials x3 (path to Flak Cannon)
2	Flak Cannon +1 Ammo Pack
3	Shock and Lightning ammo pack (ledge)
4	100 Shield Pack (end of tunnel)
5	Rocket Launcher +1 ammo pack (linking tunnel)
6	Link Gun + 1 ammo pack
7	Health Vials x3 (tunnel)
8	Minigun and 1 ammo pack
9	Mini and flak ammo (tunnel ledge)
10	Health Vials x3 (tunnel)
11	Health Vials x3 (curved ramp)
12	50 Health Pack (curved ramp)
13	Double Damage (top of folly)
14	Bio and mini ammo pack (curved ramp)
15	Health Vials x3 (curved ramp)
16	Shock and flak ammo packs (base of elevator)
17	50 Shield Pack (wooden plank)
18	50 Health Pack (near elevator)
19	Shock Rifle +1 ammo pack (base of elevator)
20	50 Health Pack (near elevator)
21	50 Health Pack (base of elevator)
22	Biorifle +1 ammo pack
23	Shock and rocket ammo packs
24	Health Vials x3
25	Lightning Gun +1 ammo pack (upper ledge)

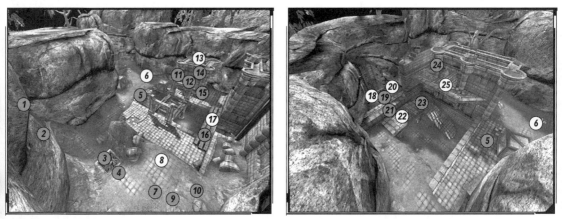

Overview

Albatross, named after the bird statues atop the ruined stonework, can be split into three sections. The main area with the crumbling wooden bridge and ropes is ideal for escaping to a narrow stream area below. Most dashing occurs near the 50 shield pack (by the lift), the double damage atop the tiny folly (a small fort structure), and the sewer courtyard (leading to a passage and a 100 shield pack). A rocket launcher stored in a small tunnel links the sewer area to an outside dell.

The third section is the dell, a small grassy courtyard where you're susceptible to enemy fire. A ramp leads to a biorifle or to an exit underneath to a shock rifle and a second lift. The ramp ends at a junction. To the right is a partially hidden alcove with the flak cannon and a lookout onto the bridged area. To the left is a large crate (useful for cover) and a main thoroughfare leading back to the bridge area, or ahead and left to a stone ruin with a lightning gun at the top.

Available Weapons

Biorifle (middle of steps near elevator, under lightning gun)

Shock Rifle (in tunnel to ramp, lower ground, under biorifle)

Link Gun (on grassy area near DD folly, overlooking bridge)

Minigun (on rocky raised corner overlooking bridge)

Flak Cannon (on rocky raised area overlooking bridge)

Rocket Launcher (under grassy area, in middle of central tunnel)

Lightning Gun (on high ledge above the grassy courtyard)

Available Power-ups

Double Damage (atop folly above bridge)

50 Shield Pack (wooden side plank near elevator, right side of bridge)

100 Shield Pack (end of curved underground stone tunnel)

Map Patrol

The double damage rotates on top of the folly near the wooden bridge. Four methods allow access to this important power-up. Method #1: Execute a lift jump from the lift adjacent to the folly, by the 50 shield pack. Control your airborne movement and land atop the folly without using the bridge. Method #2: Leap on the rope beside the bridge linking the stone columns, and double jump to the top of both columns, then up and onto the folly. Time the jumps correctly. This takes longer, leaving you open to attack. Method #3: When you've taken the lightning gun,

or you're on one of the bridge columns, dodge jump or double jump to the crate near the bridge, and then shield jump onto the folly, or double jump back onto the column nearest the folly and up into it. Method #4: Shield jump from the ground near the folly (upper ground rather than the sewer area), watching out for the gap in the stonework at the folly's front.

The vital shield pack is in a high-traffic area but easy to grab. Either run across the narrow stonework or ride the lift up, step off, and grab it. You could leap across from the bridge too; to avoid upper level fire, drop quickly to the sewer sublevel.

The 100 shield pack is in an out-of-the-way zone, under the folly in the sewer area. Run into the underground passage left of the lift, or right of the ramped grass area leading out of the sewers, around the folly. Or reach the passage entrance by dropping to the area under the bridge or enter it from near the rocket launcher. Once inside the passage, you are fairly safe.

Grab the shield pack atop a ledge leading to a short drop to the sewer stream. This is the only other exit, and may be guarded. Drop flak cannon blasts from below, pointing up at the shield pack, hunt the enemy from behind, or fire rockets or biorifle projectiles from the open grating above the exit drop into the sewer stream. The grating is next to the minigun pick-up point.

Find health packs behind the folly, on the grassy ramp leading to the sewer area. The six health vials (three on either side of the pack) make it advantageous to keep running back to this spot while securing the shield packs.

The most critical area for grabbing health packs is by the shock rifle and second lift, away from most of the action. One is by the shock rifle. Reach the two others by double jumping over the biorifle or after riding the lift. Guard this area if your opponents lack health.

Find health vials on the ramp up to the lightning gun, three more in the alcove entrance to the flak cannon, three in the bridge's middle (jump from the sides and drop into the sewer area, as these are out in the open), and six vials en route to the 100 shield pack. Snag these last six first.

A relatively safe vantage point near the bridge holds a minigun and one ammo pack. The large rock provides ample cover and enemies can attack only from below or from the flak cannon pick-up point. Reach the minigun by lift jumping, double or dodge jumping up the short hill, or after nabbing the flak cannon.

Grabbing this weapon can be stressful due to the lack of exits. Thankfully, most of the action occurs away from here. It's very close to the biorifle, so you can quickly grab a couple of pieces of firepower. Find shock core ammo and a health pack near the lift, behind the shock rifle.

The link gun and link charges, in a main thoroughfare by the crates, are picked up quickly. Snag the link gun and then move to cover. Or leave the link gun as bait for an ambush. Vary your escape route using the multiple exits (up to the lightning gun, down into the sewer, behind either crate, or down to the rocket launcher).

The biorifle, halfway up the ramp to the main grassy area from the courtyard, is very much out in the open. Snag the extra rockets near the biorifle and ammo. Approach from the lift or double (or dodge) jump up the ramp.

The flak cannon is a must-have, and there are two ways to enter the alcove where it lies: from the ramp's top leading to the biorifle or crates, or double or dodge jump over the short uphill ground near the minigun.

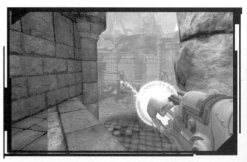

Grab this powerful weapon before your rivals do. The short tunnel with the rocket launcher joins the courtyard to the sewers. Head across and left, into the sewer passage to the 100 shield pack, as soon as you snag this.

Also grab the lightning gun early on. Pass the wind chime sound, ascend the grassy bank near the link gun, and grab the gun. Check for foes by looking (or leaping) through the gap to the left in the ruins as you ascend. The ledge makes a reasonable sniping spot.

Appropriate ammunition is placed next to every weapon—get it before your foes do. First scan the passage leading to the 100 shield pack. Find a rocket pack and flak shells halfway up the passage on a wall ledge to the left. At the end of the passage are lightning ammo and a shock core. You can single jump back to the passage from the ledge.

Find 50 bullets and a biorifle pack on the grassy ramp near the folly, and a shock core and rocket launcher ammunition to the minigun's right, up the ramp from the courtyard.

Deathmatch Dealing

Use both lifts, employing a lift jump to scare your enemy with aerial takedowns. From the lift near the folly, land on the double damage, the minigun or the link gun, then land on the bridge and escape toward the flak cannon or down to the sewers. The other lift jump allows you to double back and tackle pursuers from the rocket launcher area.

If you're stuck in a war of attrition in the lower courtyard, find the less obvious escape routes. Dodge jump up the left rock slope, avoiding the ramp to the minigun, and then flee to the flak cannon or the crates.

The exposed middle section contains crates that offer cover (it's better to be on the link gun side of the arena). Leap on the larger crate and then dodge or double jump to the lightning gun ledge. Or, double jump onto the crate from the rubble near the link gun. Try shield jumping from the grass near the bigger crate straight to the lightning gun ledge.

The shield jump can launch you out of some sticky situations if you have the health to spare. Vary your attacking strategy, attempt a surprise, or move out of the sewers by shield jumping up through the gaps in the stonework or bridge above to land in the upper grassy area.

Be aware of where you can expect the most combat. Many players use the area near the crates to reach the biorifle courtyard or the sewer and bridge, as well as the flak and lightning guns. If an enemy patrols near the crates, take the route around by the flak cannon.

The enclosed sewer area, especially in the passage leading to the shield pack or by the stream, provides an ideal opportunity to unload with your flak cannon.

The final choke point, aside from the lift leading to the shield pack, is the rocket launcher. It's the main route to the sewer. Collect the minigun and shock rifle as backup weapons, and then from the other lift, train your rockets on those attempting to sprint through this dangerous area.

After you locate the double damage, and ideally if you have the lightning gun, stand atop the folly and shoot from this elevated position; retreat to the middle of the folly to avoid return fire. You're safe from most incoming rounds unless fired from a biorifle, or from the biorifle or lightning gun pick-up location.

243

A second spot, reached only via the translocator, is a tiny area of the rock wall surrounding the arena, behind the folly. There's no room to move (leap to the folly roof if you're spotted), but it provides a good vantage point. Drop onto the health vials and packs.

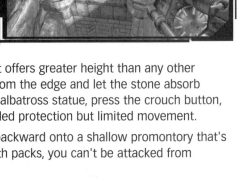

The lightning gun location is a great place to maneuver, although you are prone to attack from all directions. Retreat into the ruins to avoid gunfire or use one of the numerous escape routes.

A better sniping spot is the top of the ruins, above the lightning gun, and reached by translocator or shield jump. It offers greater height than any other camping spot and a view of most of the stage. Step back from the edge and let the stone absorb counterattacks. Fire your translocator onto the back of the albatross statue, press the crouch button, then teleport and sit on the back of the bird, giving you added protection but limited movement.

If you're using the second lift, near the shock rifle, step backward onto a shallow promontory that's ideal for sniping or hiding. You're a short fall from two health packs, you can't be attacked from anywhere except in front, and there's room to move!

From the vantage point atop the lift, or the lightning gun ledge, or the top of the ruins, double jump (from the brickwork around the lift or from the albatross statue roof) or shield jump (from the lightning gun ledge) to some upper brickwork above and to one side of the biorifle. From here, take out anyone attempting to run to the flak cannon or lightning gun, or fire into the rocket launcher area or down to the biorifle.

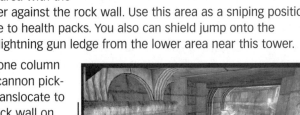

Face inward from this high brick ledge, and then double jump across or shield jump from the area with the two health packs, and land on a broken tower against the rock wall. Use this area as a sniping position until you're spotted. Once again, you're close to health packs. You also can shield jump onto the brickwork atop the second lift and onto the lightning gun ledge from the lower area near this tower.

An under-used sniping is the crumbling stone column propped against the rock wall near the flak cannon pick-up. Shield jump halfway up the column, or translocate to the top, and then drop down to a sliver of rock wall on the outer edge.

Set up camp on the ledge opposite the 100 shield pack in the sewer area to watch for chumps attempting to grab the shield pack. You can be spotted by those entering the sewer from the central area.

DM-1on1-DESOLATION

Recommended Players: 2–3

Legend

1	50 Health Pack	**14**	Link and flak ammo (lower corridor)
2	Minigun +2 ammo packs	**15**	Shock, mini, rocket ammo packs
3	Health Vials x3	**16**	Link ammo packs x2
4	Flak ammo packs x2	**17**	Flak Cannon
5	Link Gun	**18**	Adrenaline Pills x3
6	Health Vials x4 (grassy path)	**19**	Shock ammo pack x2
7	50 Health Pack	**20**	Double Damage
8	Adrenaline Pills x3	**21**	Link and flak ammo packs
9	Mini and rocket ammo packs	**22**	50 Health Pack
10	Link and flak ammo (top corner)	**23**	Health Vials x4
11	50 Health Pack (top corner)	**24**	Link and flak ammo packs
12	Rocket Launcher	**25**	Lightning gun
13	50 Health Pack (lower corridor)		

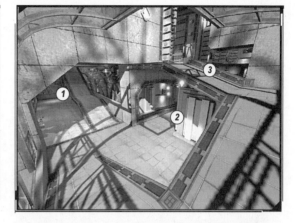

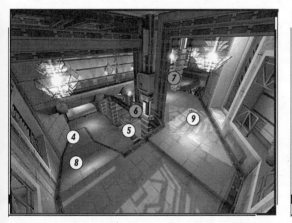

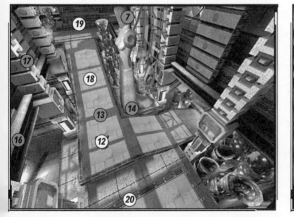

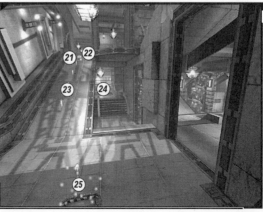

Overview

This square level contains a warren of corridors. The central ramp with the double damage ledge above is the usual combat location. Learn this two-level greenhouse map completely. Spend time in corners, watching for the enemy. Constant moving and flak cannon carnage are advisable.

Available Weapons	Rocket Launcher (flat area of main central ramp)
Shock Rifle (upper corridor near open windows)	**Lightning Gun** (corner of level, near ramp and double corridor)
Link Gun (lower double corridor near ramp)	**Available Power-ups**
Minigun (stepped fountain corridor)	**Double Damage** (on ledge overlooking central ramp)
Flak Cannon (upper corridor near double ramp)	

Map Patrol

Starting at the double damage overlooking the main ramp and working down, notice the rocket launcher on the ramp below, with three adrenaline pills on the ramp up to the top floor, across from the DD. The rocket launcher area is the main junction for the lower area. Around the top floor, turn right (if you're facing the ramp), and proceed around the left turn and upper walkway. Before you turn the corner, head down a ramp through four health vials to a lightning gun.

Turn the corner and move along the upper walkway. Find flak and minigun ammo packs, then a shock rifle. Two open windows on the main ground-level corridor are perfect for dropping presents on your foe! Turn the left corner to see a health pack on your right at a junction; on your left, the ramp leads to the rocket launcher and adrenaline pills.

Quickly check out the area near the health pack to see a short ramp on your left leading down, a walkway with minigun and rocket ammo packs, then a ramp to the ground floor. A gap near the ammo packs overlooks the ramp. Follow this ramp to the main corridor (under the open windows) and a link gun.

Pass the ramp to the rocket launcher and notice a gap to your right with odd plants poking up. This opening descends to the short ramp near the health pack. At the corner of the walkway, a route leads left, down a long enclosed upper corridor with a flak cannon and two link ammo packs, or an open-air double ramp to the ground floor, with three health vials.

The end of the corridor with the flak cannon contains a health pack. Turn left, pass link and flak ammo packs, and you're back at the double damage ledge. Take the left ledge overlooking the rocket launcher, or the corridor to the right for better cover, and the first ramp you saw down to the lightning gun.

Work counterclockwise around the main level from the lightning gun. Continue through the doorway into a double corridor. In the raised right area there are rocket, shock, and mini ammo packs, and a small drop to a corridor running past a ramp on your left (leading to the rocket launcher). There's also a ramp to a linking corridor under the main ramp with a link and flak ammo pack and a health pack. Above the double corridor are the two open windows.

Through the doorway at the double corridor's end, find the ramp with the open view leading to the upper health pack. The link gun is here, with two flak ammo packs at the ramp's base and three adrenaline pills up the ramp. Continue left past the ramp and turn the corner. A grassy lower-level path has four health vials and a doorway, which joins the linking corridor under the main central ramp with the health pack.

Continue along the ground route, past a health pack, and pass under the short ramp. At this ramp's end (find rocket, shock, and mini ammo packs along the right wall), look up to see the plant matter gap on the upper floor. Continue past the short ramp to the map's corner, to the double ramp's end and a doorway to your left.

The left corridor leads to a minigun and two ammo packs with a stepped fountain on your right. Head along this stepped corridor to a junction with a pillar in the middle. The left route leads to the health pack under the main ramp; the ramp on the right leads to the area underneath the double damage, by the rocket launcher. Double jump to reach the launcher from this area, or leap onto the bottom of the central ramp (leading to the double corridor), or head through one of the two doorways on your right. This final area contains link and flak ammo

packs and leads to a health pack and a small set of steps under the ramp leading to the lightning gun.

Deathmatch Dealing

Only the minigun has ammo packs nearby, so you'll survive longer in a close-quarter scrap if you immediately grab this weapon. The link gun is next to the flak ammo and vice versa, so watch your ammo consumption.

Head to the area near the double damage and rocket launcher at the start and lay a trap. Or set up in a sniping position (such as the double corridor, which has a fantastic view through the undergrowth) and wait for

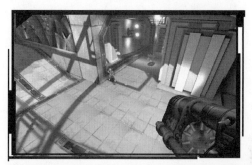

your opponent. Run down the central ramp and double jump to the plants to the right of the ramp's base, and then onto the DD ledge. Facing up the ramp from the rocket launcher, double jump onto the plants to the right, and drop to the grassy path.

Pick up as many vials and pills as possible; this is extremely important. This Deathmatch involves constant chasing and close-quarter fighting, so learn your routes. For example, zigzag if you're being chased down the flak cannon corridor, then make a left at the end. If you're far enough away, turn and devastate with the flak or drop down to the rocket launcher. Plan to lose a pursuer and turn the tables.

Make the most of the vantage points and cover. At the ramp to the lightning gun, sidestep and blast an enemy near the shock rifle from partial cover. Blast enemies with the lightning gun or shock rifle from either of the open windows, then optionally drop down and finish them. Drop flak grenades from the open ramps (near the link gun and the double ramp). Drop ordnance from the plant opening or leap down from it. Drop from the opening halfway down the central ramp to your left; you land near the double corridor and can scurry under the central ramp, down the health vial grassy path, or into the double corridor. Camp under the short ramp or the double ramp, at the fountain near the minigun, or at the corner with the pillar.

Translocating isn't an advantage in this stage. Concentrate on dropping from above. The main area is the DD ledge, but try positioning yourself over the top of the short ramp, on the lip above, or on the lip surrounding the bottom of the short ramp, accessed via the plant gap.

DM-1on1-IDOMA

Recommended Players: 2–3

Legend

1	Adrenaline Pills x3	8	Biorifle + 2 ammo packs (in tunnel)
2	50 Health Pack	9	50 Health Pack
3	Flak Cannon +2 ammo packs	10	Link Gun +2 ammo packs
4	Health Vials x4	11	Shock Rifle +2 ammo packs
5	Rocket Launcher +2 ammo packs	12	Health Vials x4
6	Minigun +1 ammo pack	13	Lightning Gun +2 ammo packs
7	Adrenaline Pills x3	14	100 Shield Pack

Overview

With wider corridors and longer areas to dash about in, Idoma is a sniper's paradise. Holding the ledge and lightning gun area assumes paramount importance. An outer corridor weaves almost completely around the exterior, with an adjacent lower floor and walkway zone. The main bottlenecks are the exits to the central tunnel.

Available Weapons

Biorifle (in middle of lower tunnel)

Shock Rifle (end of lower tunnel, in water-logged ground)

Link Gun (outer alcove opposite corridor to middle balcony)

Minigun (iron flooring area, parallel to outer corridor)

Flak Cannon (long outer corridor)

Rocket Launcher (end of lower tunnel, in waterlogged ground)

Lightning Gun (outer corridor, near shield pack)

Available Power-ups

50 Shield Pack

Map Patrol

Starting at the 50 shield pack on the large upper wooden ledge, double jump to the map's lower middle or to the lowest ground area near the central tunnel, where you find a shock rifle and two ammo packs. Or run right, through a large archway, to a lightning gun and two ammo packs. At the corner, turn left to a long outer corridor running the length of the level.

Head into the corridor to an opening on your left. This leads to a parallel area heading to the map's middle and to a ramp leading down to the shock rifle. You can see the shield pack on the starting ledge from here. The rest of the outer corridor leads to a flak cannon and two ammo packs. The parallel wooden floor leads to a minigun, one ammo pack, and an opening to the map's middle with three adrenaline pills. At the end of this flooring is a health pack to the left of the top planks.

249

Turn left at the outer corridor's end, and see a health pack and planks of wood on your left. Dodge or double jump onto the short wall. Follow the outer corridor across and descend a ramp with three adrenaline pills. To the left, the parallel flooring ends in a ramp with four health vials. These lead to a watery lower ground with a rocket launcher and two ammo packs. On the upper corridor, the ramp ends and doubles back to a ramp leading to the rocket launcher.

Through the archway on the left wall lies a crossroads. The left path leads to a corridor and a set of stairs up to the stage's middle. To the right is a small alcove with a link gun and two ammo packs. Ahead is another archway. Step through here and turn left at the health pack, and you'll see the starting point on your right. Down a ramp is the shock rifle.

The map's middle has two floors. The upper one is a balcony with a large central wall piece. On either side is a large opening, allowing you to see the ramp with the adrenaline pills over the rocket launcher, or the shield pack ledge over the shock rifle. The two corridors connect (from the link gun in a straight line to the entrance with the three adrenaline pills and the minigun flooring area). In the map's lower middle, a tunnel leads from the shock rifle to the rocket launcher. Find a biorifle and two ammo packs in the tunnel's center.

Deathmatch Dealing

The long corridors and larger areas lend themselves to the lightning gun. Pick it up as soon as the action starts. Use precise but powerful blasts, as the corridors are a little too long for the closer weapons.

You can dodge jump from the upper middle balcony to the shield pack (and back again), so you don't have to traipse around the outer upper corridor. You can quickly reach the shield pack by dodge or double jumping to the middle balcony, even from across the level. Even better is your lightning gun range: aim from the adrenaline pill ramp to the shield pack area or down the flak cannon corridor.

The next best weapon is the shock rifle. It's great for taking down enemies going for the biorifle, or to cheapshot foes attempting to grab the rocket launcher. However, the area on either side of the tunnel is a high-traffic zone and leaves you extremely prone. Stand here for only a second (shield jump up the boxes behind the rocket launcher or lurk in the shadows for some cover). The tunnel is a choke point trap, and biorifle goop won't block the large corridors.

Watch a foe run from the adrenaline pill ramp to the link gun to the top of the ramp leading to the shock rifle; have a trio of rockets waiting for him as he arrives. Turn left from the shield pack and move around the lip of the wall so you're above the health pack, looking down into the link gun alcove area. This camp spot offers an excellent panorama and good escape potential.

Translocating doesn't help much here, but you can reach the ceiling struts above the shock rifle or rocket launcher for a marvelous sniping spot. Leap to the lip above the top of the ramps, too (you can reach this area with low grav and quad jump on).

DM-1on1-IRONDUST

Recommended Players: 2–8

Unreal Tournament 2004

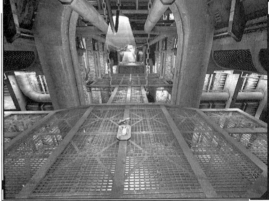

Legend

1	Flak Cannon	10	Lightning Gun
2	50 Shield Pack	11	Health Vials x5
3	Flak and rocket ammo packs	12	Double Damage
4	Link Gun	13	Rocket Launcher
5	Shock and link ammo packs	14	50 Health Packs x2
6	50 Health Packs x2	15	Shock, mini, lightning ammo packs
7	Mini and lightning ammo packs	16	Health Vials x5
8	Minigun	17	Shock Rifle
9	100 Shield Pack		

Overview

The more the players, the crazier the match becomes. Four elevators in separate corners of a T-shaped dual-level ironworks link the midsections, which are mid-sized corridors usually ending in a T-junction. The lower path generally mimics the upper one. The main thoroughfare is the area between the lightning gun, rocket launcher, shield packs, and double damage. Expect most of the action (and the winning player) to be here.

Available Weapons

Shock Rifle (T-junction opposite double damage)

Link Gun (T-junction under 100 shield pack)

Minigun (T-junction near 100 shield pack, above link gun)

Flak Cannon (T-junction along from 50 shield pack, near link gun)

Rocket Launcher (T-junction near wide upper walkway)

Lightning Gun (opposite end of wide upper walkway from rocket launcher, above double damage)

Available Power-ups

Double Damage (end of walkway below lightning gun, middle of level)

50 Shield Pack (corner near elevator and flak cannon, below lightning gun)

100 Shield Pack (large upper walkway near minigun)

Map Patrol

From the top of this two-floor ironworks, the middle section has a 100 shield pack by an elevator and a junction at the passage's opposite end. You can look down the side of the elevator shaft to a passage below, and even spot the next junction (left and right of the passage). This is viewed through gaps that look down onto a link gun on the next floor. You can drop down here. Through the two-archway junction from the shield pack are left and right passages with a minigun in the middle.

Head left at the minigun and trot around a right-bending corridor with mini and lightning ammo packs in the middle. Step onto a mesh platform through which you cannot shoot. Look through the mesh and see a 50 shield pack below and ahead of you. An elevator to your left moves you down to this point. Also on the mesh is a lightning gun. Turn right to see a wide corridor with five health vials.

Back at the minigun, head right under an arched doorway to an elevator to your right. Turn left to reach a junction with a rocket launcher and two health packs in an alcove on the right wall. Before you reach there, you can peer through the mesh floor, and even shoot through the gap to the right (which is too thin to fall down). Turn left at the rocket launcher to the wide iron corridor with the five health vials. Just ahead of the rocket launcher is another elevator.

In the middle of the wide corridor you can peer over or fall off the ledge to the ground below. The rock and mud area leads to a thin walkway and a double damage. The double damage is below the lightning gun. Drop down here to check the lower level.

Opposite the double damage is a rocky connecting area and a T-junction with a shock rifle. To the right are five health vials and an elevator leading to the junction with the arched door, near the rocket launcher. To the left is an elevator leading to the area near the rocket launcher—the quicker route to this zone.

253

On either side of the walkway to the double damage is rocky mud flooring. On the near wall are lightning, shock, and mini ammo packs. On the opposite side, two arched exits lead to the rest of the lower floor. Once through there, a passage runs left and right. Follow the junction left up a mud ramp to a right turn corridor and another right turn with shock and link ammo in the corner. The passage opens up to a T-junction with a link gun. There's a passage ahead to the left. Walk left down a passage to an elevator that goes to the 100 shield pack where you began.

Head right at the junction near the double damage drop-off; you pass flak and rocket ammo on your right and a T-junction with a flak cannon in the middle. Turn left and run up the steps for two health packs and a left turn. Head left to join the link gun T-junction.

Back at the flak cannon, head right to a 50 shield pack and an elevator to your left. This rises to the mesh walkway and the lightning gun, completing the level. Remember that you can see enemies above you here.

Deathmatch Dealing

Death dealing occurs in the area next to the lightning gun and rocket launcher as everyone waits for the double damage to respawn. Make sure you're there first! Move to the double damage, then to the 50 shield pack, and then up the adjacent elevator to the lightning gun and the 100 shield pack.

Control this area. When the double damage is recharging, patrol the upper concourse, completing your health vial collection and dealing with any enemy menace. The wide corridors discourage ambushes and allow escape (but with the increased weapon damage and armor, this shouldn't be a problem).

Secure extra lightning gun ammo under the double damage walkway and at the bend near the gun. En route to the 50 shield pack, grab the rockets at the right side of the lower junction near the double damage.

If you're adamant about using other weapons, patrol the lower ground with the shock rifle, and always look up if your enemy is upstairs. Combo through the mesh floor for a devastating strike. Know where to drop down (the area near the 100 shield pack for example) if you're being chased. Listen for elevators moving—the sound gives your opponent away. But be careful; he may be setting a trap. You should, too!

Bounce flak cannon grenades from the gaps along the mesh portions of the top corridors. Have even more fun with a translocator. Shoot it up from the 100 shield pack and stand on the edge of a red glowing cage high above, or walk along the chain that links it to the archway's top. Translocate onto the pipes above the rocket launcher or to any area with an open ceiling and set up an ambush.

DM-1on1-ROUGHINERY

Recommended Players: 2–2

Legend

1 Double Damage	**7** Adrenaline Pills x5	**13** Flak and lightning ammo packs	**19** Shock, flak, rocket ammo packs
2 Rocket Launcher	**8** Minigun	**14** Link Gun +2 ammo packs	**20** Health Vials x4
3 50 Shield Pack	**9** Rocket ammo packs x2	**15** 100 Shield Packs (basement)	**21** 50 Health Packs x2
4 50 Health Packs x2	**10** Lightning Gun	**16** Health Vials x5 (basement)	**22** Shock ammo packs x2
5 Mini ammo packs x2	**11** Biorifle +2 ammo packs	**17** 50 Health Packs x2	**23** Shock Rifle
6 50 Health Packs x2	**12** 50 Shield Packs	**18** Flak Cannon +1 ammo pack	

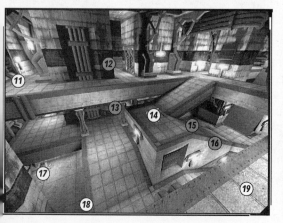

Overview

Compact and clustered with ledges and corridors, Roughinery is an ambusher's delight. The three main levels mask three main locations through which to fight. First is the 50 shield pack area, with a shock rifle below. Next is the minigun zone, complete with an elevator leading to a couple of neat upper places. Finally, the rocket launcher area boasts the heavier weapons and the double damage. A 100 shield pack is in an L-shaped basement that can usually become a tomb because it has only one exit but four entrances.

Available Weapons

Biorifle (on upper ledge around corner from 50 shield pack)

Shock Rifle (middle of red mesh, ground floor)

Link Gun (halfway up the double ramp)

Minigun (on ledge near elevator)

Flak Cannon (on ground, near hole to basement)

Rocket Launcher (on ledge under double damage)

Lightning Gun (on upper ledge near double damage)

Available Power-ups

50 Shield Pack (upper walkway path, above shock rifle)

100 Shield Pack (middle of L-shaped basement)

Double Damage (end of upper alcove, above rocket launcher)

Map Patrol

Starting atop this maze of narrow walkways, at one end of a narrow walkway with a 50 shield pack, turn right; access this area via a small ramp against the exterior wall with four health vials. Below this ramp, an undulating outer walkway contains two health packs, and the bottom floor has a shock rifle on a red mesh square.

Continue past the 50 shield pack, noting the parallel ramp to your left leading to this level. Ahead is a junction and the path goes straight or right. Head right around a large pillar to find the biorifle and two ammo packs. The path rejoins the straight route at a T-junction overlooking a series of ramps and a link gun below.

Turn left and continue to a crossroads. To the left is the ramp down to the lower level. To the right is a walkway with a ramp on your right, adjacent to the top ledge, leading to the link gun. Head along the right walkway to a T-junction. To the right is a small ledge with lightning, rocket, and shock ammo packs. To the left is a lightning gun and a ramp (as you turn the corner, you see a double damage at the end of an upper walkway) that leads down and left to a rocket launcher on a lower alcove.

If you take the road at the crossroads, you enter an open walkway. Look left and down to see a minigun, ammo, and two health packs on the ground far below. To the right, a walkway below leads to a leaning stone. You can dodge jump up the stone to the walkway you're on. Across from the walkway is the lightning gun, and ahead to the right is the rocket launcher on a lower alcove.

At the end of the walkway is a T-junction. Left is an outer walkway to a dead-end (and a drop to the left) with five adrenaline pills. To the right is a short walkway to the double damage. Remember this route to the power-up; your life will depend on it!

Back at the 50 shield pack, head down the ramp with the four health vials to the corner of the mid-level area. Left is a dip with two health packs. Right is a narrow ledge leading to an area overlooking a flak cannon. In the middle is a ramp to the ground and the shock rifle. Run over the health packs to reach an L-shaped junction with a ramp in the middle, to the right. This leads up to the walkway near the 50 shield pack.

The left mid-level route leads up a short ramp to an elevator and a minigun, with a view of much of the ground level. The outer ledge at mid-level continues to a ledge (with minigun ammo packs) overlooking the same area. Follow the ledge under the ledge with the adrenaline pills. An exit ramp to the ground is on your right, and ahead a ramp leads up to the rocket launcher and upper ramp to the lightning gun.

TIP

Elevator jump from the lift platform onto a high platform to the right where you can camp. Or, elevator jump over to the upper ledge containing the adrenaline pills for a cunning way to reach the double damage!

Back at the L-shaped junction, move down the right path with the ramp on your left to reach the middle maze. Under the ramp is a junction. Head left up a small ramp and left again to the minigun. Head left, then right, to pass under a walkway leading to the double damage. Then turn left to leap up the leaning stone slab. The end of the ledge looks out with the rocket launcher on your left.

Head right at the junction under the ramp, and you immediately come to a right turn. Ahead is a drop to a double ramp. To the right is a junction leading to a tiny ledge with flak and lightning ammo packs. From a drop-off area near the flak cannon, under the biorifle, head back to the shock rifle.

Unreal
TOURNAMENT
2004

Drop onto the double ramp and follow it up for the link gun and two ammo, and take the top walkway to the double damage. Turn left and dodge jump up the leaning stone, leading to a view of the rocket launcher and the upper leaning stone slab. Right of this is a ramp to the ground floor and two rocket ammo packs, almost under the launcher. A final ramp is above the double ramp, leading to two health packs on the ground floor.

Going around the ground floor counterclockwise from the shock rifle, note the thoroughfares to the right and left. The left has two shock ammo packs and a junction. Head left to a support column area with the elevator to the minigun or right to an area with two health packs on the left. The right path at the junction goes to a second opening that leads to the health packs and a ledge overlooking the basement.

Head into the open area for a ramp to the left (leading to the rocket launcher if you take it and turn right), and a ramp cut into the ground on your right. This leads to the basement L-shaped corridor and 100 shield pack. At the open area's far end are the two rocket ammo packs under the launcher and the ramp up to the link gun. Follow the ground passage around to the right.

The passage ends at a junction. Right is a ramp up to the link gun ramped area. Left is a hole that's another entrance to the basement and five health vials leading to the 100 shield pack. Head down there or jump over it to the flak cannon and ammo pack, two floors below the biorifle. Follow the passage around until it opens up, with two health packs on your left.

Ahead is the thoroughfare opening to the shock rifle, completing the circuit. Turn right at the health packs, and see a gap to the left, and up to the right. The right ramp leads to the link gun ramped area. The left gap allows you to drop onto the 100 shield pack in the basement, and offers a good view of the ramp down to this area. The other gap overlooking the basement is ahead and left.

Deathmatch Dealing

With this complex of walkways in such a confined area, learning where you are takes longer than usual. But learn you must, especially the leaps to the level's top. Memorize the quickest way to the rocket launcher, the 100 shield pack, the 50 shield pack, and then the double damage. Acquire these weapons (substituting the rocket launcher for the flak cannon or lightning gun as you see fit) to rule this map.

Learn the multiple paths to the double damage: the elevator jump to the adrenaline pill ledge and the upper walkway (or shield jump from the ramp between the lightning gun and rocket launcher). With the rocket launcher in hand, drop down to claim the extra rounds, and remember that the higher you are, the more advantageous combat becomes. You can see through the maze of ledges much easier if you stand by the lightning gun.

Double jump across gaps to the continuation of ledges farther around. For example, double jump across from the lightning gun and land on the rocket launcher ledge instead of weaving around. The best place to use rockets is when an enemy hits the basement looking for the 100 shield pack. Stay at the ramp exit below the rocket launcher spawn point and blast this choke point and the shield pack. There's no way out of this basement except via the ramp or shield jumping, and either way can result in a quick kill.

Double jump and move around the upper ledges, dodge jumping to nearby ledges if possible. Strafe left and right along the outer ledge between the ammo packs and lightning gun. You can see the 50 shield pack and the entrance to the basement ramp from here, allowing you to stay on top of your enemy.

Elevator jump to the upper central platform overlooking the minigun and 50 shield pack areas. Then shield jump onto the pipes riveted to the outer wall. Step up here and all the way around the shield pack area. This offers incredible views and sniping positions. A second pipe above the walkway to the double damage can be accessed only via translocator.

DM-1on1-SPIRIT

Recommended Players: 2–2

Legend

1	Lightning Gun +1 ammo pack	**13**	Shock, link, rocket ammo packs	**22**	100 Shield Pack (above, on pipe)
2	50 Shield Pack	**14**	Health Vials x2 and Minigun +1 ammo pack	**23**	Adrenaline Pills x2
3	Health Vials x3	**15**	Rocket and lightning ammo packs	**24**	Mini and lightning ammo packs
4	Shock Rifle + 1 ammo pack	**16**	Link Gun + 1 ammo pack (indented ramp)	**25**	Adrenaline Pills x2
5	Health Vials x3 (slope)	**17**	Adrenaline Pills x3	**26**	Bio and flak ammo packs
6	Biorifle +1 ammo pack	**18**	Flak Cannon +1 ammo pack	**27**	Rocket Launcher +1 ammo pack
7	Adrenaline Pills x4	**19**	Health Vials x4	**28**	50 Health Packs x2
8	Adrenaline Pills x3	**20**	50 Health Pack	**29**	Shock and link ammo packs
9	Health Vial x3	**21**	Shock and mini ammo packs		
10	50 Health Pack				
11	Bio and rocket ammo				
12	Adrenaline Pills x3				

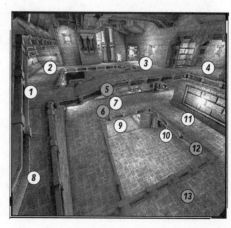

Overview

Spirit is segmented into four lower chambers, three of which house a weapon that amateur players usually rush to. A series of balconies on the floor above and a third set of walkways all contain weapons and shield packs. Plot a course up here, and combat becomes a series of shooting opportunities from the ground to the sky. Be aware of how much of the level you can see and where you can see it from, and don't be afraid to slow down the higher you go.

Available Weapons	Rocket Launcher (in quadrant, ground floor)
Biorifle (in quadrant, ground floor)	**Lightning Gun** (top floor, ledge near 50 shield pack, above biorifle)
Shock Rifle (in upper floor, middle area)	**Available Power-ups**
Link Gun (top of enclosed ramp on middle floor)	**50 Shield Pack** (next to shadowy elevator, third floor, above biorifle)
Minigun (next to elevator, above quiet quadrant)	**100 Shield Pack** (end of narrow pipe ledge, third floor, above flak cannon)
Flak Cannon (in quadrant, ground floor)	

Map Patrol

On the upper floor of this tri-level map lies the 50 shield pack on a stone pathway in the corner. A path leads left and right, along the outer walls, offering a good view of the level below. A lower walkway contains four adrenaline pills and a biorifle. Head along the right side to a lightning gun and a junction. Straight ahead, a ramp leads down to the middle floor with three adrenaline pills and a weaponless "quiet" quadrant. To the left is a walkway to the middle.

Head left and note the elevator on the left exterior wall, near the shield pack. It leads to a ramp with three health vials. Use the elevator to grab the shield pack from lower ground. Continue along the top ledge to a large opening to the rocket launcher quadrant. The linking ledge with three health vials leads to the map's middle.

At the top level area in the map's center, an alcove houses the shock rifle and ammo pack. The pass-through leads to the opposite flak cannon quadrant. Near the shock rifle, drop down a hole by the left wall to the middle center area.

Back on the top floor of the rocket launcher quadrant, find a couple of adrenaline pills on the left as you enter, and a long ramp down to shock and link ammo along the left wall to the corner. On the right are mini and lightning ammo packs and a straight ledge over to the next linking entrance on the right wall. Avoid lengthy ramp climbing by dodge jumping up the stone slab near the right path.

The final quadrant with the flak cannon below is most interesting on the third floor. Find two adrenaline pills, and on the right is the linking ledge to the map's center and the shock rifle. Move around the right ledge for a rocket and link ammo pack. A gap in the far right corner houses an elevator leading to the quiet quadrant's second floor ledge.

A pair of rusty pipes (on the left as you enter) lead up to a 100 shield pack. Try to reach this important area before your opponents. Left of the pipes is an entrance to an enclosed ramp with a link gun and ammo pack at the top, and four health vials as the ramp descends to link and shock ammo packs on the second floor.

On the second floor corner of the flak cannon quadrant, be wary; the middle section diagonally opposite you is open and a great sniping spot. A ramp on your right descends to the flak cannon, and a ledge on your left leads to the elevator to the third floor.

Continue past the elevator and grab two health vials when you reach the quiet quadrant containing the minigun and two ammo packs. The remainder of the left ledge leads to the ramp with the adrenaline pills up to the third floor and 50 shield pack area. Find a flak ammo pack on the way. To the right is a rocket and bio ammo pack and a junction. To the left, a walkway with three adrenaline pills separates the quiet and biorifle quadrants. The rest of this area consists of a ledge to a ramp and three health vials, and the elevator to the 50 shield pack.

Check the second floor middle area. Three openings allow views of every quadrant, making this a great sniping spot. Remember the hole in the ceiling! The middle section connects only via the main ledge to the rocket launcher quadrant, and when you reach this area there are two adrenaline pills on the left and a bio and flak ammo pack next to the stone slab.

261

Drop to the rocket launcher and work counter-clockwise around the ground floor; find an ammo pack next to the launcher and two health packs to the right, at the base of the ramp to the second floor. Double jump up the rubble against the ramp in the outer corner to the second floor.

In the flak cannon quadrant, the weapon spins to the right of a ramp on the outer wall leading to the ledge with the elevator to the 100 shield pack, and the doorway to the enclosed ramp and link gun. Watch for sniping from the center. Find a health pack in the corner, and a flak ammo next to the weapon. The chambers continue to the right.

Pass through water to the quiet quadrant with a left wall under a ledge above (you're underneath the minigun area) and pick up the rocket, shock, and link ammo packs. The ramp on the far wall leads to the ledge splitting the quadrants. Note a health pack on the inside corner, and three more vials as you pass through a shallow pool into the biorifle quadrant. Aside from the ammo pack next to the weapon, the only area of interest is the ramp leading left and up to the shadowy elevator. The doorway to the right links back to the rocket launcher quadrant.

Deathmatch Dealing

Don't follow the ledges blindly around. Dodge and double jump across ledge corners and drop off ramps instead of running down them.

Watch yourself as you appear in a different area. For example, if you stride to the top of the enclosed ramp and the link gun, you could be struck by an enemy on the top platforms who spotted you entering the base of the ramp. Stay flexible and dodge periodically to throw the enemy off. Pick up the lightning gun as soon as possible—it's a great asset on the upper ledges.

On the ground, combat becomes more fierce, as the four linked rooms offer little cover. Those with keen ears can tell when an opponent lands nearby and also when enemies walk through the puddles (keep your feet dry and leap these areas). Grab weapons after you snag both shield packs.

You can see both shield packs (at opposite corners of the top floor) from each shield pack spawn point. Wait for them to appear before dashing over to grab the other shield pack. Use these two instant-hit weapons on enemies lower down. Prowling the top floor is a great way to shower the enemy below with flak grenades, bio ooze, and lightning gun blasts. Stay on the outer ledges.

Also make sure you're well versed with elevator trickery. If you're being chased, head into the shadowy elevator to the third floor near the 50 shield pack, then drop down and gun the enemy waiting for the elevator to return. This works at the other elevator, too. Make sure you know where the elevator is, or you'll run for the minigun and lose your bearings; leap over the lift platform to reach the gun. Better yet is the shock rifle, allowing you to drop down through the hole or to any part of the map, although you can be seen by everyone! Try to keep your ground combat to a minimum.

Translocator fans can balance up any of the torches, on the slanted outer walls above the 100 shield pack, or above any doorway for a nasty ambush. From the walkway between the shock rifle and lightning gun, double jump to the lip of the upper wall above the ramp with the adrenaline pills on it and stand above the third floor walkway and the quiet quadrant—a great ambush point.

DM-1on1-SQUADER

Recommended Players: 2–2

Legend

1	Health Vials x5 (near Rocket Launcher and hole)	6	50 Health Packs x2 (under Shield Pack)	11	Flak ammo pack
2	50 Shield Pack	7	Shock and rocket ammo packs	12	Flak Cannon
3	Shock ammo packs x2	8	Health Vials x8 (ramp)	13	Link and mini ammo packs
4	Double Damage	9	Link Gun +1 ammo pack	14	Biorifle +1 ammo pack
5	Health Vials x5 (lower ramp)	10	Shock Rifle	15	50 Health Packs x2

16	Health Vials x6
17	100 Shield Pack
18	Rocket ammo packs
19	Rocket Launcher (near hole)
20	Minigun +1 ammo pack

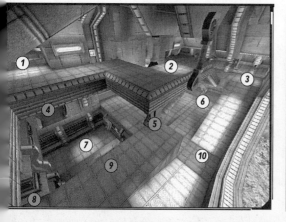

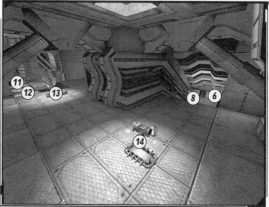

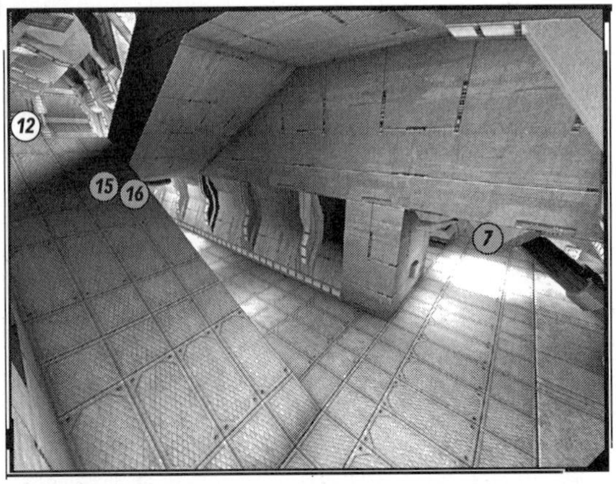

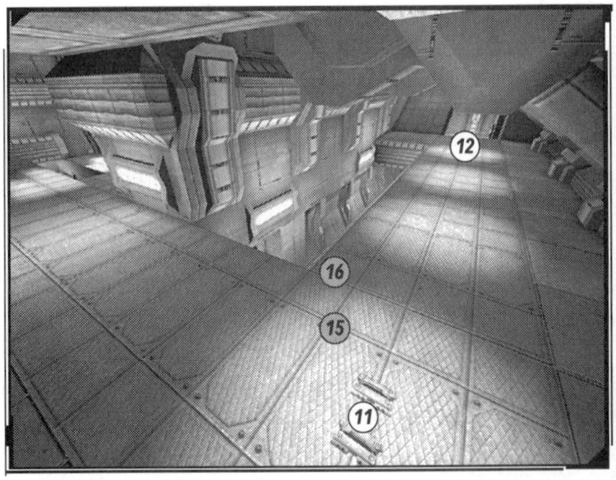

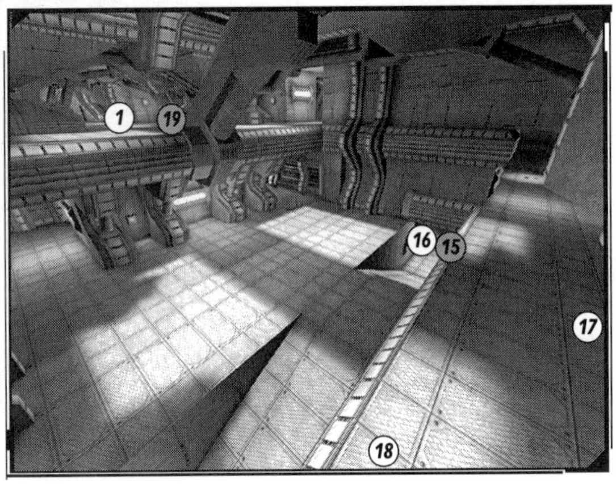

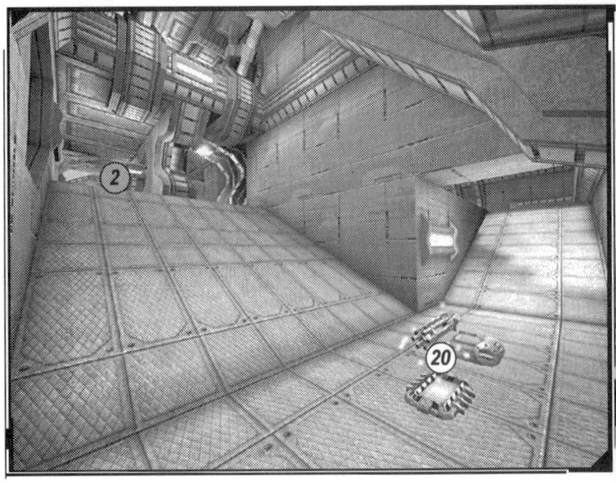

Overview

One of the best small Deathmatch maps, Squader has a central double damage that's easy to spot. Both shield packs are in large open areas: a huge courtyard with a raised area and many entrances, and a multi-level chamber with a gigantic greenhouse window. Once you secure these three items, grab the flak cannon, rockets, minigun, or the biorifle.

Available Weapons

Biorifle (spotlight in map's top corner, up ramp from flak cannon)

Shock Rifle (base of two ramps, under 50 shield pack in open chamber)

Link Gun (in hole at base of open chamber, near jump pad)

Minigun (end of left indented ramp, near 100 shield pack)

Flak Cannon (end of four spotlight corridor)

Rocket Launcher (above double damage, balcony overlooking main courtyard)

Available Power-ups

50 Shield Pack (top platform of open chamber, near large window)

100 Shield Pack (alcove on raised area of main courtyard)

Double Damage (T-junction under rocket launcher, in map's center)

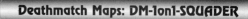

Map Patrol

In an alcove with a window lies the 100 shield pack that should top your priority list. Exit the alcove into a large enclosed courtyard with multiple exits. To your right is a doorway to a dimly lit corner with two flak cannon ammo packs. To the left are two rocket ammo packs; claim them when you're using the launcher.

In front of the rocket ammo is a drop to the top of two ramps, one running down and left, and the other down and right. The right one leads to another right corner and houses two health packs and a row of health vials to the left. The left ramp leads to a minigun and ammo pack, and a ramp heading up and right.

The middle part of the courtyard, on the same plane as the indented ramps, has two entrances, both on the far wall (on the left and right corners). Above is a balcony with two more exits (on the upper left and right corners), and another exit to the right. This sounds confusing, but the level is tight and easy to navigate. Start by checking the dimly lit corridor to the right of the 100 shield pack. To snag the 100 shield pack from the center courtyard, double jump up from the top of the indented ramps, or across the side walls above the base of the indented ramps.

Back at the top floor of the dimly lit corner and the two flak ammo packs is a ledge leading left, through four spotlights. In the middle of the farthest spotlight is a flak cannon and a junction. At the junction, a ramp to your left heads up, and in front of you is a ramp that leads down.

To your left as you run along the corridor to the flak cannon is a lower corridor. This begins at the base of the right indented ramp in the main courtyard, with a left turn and two health packs mentioned before. Run along here for six vials. Continue through the gap ahead, run under the upper ramp near the flak cannon, and end at a corner where the lower ramp near the flak cannon joins up.

Move around this corner to the left to see a large open chamber ahead and a gap to your left. The gap leads to the right indented ramp at the main courtyard. The corridor to the open chamber ends with shock and rocket ammo packs, and a drop to the right (and an area above you that you can't reach, near a 50 shield pack).

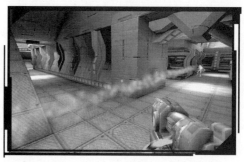

Head up the left ramp to a top ledge. Turn around to see the entire flak cannon corridor and the lower corridor with the health vials below. Find minigun and link ammo packs at the ledge's top. There's a gap to the left that leads to the open chamber, with a corridor on your left that leads to the rocket launcher and a 50 shield pack on an upper platform.

You can fall off to the right, landing near the lower corridor's opening. Take the opening to the right to a corner of the level and a spotlight. In the spotlight is a biorifle and ammo pack plus a ramp down to the left. Head down and you appear in the open chamber just above and right of the gap.

Check out the open chamber. From the top floor, walk past the left corridor leading to the rocket launcher to an opening on your left; an elevator takes you down one floor. Follow the path to the 50 shield pack and a ramp down to a U-shaped end area with two shock ammo packs in the right corner. View the lower part of the open chamber.

There's a giant window on the left and a ramp down to a shock rifle and up the other side to the ramp with the health vial and biorifle. To the right is a platform along the right wall; a corridor in the right wall leads to the double damage, to a small ramp down to the elevator on your right, and to a connecting area to the ramp leading to the biorifle.

Ahead is a hole. Drop down the left side of it to reach a jump pad and a ramp leading out (the exit is under the platform with the 50 shield pack). Find a link gun and ammo pack, plus five health vials on the way out. The ramp leads to an antechamber with two health packs and a shock rifle on the right.

Look left, at the elevator. Left of that is a hole in the wall, above the hole in the ground. The double damage spins in a T-junction across from you. Double jump into the T-junction, or use the entrance to the right of the elevator and move left. A junction on your right before you reach the DD leads to the main courtyard. Or, from the initial main courtyard, take the right raised exit and double jump or wall jump left into the gap and claim the DD.

Now take the five health vial corridor on the top floor, above the alcove where the double damage is, leading to the rocket launcher. Watch out for the hole in the floor (you can drop down onto the double damage from it); jump the hole to claim the launcher instead of sidestepping around. The rocket launcher is on the top balcony across from the 100 shield pack; drop onto the main courtyard, or check the left or right areas. To the left, an opening overlooks the flak cannon (this good ambush point also can be reached via shield jump from the cannon). To the right is the last section.

Take the right section to reach a small bare walkway with an elevator ahead. The elevator takes you down to a similar area, a ramp to the open chamber and opening next to the first elevator. One exit leads to the double damage, and two lead to a ramp down to the minigun (at the end of the left indented ramp near the 100 shield pack). Peer down at the minigun and land on it from the top bare upper walkway, or double jump over the gap to the 50 shield pack.

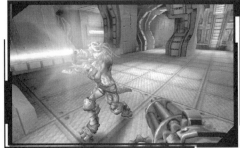

Deathmatch Dealing

The action takes place in two main areas: the main courtyard and the open chamber with the two shield packs and the double damage. The double damage's central location means you can shield jump up to the rocket launcher balcony from the courtyard, run around the corner from the chamber, wall jump in from the nearby ramped corridor, or even use the jump pad in the hole and steer yourself in.

The double damage is the most important weapon, so make some serious ambush decisions. The dark corner at the base of the ramp near the flak cannon is a good spot to catch your breath and lurk. Either of the indented ramps near the 100 shield pack are handy if your opponent is about to grab the shield pack.

Use the elevator to reach the open chamber. The open chamber has many lips to land on, such as the sill of the giant window, or the lip above the entrance to the health vial ramp to the biorifle. You could stand on the support strut overhanging the courtyard, next to the rocket launcher, but you're prone there. Instead, double jump to the lip on the sides of the walls left and right of the courtyard, then across to the raised ground where the 100 shield pack is. Or stand on the protruding wire seal above the ramp leading out of the hole.

Sit in the window sill on the ramp heading down from the flak cannon; enemies can't see you until they receive a flak round to the face. The flak cannon is excellent for this level. Use bio ooze around blind corners (such as the wall jump near the double damage or the top of the 50 shield pack platform).

You can stand behind the jump pad and defeat enemies who don't look before they fall; check for enemies in the hole before you use the pad. Zigzag along health vial corridors to avoid gunfire, and drop down from the flak cannon to

the corridor below and chase. Avoid the hole's exit ramp—it leads to a dead-end chamber where you're easily picked apart. Come up with inventive routes to the shield packs, double damage, and weapons (100 shield pack, wall jump to double damage, out and elevator up to 50 shield pack, then head for rockets or flak).

267

DM-1on1-TRITE

Recommended Players: 2–2

Legend

1	Biorifle +1 ammo pack	16	Adrenaline Pills x3
2	Adrenaline Pills x4	17	Bio and link ammo packs
3	Health Vials x4	18	50 Health Pack
4	Shock ammo pack	19	Flak Cannon +1 ammo pack, plus mini and lightning ammo packs (near window)
5	Adrenaline Pills x3		
6	Mini and flak ammo packs	20	Health Vials x4
7	Double Damage	21	Adrenaline Pills x4
8	Rocket Launcher +1 ammo pack	22	Minigun +1 ammo pack
9	50 Health Packs x2	23	Health Vial x2
10	Link Gun +1 ammo pack	24	50 Shield Pack (ramp)
11	50 Health Pack	25	Lightning ammo pack
12	Health Vials x3	26	Link and rocket ammo packs
13	Adrenaline Pills x4	27	Health Vials x4
14	Lightning Gun +1 ammo pack	28	100 Shield Pack
15	Bio and link ammo pack		

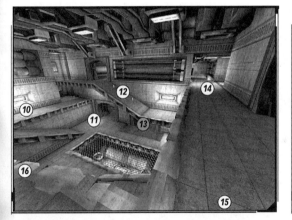

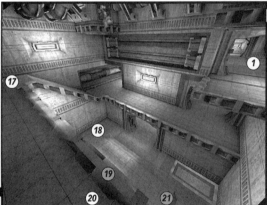

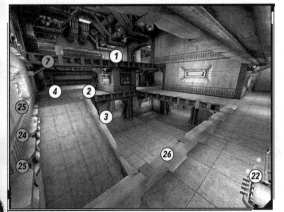

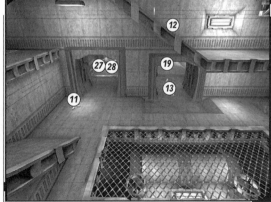

Overview

Those who enjoyed Spirit will be at home here, although the map is less confusing, and the fighting always heads up to the double damage. The other main area of combat is the doorway to the 100 shield pack. Otherwise, this is a double jumper's delight, with many lips and ledges to flit around.

Available Weapons	
Biorifle (top floor platform between quiet and rocket quadrant, near DD)	**Rocket Launcher** (middle of ground floor quadrant, below DD)
Shock Rifle (enclosed third floor corridor between flak and mesh quadrants)	**Lightning Gun** (center ledge of mesh quadrant)
Link Gun (outer wall, second floor mesh quadrant, near elevator)	**Available Power-ups**
Minigun (outer wall, second floor quiet quadrant, near enclosed shield pack ramp)	**50 Shield Pack** (middle of enclosed ramp, near minigun)
Flak Cannon (middle of ground floor quadrant, near 100 shield pack)	**100 Shield Pack** (dead-end glass room near flak cannon)
	Double Damage (top floor corner, above rocket launcher)

Map Patrol

Let's start in the bottom corner with the 100 shield pack. It's inside a small dead-end room with a large window on the left. On either side of the shield pack are two health vials. Head out the exit to a mesh floor quadrant. Just outside the door on the right wall is a health pack. Ahead is a ramp up to a link gun and adrenaline pills on a ledge to the left.

Stay on the ground and look left. There's a short ramp on the right, a doorway ahead (spot two health packs in the distance), and a doorway to the left, right of the room you were just in. Follow the four adrenaline pills through the doorway.

This leads to the flak cannon quadrant. The weapon is in the middle of the room next to an ammo pack. To the left is the window looking into the shield pack room. Next to the window is lightning and minigun ammo. In the right corner is an elevator up to the second floor ledges and the map's center. There's no other way up from here, so head through the doorway on your right, passing a health pack. This leads to the empty quadrant, bereft of ordnance except rocket and link ammo packs on the left wall. Ahead and left, a ramp leads up to the view of the double damage and the minigun behind you.

Go through the doorway and four health vials and you appear in the rocket launcher quadrant. Ammo is adjacent and two health packs lie to the left. The doorway leads back to the initial, mesh floor quadrant.

Go up the outer ramp in the mesh floor quadrant. Left is a ramp (with three adrenaline pills) up to the third floor and a shock and bio ammo pack. Turn right almost completely around for a link gun and ammo. Follow this ledge to a shadowy elevator on the left. This leads to the third floor junction with the shock rifle corridor on your left. Take the inner ramp from the mesh quadrant and it turns left to a doorway, then left again and up a ramp with three health vials on it to the junction that the elevator rises to.

Take the doorway reached by the second ramp, and you overlook the rocket launcher quadrant. Above and right is the ledge with the double damage, which you can't reach yet. Ahead and left is an alcove. Double jump there for four adrenaline pills and shock ammo. The alcove leads to a ramp down to the quiet quadrant. Take the doorway to the left, as you come in.

The doorway immediately splits into an opening to the left, overlooking the flak cannon quadrant. The ledge opposite the shield pack window ends in a ramp to the left and a doorway on the right. The ramp leads to bio and link ammo. The doorway leads to the continuation of the parallel ledge on the quiet quadrant side. Turn right at the end, and pick up the minigun and ammo pack. The ledge leads to an enclosed ramp. Look right; the ramp to the alcove with the four adrenaline pills and shock ammo is across from you.

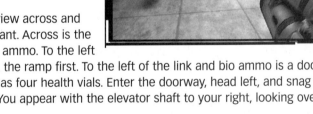

Run into the enclosed ramp, turn right, and run up through two health vials and a 50 shield pack. At the top is a lightning ammo pack. You're on the top floor. Down the walkway is a biorifle. Look left and down to the rocket launcher quadrant, and across to the double damage window. Look right and down for the minigun and the quiet quadrant.

Head into the top middle area for a view across and right, high above the flak cannon quadrant. Across is the ramp ascending to the link gun and bio ammo. To the left is a ledge with the lightning gun. Check the ramp first. To the left of the link and bio ammo is a doorway on the right, and the end of the ledge has four health vials. Enter the doorway, head left, and snag the shock rifle and flak plus rocket ammo. You appear with the elevator shaft to your right, looking over the mesh quadrant.

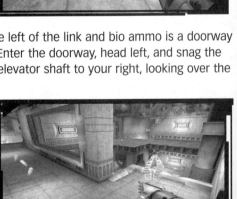

Back at the lightning gun (which you can see from the elevator), move forward to an open doorway on your left and the shock and bio ammo in the corner (an adrenaline pill ramp heads down and right). Take the left doorway down the double damage window platform and to the grand prize: three adrenaline pills, mini and flak ammo, and the double damage in an opening in the corner.

Deathmatch Dealing

The 100 shield pack is in a very risky area, easily viewed from the mesh quadrant and the ramps, but also through the window from the flak cannon quadrant. Enter this potential deathtrap only when the coast is clear, and plan an escape to the 50 shield pack and double damage seconds later.

Take to the skies from the flak cannon quadrant. Use an elevator jump to land on the third floor ledges, either at the middle of the map (for a quick leap to the double damage) or on the four health vials (or anywhere on the second floor ledge). This is great for changing direction if you're being chased, or getting across the map effortlessly. Find a camping spot in the corner on top of the three horizontal pipes.

Novice campers sometimes hide in the doorways linking the quadrants, but there's nowhere to run, so slip into the next quadrant so you can dodge incoming bullets.

Also try leaping across ramps to shorten the distance between you and your target; never run up the ramp unless you're seeking partial cover from a chasing attacker.

Run along the narrow ledges. For example, if you're at the top of the elevator in the mesh quadrant and want to reach the lightning gun, stay to the left, run to the top of the three health vial ramp, hug the left wall indent, and leap onto the lightning gun ledge.

Try the lip on the second floor underneath the double damage (you can see the rocket launcher and the minigun). Or hug the lip on the left central wall instead of double jumping to the alcove. At the alcove with the four adrenaline pills, hug the right wall lip to reach the minigun and the 50 shield pack in the enclosed ramp. Or, use the air-conditioning grill to wall jump onto the third floor. At the top of the enclosed 50 shield pack ramp, turn right, and walk along the lip above the other lip you just sped across. That's another camping spot. An indented wall on the third floor overlooks the 100 shield pack below, with a great view of the flak cannon.

Try dodge jumping to the lips on the far walls, or translocate there. Double jump from the lips near the biorifle to the lip opposite the DD window. You can even double jump across the biorifle platform to the double damage, or walk along the window sill! Take the lightning gun to camping spots such as the top of the orange elevator (for an excellent view of the mesh quadrant floors), the upper corner of the flak cannon quadrant near the door to the DD (you can see down the ramp, through to the minigun, and all the way to the DD), and even the pipe next to the DD (looking out over the rocket launcher).

271

DM-CORRUGATION

Recommended Players: 4–6

Legend

1 50 Health Pack
2 Health Vials x2
3 50 Health Pack
4 Rocket Launcher +1 ammo pack, bio ammo pack
5 Double Damage (lower level)
6 Health Packs x2 (tunnel)
7 Adrenaline Pills x5
8 Link and flak ammo packs
9 Link Gun
10 Shock and link ammo packs
11 100 Shield Pack

12 Shock Rifle
13 Health Vials x3
14 Shock Rifle (also point 21)
15 Adrenaline Pills x5
16 Adrenaline Pills x5
17 50 Shield Pack
18 50 Health Pack
19 Bio and shock ammo packs
20 Minigun +1 ammo pack and flak ammo pack
21 Shock Rifle
22 Adrenaline Pills x2 and Health Vials x2

23 Shock and rocket ammo packs
24 50 Health Pack
25 Adrenaline Pills x4
26 Shock and flak ammo packs
27 Health Vials x2 (in tunnel)
28 Health Vials x2 (tunnel)
29 Bio Rifle (tunnel)
30 Health Vials x2
31 50 Health Packs x2
32 Lightning Gun +1 ammo and one flak ammo pack
33 Flak Cannon

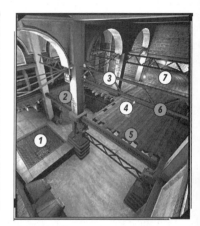

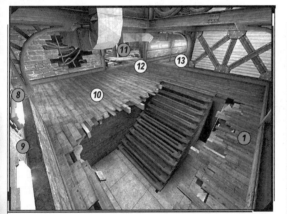

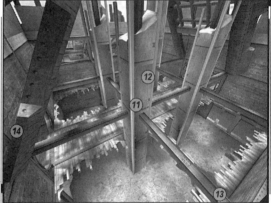

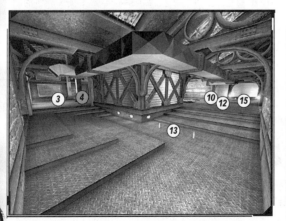

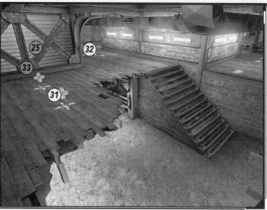

Overview

This small two-level area is full of confusing corridors. Most of the top area's floors are smashed and you can see through to the level below. If you're on the ground, you're looking for a weapon or a way up (try the stairs, elevators at the outer edges, or shortcut door near the murky sewer); expect trouble either way.

Available Weapons

Biorifle (in middle of lower floor tunnel, near double damage)

Shock Rifle (x2, upper level between red-lit junction and 100 shield pack hall; lower corridor near central grassy area and water junction)

Link Gun (below upper shock rifle, near grassy area adjacent to double damage)

Minigun (x2, upper level between 50 and 100 shield pack; upper level on raised mesh area at far end of 100 shield pack hall)

Flak Cannon (small corridor between red-lit entrance to main grass area and grassy thoroughfare)

Rocket Launcher (upper room near elevator down to double damage)

Lightning Gun (upper corridor to side of shield pack hall)

Available Power-ups

Double Damage (tunnel junction near grass, lower level)

50 Shield Pack (end of curved corridor near minigun, upper level)

100 Shield Pack (middle of map, upper level main chamber)

Map Patrol

Start at the double damage and the adjacent elevator. The power-up is next to two tunnels (to the right, containing health vials), and a grassy mound to an opening with a health pack (left). Take the elevator to the upper walkway level. You see the rocket launcher with an ammo pack and a bio ammo pack. The hole in the walkway gives a great view of the grassy area and one of the tunnels. The walkway has two exits: ahead and a curved corridor to the right.

273

Take the corridor to a red-lit T-junction on the left wall and a left corner with three health vials. The corner leads to a corridor to the shock rifle (upper floor). Turn right at the red-lit junction to peer into a balcony area. Ahead and left are a minigun and ammo. Just before the minigun, a hole lets you see a shock and bio ammo pack on the ground. To the right of the minigun is an L-shaped hole; drop into this to land at the end of a tunnel, near another shock rifle (lower floor). Turn right at the red-lit junction to see a 50 shield pack near the hole. Behind it, the curved corridor leads back to the rocket launcher and five adrenaline pills.

Continue down the walkway with the minigun. Near the far side of the L-shaped hole are two health vials and two adrenaline pills. A large opening in the left wall leads to an open area full of holes and wooden balconies. The 100 shield pack is in here, as is the main thoroughfare. We'll return here in a moment.

Continue down the minigun corridor to the end. Steps lead down to a left corner, with four adrenaline pills and a flak cannon. The room to your right has a health pack and a large hole. Drop down to the shock rifle (lower floor). You can reach the rifle (and move to this upper level) from the elevator at the room's far right side. Collect shock and rocket ammo at the top entrance.

From the minigun corridor, enter the large hole-filled hall with the 100 shield pack. To the left, a hole reveals the grassy central junction below; on the left wall, you can drop to the tunnel to the double damage. A second hole in this hall's left corner leads to the grassy central area, and a wrecked wood platform leads to a left door. Behind this is the shock rifle (upper floor), and left of that is the red-lit junction.

Right of the 100 shield pack, another hole leads to the grassy central area and an exit to the flak cannon on the lower level. A door leads to the second minigun. To the shield pack's right is a wrecked wooden walkway. Follow it to the wall, then step right to a door and turn left to reach the lightning gun and lightning and flak ammo. This room opens to the right side with two health packs and has stairs to a grassy thoroughfare below. This is a popular place to dash to the top floor. Follow the wrecked floor around the outer walls or double jump across and left from the stairs to rejoin the shield pack hall's far end.

After the shield pack hall, a mesh floor room contains another minigun and mini and link ammo packs. To the left, another hole leads to the link gun lower corridor. At the far end is an elevator descending to the link gun corridor (another way to reach this upper area), and an entrance to another curved corridor.

Run down the second curved corridor, snag five adrenaline pills, and reach that shock rifle (upper floor) again. Near the steps on the right are shock and link ammo. The shock rifle area leads back to the red-lit junction. The stairs to the right—the final access to the top floor—lead down to the link gun corridor.

The ground floor is a maze of close corridors with little room to snipe and dodge. From the double damage, take the left grassy exit, through the health pack, to a junction with stairs on the right, up to the shock rifle (upper floor). Continue right to the link gun corridor with the weapon and ammo, plus a flak ammo pack. Pass an opening on the right to the main grassy area and a short corridor to the left. This leads to the elevator to the mesh floor second minigun area. The hole above is next to the minigun.

A small tunnel at the link-gun corridor's end leads to the grassy thoroughfare, with stairs (on right) to the lightning gun corridor. Continue around the grassy thoroughfare to the flak cannon corridor with the weapon at a junction. On the right, a short tunnel leads to the main grassy area under the 100 shield pack hall (the red opening houses flak and shock ammo). Ahead are the four adrenaline pills and the steps to the minigun corridor's far end.

Back at the double damage, take the metal tunnel. Grab two health vials and a biorifle, but watch for the junction with a right opening. Continue down the tunnel (two more health vials) to the grassy area. Turn right to a water-filled junction—the right-hand curved tunnel from the double damage comes out here (grab four health vials on the way). The junction holds a tunnel alcove, a health pack, and steps to the right. The raised area holds the shock and bio ammo you saw through the hole near the first minigun.

At the raised area's far end is a door to the shock rifle (lower level). To the right is an elevator up to the end room near the minigun corridor. To the left is a large entrance to the center grassy area.

Stand in the grassy area's middle and look through the tunnel to the double damage. Above the grassy area, through the many holes in the ceiling, is the 100 shield pack hall. To the right is the entrance to the link gun corridor. Behind and left is the red-lit opening to the flak cannon corridor. To the left is the shock rifle (lower level) corridor.

Deathmatch Dealing

Find the shortcuts, learn where you'll be shot at, and remove yourself from hazardous areas. At the murky water area, use the raised area, metal beam support, and top of the door to double jump a couple of times to the 50 shield pack and minigun; this is a great shortcut. Set up an ambush at the tunnel entrances.

275

Note the locations of all the main items. Know if you can take an item by dropping or jumping to an adjacent floor instead of using stairs. At the rocket launcher, drop off the broken flooring to snag the double damage. From the raised metal minigun ledge, run toward the hole and down to reach the link gun. Cut the corners near the lightning gun by double jumping across the stairs from the upper level.

The key is sniping from the top floor to the bottom. Stand in a protected area on the top floor and blast enemies below, then retreat so return fire hits the ground. Ambush enemies running for the link gun by standing on the minigun metal platform. At the upper shock rifle, aim down the stairs to spot anyone after the double damage (although they can fire at you, too). Stand by the rocket launcher, look left at the grassy thoroughfare, and fire. Guard the 50 shield pack and watch the lower shock rifle corridor. Get both shield packs right away.

It's hard to stay safe in the main 100 shield pack hall (translocate onto the roof beams for added mayhem). The lower grassy area is an unsafe place, ideal for quick combat, but better to fire at from above. Run around the edges of the broken floors to reach a corner where enemies can't attack you from behind and aim at the hall or grassy area below. Check each upper floor and skirt the outer walls to find unexpected ambush locations, such as the metal crossbeam near the rocket launcher (move along the left wall). Or translocate up to a beam like the ones above the rocket launcher.

Expect the most action at the 100 shield pack, flak cannon, and biorifle. Unleash hot goop from your biorifle if enemies follow you down the sewer tunnels. The flak cannon becomes a ricocheting nightmare in these close areas. Brush up on your lightning gun skills; stay near the weapon—it's near two health packs and you can see much of the level, including both shield packs.

DM-DECK17

Recommended Players: 4–8

Legend

1	Shock, rocket, and sniper ammo packs	12	Flak Cannon +2 ammo packs	24	Health Vials x3
2	Double Damage	13	Adrenaline Pills x4	25	Adrenaline Pills x4
3	50 Health Packs x2	14	Link ammo packs x2	26	Adrenaline Pills x4
4	Adrenaline Pill	15	Sniper Rifle	27	Minigun ammo packs x2
5	Adrenaline Pill	16	Biorifle +2 ammo packs	28	Minigun
6	Assault ammo packs x3	17	Shock Rifle + 2 ammo packs	29	Biorifle +2 ammo packs
7	Rocket Launcher +1 ammo pack	18	Bio ammo packs x2	30	Redeemer
8	Flak Cannon +2 ammo packs	19	50 Shield Pack	31	Rocket ammo pack
9	Sniper Rifle +2 ammo packs	20	Rocket Launcher +2 ammo packs	32	Rocket ammo pack
10	Adrenaline Pills x3	21	Link ammo packs x2	33	Shock Rifle +2 ammo packs
11	Health Packs x4	22	Link Gun	34	50 Health Pack x2
		23	100 Shield Pack (under platform)	35	50 Shield Pack

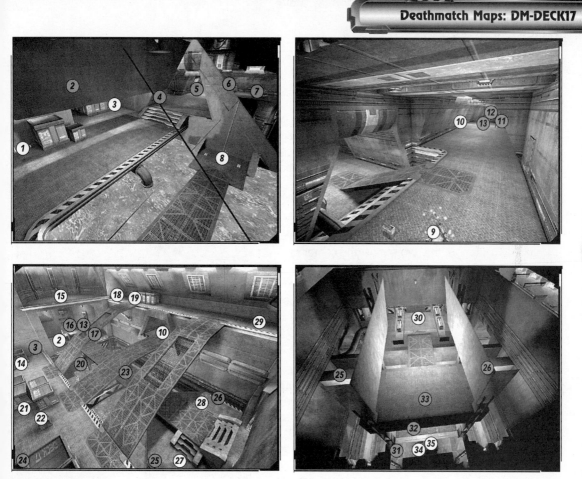

Overview

The classic Deck 16 is cordoned off, but the next deck is functional and full of weapons. Most of the action involves blasting the enemy in the circular outer corridor, or checking the huge deck and the magma pool below. Learn the location of the hard-to-reach items and consistently return to them. Find a few unexpected sniping spots.

Available Weapons

Biorifle (x2, end of main deck upper ledge; in outer circular corridor room behind double damage)

Shock Rifle (behind crates near double damage)

Link Gun (top of small crate on main deck lower ledge)

Minigun (right side of central deck platform)

Flak Cannon (x2, on platform just above small magma pond, at start of circular corridor; end of corridor, top of ramp on outer circular corridor)

Rocket Launcher (far end of magma pool, near teleporter)

Sniper Rifle (x2, on upper semicircular alcove overlooking main deck, under double damage; end of flak cannon corridor near ramp to double elevator junction)

Redeemer (secret chamber above double elevator junction, accessed via teleporter)

Available Power-ups

Double Damage (on crate, far end of central deck platform)

50 Shield Pack (x2, end of the main deck upper ledge, near sniper rifle; on stack of crates between elevator platforms)

100 Shield Pack (support strut above magma pool, lower ground)

Map Patrol

Starting on a ledge overlooking the main deck structure and three ramps, note a sniper rifle in the semicircular top alcove and double damage on a crate underneath. Reach it by double jumping to the upper ledge spanning the main deck. The deck has three crates against the left wall. Between the sniper rifle and the crates are a 50 shield pack and two biorifle ammo packs. Move to the upper ledge's end to grab the biorifle and two more ammo packs.

Head down either of the two ramps (the center one leads to a door below) to the lower decks. Near two crates at the end by the double damage area are two link ammo packs and a door (with an adrenaline pill) to a circular surrounding passage. In the lower deck's middle, on a tiny crate between two large crate stacks is a link gun with two ammo packs. In front of this tiny crate is the second door to the circular surrounding passage and another adrenaline pill.

At the lower ledge's end, which has three ramps connected to the upper ledge area, a central platform runs the length of the deck interior. Jump onto this but watch your footing as there's a lower deck and a pool of lava below. Jump in the middle and land on the narrow center support strut below the platform to get a 100 shield pack. For the moment, stay on the middle platform. A door at one end connects to the circular outer corridor and a double elevator bank, plus a hidden roof support area with the redeemer (accessible only by teleport).

The platform has a wider end near the door, with a minigun and two ammo packs. Run to the other end, under the sniper rifle, and check out the double damage atop the crates. Around the back of the single crate to the right is a shock rifle and two ammo packs. To reach the double damage, head up the nearest large deck ramp and jump or double jump from it. The double damage is on the three crates. Along the right wall is a door (and an adrenaline pill) that leads to the end of the circular corridor and a biorifle.

Head down the large passage near the double damage, stay left of a large crate stack, and claim two health packs. You're now at the start of the circular corridor. A passage in the far right corner leads to a flak cannon and two ammo packs. Note the pipe that you can use as a shortcut, and the sniper, shock, and rocket ammo packs on the opposite wall.

Head away from the lava along the circular corridor. Climb the steps into a huge passage with the two large doors to the main deck on your left. A stepped alcove to your right contains a rocket launcher and ammo pack. Continue past the second door and the corridor curves left. Find three assault ammo packs, two sets of three health vials, and a door.

The door leads to the junction with the double elevator bank on your right and the deck platform entrance to your left. Head straight up a ramp, passing the motivational screen. Atop the ramp, a long corridor leads left. Right of the ramp is a sniper rifle and two ammo packs. Run along the corridor to a gap in the left wall that leads to the middle giant ramp in the main deck, and three adrenaline pills.

Pass the door to the deck and inspect the two crates on the right wall. Between them are five health vials. At the corridor's end is a ramp, a flak cannon on a small crate, and two flak ammo packs. Follow the ramp to a curved corridor to the left. Pass through four adrenaline pills to finish the outer circular corridor at the biorifle near the double damage. Find two bio ammo packs here.

Return to the double elevator bank and ride either elevator down to the lower deck. Beneath and between the elevators is a crate stack with a second 50 shield pack on top. To reach it, double jump off a moving elevator (in either direction). Find two health packs and rocket ammo to the stack's right. Jump atop a smaller crate stack to claim another rocket ammo pack. On the opposite wall are left and right corridors to the magma pool; grab four adrenaline pills. Between the corridor entrances, a small alcove holds a shock rifle and two ammo packs.

Enter the magma pool area. A smoke vent on the left side blows you up into the main deck's middle (either to the main ledge or the platform), or you can land on the center strut for the 100 shield pack. Move to the far end of the magma pool, under the double damage, and take the rocket launcher and two ammo packs. Step into a red-glowing teleporter and into a tiny upper chamber with the redeemer! Drop down to the double elevator junction, armed to the teeth!

Deathmatch Dealing

Deck 17 is all about finding the redeemer or sniping those seeking it. Drop down and collect the 100 shield pack on the rafters under the main deck platform, then drop to the rocket launcher and into the teleporter before anyone can catch you. Grab the redeemer, but watch for enemies with the same plan. Once you take the redeemer, step onto a pipe and fire the redeemer into the main deck.

The main area is a great sniping spot; leap to the gap between the wall pipes in the corners for an unexpected camping spot. Double jump over the ramp nearest the double damage to snag this powerful power-up; this is the opposite direction from the redeemer, so choose.

Use a flak cannon on the outer corridor where there's more room. Save the shock rifle for the lower magma pit, or combo those trying to reach the 100 shield pack into the lava (try it at the flak cannon near the lava pond, and the sniper rifle at the lava ramp). Although there are two biorifles, these are useful only in certain circumstances. Confine yourself to the outer corridor, spraying goop on enemies or corners and junctions.

279

TOURNAMENT 2004

The corner of the flak cannon corridor with the sniper rifle is another great sniping spot, as you can see far down two corridors. A good place for leaping is the middle entrance to the main deck, atop the center ramp. Double jump left to the minigun. While near the minigun, use the lip to reach the link gun or just double jump across. Double jump up on the barrels to the right of the Deck 16 sign, across the barricade, and double jump atop the crates for another snipe spot. View most of the level from the shock rifle area near the DD; aim at the lower magma pool or the double elevator area.

Deck 17 is a translocator's paradise. Translocate into the redeemer area from the double elevator junction. Translocate onto the "17" sign above the door where the minigun is. From here, translocate atop the pipes running above the ledges, and camp. You're next to the ceiling and can shuffle to the shock rifle ledge! Also try translocating onto the monitor (above the door to the biorifle) or the light fittings, as well as to the large crate stack near the double damage and health.

DM-DESERTISLE

Recommended Players: 4–8

Legend

1	Link Gun +2 ammo packs	**6**	100 Shield Pack (and 50 Health Packs x2)	**9**	Adrenaline Pills x5 (and Minigun +2 ammo packs)
2	Flak Cannon +2 ammo packs				
3	Health Vials x4	**7**	50 Health Pack (and Rocket Launcher +2 ammo packs)	**10**	Biorifle +2 ammo packs (and Double Damage)
4	50 Shield Pack				
5	50 Health Pack (and shock, mini, rocket ammo packs under bridge)	**8**	Shock Rifle +2 ammo packs (and 50 Health Pack)	**11**	Lightning Gun
				12	Redeemer (on bridge)

Overview

This open-air level is a streambed that starts within a rockfall near a lightning gun and cuts through a ravine to a waterfall. From the pond below the falls, the stream flows to a shield generator marking the map's outskirts.

Use the lightning gun on the riverside, and use close-quarter weapons on the hill down to the 100 shield pack, creating two distinct combat areas. Chase down enemies going for the redeemer and double damage, but the most cunning players take advantage of the surrounding rocky plateaus.

Available Weapons

Biorifle (at junction halfway up hill, on poolside gully)

Shock Rifle (bottom of poolside gully near shield pack)

Link Gun (large rock shelf near waterfall elevator)

Minigun (stream's right side, past redeemer bridge)

Flak Cannon (stream's right side, near waterfall)

Rocket Launcher (stream's left side, near elevators)

Lightning Gun (end of stream, on right bank near wind chimes)

Redeemer (redeemer bridge's far end, above rocket launcher)

Available Power-ups

Double Damage (on rock shelf near stream)

50 Shield Pack (atop main bridge, middle of map)

100 Shield Pack (in pool at waterfall's base)

Map Patrol

Begin at the 100 shield pack, submerged in a pool near a waterfall. Head onto dry land right of the waterfall to find a health pack and elevator. The elevator leads to a rock shelf and a natural bridge over the waterfall, near a link gun. Left of the waterfall is a health pack near some rocks. On the outer edge of the gulley, opposite the waterfall is a shock rifle in a wooded area with two ammo packs.

Follow the five adrenaline pills to the cliff's midsection. A path on the left leads up. Find a biorifle and two ammo packs at this junction. To the right is a flat path overlooking the pool on your right, leading to the waterfall's top. Turn left and follow the stream under the natural bridge accessed via the elevator.

In the long grass on the stream's right side are a flak cannon and two ammo packs. Pass under the natural bridge and continue around the stream. Once under this bridge, check the health pack on your right. Dodge jump to the arch under the bridge for mini, shock, and rocket ammo. From here, run around the middle path circling the map's center.

Back at the stream, to the left of the rock in the water is a clearing with a rocket launcher and two ammo packs. Left of that is an elevator. Use this to reach the central circular path, or elevator jump and double jump atop the large central bridge and land on a 50 shield pack. A second elevator on the circular path allows you to land on the bridge or the other bridge leading to the redeemer.

Continue upstream under the redeemer bridge to a minigun and two ammo packs on the right bank. When the left bank becomes green, double jump to the circular path; there are two health packs under the redeemer bridge. From here you can bounce up the rocks to the beginning of the redeemer bridge or to the stream's end bridge. Or, cross the stream's end bridge from the opposite side, double jumping up and around from the minigun.

With the stream ended, run up the grassy bank, checking right for the lightning gun. Listen for the wind chimes—they jingle near the gun. Nearby, a wind chime arch points down the valley to the 100 shield pack pool. Pass through the arch and down the gully to reach the biorifle you saw earlier, or climb the hill to the left to reach the circular path and large bridge.

Check the level's upper areas by climbing the hill or using elevator jumps. The main huge bridge with the 50 shield pack has four health vials and lightning gun ammo in the middle. The plateau at the far end is a great sniping spot. Drop to the link gun above the waterfall with three ammo packs (also reached via the pool elevator), or to the other side and long rock shelf. This is completely exposed, so watch your step.

Reach the double damage by dropping from the main bridge or the redeemer bridge, or by elevator jumping from the upper elevator on the circular path. The redeemer bridge entrance is next to the main bridge, near the 50 shield pack. Run to the redeemer on the other side—out in the open.

Deathmatch Dealing

The circular object above this valley and wooded area is an energy field that prevents you from venturing too far into the rocky outer area, and it cannot be deactivated. Concentrate on the flak cannon and rocket launcher on the riverbed; most of the action occurs here. Take a nearby elevator and jump onto the central natural bridge to get the 50 shield pack. The 100 shield pack, at the bottom of a pond near a waterfall, is great, but players running for it could be ambushed.

The map contains many sniping spots, such as the central bridge's far end, the area near the double damage, and any of the natural bridges. You can snag only the DD and 50 shield pack in quick succession. Ignore the flak cannon, biorifle, or link gun unless you're heading down the steep hill into close combat or toward the 100 shield pack. Otherwise, use long-range fire, such as shock comboing punks off bridges, or aiming the lightning gun from a secure location.

You can claim the redeemer (although competent rivals guard it), double jump to the double damage, and then launch it, but it's better to move and shoot from a low-traffic area, such as the rocks near the link gun. Remember the alternate route: shield jump from the double damage plateau up to the redeemer.

For the most impressive sniping spot, double jump from redeemer to the upper overhang above the lightning gun, and slide down to the lip. You won't fall. Bound across to the outer area above and right of the wind-chime archway. Stay up here and plug away, overlooking the entire level. Run around the rock plateaus to the edge of the shield generator, and dodge shield jump (or double jump) across the crevasse downstream of the 100 shield pack to the waterfall elevator. All this area is perfect for sniping or letting off the redeemer. Top that by translocating or double jumping from the plateau above the wood to the top of a tree! You can even double jump across the tops of the trees if you're skilled enough!

DM-GOLIATH
Recommended Players: 4–8

Legend

1. Health Vials x2 (connecting tunnel to DD room and #28)
2. Bio, link, mini ammo packs (central area)
3. 50 Health Pack
4. Biorifle
5. 100 Shield Pack (on upper mesh walkway)
6. Link ammo packs x2 (on mesh walkway)
7. Lightning Gun
8. Bio, Flak, lightning ammo packs
9. Link Gun (in connecting tunnel)
10. 50 Health Packs x2
11. Flak Cannon
12. Shock and mini ammo packs
13. Shock and rocket ammo packs
14. Rocket Launcher (middle of central area)
15. 50 Health Packs x2 (inside central area)
16. Rocket and lightning ammo packs (on mesh ledge)
17. Adrenaline Pills x3 (upper central opening)
18. Shock ammo packs x2 (floor with opening high above)
19. Shock Rifle
20. Bio and mini ammo packs
21. 50 Shield Pack
22. Health Vials x6
23. Link Gun (inside connecting tunnel)
24. Minigun (below mesh plinth)
25. Redeemer (between roof joists and platform)
26. Shock, link ammo packs
27. Double Damage
28. Health Vials x2 (leading to #1)
29. Bio and mini ammo packs
30. Bio, rocket, lightning ammo packs
31. Adrenaline Pills x3, Health Vials x2 (upper secret area)
32. Bio, flak, rocket, lightning ammo packs (upper secret area)
33. 50 Health Pack (upper secret area)

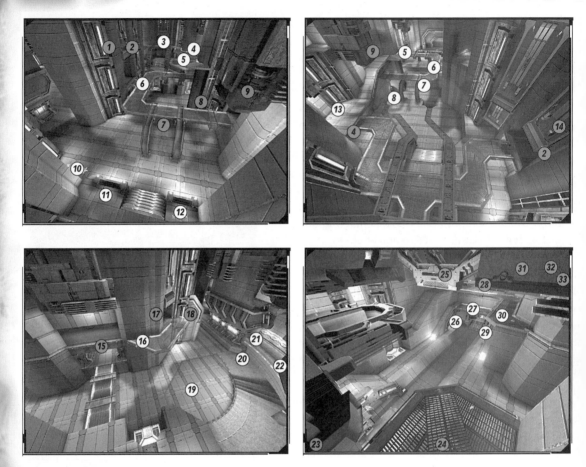

Overview

Goliath is divided into three main areas linked in a circle, with a central tower in the middle and snaking walkways all over. As usual, the impressive power-ups are atop walkways or ledges, including a well-hidden redeemer within jumping distance of the double damage. The middle elevator leads to a third floor hidey-hole if you elevator jump. The only way to the 100 shield jump is via that balcony platform; keep zigzagging because you're more susceptible to snipers than usual.

Available Weapons	
Biorifle (raised corner of the 100 shield pack chamber, near lightning gun)	**Minigun** (in left corner near tunnel entrance opposite the double damage)
Shock Rifle (in chamber's middle near the 50 shield pack)	**Flak Cannon** (next to teleporter on opposite side of 100 shield pack chamber to biorifle)
Link Gun (x2, middle of small U-shaped tunnel near double damage or by 100 shield pack; near mesh walkways)	**Rocket Launcher** (2nd floor of middle thoroughfare, near central elevator)
	Lightning Gun (between two ramps, under 100 shield pack)

Redeemer (on high ledge just under whirring cylinder, above double damage)

Available Power-ups

Double Damage (on mesh balcony above teleporter, below 3rd floor ledge)

50 Shield Pack (in curved ground alcove near six health vials and shock rifle)

100 Shield Pack (on top of upper walkway above lightning gun)

Map Patrol

Starting at the 100 shield pack, follow the walkway down the right outer wall to a yellow-lit alcove with flak, rocket, and shock ammo packs. Take the walkway junction left, to the large tunnel entrance on your right and an identical walkway ahead. Both end at tunnels.

The beginning of the right tunnel holds a health pack. Pass through four health vials out to another gigantic chamber. Note a U-shaped walkway in front of you, and a rotating shaft above your head (don't touch that!). Drop into the middle of the "U" to claim the double damage on a mesh balcony below. Follow the mesh walkway around to the left of the double damage to shock, bio, and rocket ammo packs.

Now move back to the two tunnel entrances on the walkway near the 100 shield pack, and take the other one. There's a corner to the left, and on the right wall are mini, link, and bio ammo packs. There's also a junction with a rocket launcher to the left. Go right, following the three adrenaline pills to an outer balcony overlooking the 50 shield pack alcove. Drop down or head right to grab the lightning and rocket ammo packs. The balcony stops, so hug the right wall and move around the lip to the trio of ammo packs near the double damage.

An important elevator is in the shadows at the rocket launcher, but don't enter it yet. Head past the rocket launcher to the junction. A hole in the wall looks out on the curved 50 shield pack alcove. Two shock ammo packs lie under the hole. To the left is a mesh walkway under the 100 shield pack. You can't reach the pack, but you can pick up two link ammo packs. Take either walkway into a connecting tunnel containing a link gun and out to the other side where you got the link ammo.

Move to the rocket launcher, ride the elevator up, and elevator jump up to a hidden third-floor room above the rocket launcher. The lift platform stops at the rocket launcher, so jump! The room holds a health pack and a view of the 100 shield pack on the ledge's left side. To the left are lightning, rocket, flak, and bio ammo packs. A small ramp has three health vials and two adrenaline pills at the top. The ramp goes down to a small mesh ledge overlooking the double damage below. Snag the double damage. Turn left and shield jump from this upper ledge to a higher platform that's part of the cylinder whirring mechanism to find the redeemer!

Move back to the double damage area and take the ramp to the ground floor; check the elevator and the water-soaked channel. Teleport to a flak cannon to the side of the arena with the lightning gun, under the 100 shield pack. An identical teleporter returns here. Double jump up the opposite sloping sides to a minigun and a tunnel entrance.

The tunnel bends left to a link gun and left again out to a short mesh walkway and into the central thoroughfare. A large exit corridor lies at the minigun. Run under the mesh walkway to a huge open area. To the right is a small elevator up to the raised area near the mesh walkway on the right. Head left, around a large curved alcove and steps, and find six health vials leading to a 50 shield pack. The middle of the chamber holds a shock rifle. On the opposite wall are minigun and bio ammo packs. At the far end of the corridor are two shock rifle ammo packs.

To the left, a ramp leads to the central thoroughfare. The elevator to the hidden room is on your left. The thoroughfare splits, and the left route joins the mesh walkway at the shield pack alcove chamber with two health packs on the way. The other route leads you to the other side of the 100 shield pack chamber, opposite the teleporter and across from a biorifle.

At the two shock ammo packs, double jump onto the raised area. Head left around the corner (past two health packs) to the 100 shield pack chamber. The power-up is up and left on the high walkway. Head up the steps on the right. Turn left to nab mini and shock ammo packs and right to steal the flak cannon; then go through the teleporter to exit under the double damage.

Head into the room's center. Under the circular mesh walkway to the first link gun is a U-shaped double ramp. Between the ramps is a lightning gun. On the other side is an elevator to the left and right. Elevator jump off either to land on the mesh walkway. On the right are flak, bio, and lightning ammo packs. On the raised area above the elevators are steps. Head left to return to the middle thoroughfare. Head right to secure the biorifle.

Deathmatch Dealing

Don't be put off by the map's sheer size. The higher you are off the ground, the more probable your victory. Focus on the double damage and the middle elevator that leads to it. The double damage is easily grabbed from its balcony at the ramp's top; head to the secret third floor to secure ammo and leap for the redeemer (with a careful shield jump) hidden in the whirring cylinder above. Try shield jumping to the upper ledge, too.

Regular combat continues along the ground, with shock rifle and lightning gun aficionados taking posts at spots such as the ground elevator near the double damage overlooking the 50 shield pack alcove, the end of the curved shallow steps near the shock rifle (peer through the gap and tag those attempting to reach the flak cannon), and the biorifle (there's a great view across to the flak cannon and the building's middle).

For a sniping point that's difficult to spot, you need extra height. Try the 100 shield pack area, the link gun chamber under it (use the interior to sidestep into cover), even the third floor central tower opening overlooking the biorifle (accessed from the central elevator). From the second floor gap, above the two shock rifle ammo packs, double jump diagonally right to the sloping sides of the central building.

Creep to the building's end and snipe down to the 50 shield pack, or drop to the second floor balcony and head back to the rocket launcher. Or double jump across the gap between this and the outer wall. Land on a tiny lip and head left to a view of the 100 shield pack area; great for sniping! Head right until you're almost on top of the 50 shield pack for a good line of sight to the base of the double damage chamber.

On the ground at the 100 shield pack chamber, shield jump onto the curved walkway supports and bound to the top. Also try elevator jumping on them or double jumping from the raised area near the flak cannon. Don't forget the lip of the central building on the ledge by the double damage. Hug the left wall and creep to the continuation of the platform; double jump across to secure the 50 shield pack.

DM-HYPERBLAST2

Legend

1 Flak Cannon +2 ammo packs (lower corridor)	**6** Adrenaline Pills x3	**13** 50 Shield Pack	**20** 50 Health Pack
2 Biorifle +2 ammo packs (lower corridor)	**7** Link Gun +1 ammo pack	**14** Adrenaline Pills x3	**21** Health Vials x5 (left side)
3 Adrenaline Pills x3	**8** 50 Health Packs x2	**15** 50 Health Pack (inside arm)	**22** Bio ammo packs x3 (left side)
4 Rocket Launcher +2 ammo packs	**9** 50 Health Packs x2	**16** Adrenaline Pill	**23** Minigun +2 ammo packs
5 Shock Rifle +2 ammo packs (back of craft exterior)	**10** Link Gun +1 ammo pack	**17** Health Vials x5 (right side)	**24** Adrenaline Pill
	11 50 Health Pack (inside arm)	**18** Bio ammo packs x3 (right side)	**25** Link Gun +2 ammo packs
	12 Adrenaline Pills x3	**19** 100 Shield Pack	**26** Adrenaline Pill

Overview

Those with awards from previous tournaments should welcome the return of this old favorite, now altered to avoid needless sniping. Lack of the double damage and sniper rifle adds an air of ease, until you realize you're one wrong jump from deep-space oblivion! Use the inside and outside of the ship to collect the necessary armor for a win, and know which windows to jump though and which corridors to avoid. Note the normal gravity inside the ship, and low gravity around the exterior.

Available Weapons

Biorifle (end of lowest corridor, near open window and embedded ramp)

Shock Rifle (aft of ship's exterior, above 100 shield pack)

Link Gun (x2, exterior end of each arm)

Minigun (end of 50 shield pack corridor interior)

Flak Cannon (end of lowest corridor, near open window and embedded ramp)

Rocket Launcher (middle of upper exterior superstructure)

Available Power-ups

50 Shield Pack (middle of interior corridor overlooking exterior arms)

100 Shield Pack (middle of semicircular corridor)

Map Patrol

Starting outside in deep space, stand and view the exterior of the hyperblast cruiser from the stern—the circular area with the shock rifle and two ammo packs. Look forward and down to see two decks on the other side; one contains a link gun. You can float to these or to the semicircular walkway under you, which has the 100 shield pack. The opening is opposite the deck openings. Leap off the side and glide through any of the walkway's front windows.

Move to the middle of the ship's exterior, above the two decks, and snag a rocket launcher and two ammo packs. Find two sets of four adrenaline pills on the outer edges. Now drop down the two frontal "arms" and down either of the giant ramps (used to reach the rocket launcher). Below each ramp are two health packs; behind you doors lead to the craft's interior.

On the interior sides of the arms are two openings with a platform. These lead to the inner arm corridors and a ramp to the lower deck. An additional opening on the right arm (if you're looking forward toward the hyperspace hole) lets you land a little farther along the arm's interior. Atop the end of the superstructure arm is a link gun on each side. Beyond that is the front of the arms—unsafe but reachable. You could land on one of two space fighters flying under the hyperblast cruiser, but once you land on them you're too low to jump back. Look back at the ship's sides under the rocket launcher to see the upper empty corridor and the 50 shield pack corridor.

289

Starting inside the craft at the semicircular corridor and 100 shield pack, double jump to the upper deck, lower deck, or two side platforms at each end of the lower deck. Now check the corridor's interior curves to find five health vials and three bio ammo packs on each side and a health pack behind the shield pack.

The ship has four internal corridors and two internal arm corridors. Access the three main corridors from the semicircular corridor. At each end is a junction with a ramp to an empty corridor and access outside to the top of the ship; there's space on either side to reach the arm and a 50 shield pack corridor, and another link gun corridor to the left or right. The link gun corridor has a short ramp with an adrenaline pill and a link gun with two ammo packs. To one side, an open window overlooks the 100 shield pack. Drop to the shield pack or the three platforms of the lowest corridor. At the corridor's end, another ramp leads to the other arm and the end of the 50 shield pack corridor, and to a door to the semicircular corridor.

Head up the ramp and check the empty corridor. The middle window looks out on the space fighters and the drop to the three arm platforms. Down at the corridor below, find an adrenaline pill, a junction, three more pills down a ramp to a 50 shield pack, and an identical ramp with pills on the other side. At the 50 shield pack, view the maneuvering space fighters below, and double jump to the platforms left and right leading to the arm corridor interiors. At the junction gap for the left arm, find a minigun and two ammo packs.

Check either interior arm corridor. Each has a ramp, a health pack, an open window with a platform (leap onto the 50 shield pack or the opposite arm platform); the right arm has an additional platform. Both have teleporters, but these are disabled.

Step down the embedded ramps to the lowest corridor, which connects with the other end. Find a flak cannon and two ammo at one end (under the minigun), and a biorifle and two ammo at the other. Three window exits work for sniping or suicide; look up to see the 100 shield pack area. Return to the action via a ramp.

Deathmatch Dealing

If you get the shock rifle and ammo, patrol the exterior, comboing slower-moving punks into oblivion. A link gun or the minigun also works well. Overpower a rocket-launcher-toting foe by instant-hit peppering.

When you're exiting the craft, usually on a door above the arms, turn and check for ambush above you; the slow-mo combat outside is perfect for this. If you have the shock rifle, jump to the arms' far end, turn around, and plug leaping foes with single-hit strikes. Also try this by the link guns, using the spotlights for cover.

Try to reach the 100 shield pack as soon as possible, and remember you can fly in from any exterior window or opening. Hunt down foes along the corridors, heading for the 50 shield pack (which is likely to have been taken). Avoid the middle of the corridors.

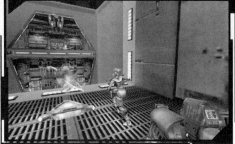

Spread biorifle goo on enemies exiting the indented arm ramp or trying to land on a ledge from outer space. Weapons grabbed outside are more impressive on the inside; rocket launchers and shock rifles shooting down the corridors are devastating. Take the health vials while heading for the shield pack; set up a snipe point outside, overlooking the window by the shield packs. Outside hiding spots are scarce unless you count the satellite dish and protruding superstructure on the underside, near the ledges for the lower corridor.

Inside however, the hiding spots become more interesting. Use the low outside gravity to bounce on an outside ledge, and steer onto pipes and ceiling structures on the corridor. Do this near the biorifle or flak cannon corridor, move in the darkness across the ceiling pipes, and lie in wait. Or wait on the jutting bank of wires above this corridor's center.

Translocate to the steam pipes in the arm corridor and to the pipes above the 50 shield pack. Use the interior ramps at the end of the two corridors to reach the top corridor, double jumping to the pipes, then to the lip above the doors opposite (leading to the semicircular hall and 100 shield pack). Steer in from outside or translocate to the top of the lights on the outer walls of the 100 shield pack area, or to the tiny platform above the 100 shield pack.

DM-METALLURGY

Recommended Players: 6–10

Legend

1	Lightning Gun +2 ammo packs	9	Rocket Launcher	16	Health Vials x3 (lower inner area)	23	Assault ammo packs x2
2	Rocket ammo pack	10	Rocket ammo packs x2	17	Health Vials x3 (inner platform)	24	Bio ammo packs x2
3	Rocket ammo pack	11	Minigun +2 ammo packs	18	50 Health Pack	25	Biorifle
4	Link Gun (also #20)	12	Health Vials x3	19	Double Damage	26	50 Shield Pack
5	50 Health Pack	13	50 Health Pack	20	Link Gun	27	Adrenaline Pills x3
6	Minigun +2 ammo packs	14	Shock ammo packs x2	21	Link ammo pack	28	Rocket Launcher
7	Adrenaline Pills x3	15	Shock Rifle	22	Link ammo pack	29	Assault ammo packs x2
8	Flak Cannon +2 ammo packs						

291

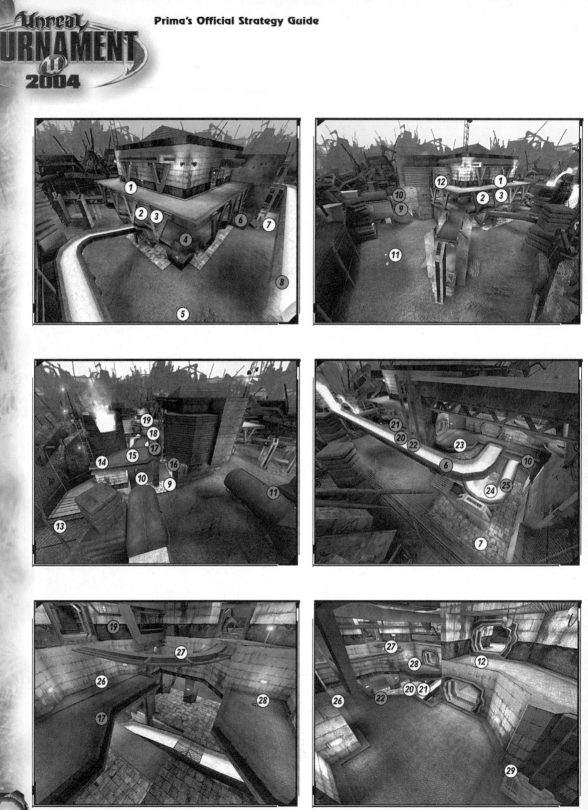

Overview

In this large smelting building, chutes of lava add an additional sense of danger to a maze of connecting ramps, ledges, and corridors. You have only two power-ups: a 50 shield pack reached by almost every entrance, and a more-difficult-to-reach double damage. Lower down are platforms clutching the exterior and large outer grounds near an interior series of chambers, where you're most at risk from snipers above. The height and numerous angles of attack and camping posts make this a deadly deathmatch until you figure your way around.

Available Weapons

Biorifle (lower ground area, near second minigun set)

Shock Rifle (top of ramped walkway, under double damage ledge)

Link Gun (ground floor on tile, near multiple ramped exits)

Minigun (x2, next to elevator shaft outside; ground floor raised area in smelting side chamber)

Flak Cannon (between two fuel trucks, outside)

Rocket Launcher (x2, alcove in shield pack room under lightning gun; on tiles at base of steps to shock rifle walkway)

Lightning Gun (upper ledge above rocket launcher)

Available Power-ups

Double Damage (on upper ledge overlooking shock rifle walkway)

50 Shield Pack (in middle area, 2nd floor, accessed via numerous entrances)

Map Patrol

Beginning at the top of the smelter, at the long ledge with the lightning gun and two ammo packs, peer down at the ore chute (drop onto the edge for a haphazard sniping point) and turn right. Jog to the right corner and peer down to an outer elevator shaft and platform with a minigun to the right on the ground below. You can elevator jump from the lift platform up to this ledge if you time it right.

While on the upper ledge, turn right and head through the door. An L-shaped walkway contains three health vials, and an elevator to your left descends a level to the smelter shield pack area. Use the elevator to reach the ledge and the lightning gun. Now return to the lightning gun and head left.

Turn the left corner, and move along the ledge to a door on your left. Peer out to see a flak cannon with ammo near two fuel trucks on the ground below. Enter the door and you're above the shield pack area. From here, step left to the rocket launcher alcove, step right and double jump to the 50 shield pack or the ground, or follow the beam. The beam has three adrenaline pills and leads to a door and a small ledge with the double damage. Peer left over the DD ledge to spot the lower ramped area and shock rifle walkway and a door on the left wall. This door leads to two minigun ammo packs and the shield pack area near the elevator to the lightning gun.

Head through the door to the right of the DD ledge and into the smelting side chamber. You're on a tiny ledge above the pouring ore. Drop to the ledge below or check the hole in the outer wall, which is an elevator shaft to the ground. To quickly snag the DD, use this lift platform; it's adjacent to the biorifle on the ground level.

Drop to the lower level ledge, just below the DD ledge, in the smelting side chamber. Find two assault ammo packs and two doors. The door ahead leads around the outside of the plant, with an open area to the left, to the ground below. Before you reach the right corner, turn and look out at the trucks and flak cannon to get your bearings. After the corner, a door on your right is flanked by two rocket launcher ammo packs. This is under the lightning gun and leads to the rocket launcher alcove, which is above the link gun by the ore chute below.

Continue past the rocket launcher door to see the outer elevator shaft and platform down to the minigun. Make a right, and through a door is the central 50 shield pack area. Walk out the door opposite and you're just below the DD ledge, back where you started on this floor. Under the DD ledge is a health pack and the door to the smelting side chamber. To the left is the shock rifle walkway.

Grab the shock rifle and two ammo packs, and look over the edge at the health pack and ramp below. Follow the ramp down (optionally jump down to the two rocket ammo packs) to the health pack and down the steps to the ground.

Left is the plant's ground level. Ahead is a hilly gravel area with a minigun, two ammo packs, and the outer elevator shaft. On the left are two ramped entrances to the inside and the underside of the ore chute in the middle. At the far end of the perimeter is a health pack. Turn the left corner again for the flak cannon, two ammo

packs, and the trucks on the right, and another three plant ramp entrances on your left. Continue to the smelting side chamber on the ground floor. Enter the base: either climb the steps to the left to claim the minigun and two ammo packs, or descend the indented tile ramp. Three adrenaline pills are at the corner, which leads to the biorifle, two ammo packs, and an elevator to the DD ledge.

Ahead and right are three health vials, and at the far side are two rocket ammo packs and the launcher on the left, next to the shock rifle ramped area. Head back into the lower ground area. The elevator opposite the health vials leads to the raised ground area.

At the elevator's top is a tiled floor and a ramp down. Left is a mesh walkway to the right with three health vials. This leads back to the second minigun. Back at the elevator, cross the ore chute over the mesh and you're at the link gun. Two link ammo packs and another ramped

exit lie to your right. The link gun overlooks the three ramped exits to the trucks and flak cannon. Don't forget the elevator to the left, ascending to the shield pack.

Deathmatch Dealing

Falling in the lava chutes is even more deadly than a rocket to the torso. Use the shock rifle to blast enemies into the chute below (it doesn't count as a frag for you, but drops your opponent down a point). Otherwise, work on a quick and competent route between the shield pack, double damage, and a meaty weapon such as the rocket launcher, lightning gun, or flak cannon.

While on this circuit, stop and snipe from various points, such as the tiny upper alcove near the DD, the alcove above the rocket launcher in the shield pack chamber, and anywhere along the upper platforms that gives a view of the outside ground. Stay on the upper levels, peer down or across at your foes, and listen for elevators moving; set a trap by activating an elevator, dropping off it, then training your guns on enemies coming in to check.

Numerous unsafe but cunning sniping points dot the main platform and smelting building. For example, you can leap from the double damage balcony to the giant smelting cylinder to the right. Land on the lip! Double jump to the lip to the left, then drop to the barbed wire fence. Walk around this until you reach a large rusting tank across from the shock rifle. Dodge jump, shield jump, or double jump to this cylinder from the shock rifle, too. This spot is sweet for checking the double damage, the lower rocket launcher, and the outer elevator area to your right.

The lightning gun is another key area from which to leap. Round the corner to the left and shield jump up on the pipe. Scramble onto the rooftop and fight; drop onto the platforms below, including the double damage one. Find incredible sniping potential here! Jump to the outer elevator, and elevator jump (or double jump) to a pipe on the outer edge, behind the elevator for a good view of the level.

DM-MORPHEUS3

Recommended Players: 2–8

Legend

#		#		#		#	
1	Adrenaline Pills x3	9	Mini ammo pack	17	Double Damage / Big Keg-O-Health	24	Assault ammo packs x2
2	50 Health Packs x2 (under roof)	10	50 Health Packs x2 (under roof)	18	Link Gun (red building)	25	Sniper Rifle (inside blue building)
3	Redeemer	11	Adrenaline Pills x3	19	Link ammo packs x2	26	Sniper ammo packs x2
4	Rocket ammo pack	12	100 Shield Pack	20	Ion Painter	27	Adrenaline Pills x2 and Assault ammo packs
5	Rocket Launcher	13	50 Health Packs x2 (under roof)	21	Rocket Launcher +2 ammo packs	28	Adrenaline Pills x2 and Assault ammo pack
6	Rocket ammo pack	14	Shock ammo pack	22	Adrenaline Pills x3	29	Adrenaline Pills x2 and Assault ammo pack
7	Mini ammo pack	15	Shock Rifle	23	Minigun (inside yellow building)		
8	Minigun	16	Shock ammo pack				

295

Overview

A classic returns! High above the stratosphere on the edge of space are the roofs of three colossal skyscrapers. There's a central platform and helipad, above which are windows leading to an interior floor, a ramp to a balcony, and a roof above that. There are even power-ups on the antenna towers! The low-grav mutation is on by default, so adjust your jumping accordingly and don't fall.

Available Weapons

Shock Rifle (middle of blue skyscraper roof)

Link Gun (interior of red skyscraper, left of window)

Minigun (interior of yellow skyscraper, left of window)

Rocket Launcher (middle of blue skyscraper roof)

Sniper Rifle (interior of blue skyscraper, left of window)

Redeemer (atop yellow tower top)

Ion Painter (on helipad below all three buildings)

Available Power-ups

Double Damage (randomly appearing with big keg-o-health atop blue tower)

100 Shield Pack (atop red tower)

Big Keg-O-Health (randomly appearing with double damage atop blue tower)

Map Patrol

The three buildings are identical except for height (red is shortest, blue is next, yellow is tallest), so the descriptions are for each building interior and exterior.

Starting from the lowest point, on a walkway below all three skyscraper roofs, there's a rocket launcher and two ammo packs. Along the walkway are three adrenaline pills and a jump pad up to a helipad. On the helipad is the ion painter. Due to the gravity, the jump pad takes you to the rooftop of the building you steer near, so for a quick ion painter grab, drop onto the helipad instead of using the pad.

Inside each building are two advertising screens on a wall, a leaderboard screen, and an open window. The red and blue buildings look out on the rocket launcher below. The yellow window looks out on the helipad below. Double jump to each of the other buildings' balconies from the window.

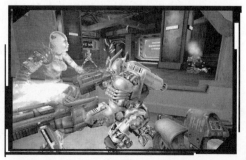

Each building has a weapon left of the window and two ammo beside the adjacent pillar. The red building has a link gun, the blue building has a sniper rifle, and the yellow building has a minigun. In each building, a corridor exits to the balcony ramp with two adrenaline pills and an assault ammo pack. Up on each balcony are two health packs.

The other way to the roof is via the roof ramp, each with three adrenaline pills. The blue roof contains a shock rifle and two ammo packs. The red roof has a minigun with two ammo. The yellow roof has a rocket launcher with two ammo. Double jump from the blue roof to reach the red roof. Use the red roof to reach the blue roof's lower antenna ledge and the yellow roof. Double jump from the yellow roof to reach the roof of the red building and the blue building's upper antenna ledge.

Double jump vertically to reach the three-ledged antenna points atop the roof. The blue roof has a double damage and a big keg-o-health randomly appearing. The red roof has a 100 shield pack. The yellow roof has a redeemer. The higher the building, the higher the ledge you can reach if you're leaping from building to building.

Deathmatch Dealing

Though the ion painter is an easily obtainable weapon with devastating potential, be careful. Because it emits a laser and takes seconds to fire, you can be picked off before you even fire it. Therefore, drop down to snag the ion painter first, then take the rocket launcher, jump pad up, and fire it either into a nearby window or on a roof. As you're firing, stand with the laser pointing to the ground, ideally in cover, then quickly flick the laser out at the last possible second.

Understand the differences in height of each skyscraper so you can double jump to other parts of adjacent buildings. For example, the yellow skyscraper is the tallest, so you easily can bound over to the blue building's antenna tower; this arching jump may be easier than jumping up on the spot to reach the two ledges before the power-up atop each antenna tower. The grand prize is the redeemer, which is an easier weapon to let off. Wait for a group to congregate on a building, then fire the redeemer from a safe point (under the roof ramp for example). If you're steering the rocket, aim for the upper balcony or window, depending on where the enemies moved.

Although a large part of the game is securing the added health, armor, and double damage atop the towers, reaching them can be a problem, so check these locations from a sniping point. The best places from which to snipe are the backs of the balconies near the indented ramp or the windows inside. Step into the shadowy interior and use the side walls as cover; you still have a good view.

If you're attacking amateurish enemies, employ instant-hit weapons, especially when leaping from building to building. Although the rocket launcher is more powerful, the giant jumps make hitting more difficult, so train a shock rifle or minigun on them instead. The shock rifle is especially amusing if you can predict an enemy's movement; the low gravity propels them much farther than normal—sometimes off the buildings entirely!

Stand atop the roof ramp. You can hide behind the antenna tower of the building in front of you and sidestep left and right to the ramp's top and mid-section. You can be ambushed only by enemies coming around from behind. The balcony and roof areas are very open, so head down the indented ramp for cover. Check the middle platform below for enemies trying to grab the rocket launcher; use a shock combo to send them flailing into the stratosphere.

Quickly check the leaderboard sign inside the buildings; see who is in first place and go after him. Coat the ground in biorifle ooze, especially around blind corners, the top of the indented ramp on the balcony, the antenna, the helipad, and the window ledges.

Make single jumps to adjacent buildings instead of double ones at times, as double jumps may leave you sliding down a wall. Double jump at different times as well to increase your distance; the low gravity really makes a difference. You can even shield jump to the antenna's tip, standing on the light!

DM-RANKIN

Recommended Players: 2–8

Legend

1	Health Vials x3
2	Health Vials x3
3	Lightning Gun +2 ammo packs
4	Adrenaline Pills x3
5	Health Vials x2
6	Health Vials x4
7	Shock ammo pack
8	Shock Rifle
9	Shock ammo pack
10	50 Health Pack
11	Link ammo packs x2
12	Link Gun
13	Adrenaline Pills x3
14	Double Damage
15	Health Vials x3
16	Link Gun +2 ammo packs
17	50 Health Pack
18	50 Health Pack
19	Adrenaline Pills x3
20	100 Shield Pack (basement dead-end)
21	Rocket Launcher
22	Minigun +2 ammo packs
23	Rocket ammo pack
24	Rocket ammo pack
25	Bio ammo packs x2
26	Biorifle
27	50 Health Pack
28	Assault and shock ammo packs
29	50 Health Pack
30	Flak Cannon +2 ammo packs

299

Overview

Rankin is an abandoned factory in a severe electrical storm. The three main sections are a sub-basement with exceptional weapons and power-ups, a slightly higher area with a shock rifle and double damage, an upper series of corridors, and an open courtyard that connects with two long upper corridors. Try to balance obtaining powerful weapons with being blasted trying to reach them.

Available Weapons	
Biorifle (2nd floor corridor linking upper areas of shock rifle and rocket launcher areas)	**Flak Cannon** (in thoroughfare, on ground floor, near double damage)
Shock Rifle (on ground tile chamber near double damage)	**Rocket Launcher** (end of lower sub-basement area, near shield pack)
Link Gun (x2, under wooden ramp above rocket launcher; in small side room near shock rifle chamber)	**Lightning Gun** (3rd floor balcony overlooking both the DD and flak cannon)
	Available Power-ups
Minigun (3rd floor balcony overlooking rocket launcher)	**Double Damage** (in curved corridor, ground floor, between shock rifle and flak cannon)
	100 Shield Pack (dead-end in sub-basement, across from flak cannon)

Map Patrol

Starting on the ground floor, at the 100 shield pack at the end of a dead-end corridor, look across the corridor junction to a tunnel. There's a ramp in the distance up to the flak cannon thoroughfare. Look at the hole in the ceiling; use this to fall from the biorifle corridor above. From the shield pack, look left at the intersection. At the corridor's end is a rocket launcher. Wooden planks propped on either side of it serve as ramps to the second floor junction (and the link gun to the right). Behind the planks are two rocket ammo packs.

Back at the intersection, the adrenaline pill bridge is above you at the other end of the link gun junction (drop down from here to claim the shield pack). Run up the stairs to the right, under the bridge and into the courtyard with the shock rifle and two ammo packs on the lower paved ground. To the right is a health pack, and on either side of the bridge (which leads up a ramp with three health vials) is a propped sheet of metal from which to wall jump up to reach the bridge. Turn left and check the courtyard's far end; a curved tunnel with three adrenaline pills leads into the flak cannon thoroughfare.

On the other side of the shock rifle courtyard, near the health packs, two sets of steps climb to the raised area. To the right is an elevator to the second floor balcony overlooking the courtyard. To the left is a raised area next to the shock rifle, which ends in a left corner with two health vials on either side of a double damage.

Back at the raised area, the door leads into a small side room with two large windows. To the right is the second link gun (lower floor) and left are two link ammo packs. There are two more exits: the ramped corridor on the left with four health vials, leading to a junction where the second floor courtyard balcony ends, and a smaller brick corner to the right, leading to the biorifle corridor and a door to the bridge you ran under to the shock rifle.

Head around the double damage or pill-filled curved corner to the flak cannon thoroughfare; both passages open to this spot. Find two flak ammo packs near the weapon and two more exits, as well as a propped metal sheet to wall jump up onto a surrounding balcony. The left exit (if you entered from the double damage corner) leads back to the 100 shield pack (which you can see from here). The right route heads into a brick corner with a tile ramp and three adrenaline pills, then opens up into the link gun courtyard, above the hole leading to the rocket launcher.

Left of the tile ramp is a health pack and the adrenaline pill bridge. Cross it, and note an identical third floor bridge above. On the other side is a balcony with two doors, one on either end of the rocket launcher hole. They both lead to the long biorifle corridor. In the corridor, between the doors, is a wooden plank ramp up to the third floor and the bridge above the adrenaline pill bridge. Under this third floor platform you can wall jump up a propped metal sheet to the third floor (very difficult). Also find a hole with a health vial in the right wall, down to the 100 shield pack, and the biorifle with the two ammo packs. Continue down the corridor to the two exits at the shock rifle chamber.

At the upper link gun courtyard, check the link gun under the wood ramp, with two ammo packs nearby. The shallow ramp to the right leads to a landing. Once on the wood, turn left to see a health pack and a wood ramp up to the third floor. Turn right, looking over the tiled ramp, and notice a plank to run up to the third floor overlooking the rocket launcher.

Take either ramp (the wooden one above the link gun or the plank) to reach the third floor balcony. Find a minigun and two ammo packs here. Head left and check the corridor to the left of the third floor bridge. This ends at the lightning gun area, but a hole in the left wall leads to the shortcut across the flak cannon thoroughfare.

301

The bridge to the right, near the minigun, leads to the walkway over the biorifle, which is to the left if you drop down. On the end of the walkway (visible from the corridor below) is a health pack and shock and assault ammo. Back at the minigun, look at the opposite wall left of the upper windows. Double jump to a vent leading to a hole dropping you at the end of the biorifle corridor.

Back at the second floor entrance to the flak cannon thoroughfare, move left around the outer balcony and the three health vial ramp to the lightning gun; or take the plank ramp to the hole in the right wall (connecting the third floor corridor near the minigun), then take a plank across to the lightning gun, flanked by two ammo packs. Left of the gun are planks and a hole to drop into the double damage corner. To the right is a junction where the third floor corridor ends and the ramp down to the shock rifle chamber connects to the bridge. Don't forget the connecting walkway to the balcony overlooking the shock rifle (check left for a second hole down to the DD), and the long enclosed ramp in the walkway's far end, down to the lower link gun.

Deathmatch Dealing

Unlike many multitiered deathmatch maps, most combat takes place on the ground and sub-basement areas, due in part to the abundance of weapons and lack of accessibility upstairs. You always find enemies near the rocket launcher, shock rifle, and 100 shield pack, and up the raised part of the shock rifle chamber to the double damage.

Because of this constant battling, you must discover alternate methods of reaching these areas without being torn apart. The 100 shield pack is a dead-end; stand at the flak cannon thoroughfare and trap anyone moving in there who didn't check the surrounding areas. One way is to drop in from above; even after an opponent picks up the shield pack, you can ambush him by dropping in from behind.

Dodge jump across the gap with the double damage below, in the area of the lightning gun, to throw off a pursuing enemy, then double back around and hunt him down instead. Various areas allow you to drop down and outfox an opponent. Remember that you can double jump many of the areas, such as the top balcony to the bridge near the shock rifle. Spend most of your time trying to dodge jump or shield jump up the metal sheets—an effective way to gain height.

One of the best sniping spots is the black corner under the link gun under the wooden ramp; you can check out the upper balcony level, but you can't escape when spotted. Move farther up to the third floor and stand on the lip of the window that's opening and closing, then shield jump up to the lip of the air duct and open grating for fantastic views of the rocket launcher below. Or grab the double damage and then go on a flak cannon rampage; the items are near each other, and the numerous corners make this weapon advantageous even on normal power.

DM-RRAJIGAR

Recommended Players: 2–8

Legend

1	Health Vials x4	**7**	Adrenaline Pills x4	**13**	Health Vials x4	**19**	Shock, flak, rocket, lightning ammo packs
2	Biorifle +1 ammo pack	**8**	Health Vials x4	**14**	100 Shield Pack	**20**	50 Health Packs x2
3	Lightning Gun +2 ammo packs	**9**	50 Health Packs x2	**15**	Health Vials x4	**21**	Adrenaline Pills x4
4	Health Vials x4	**10**	Adrenaline Pills x4	**16**	Flak Cannon +2 ammo packs	**22**	Health Vials x4
5	Double Damage	**11**	Assault, bio, link, mini ammo packs	**17**	Biorifle +2 ammo packs	**23**	Rocket Launcher +2 ammo packs
6	Link Gun +2 ammo packs	**12**	Shock Rifle +2 ammo packs	**18**	50 Health Pack		

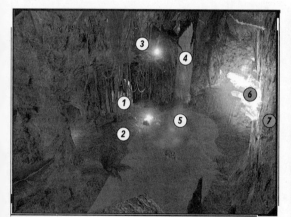

Overview

This intricate cave system features a subterranean stream running the map's length, as well as an ancient mine-workings nearby. There are three main chambers: a large area with a minigun and a flak cannon, a rocket-launcher mine works, and a waterfall with double damage. Circling the entire lower area are balconies and overhangs with multiple tunnels. Once you realize where every connecting chamber leads, you can avoid this map's many dangerous open areas.

Available Weapons

Biorifle (x2, on bank near to waterfall and double damage; on main upper balcony junction, above flak cannon)

Shock Rifle (on overhang ledge between shield pack and double damage, above stream)

Link Gun (on overhang balcony overlooking waterfall)

Minigun (on bank of stream across from flak cannon, near shield pack)

Flak Cannon (on opposite bank of stream near junctions, near shield pack)

Rocket Launcher (in middle of mine-works chamber, across from flak cannon and DD)

Lightning Gun (on high ledge above stream, overlooking link gun)

Available Power-ups

Double Damage (submerged in water, near waterfall at stream's end)

100 Shield Pack (submerged in water, under bridge, at stream's opposite end)

Map Patrol

Start this crazy mine maze at the stream alcove (ground level) at the end of the minigun cavern. Above you, a rocky path links the flak cannon thoroughfare and the double health pack on the rock balconies above the minigun. Splash through the water to the other side of the map and you pass two giant open areas: the flak cannon thoroughfare on the left, and the minigun cavern to the right. Continue upstream as it curves left in a narrow gorge, which is open above you (leaving you open to attack).

In the stream gorge, a tunnel to your left with health vials leads to a junction. Continue to the double damage waterfall cavern. Note the alcove to the right, the two large cave entrances to your left, and the tunnel behind the waterfall. There are ledges above, too.

Back at the 100 shield pack, head into the minigun cavern, turning right as the stream flows into the giant open areas. The minigun cavern is the right bank, while the flak cannon thoroughfare is the left. Near the minigun are two ammo packs, a ledge above, and two tunnels. Face away from the stream and inspect both tunnels. The right one curves to the right with four adrenaline pills. Turn at the second pill to see a long wood plank leading to the double health packs and a vantage point overlooking the flak cannon. The tunnel continues over

the shield pack (drop to the left to land on it), then follows a trail of four health vials to the flak cannon.

The left tunnel near the minigun leads up a mine tunnel with rusting flooring pieces and four health vials. Up at the tunnel's top exit is an overhang with a shock rifle and two ammo packs. On the same level as the rifle is a continuation of the double health pack ledge and a natural balcony all around the flak cannon thoroughfare below. Continue from the tunnel exit past the rifle to view the DD waterfall and a downward tunnel ahead, with adrenaline pills, leading to the waterfall.

Back on the ground near the 100 shield pack, turn left and check the flak cannon thoroughfare. Head up the bank by a fallen rock to claim the gun and the two ammo packs. Aside from the overhang walkway above, there are four ground exits. The left one leads to the path above the 100 shield pack you previously checked.

The middle left and right tunnels lead to the rocket launcher mine-works courtyard. The middle right tunnel also has an opening to an elevator and junction. To the left is the DD waterfall and a biorifle (lower level). Past the elevator are four health vials and the opening into the stream gorge you saw from the opposite direction. The tunnel also splits again near the stream gorge, in the right wall. This leads back to the flak cannon and is the right tunnel entrance. The elevator leads to the upper balconies, overlooking the flak cannon with the biorifle (upper level) to your right.

Back on the ground, inspect the rocket launcher mine-works. Inspect the ground exits. Head left to an alcove with two crates and a mine cart. Take a left down a short tunnel to an elevator. The lift platform drops you at the biorifle (upper level) on your right, the balcony above the flak cannon, and the balcony of the rocket launcher on your left. Elevator jump to reach a secret third-floor alcove. Flak, shock, lightning, and rocket ammo packs and a health pack await in a root-infested area. Drop onto the elevator, or down to the biorifle from a hole in the ceiling.

At the rocket launcher (with its two ammo packs), move to the tunnel that's left of the mine wheel. This leads to a smaller elevator. Stand on it and turn right. Step out onto the balcony above the mine wheel. Find two health packs here and a tunnel on the opposite wall heading down. Follow it through four adrenaline pills, and the tunnel splits to an upper and lower level.

Take the lower route around and emerge behind the waterfall, near the DD. Jump to the upper level and it curves to the right, allowing you to exit over the DD, behind the waterfall. Either drop down on the DD, or double jump to a link gun and two ammo packs on a crystal-glowing balcony that overlooks the entire DD waterfall area. Left of the link gun, a tunnel links to the shock rifle overhang. Pass over the plank to reach the tunnel and through the four adrenaline pills. Or, double back at the tunnel, leading down to the water's edge by the DD.

The final exit from the rocket launcher mine-works is on the right and leads to the double damage waterfall. The tunnel behind the waterfall is on your left. A second biorifle (lower level) is at the water's edge, with an ammo pack.

Back at the shock rifle overhang, peer to the left. A couple of planks lead to the other balcony area, and another two to the right of them. Between them on the opposite side are mini, link, bio, and assault ammo packs. You can double jump toward the tunnel leading to the link gun from here. Turn and look down with the flak cannon under you, to the right. Walk around the balcony to the biorifle and two ammo packs (upper level).

This area has a host of cave entrances, but knowing what lies beyond is more important. To the right of the biorifle (upper level) are two planks of wood across to the balcony you're on (near the clump of ammo). The cave to the planks' right leads to the elevator with the secret third floor alcove. Move to the biorifle and check the entrance to the right of the glowing crystal pillar. To the right is an upper corridor only accessed from this area. A hole in the left around the pillar overlooks the rocket launcher mine-works, but the corridor continues through four health vials to a lightning gun on a high ledge with two ammo packs. Drop to the waterfall, or snipe the link gun and shock rifle balconies from here.

The biggest hole, left of the crystal pillar, leads to the rocket launcher mine-works. On the left wall is a hole down to the elevator linked to the mine-works. Left of that is a small balcony with the flak cannon to the left, below. Double jump to the double health pack area or to the bridge over the 100 shield pack; or snipe down the steam below or across to the shock rifle.

Deathmatch Dealing

The complexity of the map takes some getting used to. However, once you realize how everything links up, you can use this to your advantage. The view is excellent, and the chance of ambush is minimal, especially if you're at the upper tunnel exit, because you quickly can double jump to the adjacent ledge on the left with the link gun. Escape from the lightning gun perch by double jumping onto the link gun area, or to the right, onto the shock rifle overhang.

In the rocket launcher mine works, there are enough entrances to be overwhelmed by enemy fire, so try a little camping, sniping enemies on the ground and balcony from the dark area behind the mine-wheel mechanism. Or stand on the crate to the right, hiding behind the steel support. Step into the dark alcove near the mine cart and lie in wait; of course, if you're spotted, you're trapped!

Watch your step, especially on the second floor natural rock balconies. Know where your feet are before you start blasting enemies on the ground and moving across the balconies at the same time. Flak cannon assaults are also popular up here, usually in the connecting corridors. Change to the shock rifle and combo fools off planks or those heading for the double damage or shield pack below. These power-ups are in high-traffic zones, so lie in wait and blast apart enemies as they spot the power-up from a distance and run in.

Close assault is possible along the upper balconies for those armed with a biorifle. Enjoy all the damage potential without the danger, because you're up one floor from the exploding goop. Place ooze on corners or at the top of elevator shafts. Listen for the faint sound of a lift to know approximately where your foes are. Finally, shield jump to a well-camouflaged ledge above the shield pack and the bridge and set up camp!

DM-SULPHUR

Recommended Players: 2–6

Legend

1	Shock and link ammo pack	7	100 Shield Pack	13	Biorifle / Minigun (each end)	19	50 Health Pack
2	Lightning ammo pack	8	Flak Cannon	14	Adrenaline Pills x3	20	Shock Rifle
3	Flak ammo pack	9	Flak ammo pack	15	Mini ammo pack	21	Bio ammo pack
4	50 Health Pack	10	50 Health Pack	16	Link Gun	22	Mini ammo pack
5	Lightning Gun	11	Shock and link ammo pack	17	Bio ammo pack	23	Redeemer (on antenna)
6	Rocket Launcher	12	Adrenaline Pills x3	18	50 Health Pack		

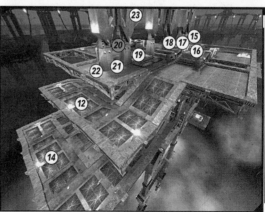

Overview

A multilayered rig in the middle of a murky sea, Sulphur is a surprisingly compact level, featuring only three main floors and an antenna, all interconnected. Campers sometimes use the jump pads, so take the more traditional metal platforms up and around. Each side of the rig is identical except for weapons and items. With no shield packs, combat is more precarious than normal, and powerful items lie at the bottom and very top of this structure.

Available Weapons	Lightning Gun (mid-level platform, middle of interior platform)
Biorifle (corner of lower ramped platform)	**Redeemer** (middle of antenna platform, map's highest point)
Shock Rifle (bridge on top platform)	**Available Power-ups**
Link Gun (bridge on top platform)	
Minigun (corner of lower ramped platform)	**Double Damage** (platform above flak cannon, randomly spawned)
Flak Cannon (middle of lowest platform)	**Big Keg-O-Health** (platform above flak cannon, randomly spawned)
Rocket Launcher (mid-level platform, middle of interior platform)	

Map Patrol

Starting on the rig's bottom level, under the double damage/keg at the flak cannon, the platform runs perpendicular to the double damage/keg platform above. Both ends of the flak cannon platform end at a T-junction with a lightning ammo pack at one end and a rocket ammo pack at the other. Each T-junction has a jump pad propelling you to the top floor. From the rocket ammo jump pad you land near the link gun; land near the shock rifle from the other.

Turn right at either T-junction and the lowest platform moves under an upper platform with a health pack under it and ends in a junction. Turn left at either T-junction; the platform meets the junction with the health pack and dumps out in an elongated ramped square. Take either ramped square to the corner to find a biorifle (if you traveled left from the lightning ammo) or a minigun. The ramped square turns left, heads up steps and through three adrenaline pills to another left corner, and up to the next floor. At the second pill is the DD/keg platform; head across, over the health packs below and the flak cannon at the rig base. Take two flak ammo packs on the way to the opposite ramped area.

At the top of either ramp is a mid-level platform. Head straight to pick up a link and shock ammo pack (on each side), then go up the mid-ramped platform to the next level. Head left for a weapon—either a lightning gun or a rocket launcher. You can double jump or fall onto the DD/keg platform or the jump pad ledges from here. When you're done, head to a jump pad, down to the lowest platforms, or up to the mid ramped platform steps; grab three adrenaline pills as you reach the top level.

The top platform is a little wider. To the left is a raised area with a health pack; there's also a bio and mini ammo pack on either side of an iron support leading to a jump pad. Head forward and cross a small bridge containing either a link or shock rifle (depending on the side). If you use the low jump pads, you land on the outer ledge. Reach a higher antenna area via a jump pad at the bridge's other side, or reach the bio and mini ammo. You can also drop to the mid-ramped platform or through the gaps in the top platform.

Topping the highest platform is the antenna. On each end of the platform are two health vials. Move around a pipe to a middle area holding a redeemer; use secondary fire!

Deathmatch Dealing

There's much to be said for staying low in the rig's lower and mid-level interiors, which house all but one of the preferred weapons. At the match's start, you can either jump from the top floor to the antenna platform and secure the redeemer, or drop to the bottom floor to grab the big keg-o-health or the double damage.

Anyone going for the redeemer is prone to attack, so look up, and light up your foe with lightning rounds or with the shock rifle. The rifle is always a pleasure to use—bounce the enemies into the murk below. If you're after the redeemer, stand at the pick-up point, crouch and then fire so you're not tagged from below; use the bottom of the antenna platform for protection.

Translocating is helpful to flit from one floor to the next instead of using the outer ramps or jump pads. But the translocator really becomes helpful if you're after a high teleport at the rig's top; point and fire from the redeemer platform, then teleport up to the three-pronged supports for the final antenna, at the structure's top.

Mainly though, combat consists of jumping up pads (train weapons at landing spots, such as the platform near the tiny bridges on the top floor) or dropping through openings to the lower decks. Drop on an outer ramped platform and peer into the base; line up instant-hit weapons from here. Or try the middle gap on the top floor; this is an alternate escape route and sniping point. Mainly though, practice running around the different decks and double jumping across the open spaces and land on a platform below; doing this effortlessly without looking for the landing spot is the key to escape and victory.

309

Capture the Flag Maps

CTF-1on1JOUST

Recommended Players: 1–2

Legend

1 *Lightning Gun*
2 *Rocket Launcher*

Overview

This map is suitable for two teams of two (maximum). You start at one of two alcoves leading to a main corridor. There's the same structure at the corridor's other end, with a flag at either end, and that's the extent of this level! This is a great way to practice fleeing with flags, shooting from the hip, and wall dodging.

Available Weapons

Rocket Launcher (x2, right of the home flag, if facing the enemy flag)

Lightning Gun (x2, left of the home flag, if facing the enemy flag)

Base Patrol: Level Check

You spawn on either side of your own flag. When you turn at the junction, you see a long corridor to the other flag and base. This is an elongated "H" shape, with a lightning gun (to the left of your own flag if you're looking toward your opponents) and a rocket (on the other side).

Flag Waving: Victory!

The action always centers around the main corridor and involves lightning gun and rocket fire. Become proficient in both weapons before you try this level. Fire lightning guns from the hip or you'll be outclassed in seconds. Predict where your opponent will move and fire at the spot he will be going to. If your foes aren't zigzagging down that corridor … victory is easier!

Always move and shoot. Never stand still or you'll be toasted. Don't wait at your flag either, as this just prevents you (and possibly your teammate) from getting anywhere near your foe. Zoom toward the opposing flag as quickly as possible, using a mixture of translocating and running/jumping to reach it. Bind your keyboard to flick between translocator and weapon to be quicker on the draw.

Learn to wall dodge (see the Training section for details) and avoid the barrage of fire. Throw your translocator over your enemy's head. If he ignores it, warp and attack him from behind. If he fires on it, attack him while he's preoccupied. Nasty!

CTF-ABSOLUTEZERO

Recommended Players: 8–16

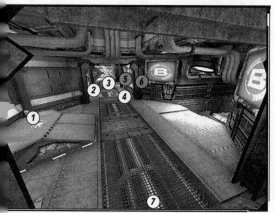
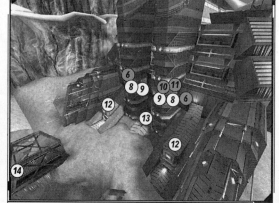

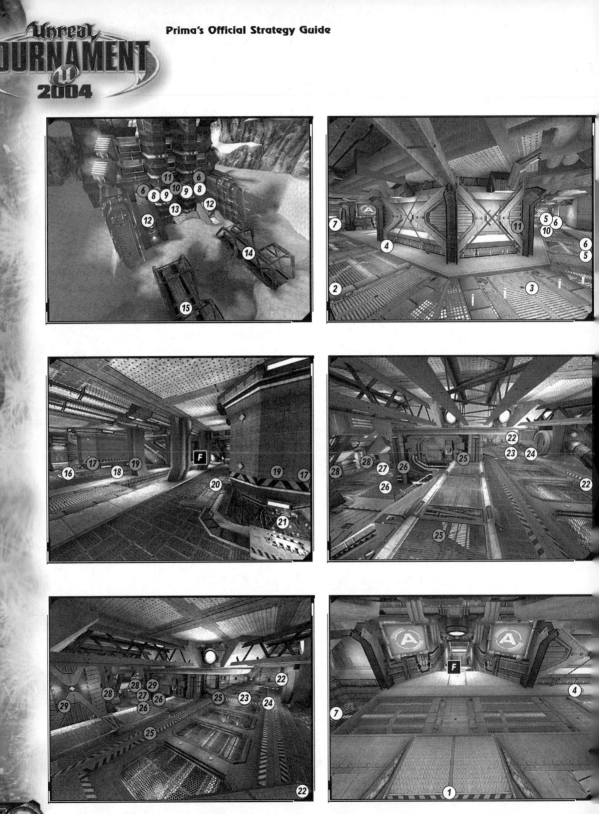

Legend

1	Link gun (end of upper ramp to flag)	**8**	Flak and Rocket ammo (near upper entrance)	**15**	Redeemer (middle of bridge)	**24**	Assault ammo pack x2 (near turbine)
2	Minigun ammo pack (upper corridor)	**9**	Bio and Shock ammo (on alcove)	**16**	Shock Rifle (back side of left vat)	**25**	50 Shield Pack (one under each set of stairs)
3	Health Vials x5 (upper corridor)	**10**	Sniper Rifle (middle of upper corridor)	**17**	50 Health Pack (side of left or right vat)	**26**	Rocket ammo pack (either side of launcher)
4	Link ammo pack x2 (upper corridor)	**11**	Double Damage/100 Shield Pack (central alcove)	**18**	Shock ammo pack x2 (side of left vat)	**27**	Rocket Launcher (entrance)
5	Flak and Rocket ammo (near upper entrance)	**12**	50 Health Pack (over each lower entrance)	**19**	Adrenaline Pills x4 (front of vat)	**28**	Adrenaline Pills x3 (entrance corridor)
6	Sniper ammo x2 (near alcove)	**13**	Big Keg-O-Health (outer base center)	**20**	Bio ammo pack x2 (side of right vat)	**29**	Link ammo x2 and minigun ammo pack (corner of entrance corridor)
7	50 Shield Pack (each end of upper corridor)	**14**	Ion Cannon (middle of bridge)	**21**	Biorifle (back side of right vat)		
				22	50 Health Pack (in corner)		
				23	Flak Cannon (near turbine)		

Overview

Take two large, three-tiered fortresses, build them in an inaccessible artic tundra, then construct two small bridges between them for a map that's most frantic when teams try to cross the bridges—especially as the two most devastating weapons are there! The bases have four proper entrances, two balconies, and a gap behind the flag for translocating fiends to get their fix.

Available Weapons

Biorifle (x2, behind left vat, on 2nd floor)

Shock Rifle (x2, behind right vat, on 2nd floor)

Link Gun (x2, U-shaped 3rd floor, opposite left ramp down to flag)

Minigun (x2, U-shaped 3rd floor, opposite right ramp down to flag)

Flak Cannon (x2, 2nd floor, bottom of center stairs)

Rocket Launcher (x2, ground floor, inside base entrance)

Sniper Rifle (x2, middle of 3rd floor corridor, near two outer balconies)

Redeemer (on middle of right bridge, from red base facing blue)

Ion Painter (on middle of left bridge, from red base facing blue)

Base Patrol: Level Check

Each of the two identical bases has three floors. On the top floor, starting on the right side, the top level is U-shaped with a number of exits. At "A" on the base's right side, a ramp leads down to the main second floor and flag. On a mesh alcove behind you is a 50 shield pack, and to the right is a minigun. Move toward the left corner and pick up two link gun ammo packs, a minigun pack, and five health vials around the corner.

On the main corridor, find rocket and flak cannon ammo near the first exit on your right. This leads outside to a long slope that ends atop the base's bottom entrance and is a great alternate way in and out of the base. Continue and you pass two sniper rifle ammo packs and another entrance in the right wall.

This leads to the first of two adjacent balconies offering fine sniping with a great view over the middle of the level to the opposing base. Find shock and bio ammo on this balcony. The next balcony is identical, down to the ammo you find. Between the two balconies, though, is a sniper rifle and a box-shaped alcove with either 100 shield pack or double damage. Grabbing this is of paramount importance.

Past the entrance to the other balcony are two more sniper ammo packs, then another sloping exit down to the other bottom entrance. The ammo packs are the same for the rest of the corridor: rocket and flak, five vials, a minigun, and two link gun packs. At the mirror-image end is a link gun to the side, a sloped ramp heading down to the flag, and another 50 shield pack at the far end.

Down the ramp to the main second floor, find the flag at the far end, between the ramps to the top corridor, and in front of a generator wall with a gap in the floor. In front of it is a staircase, and these are the only ways to reach the flag. Check out the flag chamber further, and notice two smelting pods attached to the ceiling. Clustered near each are four adrenaline pills, and around the back of the left one is a biorifle. Along the right side are two bio ammo packs and a health pack along the left side. Around the back of the right one is a shock rifle, and along the left side are two shock ammo packs and a health pack to the right.

At the base of the steps lies the raised part of the first floor. In front of a generator fan is a flak cannon, and next to the fan are two assault rifle ammo packs. On either side of the cannon in the corner is a health pack, and between them and the center stair entrance are some barrels in the shadows—a reasonable, if predictable, hiding spot (although you can translocate up to the pipes feeding the fan and camp out here).

Around either side of the central stairs is an open set of steps leading down to a main entrance in the middle of the far wall. Under each set of steps is a 50 shield pack—well worth securing. The stairs afford partial cover. On the way out of the main door to the entrance corridor, find a rocket ammo pack on either side of the rocket launcher, which is just inside the door. Secure this weapon.

Out in the entrance corridor, which exits on the sides of the map in front of either bridge, find six adrenaline pills (three each side of the center door), two link ammo packs, and one minigun ammo pack in each corner. Head up a ramp (when entering a base, walk down this ramp rather than jumping from the top to avoid excess gunfire), and you're out of the base, facing one of the bridges and the opposing team's structure.

Before you dart out to invade your opponents, check the back and center of your base's exterior. Find a health pack atop each lower entrance, a ramp to the third floor, and a big keg-o-health in the base's middle—snag that immediately! Finally, wander on the bridge to take an ion painter (left bridge, when facing the blue base from the red one) or a redeemer (right bridge, same view). This leads to a frantic outdoor fight!

Flag Waving: Victory!

The power-ups are incredibly critical on this map, especially due to the high concentration of nasty ordnance next to each other (such as the two ultra weapons on each bridge). Your team must spawn, then attack and secure the bridge within seconds. Your opponents will attempt the same plan. The bridge is open, so have some of your team watch for snipers on the balconies opposite. Those securing the map's middle must collect a 50 shield pack (which is why there are four in each base), the power-up on the middle of the third floor, and then drop to collect the big keg-o-health.

Have the most amped-up teammate run point on the bridge. Use the ion painter and redeemer as soon as you can, but not in extremely close quarters! Try clearing out the third floor balcony or a base entrance (ideally figure out a base entrance and fire both nasty weapons at it while your team charges the other side). Actual base infiltration tactics vary, but teams work better than single mavericks.

Translocate your team, in two mini-squads of two or more, to two different base entrances, depending on the defensive firepower you're facing. Breach the bottom left and top right entrances at the same time to throw the enemy into confusion, especially if you're translocating up into the balcony too! Translocate across the bridge and onto the balconies or third floor to avoid the pain of the biggest guns.

Grabbing the flag is something of an art. Appearing from the ground floor up the main central stairs is just asking for a shock combo, unless you flick-turn at the base of the steps and translocate up to the flag. For a great and easy shortcut, run up the ground steps (or around for a shield pack if one's there), and when you reach the flak cannon, bounce the translocator up and off the fan generator's top and onto the flag area.

If you're defending the flag, you can position a couple of defenders on the ground floor (rockets at the main door choke point work well). For better coverage, however, put a couple of teammates behind the vats on the second floor and use nonranged sniper attacks on enemies leaping or translocating up the stairs. When you see enemies coming down from the upper ramps or warping up behind the flag, give chase or dish out shock combo damage. Spattering the ground near the flag with biorifle ooze is also a must. Take up a sniping position near the adrenaline pills next to the vat; there's a great long view of the ramp to the third floor and the top of the steps.

Got the flag, hero? Then jump, wall dodge jump onto the bridge's top, and it's only three jumps back to your own base. Only proficient players can wall dodge jump onto the bridge's top; practice this and if you can't achieve it, you must rely on dodge jumping and teammate back-up.

Unreal TOURNAMENT 2004

Back up your team by using the sniping points on the upper balcony and acting as a spotter. This allows you to keep a running commentary on who's moving to which position. Duck and use the balcony lip for cover from the ground (although enemies could shock combo you from here), or step out to the upper balcony entrance and snipe with a clear view of the bridge.

TIP

Translocate onto the horizontal metal rods poking out of each base. You can reach the top of the base's front part with a commanding sniper's view.

CTF-FACECLASSIC

Recommended Players: 6–10

Legend

1   Sniper ammo pack x2 (left rear of tower top)
2   100 Shield Pack (right rear of tower top)
3   Sniper ammo pack (right of tower top)
4   Sniper Rifle (tower top)
5   Sniper Rifle (upper tower alcove)
6   Sniper ammo pack x2 (lower tower alcove)
7   Redeemer (lower tower alcove)
8   Double Damage (above base entrance)
9   Assault ammo pack (left front of base)
10 Assault ammo pack (right front of base)
11 Sniper Rifle +1 ammo pack (right back of base)

12 Adrenaline Pills x5 (behind rocks)
13 Link Gun + 2 ammo packs (left back of base)
14 Big Keg-O-Health (middle of map), and 50 Health Pack x2 (right and left of entrance)
15 Assault ammo pack (on mantle)
16 Rocket Launcher +2 ammo packs (near flag)
17 Adrenaline Pills x4 (side of base)
18 Shock Rifle +2 ammo packs (opposite side of base from flag)
19 Adrenaline Pill (back of alcove)
20 Sniper ammo pack x2 (side of alcove)
21 Sniper ammo pack (front of alcove)

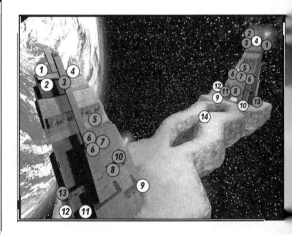

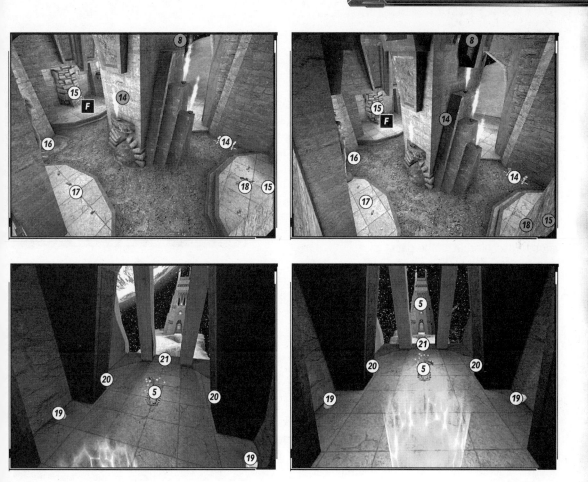

Overview

You wanted the best, you got the best: the craziest CTF flag above the world! Retooled from the original *Unreal Tournament* competition, this version of Face is closest to the original, from the multiple sniper rifles on the upper areas of the base tower to the crazy pathways across outer space to the rival's monolith. The four chambers above the main flag area enable snipers to ply their trade, while the race for the keg-o-health begins. The players with finest dodge jumping and backpedaling skills win this one!

Available Weapons

Shock Rifle (x2, inside base, between side teleports)

Link Gun (x2, rear right of base, outside)

Rocket Launcher (x2, inside the base, to the flag's left)

Sniper Rifle (x6: x2 rear left of base outside; x2 3rd alcove from ground; x2, roof)

Redeemer (x2, 2nd alcove from ground, accessed via teleport/translocator)

Base Patrol: Level Check

Each base is identical and cramped compared to some of the more recent maps, but for sheer insanity and snipe-tabulous combat, it can't be beat! Run counterclockwise around the exterior of your base from the right to find assault ammo at the near right corner and a link gun with two ammo packs at the far right corner. Run to the back of the tower base to find five adrenaline pills. In front, by the far left corner, find a sniper rifle with an ammo pack. At the near left corner (left of the base entrance) is another assault rifle ammo pack.

The route to and from each base is a nasty gauntlet: a completely open jaunt along one of two stone paths that meet in the middle at a big keg-o-health. Don't fall off the sides (or anywhere away from the ground unless you're dodge jumping and then translocating back again) or you'll fall out of the floating level and depressurize.

Instead, inspect your tower base. The only entrance (via the ground) leads to a single chamber with an opening in the middle (the doorway is around the opposite side). Your flag is to the right as you enter, with two health packs on the right wall.

Follow the interior of the base around to the back, opposite the entrance, and see a rocket launcher and two ammo packs on the right wall. Four adrenaline pills are opposite the doorway to a middle teleport, and on the base's left side are two teleports in each corner, with a

shock rifle and two ammo packs between each teleport. There are two health packs as you reach the entrance again. Don't forget the extra assault ammo packs; one on the altar behind the flag, the other on the altar behind the shock rifle.

Before you check out the three teleports, translocate to the mesh platform above the entrance. This leads to a cubbyhole containing a double damage. This groovy sniping hole offers a view of the same cubbyhole on the opposite base and all the rooms above inside the tower. It's even better for blasting down on enemies breaching your entrance, and two rocket ammo packs keep the missiles firing.

Looking at the shock rifle and two teleports, take the left one; you appear at an alcove up from the double damage cubbyhole. On either side of the teleport (landing you back in the central base room) are sniper ammo packs, while a redeemer awaits at the front of this area. You can teleport back or drop down from here, but be careful and watch your position—you'll be prone. You can see everywhere except the floor of the base's interior.

Take the right side teleport to appear on an upper alcove, above the ledge holding the redeemer. Snag two adrenaline pills, a sniper rifle, and three sniper ammo packs while you're here. A fall off here means severe scraping and death, so try teleporting back the way you came, or use this as a sniping post.

Take the teleport inside the doorway in the middle of the base to reach the tower's top! Up a couple of steps is a sniper rifle. To the left in the corner are two sniper ammo packs, a 100 shield pack on your right, and another sniper ammo pack next to that. From the base's top (and the alcove below with the sniper rifle), you can aim and spot enemies anywhere except behind the opposition's base, but you're prone to enemy fire just as easily as the other locations.

Flag Waving: Victory!

The gameplay is simple, and the flag capturing difficult, but a great tower defense is a must. Before the match starts, know your role and stick to it. If you're after the flag, dash out without delay, pausing only to grab the link gun or shock combo. Use these and the rocket launcher to blast close-combat enemies as you run to the big keg-o-health. Bag this if you can, or snipe at it to prevent the enemy from reaching it.

Translocate to the enemy base, and try to head through the main entrance. Or translocate up the ledges along the left side of the tower's front, or into the cubbyhole with the double damage, or the alcove with the redeemer in it, and teleport into the base. With a helper in tow, you can wreak havoc before you dash back to the base with your takings. The defenders at your base should offer you covering fire for the deadly journey back; perfect your dodge jumping without leaping into space!

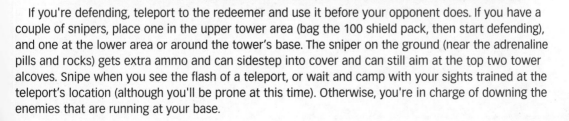

TIP

Do you have the flag but are waiting for yours to be returned? Take refuge behind the base (as this is a spawn point) rather than heading into a teleported alcove.

If you're defending, teleport to the redeemer and use it before your opponent does. If you have a couple of snipers, place one in the upper tower area (bag the 100 shield pack, then start defending), and one at the lower area or around the tower's base. The sniper on the ground (near the adrenaline pills and rocks) gets extra ammo and can sidestep into cover and can still aim at the top two tower alcoves. Snipe when you see the flash of a teleport, or wait and camp with your sights trained at the teleport's location (although you'll be prone at this time). Otherwise, you're in charge of downing the enemies that are running at your base.

The other sniper should keep moving from alcove to alcove, taking potshots at spawning enemies, those in the base, and anyone on the first two alcoved areas. Working in tandem with a second or third sniper means you have less ground to aim at. Once someone grabs the flag, switch to other ordnance and give chase, or if you're being picked off, plug the enemy in the back (but at least one teammate must be on the ground to return the flag). Offer covering fire to a returning flag carrier.

TIP

Translocate up the left ledges of the tower's outside, or the ledges behind the tower, for a fun alternative to regular warping.

Although the enemy will spot you from upper vantage points, you could drop down and stand on the rocks at the joining of the paths, near the base, then translocate up and ambush or fire at enemies running past you. There's a rock area behind the base too, but this rarely used area is very sheer, and you may slide to your doom!

With your friends blasting enemies near your base, if you're carrying the flag, dodge jump and backpedal over to your base and take down pursuing enemies with extreme skill! Learn that level!

CTF-GRASSYKNOLL

Recommended Players: 6–10

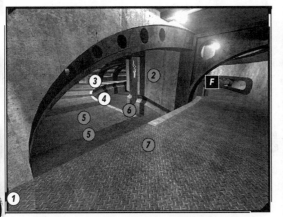

Legend

1 Link Gun + 1 ammo pack (corner near base inner entrance)

2 Biorifle +1 ammo pack (corner near base inner entrance)

3 50 Shield Pack (top of elevator)

4 Bio and shock ammo pack (under Shield Pack)

5 Health Vial x3 (each side of elevator entrance)

6 Minigun + 1 ammo pack (lower entrance)

7 Rocket Launcher + 1 ammo pack (lower entrance)

8 Mini and rocket ammo pack (bend of ramp)

9 Flak Cannon + 1 ammo pack (upper side entrance)

10 Assault, mini, lightning ammo (lower ramp)

11 50 Health Pack (corner of ramp)

12 Adrenaline Pills x4 (near copse of trees)

13 100 Shield Pack (near minefield)

14 Lightning Gun (middle of woods)

15 50 Health Pack x2 (middle of knoll)

16 Double Damage (top of knoll)

17 50 Health Pack (top corner of ramp)

18 Flak and lightning ammo packs (bend of ramp)

19 Shock Rifle + 1 ammo pack (side entrance)

Overview

This small base has a wide open view of a large grassy hillock (the "knoll"). This accommodates a different type of strategy: waiting at the base and reacting to dodge-jumping fiends coming over the brow of the knoll. The red team's shortest distance to the opposing base is along the map's right side, while the blue team should hug the trees to the left. On the far side, away from the double damage atop the knoll, lies a 100 shield and mine field that shouldn't be tampered with. The keys to victory are using the trees and boulders as cover and mastering the subtleties of translocating through tight windows.

Available Weapons

Biorifle (x2, on interior upper entrance to base, right side)

Shock Rifle (x2, on left [blue] or right [red] fortification, near lower side entrance)

Link Gun (x2, on base's interior upper entrance, left side)

Minigun (x2, low ground base entrance, right of center entrance)

Flak Cannon (x2, on left [red] or right [blue] fortification, near lower side entrance)

Rocket Launcher (x2, low ground base entrance, left of center entrance)

Lightning Gun (in copse of trees, toward the middle of map)

321

Base Patrol: Level Check

NOTE

The following is a description of the red base. The blue base is identical but mirrored.

Each base has three main outer areas. First is the left side, accessed via an entrance to the left of the main central lower entrance. This leads left, up a ramp to a health pack in the corner and a left turn. Head up a few steps to a quick 180 turn (pick up the rocket and minigun ammo packs) and dash into the base's far upper corner and the upper inside corridor running to the semicircular center. Just as you enter the base, claim a link gun and ammo pack.

Or you can dash left, across a flat raised ramp to the base's lower side entrance (which is still above the main central ground entrance) and grab a flak cannon and ammo pack. As you reach the cannon, either head through the entrance or dash around the lip of the center balcony (outside, above the main entrance) to the right balcony area. Translocating around these parts makes ramp-running redundant, so aim your translocator at the base entrances.

On the base's right is an elevator on the outside right flank, so watch for incoming enemies (or your returning flag carrier). Normally though, expect translocator fire up and over the base. This lift is the only external way to reach the right side of the base, which is smaller than the left. Head to either of the interior base entrances, either leaping down or around the 180 turn to your left (which has lightning and flak ammo). Before you turn left into the entrance, grab a shock rifle and ammo pack, or use the left turn upper balcony with the health pack in the exterior corner and a biorifle just as you head inside.

The other way to enter the base is to translocate through the large horizontal slit window, or head past the sand bags and through the main entrance under the flag. As you enter, find a minigun on the right and a rocket launcher on the left, each with an ammo pack. Run to the rear of the entrance chamber to discover two small alcoves on each side with three health vials. An elevator heads to the inner balcony overlooking the flag and a 50 shield pack. Scoop up shock and bio ammo on the thoroughfare, just below the shield pack.

The flag is in the main interior. Coming from the upper side entrance, follow the upper curved balcony around to the elevator exit and shield pack, then drop or jump across to the lower thoroughfare and up the ramp to the flag; or run around the connecting balcony next to the slit window and grab the flag. If you're entering via the lower side entrances, the thoroughfare is the easiest route, otherwise translocate up to the curved balcony and shield pack before you nab the flag.

Out in the open is a long rise up to the brow of a hill. To the right (from the red base) at the top is a double damage power-up: very exposed and usually guarded by snipers. To the left of that is a copse of trees, near two health packs. Over on the clearing's far left is a deadly minefield, a few crates near a lamppost, and a 100 shield pack. In the middle of the woodland find a lightning gun. Finally, to the left of the base are four adrenaline pills out in the open near a few trees.

Flag Waving: Victory!

Base defending is simpler because you have more time to aim at incoming enemies. It's best to dash out and claim the lightning gun, then retreat to the base to shoot enemies when they head over the rise, through the woodland, or around the rocks. But shock firing or combos work in a pinch if you can predict where your foes will be.

Use the base's side fortifications as lookout posts, retreating into the main base if you're overrun. Other viable guarding positions include the openings along the upper outer balcony, the horizontal slit near the flag, and the front central area with the sandbags, where you can retreat for more weapons and create a choke point. You can even translocate above the upper walkway or to the outcropped cement overhang near the antenna.

> **TIP**
>
> Two other areas make good guarding points. The first is the doorway surrounding the lower side entrance (either side), which offers a good view of the grassy knoll.
>
> You can also translocate to the tops of the large conifers. This is an unexpected place to stand, if a bit impractical. Still, some of the trees offer incredible views into the opposing base for outrageous sniping fire!

If you're covering the flag from the base's sides, blast incoming enemies from the vantage points, then gradually fall back to the base as the enemy reaches it. To enter a base in one piece, you must dodge jump up and around or through the knoll, or shoot an incredibly long translocator shot that lets you warp to the enemy base (or almost there; you can reach the opposing base in around three translocator shots). Try to land the translocator pod at the base's foot in front of the fortification where enemies at vantage points can't see you.

Or try using your shield gun when entering, as long as a partner shoots for you. That way you reach the flag with minimal health loss. Finally, nothing beats translocating through the slit window and then varying your escape route.

323

If you're moving back to your base with a flag, you'd better hope your team is providing covering fire. Head directly into the middle of the trees (if you're without the translocator, attempt short translocator hops), and then take a breather behind one of the rocks (peer out from behind to snipe or ambush). Then dash back, listening to your teammates' intel about which entrance is least problematic. Split your team up when you're charging in, don't move in bunches due to the large expanse of ground, and try to control the lightning gun and 100 shield pack (but don't head out of your way to reach these).

CTF-GRENDELKEEP

Recommended Players: 4–10

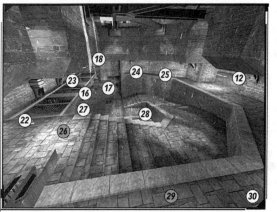

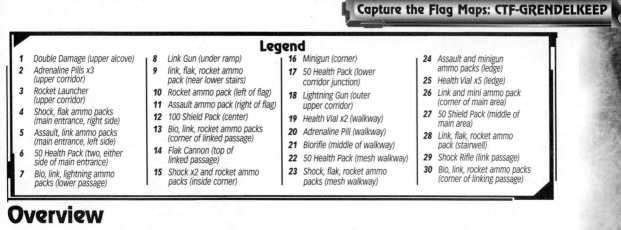

Legend

1	Double Damage (upper alcove)	**8**	Link Gun (under ramp)	**16**	Minigun (corner)	**24**	Assault and minigun ammo packs (ledge)
2	Adrenaline Pills x3 (upper corridor)	**9**	link, flak, rocket ammo pack (near lower stairs)	**17**	50 Health Pack (lower corridor junction)	**25**	Health Vial x5 (ledge)
3	Rocket Launcher (upper corridor)	**10**	Rocket ammo pack (left of flag)	**18**	Lightning Gun (outer upper corridor)	**26**	Link and mini ammo pack (corner of main area)
4	Shock, flak ammo packs (main entrance, right side)	**11**	Assault ammo pack (right of flag)	**19**	Health Vial x2 (walkway)	**27**	50 Shield Pack (middle of main area)
5	Assault, link ammo packs (main entrance, left side)	**12**	100 Shield Pack (center)	**20**	Adrenaline Pill (walkway)	**28**	Link, flak, rocket ammo pack (stairwell)
6	50 Health Pack (two, either side of main entrance)	**13**	Bio, link, rocket ammo packs (corner of linked passage)	**21**	Biorifle (middle of walkway)	**29**	Shock Rifle (link passage)
7	Bio, link, lightning ammo packs (lower passage)	**14**	Flak Cannon (top of linked passage)	**22**	50 Health Pack (mesh walkway)	**30**	Bio, link, rocket ammo packs (corner of linking passage)
		15	Shock x2 and rocket ammo packs (inside corner)	**23**	Shock, flak, rocket ammo packs (mesh walkway)		

Overview

It takes a few matches to learn the layout of this gloomy, enclosed series of catacombs, but stick with the map and realize the potential of lightning gun sniping across vast interiors and the multitude of ways through the level. There are no real choke points and many junctions to check out, meaning your team is likely to steal the flag (or have it stolen) often. Patrol the iron walkway because it's the best way to reach the rest of the level quickly. It's above the 50 shield pack in the main stepped chamber.

Available Weapons

Biorifle (x2, middle of curved ledged chamber)

Shock Rifle (x2, next to elevator in lower right-side passage)

Link Gun (x4: x2 under the central steps in the flag room; x2 start of curved ledge in stepped chamber)

Minigun (x2, to the left, in the stepped chamber if you enter from the main central entrance from the flag room)

Flak Cannon (x2, top of shallow ramp halfway along the lower right-side passage)

Rocket Launcher (x2, upper flag room balcony, middle of corridor near double damage)

Lightning Gun (x2, upper left exit of flag room, next to curved ledge)

Base Patrol: Level Check

Picture this large enclosed zone as three interconnected chambers: the flag room with multiple entrances and an upper corridor leading to double damage; a curved ledged chamber accessed via the left side of the flag room; and the large stepped chamber with the upper curved balcony and shield pack (plus a lower passage and elevator on the right, accessed via the middle and right entrances).

The middle area links both chambers to the identical two chambers on the other side; it's the only entrance to the other side, aside from the lower right passage leading back to the lower part of the curved corridor. Learn this map by using the guide maps, or use the "ghost" cheat and pan all the way out!

From the flag, the main outer ledge leads up and around both sides. To the left is a ramp to an elevator and the entrance to the curved ledge chamber. Claim the lightning gun. To the right is a ramp to an elevator and the right side of the larger stepped chamber. Claim a health pack. Then turn left to see a long iron walkway that leads to the lightning gun pick-up (with rocket, flak, and shock ammo halfway along). The walkway offers a great view of the steps, the middle of the map, and the lower right-side passage.

Back at the flag room, take the middle steps to the doorway to the lower part of the large stepped chamber. Left of the doorway are a health pack, assault, and link ammo. Right of the doorway are shock and flak ammo and a health pack. This area is useful if you're being chased or want to vary your movement, because you can leap to either of the elevators, down to the lower ground area, or to the flag. Heading away from the flag allows you to enter the large stepped area the quickest and claim the items inside.

On the lowest ground, a stone slab runs along the outer edge of the thoroughfare between the flag and lower area. Use this to double jump onto the flag ledge. Under the steps is a link gun. The left route snakes right (past rocket, lightning, and link ammo), up steps, and through a doorway to a junction. Head right, into the large stepped chamber. Go to the curved ledge chamber and the intersection of the opposite base's lower right-side passage. The right route snakes left (past a link, bio, and lightning ammo pack stash) and straightens out into the lower right passage.

The final area to explore in the flag room is the double damage area above the flag. Access it by translocating (with far less hassle), or take one of the elevators to the sides and lift jump back at the top. Run around the T-shaped corridor and find a rocket launcher at the junction. Head down the small corridor to the alcove containing the double damage. This area affords limited sniping opportunities (mainly at the sides, as you can see into the main chambers along the outer walls), or an ambush down from above, as you can see into the main

flag room from two openings in the upper passage. Stand on the metal rod under the double damage and drop off to ambush the unwary.

Moving into the upper curved balcony (accessed via the left route from the flag room, or the left upper and lower doors of the stepped room), the lower ground area consists of a staircase going up to the right, with two shock and one rocket ammo pack at the bottom. This staircase leads to the middle of the map, as does the upper curved balcony.

From the lightning gun, the curved balcony contains of four health vials, two adrenaline pills, and a biorifle before you reach the top of the stairs and the middle of the level. The lowest area allows you to pass to the right of the steps to a flak cannon, then down a ramp to the lower right-corridor with bio, link, and flak ammo packs, leading to the opponent's base. At the elevator, which leads to the right side of the stepped room (or left if you're nearer your opponent's base), find a shock rifle.

In the stepped chamber, assuming you're entering from the flag room, find a 50 shield pack to your right and a minigun on your left. Near the shield pack is link and minigun ammo. Near the elevator is flak, link, and rocket ammo.

The main steps in the room's center lead to two square landing sections on the way up. At the top floor is the health pack you saw earlier, and the upper entrance to your base. Reach the opposition's base by running around the right curved ledge with the link gun at the start. You reach the map's center, or you can continue around the curved ledge and nab five health vials and minigun and assault rifle ammo.

Finally, when you reach the map's center, find a 100 shield pack (unless it's been grabbed) and a choice of four directions. If you're approaching from the stepped chamber, the enemy stepped chamber is in front of you, while the curved ledge is on your right. Check the flags billowing on the right wall of the curved chamber to make sure you're assaulting the right base!

Flag Waving: Victory!

The complicated maze-like nature of this level makes defense difficult and assaulting problematic. Spend most of your time on the top circling corridors. There's a variety of corridors to which you can translocate (you need never run up any stairs unless you're carrying the flag), power-ups you can take, and a number of escape routes.

Begin your attack by having at least two of your team dash the opposition's flag area, taking care to reach the middle of the level and the 100 shield pack before your opponents. With so many entrances to the flag room, you can jump in from almost anywhere, but check the double damage area for power-ups and the rocket launcher; leap in from the upper side entrances.

The lower right corridor is long and open, allowing chasers to easily strike you. Dodge jump away from the flag and create a flitting route through the level, such as dashing up the curved corridor stairs, through the middle, and down into your own stepped chamber, through the middle doorway and onto your own flag.

Translocate and hide above the 100 shield pack in the rafters or the lamppost above the power-up, then aim at incoming enemies from all directions. Place snipers and defenders in the stepped chamber, ready to be pushed back if necessary. Place one teammate at one end of the iron walkway, one at the other, and a third covering the lower area; this is the most effective way to cover all entrances to your base.

327

The walkway is also an excellent vantage point as you can see most of the paths, both shield packs, and many of the weapons and health power-ups. Try mixing up your attacks, too. Chain link guns from this area, or knock the enemy off the curved ledges with shock combos. Hiding behind the center door near the health pack, in the flag base, allows you to ambush enemies coming in from a couple of locations. Mainly, though, have teams of two translocate to the flag and back each other up while varying the routes back home.

CTF-JANUARY
Recommended Players: 8–16

Legend

1	Flak and rocket ammo pack (end of dock)
2	Sniper Rifle (under pipe)
3	Shock ammo pack (dock)
4	Health Vial x3 (upper ledge)
5	Lightning ammo pack (upper ledge)
6	Double Damage (top of submarine)
7	Adrenaline Pill x6 (around crate)
8	Sniper ammo pack x2 (on crate)
9	Shock ammo pack (behind crate)
10	50 Health Pack x2 (near pipe)
11	Minigun + link and flak ammo x2 (on mesh platform above water)
12	Link ammo pack (corner passage, near base entrance)
13	Mini and lightning ammo (near link gun)
14	Link Gun (top of ramp)
15	Assault ammo pack (main corridor)
16	Rocket ammo pack x2 (main corridor)
17	Lightning ammo pack x2 (entrance near boxes)
18	Adrenaline Pills x2 (each base ramp)
19	50 Health Pack x2, under each base ramp
20	Flak Cannon + 2 ammo packs (under flag)
21	Bio and lightning ammo pack (near rocket launcher)
22	Rocket Launcher (dead-end room)
23	Lightning Gun (above ramp near hole)
24	100 Shield Pack (underwater passage)
25	50 Health Pack (corner near ramp)
26	Lightning Gun (top of ramp)
27	Health Vial x4 (ramp)
28	Shock Rifle (near boxes)
29	Shock ammo pack (on box)
30	50 Health Pack (box room)
31	50 Health Pack (under fan at junction)
32	Link ammo pack (corner near base entrance, same as 12)
33	Rocket ammo pack x2 (upper room corner)
34	Big Keg-O-Health (upper room)
35	Biorifle (in crate)
36	50 Shield Pack (above crate)

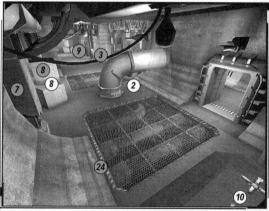

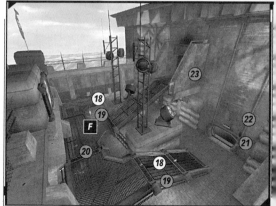

Overview

Another reworking of an old *Unreal Tournament* favorite, this map offers a small, well-fortified base with good prospects for defense. Following that is a range of interlocking corridors designed to be a maze to the unwary, while offering great hiding for the knowledgeable. Finally, the submarine dock in the map's center offers roof supports to which to translocate and a special double damage in the sub tower.

Available Weapons	
Biorifle (x2, inside crate in upper room near flag base)	**Flak Cannon** (x2, under flag in base)
Shock Rifle (x2, near crate in storage room, in connecting zone)	**Rocket Launcher** (x2, in dead-end room near right base exit)
Link Gun (x2, in short corridor between two connecting zone entrances to base)	**Sniper Rifle** (x2, under pipe near dock main entrance)
Minigun (x2, on mesh platform over water exit)	**Lightning Gun** (x4: x2 at top of base ramp in upper room near hole; x2, in short U-shaped corridor in connecting zone)

Base Patrol: Level Check

Let's split this level into three different zones. The first is the base. The second are the connecting corridors to the central submarine dock. The third is the dock. Aside from some confusion over where the snaking corridors in the middle section lead, the map is straightforward, and both teams' areas are identical. We'll start with the base and flag area.

Each base has three entrances. The two on the ground to the far left and right are the usual locations for enemy incursions. The top entrance, connected to the flag by a straight mesh walkway, is used only by translocating enemies or members of your team grabbing the items and power-ups.

Out in the courtyard, a mesh ramp leads up to a walkway junction (left or right, depending on the entrance) opposite each entrance. The mesh walkway continues to the flag, and then ramps up to the power-up room. Under each initial ramp is a health pack. There's also a flak cannon and two ammo packs under the flag. On each ramp leading to the flag are two adrenaline pills.

The ramp to the power-up area leads to a room with a lightning gun and a hole; it's useful for chasing flag carriers or translocating from below. Run around the hole to the left, and grab two rocket launcher ammo packs and a big keg-o-health in the far corner. Run around the hole and right, and check the boxes. Find a 50 shield pack and a biorifle in this corner (the shield pack is on the boxes).

TIP

The base is a veritable smorgasbord of warping locations and areas from which to guard. You can translocate all around the outer crenulations of the exterior base wall. Warp to the top of either of the two radio masts (land on one of the mini dishes halfway up first, then teleport to the tip of the radio mast, and double jump over and land on the other).

Or translocate up to the buttress wall adjacent to the upper room entrance, and again up and onto the structure's top (the long wall above you), giving a supreme view of the area below. You also can move onto the ledge above the doorway to the room to blast incoming enemies using the hole as a shortcut to the flag.

Now for the middle corridor section. If you're looking from the flag room to the level's middle and take the right door, you emerge in a connecting corridor with a doorway ahead and the corridor to your left. On the right wall are bio and lightning ammo packs. Enter the doorway into a dead-end room holding a rocket launcher. Turn left down the corridor, and pass a pulsing conduit (a visual and color-coded location, showing you that you're near the base). The corridor turns right, at a link gun ammo pack.

Continue down this corridor to pass under the hole in the ceiling. If you're going the other way, this is where you'll translocate for a quick flag snag, and you may wish to leave via this hole; check the light shadow of the ground so you know where it is. This part of the corridor ends with a junction to the left, with steps straight ahead. The steps lead to the middle of the connecting area.

Go left toward a wooden crate; behind it on the right wall is a link gun. The passage's left side holds minigun and lightning ammo packs, and ahead of this corridor section are steps down to a four-way junction. There's a health pack in the middle of it; use this, the two pulsing conduits ahead of you, and the shadow of a rotating fan above you as landmarks.

If you take the left entrance out of the flag fortress, turn immediately left, descend a few steps and pass two conduits, then turn right, you reach the intersection with the health pack. If you move into the doorway with the conduits on either side, you reach a storage room with a health pack, a shock rifle, and ammo near some crates. Optionally translocate to the top of the crate stack for a decent camping spot.

Or, head up the ramp with the line of four health vials to a small U-shaped raised corridor. At the corner is a lightning gun, with a health pack in the adjacent corner. Follow the corridor around to immediately spot two lightning gun ammo packs; drop down some crates to the main connecting corridor area. Use the location of the two lightning ammo packs to orient yourself in the map. Move around this raised corridor and down the ramp to the shock rifle storage room by double jumping up from the two crates.

331

Go through the entrance to the right of the pulsing conduits, from the shadow of the fan and the health pack crossroads, to reach a double set of short steps and the word "DOCK" on the left wall. This is the main route to the middle of the map, but first let's check the main connecting area. If you're at the open end, looking toward the mesh ramp at the other end, you walk past a stack of three crates that you can double jump over. At the junction with the stairs on your right (which lead to the hole in the ceiling), check the left wall for two rocket ammo packs. At the mesh ramp, a platform above the water contains a minigun and two ammo packs, plus two flak cannon packs. The water under the minigun leads down an underwater shaft to the main dock.

The rest of the connecting zone between dock and base is one large corridor. Run past the "DOCK" sign, turn right, turn the corner to the right (a stack of three crates contains assault ammo on one crate corner and shock ammo behind in the shadows) and you enter the dock's main entrance. The submarine should be visible. Check the rest of the corridor for a second stack of crates to the right of a pipe. Atop the crates are two sniper ammo packs and six adrenaline pills are around the right side. The sniper rifle is under the pipe. The end of the corridor has a second smaller door leading to the dock, and two health packs.

Once in the dock, find a color-coded jump pad (which works for both teams) to the right, along the dockside. This allows you to land on the submarine (although translocating or double jumping works just as well). In the far right corner is a rocket and flak ammo pack. Head left along the dockside, and you pass a shock ammo pack and a ramp into the water.

Jump into the water to swim around or under the submarine. To access the underwater area of your opponents' (or your own) base, look for the color-coded light at the left side of the main entrance, underwater. That's the entrance. Follow the broken pipe along, and halfway through is a 100 shield pack—a must-have power-up!

Finally, the submarine holds a surprise; at the top of the center tower is a double damage (translocate to grab it). Translocate around the upper ledge above the doorways, onto the top of the dock's sides, then around the ledge and roof supports. Each side offers a lightning ammo pack and three health vials.

Flag Waving: Victory!

With a multitude of methods for reaching the flag, your team must be ready to launch into action and hold a number of important choke points. The choke point closest to your foe's base is the main dock doors. Use the sniper rifle and other nearby ordnance to assault the enemies as they teleport over the main submarine. Have an attacker on point translocate to the double damage before the enemy, then mount an assault on the enemy base (ideally via the underwater entrance to get the 100 shield pack too!). Meanwhile, let sniping shots ring out around the dock.

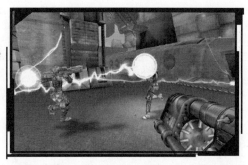

Back up if you're swamped. The enemy can enter your base from two locations: the main corridor steps with "DOCK" on the wall, and the water exit under the minigun. Point all available defenders there, especially with rockets and shock rifles (although the crates afford great cover for lightning gun sniping), and your foes will have a horrendous time reaching you.

Have a couple of your best defenders at the flag. Train your eyes on the two lower entrances, ideally from the flag area, and have one teammate checking the upper room for someone translocating through the hole.

If you're attacking the base, send your main force into the large corridor to push the enemy back, while a couple of quick movers translocate up and through the water exit. Send a decoy to leap around the main connecting zones and draw fire away from a second attacker, who can translocate up through the hole or head through the less frantic left entrance (under the rocket launcher room).

Got the flag? Radio for help, head up the ramp to the hole (reverse up there to check whether the big keg-o-health can be stolen), and dive for the underwater exit if you have backup to pass the flag to or to take care of pursuers. Diving under the submarine affords you cover, and once you're in your own connecting corridors, the flag's as good as yours. You could attempt to run around the main corridor, but this is best attempted after zooming around to the health pack crossroads, then back into the enemy base to confuse them, attempting to shake the enemy off your tail.

CTF-MOONDRAGON

Recommended Players: 8–12

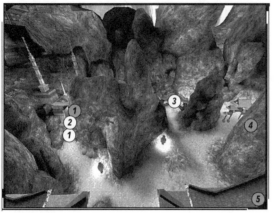

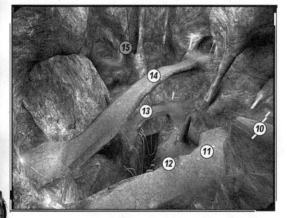

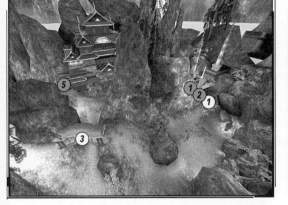

Legend

1	Adrenaline Pills x2 (temple passage)	
2	50 Shield Pack (temple passage)	
3	Lightning Gun (on bridge)	
4	50 Health Pack x2 (near archway)	
5	Minigun +2 ammo packs (stairs by side entrance)	
6	50 Health Pack x2 (in corridors above flag)	

7	Shock Rifle +2 ammo packs (entrance chamber)
8	Flak Cannon + 2 ammo packs (lower corridor junction)
9	50 Health Pack (top of stairs, each side)
10	Health Vial x5 (cave upper ledge)
11	Rocket Launcher +2 ammo packs (cave walkway)

12	Health Vial x6 (base of cave)
13	Rocket Launcher +2 ammo packs (opposite cave walkway)
14	100 Shield Pack (center of upper cave walkway)
15	Redeemer (upper secret alcove)

Overview

This weird level of ornate Asian-style buildings built on a near-vertical hill has an array of steep corners and a central cave system with more areas to explore than is immediately obvious. The flag is entombed in a few corridors in the large pagodas. It's best to catch the enemy from the upper square balconies atop the base. After you've memorized the three main routes to the caves, check the central cavern for a special "redeemable" prize in a high, U-shaped chamber!

Available Weapons

Shock Rifle (x2, inside welcoming room, near entrance #2 and above entrance #3)	**Rocket Launcher** (x2, ledge on either side of the cave)
Minigun (x2, bottom of steps to entrance #2)	**Lightning Gun** (x2, on bridge overlooking base)
Flak Cannon (x2, top of first step of steps and through double arch, near entrance #1)	**Redeemer** (inside upper U-shaped side tunnel in cave)

335

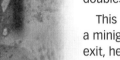

Base Patrol: Level Check

Four entrances lead to each team's pagoda, which in turn leads to a series of tight corridors all bisecting the flag room. The low front entrance leads to the grassy hill and the left route, past the lantern on the right to the narrow temple walkway with the 50 shield pack and four adrenaline pills. To the right of this entrance is a hill that leads under the lightning gun bridge. Before you head under the bridge, make a right turn to head through a passage leading to an ornate archway and two health packs. This road heads left to the lightning gun bridge, or doubles back right to the other ground entrance.

This other ground entrance features a set of steps with a minigun and two sets of ammo at the base. When you exit, head up the hill and around to your left to reach the archway and health packs; or make a sharp left through a gap between the base and the rock wall, and end up in the middle area outside the base.

The third entrance is above the one with the minigun and ammo. Translocate (or spawn) to this point and you're on a square stone balcony. Views to the left (if you're facing away from the entrance) include the route to the shield pack temple, the first lower entrance, the lightning gun bridge, and both paths to the arch; this is a good lookout spot if the enemies have breached your side of the map.

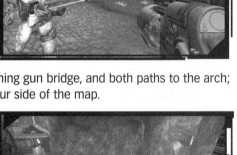

The fourth and final entrance is above the lowest first entrance but is only accessible (from the outside) via translocator. It is an identical square balcony offering views of the shield pack temple and partial views of the lightning gun bridge. This is a prime sniping spot. Or translocate down and chase the enemy from here.

TIP

You can translocate farther up the exterior of your base temple, along the ornate eaves at roof level. Try this to get a panorama of the level. You also can stand atop the lowest entrance on a short ledge (and spawn point) for the best views of the hillside.

To reach the flag room, make an immediate right up the steps and through either archway. You see another two archways and steps to the left. The steps lead to a connecting room with two health packs. Head through the second set of archways to reach a small area with the flak cannon (and two ammo packs), and two more archways on the opposite wall leading to a second set of stairs to the left. This leads to the connecting room, too. Head left up the stairs to the flag room.

If you're moving to the flag room from the second entrance near the minigun, move through the corridor, down some steps to a large welcoming chamber containing a shock rifle with two ammo packs. Step through either archway to your left and you're in the flag room (the entrance to the right heads back to the first exit).

From the third and fourth entrances, head down the steps to a walkway above the welcoming room with the shock rifle. Follow the walkway through the single upper doorway to reach the balcony above the flag room.

You see another balcony on the opposite wall, two exits from the upper balcony (which you entered from entrances #3 and #4), and a single entrance in the lower wall under the balcony, near the flag. These unexplored areas contain health or you can disorientate a pursuer in here after the flag has been taken.

Walk through the lower middle doorway and see stairs left and right, both of which go to the balcony above the doorway through which you just walked (find health packs at the top of each set of stairs). The balcony overlooks the flag room and can be used by a fleeing flag carrier to "mix up" the escape route. If you go up a farther flight of steps (where you turned at the health pack), you reach the upper balcony and the walkway back out to either entrance.

Back on the ground, the two temples are linked by a cave system with three entrances. These are set up differently depending on the base you're moving toward. If you're going from red to blue, there's a mid-level entrance on the left. This leads to a ledge with a rocket launcher and two ammo packs along the tunnel's left side. Translocate left to a narrow plinth with five health vials. Drop to the right for six health vials under the main upper walkway. Don't drop down farther or you'll fall into the pit with the tree vines and die.

The second and third tunnel entrances (going from red to blue base) are above and below each other. The lower route takes you across the tunnel's right side, where a second rocket launcher and two ammo packs lie. Head left as you enter to snag the six health vials. The upper tunnel spans the middle of the cave area and has a 100 shield pack in the middle. Check the view of the two ledges below and a strange opening to the right.

Translocate or double jump from the red base entrance to this opening on your right, which leads to a U-shaped tunnel hiding a redeemer! Drop to the ledge below when you grab it, unless you want to shoot it from the safety of this cave (make sure you're precise with the steering). When you're moving from the blue to red base, the three entrances are easier to reach (you don't have to climb

the rocks near the statue as you do at the red base area). The left entrance leads to the lowest ledge; the middle and right side entrances near each other lead to the shield pack and middle ledges. Finally, you can double jump to the redeemer if you turn left and leap just before the shield pack.

> ### TIP
>
> You can translocate back onto a ledge in the cave once you fall or jump off (a great dodging tactic). In addition, try double or dodge jumping (or translocating) to the other ledges to vary your exit strategies and pick-ups.

Flag Waving: Victory!

A translocator's dream, Moon Dragon is rewarding if you reach the many vantage points and learn when and where to guard. Start by translocating up and onto the dragon heads flanking the flag inside the base. You're hard to spot and can ambush flag gatherers. Wait here in your opponents' base for the flag to respawn, then grab it!

Once the flag is stolen, it's extremely easy for the flag carrier to hide, take alternate routes, and even mess about inside the base, so concentrate on stealing your opponent's flag instead. Avoid defensive snipers by entering via the ornate archway, then translocate up and over the wall to the side entrances, which aren't as well defended.

Try an infinite number of double-back techniques here (translocate to the top side entrance, then drop to the lower entrance, for example). Remember that your translocator can fly, so you can pretend to head for the first low entrance, then translocate up and over the side wall. The fourth entrance near the rock wall is excellent for camping (defense) or translocating to (offense).

Translocating around the rocks surrounding your base works for both attacking and defending. Attackers attempt this to appear too randomly to be shot at, while defenders find countless spots to camp and blast the flag carrier. There are numerous places to land. Sheer translocating madness! Find your spot and sit there, checking the enemy's movements, radioing in, or chasing as appropriate. If you're attacking, use your translocator to scale various walls while remaining hard to predict.

Inside the cave, the vials atop the high ledge are a great defense spot if you're backing up a flag carrier, but otherwise, your main choke point is the cave entrance (all three on each side). Defenders shouldn't venture too far forward from this point. Plug the entrances with rocket fire from a high vantage. Otherwise, approach the opposing base in two or more directions, and guard the flag from a view of all four exits—the top of the side entrances. With friends here and by the tunnel, you should never let an enemy through.

CTF-SMOTE

Recommended Players: 6–10

Legend

1. Rocket Launcher +2 ammo packs (main entrance inner chamber)
2. Shock, link x2 ammo packs (main entrance outer chamber)
3. Adrenaline Pills x2 (main entrance outer chamber)
4. 50 Shield Pack (connecting tower corridor)
5. 50 Health Pack (tower stairwell)
6. Health Vials x4 (above tower entrance)
7. Link Gun +2 ammo packs (upper dungeon chamber)
8. Minigun +2 ammo packs (dungeon chamber)
9. Health Vials x3 (lower side exit)
10. Shock Rifle +1 ammo pack (above lower side entrance)
11. Adrenaline Pills x3 (clifftop near lava)
12. 50 Health Pack (rock corner)
13. Sniper Rifle + 1 ammo pack (above main base entrance)
14. Assault, minigun x2, rocket x2 ammo packs (dark corner near sniper rifle)
15. Adrenaline Pills x3 (rickety bridge)
16. Double Damage (small side cave)
17. Health Vials x3 (walkway to cave)
18. Assault, shock, mini, rocket ammo packs (cave entrance)
19. Big Keg-O-Health (upper end of central fire corridor)
20. Assault, link, mini (red side); Assault, shock, rocket (blue side) ammo packs (middle entrance)
21. Biorifle + 2 ammo packs (base of central fire corridor)
22. Adrenaline Pills x4 (middle of central fire corridor)

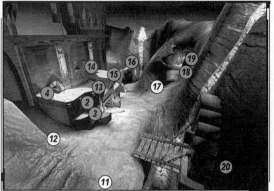

Overview

Smote has two opposing fortresses bisected by a central folly (a small fortification). Learn your fortress's interior layout, which is identical to your opponents' save for the lowest dungeon exit. Memorize the linking passages and the quickest route to the exterior near the folly. A cave to the side holds a double damage and two folly entrances: one to a big keg-o-health and the other through a main drawbridge where most of the fighting occurs.

Available Weapons

Biorifle (in connecting chamber of folly, center of map)

Shock Rifle (x2, around stone side walkway of base)

Link Gun (x2, in antechamber below flag)

Minigun (x2, in connecting dungeon junction room)

Rocket Launcher (x2, far stepped wall of base entrance, inner room)

Sniper Rifle (x2, on top of base entrance, upper nest)

Base Patrol: Level Check

> **NOTE**
>
> The base interiors are identical for each side, but the exterior trails and caves are mirrored; remember this when you switch sides!

Starting in the flag room, you notice a grill on the ground in front of the flag. The opening leads to the lower dungeon corridors. If you're facing the flag in this room, check out four raised corner areas (behind and left in this darkened corner are mini, link, and assault ammo packs). A side entrance to the left leads to an elevator and a sniper tower.

The doorway behind you leads to the main entrance room. This entrance chamber contains a rocket launcher and two ammo packs, a door opposite the rockets (the initial castle entrance), and a doorway to the dungeon. The main castle entrance has a doorway to the outside and the folly that separates the two bases. Inside the entrance are two adrenaline pills and two link and one shock ammo packs.

Now explore the dungeon! Head from the entrance under the flag and grill, or from the doorway heading right and down the steps by the rocket launcher (down through two portcullises). Both routes lead to a small underground room (usually a spawn zone) with a minigun and two ammo packs. If you're trudging down here from the flag grill entrance, expect a short curved set of stairs leading to an antechamber with one exit to the left (down to the room with the minigun). The antechamber holds a link gun and two ammo packs.

The small underground room contains three exits. To the right (if you came down the portcullis steps) is a doorway to a skull torch and a corner. This turns left (red) or right (blue) and leads down a narrow lava walkway with three health vials, and outside to the lower side entrance of each base.

Just outside the lower side entrance is a rickety bridge with three adrenaline pills. Run up there and into the cave at the path's end for a double damage power-up. You also have a commanding view to the right (red) or left (blue) of the main castle entrance. You can run up to the map's center from this lower side, but first get a shock rifle and ammo from the stone balcony above the lower side entrance. Don't stray off the rocky pathways and into the lava pools!

Back in the flag room, the elevator exit leads to a sniper tower. At the base is a health pack, with three health vials on a plinth over the doorway. Brutalis' corpse hangs inside the tower for all to see! At the top of the spiral staircase is a doorway to a short tunnel with a 50 shield pack. This tunnel leads outside to a sniper's nest above the main entrance. This has commanding views of the folly drawbridge, as well as a sniper rifle and ammo pack. There are also two rocket ammo packs, a link, and assault rifle ammo in the corner beside the entrance.

Dropping down from the main entrance, check the area to the right (red) or left (blue) of the folly drawbridge. There are two dead-end paths, one at the side of the base with a health pack, and the other overlooking a lava pool with three adrenaline pills. Then check the folly. To the left (red) or right (blue) of the main base entrance, a diagonal path leads to a wooden-support encased cave entrance that joins the far end of the corridor inside the folly. En route are three health vials and a small alcove to the entrance's right (red) or left (blue) that contains rocket, shock, mini, and assault ammo goodies.

Head up the folly drawbridge (there is one from each base) to reach a connecting room with a corridor to your left (red) or right (blue). In an alcove as you enter the room grab the mini, link, and assault ammo (red) or the rocket, shock,

and assault ammo (blue). There's only one hellish corridor—the two areas of the map join here.

The connecting chamber contains a biorifle with two ammo packs. Run up the two linked stair sections, grab the four adrenaline pills, and at the far end is a big keg-o-health. At this T-junction, head right to the blue base or left to the red.

341

Flag Waving: Victory!

Smiting your enemy here is an exercise in cunning. Remember that the base entrances are easier to defend than the interior. Stick a couple of your defenders at the sniper rifle nest above the main entrance, and a couple with the shock rifle above the side entrance. Your enemy can't reach the base without moving into either of these entrances (or translocating to the upper entrance and down the sniper tower), so waylay the enemy here. If your flag is captured, head to the sniper nest to spot the fleeing flag carrier. He or she can head only toward the cave and keg-o-health or the main folly drawbridge, so create well-guarded choke points there.

Dash into the folly for the biorifle, then coat the exterior paths or base entrances with it. The abundance of rocket ammo (the rocket near the main entrance with two ammo boxes, plus another two near the sniper rifle), makes the drawbridge and upper cave entrance even more hectic to guard. Just watch out for translocators warping in from the drawbridge or over the entrance and onto the roof—try leaving your translocator pod in a dark corner near the sniper tower for a quick additional flag-steal.

Shock combo from the base's side, knocking opponents into the lava. Or translocate onto the side of the rock wall near the double damage cave and run along this high area for a fantastic view of the entrance. Sit at a great vantage point (any of the square protrusions on the front of the base), then drop down and follow anyone who makes it through your barrage.

Those on attack should split themselves up into two charging units, and one teammate should secure the double damage while another grabs the keg-o-health. Then dash out from both exits, translocating like mad. You may want sharpshooters backing you up with splash damage weapons aimed at the sniper nest.

The main entrance is easier to enter, but don't dash into the flag room. Instead, zip around the dungeon, enter via the sniper tower, and learn the layout to quickly zoom around and out-fox your followers. With the flag, you need some backup to escape an even moderately defended base. The folly drawbridge is the shortest area of open cover you have to dash through. Have your teammates cover you the rest of the way.

Finally, note the many areas on each base to which you can translocate and ambush your foes. You can stand atop many places. The giant archways at each of the folly entrances, above the drawbridge, are fantastic sniping spots. Other exceptional sniping spots are the rock with lava spilling behind it or any parapet at the base's front.

Double Domination Maps

DOM-ACCESS

Recommended Players: 6–10

Legend

1	Minigun (in spawn point)	**11**	Flak ammo (middle corridor)
2	Minigun (in spawn point)	**12**	Flak ammo (middle corridor)
3	Minigun (in spawn point)	**13**	Link Gun and Flak ammo (middle corridor)
4	Minigun (in spawn point)	**14**	Shock, rocket, link ammo (middle corridor)
5	50 Health Pack (top floor)	**15**	50 Health Pack (bottom floor)
6	50 Shield Pack (top floor)	**16**	Shock Rifle (bottom floor)
7	Rocket Launcher	**17**	50 Health Pack (bottom floor)
8	50 Health Pack (top floor)	**18**	Assault, rocket, shock ammo (bottom floor)
9	Mini, flak, bio ammo (middle corridor corner)	**19**	Flak Cannon (bottom floor)
10	Biorifle (middle corridor corner)	**20**	Bio, link, lightning ammo (bottom floor)

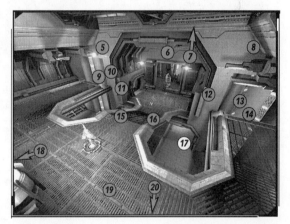

Overview

Access is aptly named, as both teams drop down from side ledges to a central room with a large ground switch in the middle. Standing on the switch flicks the doors to a domination chamber from open to closed, and closed to open for the opposite chamber—only one route can be opened at once.

Four ramped tunnels lead to each chamber, which is a floor with four elevator platforms and an upper walkway with the letter on it. Above (accessed by the elevators in the far corner of each chamber) is a long elevator leading to a ceiling walkway, which links both chambers and dips in the middle, allowing access via the ceiling of the central room for surprise attacks.

Available Weapons

Biorifle (x2, end of near right, or far left tunnel, at corner leading to domination room)

Shock Rifle (x2, in alcove between two lower ramp exits, in domination room)

Link Gun (x2, end of near left, or far right tunnel, at corner leading to domination room)

Minigun (x4, two on each spawn point ledge)

Flak Cannon (x2, on opposite side of lower ground floor, in domination room)

Rocket Launcher (in middle of secret ceiling passage, above center switch room)

Spawn Point Strategies

Both teams begin at identical spawn points on opposite sides of the map's middle section, in a long thin ledge with two miniguns. The open side of the ledge offers views of a screen showing points "A" and "B" on opposite walls to the left and right. The screens are above entrances. Nab the weapons and get going. Those timid enough to stay at the spawn point can peer down at the enemy and blast them as they pass, but this area is rarely visited.

TIP

Even without a translocator (which isn't allowed on the default setting) you can shield jump onto the top lip of the doorway, then double jump and back into the spawn ledge. Or your opponents' spawn ledge! When you've had your fill, leap back onto the top lip of the TV screen and wait for an ambush chance.

Assuming you aren't spawn camping, your team must quickly ascertain which points to secure first. The center room has a giant switch that you press with your feet. This flicks a series of flashing arrows along the floor. If you're quick at the start of the match, you can drop through to the middle of the corridor, look through the doorway into the middle room and check which way the arrows point, then dash to the door at the end of the initial corridor under the TV screen, before it closes.

Four doors are on the left side of the middle room, and four doors opposite, on the right. Each set of four leads to a domination chamber. On each side, there's a door near your spawn point, two doors after a short downward ramp, and a final door near your enemy spawn point. Dash in the direction of the arrows before the enemy enters the main room (or your own teammates) and presses the switch.

The four doors close and the four opposite doors open when the switch is pressed. The doors close immediately, and you can't wedge a door open with your body to let others through. The doors seal. So the game becomes the holding of the two domination chambers, but also who can keep the doors to the chambers open and send their teams through.

The lack of weapons in the middle room means you can't hold it for long (as you're in range of the spawn point), so try this tactic: Drop, check the open doors, and have half your team run down the near door toward the first chamber. The rest charge into the middle room, commandeer the switch, and, while one guards the switch, the others peel off toward the second chamber. You can win in moments if you're all working together!

Otherwise, use the TV screens in both the spawn corridor area and inside the middle room to check which chamber needs your attention, quickly press the switch if needed, and run to it.

The Domination "A" and "B" Chambers

If you take the left corridor nearest your spawn point (or the right corridor farthest from your spawn point) and run past the doorway, you run down a shallow ramp to a link gun surrounded by ammo on the left wall. This tells you there's two flak ammo packs, plus a link ammo pack. As you turn the corner, you run out into one of the domination chambers. Ahead is a tunnel and a right corner (leading to the left corridor farthest from your spawn point). Turn left as the two paths merge, and you can run up a shallow ramp to the "A" or "B" point.

If you take either of the middle two corridors, you run down a steep ramp that could end in a sealed door. In fact, it's a great trick to follow amateur players who run into an open middle corridor, then shut the doors at the switch, wait for them to run back out, and gun them down or trap them with flak grenades. At the base of either ramp is the entrance to the domination chamber, below the upper ramp.

If you take the right corridor nearest your spawn point (or the left corridor farthest from your spawn point), and run past the doorway, you jog down a ramp to a biorifle. There's a bio ammo pod, three flak ammo packs, and a minigun pack. Grab what you need, turn left and run right onto the upper ramp with the "A" or "B", and down the link gun tunnel. You're now in a domination chamber.

345

To keep the chamber, you must first locate the entrances. Start on the lower ground level as you emerge from any of the middle ramp tunnels and grab two health packs. Turn to face the middle of the room, then look behind. Between the lower ramp entrances is a shock rifle. Run across the room for a flak cannon; this weapon is useful as it has the most available ammo. Grab and protect this weapon. Either side of the flak cannon are three ammo pick-ups: assault, rocket, and shock on the right; link, bio, and lightning (which isn't available as a gun) on the left.

There are two elevator platforms ahead left and right, and two to the sides left and right. The ones to the sides ride up to the upper mesh walkway and the domination area you're defending. The two ahead, on either side of the flak cannon, head to a secret corridor linking both domination zones!

NOTE

It makes sense to drop down from the mesh ramp and the "A" or "B" above after you've claimed it to grab the flak cannon and shock rifle, as you'll already have stocked up on ammo. Use the elevator to return.

TIP

A key way to keep your opponents away from your letter is to fire up from below with shock combos or flak grenades. Knock them off as they rush for the letter, and finish them!

Total Domination

When you've breached the domination room and taken the letter, view the other room opposite on the TV screen. While half your team stays to defend, the remaining teammates can mount a charge. If you're defending a chamber, the attackers can storm in from many entrances. Station one teammate at the floor, shooting flak at those descending the ramp. Place another on the mesh with a shock rifle, blasting those off the ramp with combos, and devouring those entering from below (also with combos) by aiming from the area to the left or right of the letter. If anyone enters the room and tries to reach the long elevators up to the secret corridor, let your team know!

Instead of defending all the elevators from the room, make sure enemies don't reach them. The lower entrance should be well covered. Blast anyone using the small elevator to reach the letter mesh walkway. Place your final teammates on the secret ceiling platform. Ride up one of the long elevators, run around the health pack, grab the 50 shield pack, and stand guard here. It helps if you have two teammates; one to drop goop, shock combos, or flak on the letter walkway below, and the other to watch the secret corridor behind you for enemies.

The secret corridor is the easiest way to reach the other domination chamber without the door sealing. If the enemy is fiddling with the door, make sure you have a letter well guarded, then run your team up the elevators and down the corridor. There's a dip in the middle and a rocket launcher. Grab it, fight any defenders up here, and either run to the opposite end and drop down to claim the other chamber, or use one of the four holes in the corridor sides near the rocket launcher to drop down into the middle room for a surprise attack.

Mix up the route to the other room while keeping the first chamber well guarded; that way, you'll win!

TIP

Skillful players can peer over from the ceiling secret platform, watch an enemy run to the long elevator below, dodge jump and wait for it to ascend, and flak cannon the punk into pieces! You also can fall off the ceiling platform near the 50 shield pack and land on one of the two jutting lights—a good camping spot. Finally, remember to double jump across from the left or right of the letter, to the base of the upper ramp near the TV screen.

DOM-ASWAN

Recommended Players: 8–12

Legend

1	Bio ammo x2 (inner passage)	**14**	Rocket Launcher and 2 ammo (connecting tunnel)
2	Shock Rifle and 2 ammo (under spawn point)	**15**	Rocket, link, shock ammo (temple room)
3	BioRifle (inner passage)	**16**	Lightning Gun and 2 ammo (temple room)
4	Link Gun (courtyard)	**17**	Health Vial x3, Adrenaline Pills x2 (temple room)
5	Double Damage	**18**	100 Shield Pack (temple room)
6	50 Health Pack (inner passage)	**19**	Health Vial x3, Adrenaline Pills x2 (inner passage)
7	50 Health Pack (inner passage)	**20**	Minigun, 2 ammo (temple room)
8	Biorifle (inner passage)	**21**	Flak Cannon and 2 ammo (connecting tunnel)
9	Bio ammo x2 (inner passage)	**22**	Link, bio, flak ammo (temple room)
10	50 Health Pack (inner passage)		
11	50 Health Pack (inner passage)		
12	Link Gun (courtyard)		
13	Shock Rifle and 2 ammo (under spawn point)		

347

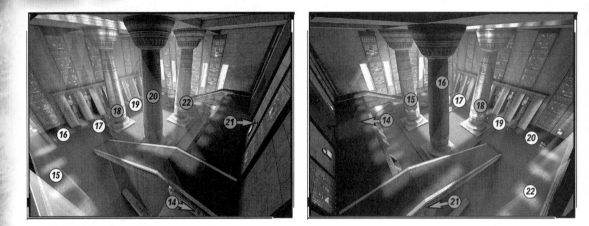

Overview

This large map has spawn points on the sides of a main courtyard. The courtyard leads to an identical huge chamber. The ground entrance to the chamber has a route straight ahead, or two side corridors leading to side elevators and a walkway where the letter is. Beyond the main entrance is an adjacent doorway into a huge domination chamber with two large ramps left and right. Turn 180 degrees and follow them up to the letter. Finally, two tunnels lead to each domination chamber, both zigzagging to the left and right of the room. Don't forget the raised area in the middle of the map, with the double damage!

Available Weapons

Biorifle (x2, in the right corridor to the side elevator, under the letter)

Shock Rifle (x2, below the spawn point, near both tunnel entrances)

Link Gun (x2, in the main courtyard)

Minigun (x2, in the huge chamber, back and right)

Flak Cannon (x2, in the left-hand side tunnel, if viewed from the spawn point)

Rocket Launcher (x2, in the right-hand side tunnel, if viewed from the spawn point)

Lightning Gun (x2, in the huge chamber, back and left)

Spawn Point Strategies

Get your bearings by realizing that both teams' spawn points are on opposite sides of the main square courtyard, with the "A" on the left for the red side, and on the right for the blue. This is important for securing weaponry (your ledge contains only two teleports and a view, mainly to stop sniping), as you can leave the spawn point via the opening onto the main courtyard, or teleport there.

If you teleport through the left teleport (red team), you appear on the ground next to the main courtyard's raised area, standing to the right of the ground entrance to "B." If you teleport through the right teleport (red team), you emerge on the ground next to the main courtyard's raised area, standing to the right of the ground entrance to "A."

If you teleport through the left teleport (blue team), you end up on the ground next to the main courtyard's raised area, to the left of the ground entrance to "A." If you teleport through the right teleport (blue team), you end up on the ground next to the main courtyard's raised area, to the left of the ground entrance to "B."

Why do you need to know this? Because once you figure out where you are before you teleport, you can immediately secure nearby weaponry and the letters themselves. Learn these appearance points as they can determine how you reach either letter and guard it.

If you drop from your starting point, you land on a shock rifle with two ammo packs. Grab this, and either run into the open courtyard for the link gun and two ammo packs, or turn left or right and look at the ramp leading to an underground passage (one on each side of you, leading to "A" or "B" zones). The left passage leads to "A" (red team) or "B" (blue team). The right passage leads to "B" (red team) or "A" (blue team). Locate the letter in need of your help, and use the appropriate tunnel.

No matter what team you're on, the left tunnel starts with a ramp, turns right and leads to a rocket launcher with two ammo, then turns left and rises up into the left-bottom entrance to the domination chamber: a gigantic hall with columns and a host of goodies.

Meanwhile the right tunnel starts with a ramp and turns left, leading to a flak cannon with two ammo ahead at right, leading to the right-bottom entrance to the opposite chamber, again with a host of pick-ups.

Use the main ground entrance underneath the letter. Run into the entrance and continue into the domination chamber (nab the pick-ups), or turn left or right for a narrow enclosed corridor with a small elevator platform at the far end. Either platform raises you up onto the open walkway and the letter. Turn left if you want health (find two health packs here), and right if you want goo (the biorifle and two ammo packs are on the right).

TIP

A quick way to know which domination chamber is which is to check the sunlight. "A" is in the sun, while "B" is in shadow.

349

Spawning tactics for your team can vary wildly with so many possible routes to take to secure a letter. One plan is to split up every team member and appear in a host of locations, then converge on a chosen letter, secure it, and send half the team to take the other letter. Another school of thought is to all pile out of the spawning point, taking one route to a letter, and guard that while the rest of the team stocks up on ammo and weapons and takes the other letter.

TIP

Remember that you can wait at ambush points above the entrance to each side tunnel by walking around the edge of the ramp and onto the lip under the TV screen. Each TV screen on this level shows the color of the team holding the letter, and signifies which letter you'll reach if you move through the area.

The Domination "A" and "B" Chambers

Once inside the domination chamber, check out the minigun and two ammo packs in the far right corner. Stretching left from that are three health vials and two adrenaline packs, with a 100 shield pack in the center. On the other side are more vials and pills and a lightning gun with two ammo packs. Grab all of this when you can, or if you need these particular weapons. Make sure you have a teammate running for the 100 shield pack in each chamber so the enemy can't make running attacks on your secured areas.

There's a stack of ammo on the left and right walls near the lower ramp (rocket, shock, and link ammo on the left, and lightning, flak, and bio on the right). Run over this as you're dashing for the only way up to the letter within the chamber: one of two large ramps. At the top, you face a central doorway up some steps to the letter. The walkway overlooks the main courtyard, so you can fall off or onto the courtyard's raised area. You can also fall through the gaps near the inner wall, landing at the lower corridor (near the biorifle).

TIP

Want double damage? Then from either letter, dodge jump across to the middle (you'll come up short if you double jump) and pick it up. Then dish damage around—the upper area with the DD is a little too out in the open.

Total Domination

To stay on top of this map, pick a main area to defend and go for it. You should have a teammate at the chosen letter, but threats come from the two side elevators and main chambers behind you. So until you secure one letter, have most of your team charge the initial area leading to the letter, usually from different angles. When you're guarding a letter, make use of the height and use the lightning gun to plug enemies spawning or running below, drop biorifle goo at the side elevators to hamper enemy progress, and create a choke point behind you. Keep at least three of your team at the letter to waylay the enemy.

It's also advisable to patrol the large domination chamber, as you can control most of the weapons and items (including that useful 100 shield pack). When you spot multiple foes running into this area, retreat up the ramp to the letter, giving you height advantage (rockets and flak grenades work well when lobbed down), and making the foes attempt to reach you from the ramp. Knock them off with shock combos.

Shock combos also work well when aimed up from the main courtyard to the letter, especially if it's guarded by a well-hidden foe. Annoy and destroy from here while the rest of your team pours into the elevators or main chamber. Sidestep to the tunnel ramp entrance and cover if you're facing retaliation. Ambushing from the main lower entrance near the side elevators is also a great plan as you can use the cover. Also, don't forget that the side tunnels are almost always never guarded, although watch for chasing foes who try to ambush you.

Use lightning guns without the target sight, as the action is too quick for sniping. However, lurking at the back of the large chamber can help your team (if you let them know where the enemy is moving in from). What you really need to do is swarm your first letter, and then have a couple of teammates dodge jump to the double damage, through the main door, and take two routes to the other letter before the opposition even has time to react!

DOM-ATLANTIS

Recommended Players: 4–8

Legend

1	50 Health Pack (in fountain)	**10**	Bio ammo (in cave)	**18**	Adrenaline Pill (on walkway)
2	Rocket Launcher ammo (corridor)	**11**	Lightning Gun and 2 ammo (on walkway)	**19**	Link ammo (in cave)
3	Rocket Launcher (corridor)	**12**	50 Health Pack (in cave)	**20**	50 Health Pack (in cave)
4	Rocket Launcher ammo (corridor)	**13**	Adrenaline Pills x3 (cave entrance)	**21**	Biorifle (in cave)
5	50 Health Pack (in fountain)	**14**	Shock ammo (on grass)	**22**	Link ammo (in cave)
6	Bio ammo (in cave)	**15**	Minigun (on grass)	**23**	Adrenaline Pills x3 (cave entrance)
7	50 Shield Pack (top of archway)	**16**	Shock ammo (on grass)	**24**	Minigun ammo (on grass)
8	Adrenaline Pill (on walkway)	**17**	Adrenaline Pill x2 (on walkway under arch)	**25**	Minigun ammo (on grass)
9	Link Gun (in cave)			**26**	Shock Rifle (on grass)

351

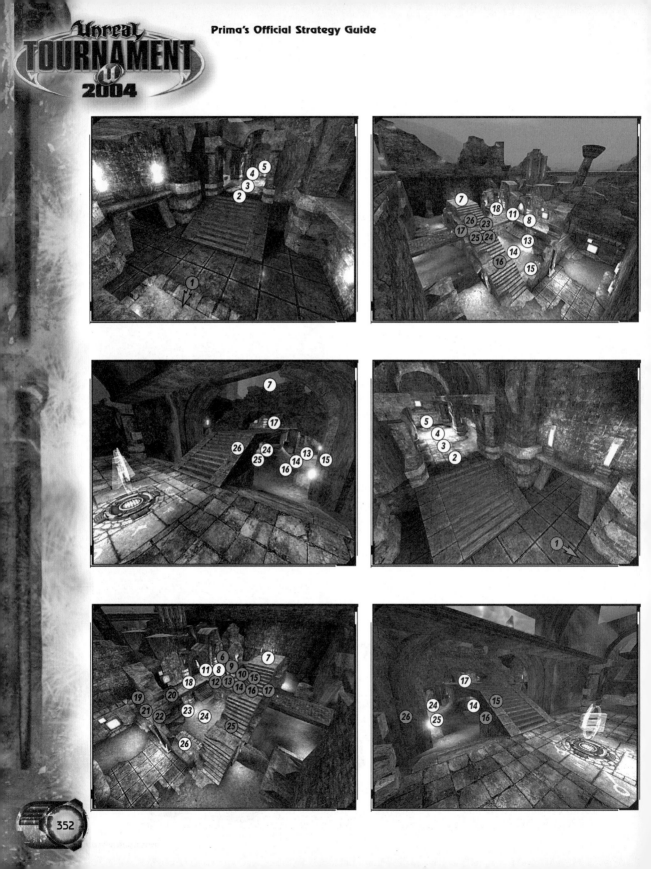

Overview

This undersea maze is confusing until you realize the entire level is much smaller than you'd expect, and contains two sets of identical areas. Two stepped corridors to the sides of the main area link domination chambers "A" and "B," while the rest of the access points are through the middle of the level, via one of two holes to a tunnel below the central ruins, or up a small set of steps, around the central tower, and back out the other side. The chambers are grassy with a long T-shaped walkway and a letter at one end.

Available Weapons

Biorifle (in the underground cave area, right and center of level—if in the "B" arena, facing the "A" arena)

Shock Rifle (x2, on the left side of the domination grass area, below the walkway)

Link Gun (in the underground cave area, left and center of level—if in the "B" arena, facing the "A" arena)

Minigun (x2, on the right side of the domination grass area, below the walkway)

Flak Cannon (in the middle of a side corridor)

Rocket Launcher (in the middle of a side corridor)

Lightning Gun (x2 on the upper walkway, near the central tower)

Spawn Point Strategies

This maze-like level doesn't always start in the same place. In fact, you can to appear in three main areas (on opposite sides for each team). You could appear at one end of a raised stepped corridor surrounded by water, at one side of an underground tunnel, or above the tunnel by a giant stone tower surrounded by ruins. What looks to be a confusing mass of small corridors is in fact a series of linked areas all leading to a grassy undersea courtyard, on either side of the central tunnel (with ruins atop) with each letter at the far end.

If you enter the raised stepped corridor that has a TV screen with "B" to the right or "A" to the left, you find health packs at each end and a waterfall. The main connecting corridor has a rocket launcher with two ammo packs at the top of the steps. The corridor opens at the other end to the chamber holding the letter shown near the doorway you entered. The corridor at the opposite side that has a TV screen with "A" to the right of the entrance and "B" to the left is identical except it contains a flak cannon and two ammo packs.

> ### TIP
>
> The small waterfall with the health pack below it has a ledge above, and you can jump from the top of the steps onto the ledge for a commanding view of the area and guard the weapon. Stand over the door so you aren't spotted, and ambush those wandering under you.

When you exit one of these side corridors, you appear on a small upper area (the side of it is a good place to set up an ambush) with three main exits. Depending on which exit you take (there are four, two on each side of the map), you'll find steps up to a walkway next to the central tower, and two adjacent routes: steps up to a large arch you climb on to reach a 50 shield pack, or steps down to the grassy domination area.

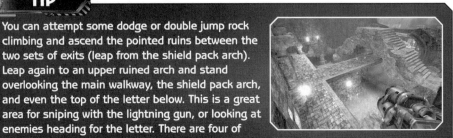

TIP

You can attempt some dodge or double jump rock climbing and ascend the pointed ruins between the two sets of exits (leap from the shield pack arch). Leap again to an upper ruined arch and stand overlooking the main walkway, the shield pack arch, and even the top of the letter below. This is a great area for sniping with the lightning gun, or looking at enemies heading for the letter. There are four of these vantage points (two identical, two mirrored) on the map! Also, try double jumping to the top of the doorway leading to the side corridor for another sneaky camping spot!

If you're on the upper walkway adjacent to the ruins, prowl around this area, moving to the junction where a lightning gun and two ammo packs wait. Find an adrenaline pill on either side of the gun. Look toward the middle ruins, peer into a gap below and see the main central tower; this is the spawn point mentioned earlier, although there's not much time to try spawn camping.

The tunnel area has six entrances, all accessed from the ground. The tunnel runs across the middle of the map under the ruins, and it's less complicated than it first appears. On each domination grass area, you can move under the walkway holding the lightning gun and enter the tunnel from a left hole, a right hole, or a set of steps in the middle. The steps lead to a platform around the central tower, where you can sprint into the opposite domination chamber, or fall between the platform and tower into the middle of the tunnel.

Take either hole entrance (two on each side) and you pass through three adrenaline pills as the tunnel bends around to a weapon—either the biorifle or link gun. If you're entering via the "B" area, the link gun is down the left hole and the biorifle is down the right hole. On each side of the weapon are two ammo packs of the opposite weapon.

If you're standing by one of these weapons, you can dash across and up the opposite hole to the other arena, or turn and run toward the middle of the map, through a narrow tunnel linking the other weapon, and around the central tower. Then you can grab the opposite weapon and head out of either hole on the opposite side.

The Domination "A" and "B" Chambers

The two chambers where the letters float are a lot more open, with the letters spinning at the very end of a long walkway. There are three ways to reach the letter: via the walkway under the shield pack arch, or up steps on either side of the walkway, from the grassy ground below.

Inspect the ground. In the area below and around the entrance to the side corridors and lightning gun walkway are two ammo packs with a weapon floating in a rectangular slab. The shock rifle is near the minigun ammo, and the minigun is near the shock rounds. Finding the right gun for the job depends on your location, but the shock rifle is always on the left slab if you're facing the center of the level.

Total Domination

The actual domination areas are reasonably easy to both defend and regain ammunition. You only use the rocket launcher and flak cannon at the beginning of your spawn, as the corridors are far away from the action. Flak is your friend in the corridor and underground, however—as is biorifle goop for spreading around blind corners or exits (such as the area out of a hole). However, a mixture of minigun, shock combo, and lightning sniping from the letter always wins through if your team is proficient enough and takes turns in grabbing extra ammo.

Don't forget to use the multitude of entrances to each domination area. Defenders should keep their strength by waiting at the letter itself to avoid enemies sneaking in behind them. A few good shock combos or lightning rounds from the letter, atop the shield pack arch, or on a perched point you double jump to are all great ways to increase security.

If you're hell-bent on taking over a letter, you need to soak up some damage when your team runs in. Try at least two players at a time, and shock combo the letter area to knock the enemy about, then approach from either set of steps to claim the area. Throw off your enemy by running in from the upper walkway and dropping down, or leaping up onto the shield pack arch, down to the walkway, and down to the letter (either onto the grass or down the middle steps).

DOM-CONDUIT

Recommended Players: 6–10

Legend

1 Link Gun and 2 ammo (team spawn)	10 50 Shield Pack (lower level)	20 Health Pack x2 (upper level)
2 Flak Cannon and 2 ammo (team spawn)	11 Minigun and 2 ammo (lower level)	21 Shock Rifle and 2 ammo (upper level)
3 Shock Rifle and 2 ammo (lower level)	12 Adrenaline Pill (central under area)	22 Health Vial x2 (upper level)
4 Rocket Launcher and 2 ammo (lower level)	13 Adrenaline Pill (central under area)	23 Minigun and 2 ammo (upper level)
5 Health Vial x2 (lower level)	14 Adrenaline Pill (central under area)	24 Health Vial x2 (upper level)
6 Health Vial x2 (lower level)	15 50 Shield Pack (upper level)	25 Biorifle and 2 ammo (upper level)
7 50 Health Pack x2 (lower level)	16 Adrenaline Pill (upper level)	26 Rocket Launcher and 2 ammo (upper level)
8 BioRifle and 2 ammo (lower level)	17 Adrenaline Pill (upper level)	27 Link Gun and 2 ammo (team spawn)
9 Health Vial x2 (lower level)	18 Adrenaline Pill (upper level)	28 Flak Cannon and 2 ammo (team spawn)
	19 Health Vial x2 (upper level)	

355

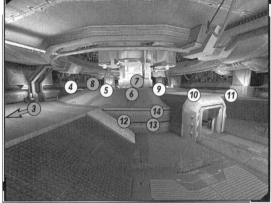

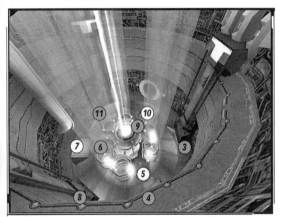

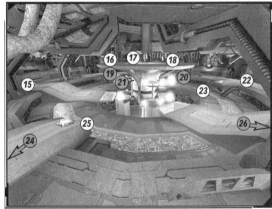

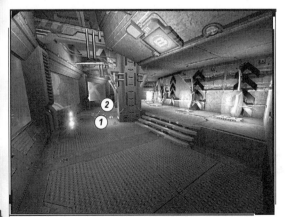

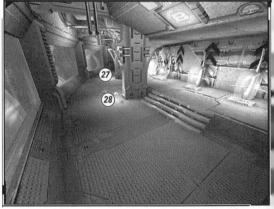

Overview

The cunning placement of the two domination chambers at the base and top of the gigantic tube-like conduit adds a cerebral aspect to this zone. The spawn point is inaccessible after you teleport out of it to one of six locations. The lower base has three entrances to the first chamber under the center of it, and six elevator tubes to reach between the areas. The top is a large circular platform and balcony with jump pads to the highest point—a completely circular platform with the other chamber.

Available Weapons	
Biorifle (x2, one on lower outer room, one on inner upper circular balcony)	**Minigun** (x2, one on lower outer room, one on inner upper circular balcony)
Shock Rifle (x2, one on lower outer room, one on inner upper circular balcony)	**Flak Cannon** (x2, inside spawn point chamber)
Link Gun (x2, inside spawn point chamber)	**Rocket Launcher** (x2, one on top of lower doorway, one on outer upper circular balcony)

Spawn Point Strategies

The two spawn points are self-enclosed curved chambers with six teleportation chambers along the far wall, up a few steps. You never return to the spawn point until you die, and the room is sealed from the main conduit area, so pick up the flak cannon and link gun at the spawn area, plus the two ammo packs near each, then choose one of the six teleports. The left three transport you to the conduit's base. The right three teleport you to the conduit's upper balcony.

   Choosing the correct teleport is important to your team's well-being. If you seek the letter "A" (ground level), take one of the left three teleports. If you seek the letter "B" (upper top of conduit), take one of the right three teleports. The exact destinations of each of the teleports are:

Teleport 1 (red team) ports you to the ground, to the left of a shock rifle and two ammo packs.

Teleport 1 (blue team) ports you to the ground, to the right of a shock rifle and two ammo packs.

Teleport 2 (red team) ports you to the ground, to the left of a biorifle and two ammo packs.

Teleport 2 (blue team) ports you to the ground, to the right of a biorifle and two ammo packs.

Teleport 3 (red team) ports you to the ground, to the left of a minigun and two ammo packs.

Teleport 3 (blue team) ports you to the ground, to the right of a minigun and two ammo packs.

Teleport 4 (red team) ports you to the upper circular area, to the left of a shock rifle, two ammo packs, and a jump pad to the letter "B."

Teleport 4 (blue team) ports you to the upper circular area, to the right of a shock rifle, two ammo packs, and a jump pad to the letter "B."

Teleport 5 (red team) ports you to the upper circular area, to the left of a minigun, two ammo packs, and a jump pad to the letter "B."

Teleport 5 (blue team) ports you to the upper circular area, to the right of a minigun, two ammo packs, and a jump pad to the letter "B."

Teleport 6 (red team) ports you to the upper circular area, to the left of a biorifle, two ammo packs, and a jump pad to the letter "B."

Teleport 6 (blue team) ports you to the upper circular area, to the right of a biorifle, two ammo packs, and a jump pad to the letter "B."

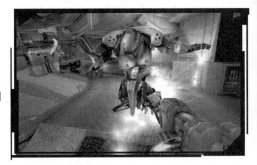

Now that you know where you appear, head for your preferred weapon. Each of the upper balcony weapons sits in front of a jump pad that you can climb the sloping sides of and leap to letter "B." You don't have run around looking for a jump pad; you can dash here to secure the circular platform.

The Domination "A" and "B" Chambers

The conduit is split into two main areas, accessed via teleport and/or a pod of six elevators in the center of the chamber. Along the base of the conduit is a massive circular room segmented into ramps and dips and an upper middle area where the lifts are. A shock rifle, minigun, and biorifle are on the outer edge of this area, reached by running up and down the ramps around the perimeter, or cutting across to the other side.

The outer undulating ground has three dipped areas. Each dip has a doorway on the inside, leading to the lower domination chamber, which is under the bank of elevators and accessed through any of the three doorways. Above each doorway is a rocket launcher and two ammo packs (between the shock rifle and biorifle), two health packs (between the biorifle and minigun), and a 50 shield pack (between the minigun and shock rifle). Near each item on top of the three doorway entrances are two health vials. At the center of the lower area are three sets of two elevator tubes. The tube on the right has an elevator waiting (unless it is in use) while the tube on the left has an elevator above. This is the only way to reach the top, unless you teleport from your spawn point.

On the top floor of the conduit, accessed via spawn teleport or elevator, are the top of the lifts, underneath an upper circular platform. This is the "B" letter domination chamber, and it's completely open from all sides. It is reached via one of three jump pads spaced at equidistant lengths around the upper deck. In front of each jump pad (which can be accessed via the side sloping supports fitted to it) is a weapon detailed in the teleport list. Behind each jump pad on the exterior balcony are two health vials.

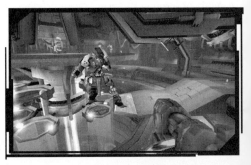

Just as on the lower floor, but sitting near a ramp on the outer balcony, is a shield pack (between the shock rifle and biorifle), a rocket launcher (between the biorifle and minigun), and two health packs (between the minigun and shock rifle). The upper platform contains three adrenaline pills.

Total Domination

Holding both the chambers is extremely difficult for two reasons. There are three entrances all around you, so you can't back up and wait for an attack; it could come at any time in any direction. The second problem is that there's no ammunition or weapons near the chambers, meaning guards always run out of guns and ammo. This is great for attackers who can wait them out!

To storm a chamber, make sure you agree on your tactics first. You can all pile into the left or right three teleports and take one area first then keep it for as long as it takes to grab both, or split up to take both at once. Both chambers require similar tactics if you're storming them. If there are three attackers, you can elect to dash in (or jump in) from all three entrances (or pads) at once and overrun the defenders from all sides. Mix this up with a strategy of all attacking from the same place. Flak cannon shots work well in these close quarters, although there's nothing quite like a shock combo to knock an enemy off the upper platform!

Take the elevator back down—don't jump or you'll suffer serious damage. Don't spend too long traipsing around the sides of the levels collecting weapons (although you may want to grab the biorifle or shock rifle on the top deck, then go for the shield pack that's nearby, before mounting an assault); you need to constantly reach the chambers to help your team out.

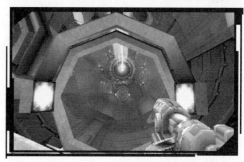

If you're defending from a letter and run out of ammo, run out or drop off to the nearest weapon, throw away your current weapon and grab a new one (if it is of the same kind), and dash or leap back. Also leave goop from your biorifle on the jump pads and landing spots on the upper platform to help your team out. The tight quarters make combat even more frantic than usual!

TIP

Peering down from the top deck to the bottom level isn't a good plan as you can't really damage anyone before you're spotted and fired on. However, you can fall off the top deck, moving toward the outer wall as you go, and land on top of a large circular duct (of which there are two). You're hard to spot here, so blast on the punk below!

With shield jumping skill, you can move to the outer balcony on the top floor, then leap to the sloping support beam from the slope on the outer wall, then double jump onto the top of a partially shielded light fixture on the outer wall. Bring out your shock rifle; there's even a view of the platform from here!

DOM-RENASCENT

Recommended Players: 4–8

Legend

1	Adrenaline Pills x8 (woodland glade)	7	Shock Rifle (woodland glade)	13	Rocket ammo x2 (rock near bridge)
2	50 Shield Pack (cave)	8	Shock ammo (woodland glade)	14	Rocket Launcher (rock near bridge)
3	Minigun and 3 ammo (ravine)	9	Double Damage or 100 Shield Pack (top of bridge)	15	Flak ammo (platform)
4	50 Health Pack x2 (cave)	10	Link ammo (grass)	16	Flak Cannon (platform)
5	Adrenaline Pills x3 (bridge)	11	Link ammo (grass)	17	Lightning Gun and 1 ammo (forest glade)
6	Shock ammo (woodland glade)	12	Link Gun (grass)		

Overview

This once-sacred ground is now a carnage-filled gorge of terror! Imagine this level as a giant dog bone with a central lower gorge linking both spawn points. Identical structures at each end lead to an upper cliff face on either side of the gorge that houses the letter. The left side is a jump pad stepped zone, while the right is a slope heading up and left. Either cliff has a center letter overlooking the other with a floating stone structure in the middle that cannot be reached. On the cliff is a copse of trees, a square platform affording height, and a rope bridge on the left leading to a special item.

Available Weapons

Shock Rifle (x2, on ground in gorge, near large tattooed tree)

Link Gun (x2, rear of gorge, between rock island and jump pads)

Minigun (middle of gorge)

Flak Cannon (x2, on platform on upper cliff, overlooking letter)

Rocket Launcher (x2, on rocky outcrop near rope bridge)

Lightning Gun (x2, behind sacred trees on right slope)

Spawn Point Strategies

Your team appears on the grass at the far end of the gorge, or on a couple of short rock outcrops that you can drop off onto the ground. Check out your base (such as it is—it's just one end of the gorge) and notice three distinct routes out of it.

To the left is a rudimentary trio of rock steps containing two jump pads in the form of a circular glowing cauldron of green fire. Find a link gun and three ammo packs. Bounce up the jump pads (side jump from the lower to the higher) and land on the left cliff top with letter "A" ahead if you're red ("B" if you're blue).

Ahead of your starting point, if you're at the back of the base, is a rock island. This holds a double damage (if you're red team) or a 100 shield pack (if you're blue). It's accessed via a rope bridge from the right cliff face. Ignore the rock if you're on the ground, and inspect the immediate area. Ahead is a giant tree with a marking on its trunk. Beyond that is a shock rifle and two ammo packs (one left and one right of the tree).

The middle of the gorge (where both teams can easily meet) contains a single minigun and three ammo packs. To the sides, in an alcove directly under the rock with the letter above it, is a 50 shield pack (under "A") and two health packs (under "B"). Continue to reach your opponents' spawning area, but the place is too big to spawn camp.

The final lower area is the route to the right side cliff face. Head right from the far end of your spawn point, go under a rope bridge, and start to climb a slope. To the right is a sacred glade, with trees and twinkling lights. Behind the trees on the right outer wall is a lightning gun and one ammo pack. Continue up the slope as it bends left past another tree to the top of the right cliff face and the letter "B" area. Most of the action happens on top of the two cliffs.

361

Unreal Tournament 2004

The Domination "A" and "B" Chambers

The cliff faces containing the "A" or "B" letters are exact mirror images. The description starts at the top of the right-side slope. Pass the huge tree, and see a copse of similarly sized trees ahead, with a jump pad in the middle. On the ground in the copse are eight health vials. Leap on the jump pad, and land on an upper square-shaped platform with a flak cannon in one corner and one ammo in another. The open area makes flak blasts a little obsolete, so use it only on anyone heading for the letter, which is on the cliff edge in the middle of the area.

You can see (and shoot) the opposition on the other cliff face all along its edge, so watch yourself! Check the other letter immediately, and send off teammates to win it, but only if they enter the cliff face from the jump pads or right slope. You can't jump across the gorge to the other letter. The far end of the cliff leads to the opposition's jump pads and rocky steps.

The final area is left of the letter, and left of the top of the right slope. Move to a rock outcrop with a rocket launcher on a small rock platform to your left. Pick up the two ammo packs from the cliff nearby, and then run onto a rope bridge you saw from below. Find three adrenaline pills as you go, a double damage at the top (if the rope bridge is above the red team), or a 50 shield pack (if the bridge is above blue). Double jump from the rock island to the jump pads area of the opposite cliff for another route.

Total Domination

Keeping both domination areas under your control is extremely difficult, as the opposing team can see where you're positioning your troops but can attack only via either side. This is your only advantage—you know to expect enemies from the jump pads and steps or the slope. With this in mind, split your team into two equal groups. Have the first team secure the double damage (or prevent the enemy from obtaining it) and capture the first letter, while the other squad does the same on the other side. The extra health and items mean you don't need to come down to take more ammo or armor, and you can set yourselves up to waste enemies coming in from either side, with a couple of sharpshooters tagging enemies on the other side.

Learn to use the lightning gun without its scope. Point shock combos at your letter, and bounce incoming punks into the gorge before they reach it. The gorge is full of ammo and health, but it's not really useful to stay there, as there's armor up and over the bridge. But you could drop down and heal in a pinch. However, you're best off with suppressing fire with rockets near the launcher pick-up itself, a shock combo or two for those leaping up the jump pads, and lightning shots from the central copse of trees or upper platform to see off the rest.

Bombing Run Maps

NOTE

During single-player games and online multiplayer, you will encounter Bombing Run levels besides the ones listed below. The following levels are new for *Unreal Tournament 2004*. For information on previously created levels, please consult *Prima's Official Unreal Tournament 2003* guide. Bombing Run levels in the single-player game include ELECFIELDS, SKYLINE, SLAUGHTERHOUSE, TEMPLEOFANUBIS, and TWINTOMBS.

Each of the Bombing Run maps feature scenery and bases identical to each other, joined in the map's middle. This means strategy and descriptions apply to both "sides" of the map, and work for both teams identically. Minor differences are mentioned where necessary.

BR-BRIDGEOFFATE

Recommended Players: 8–12

Legend

1. Link, flak, lightning ammo packs (base)
2. Shock, mini, rocket ammo packs (base)
3. Shock Rifle +2 ammo packs (main hall)
4. 50 Health Pack (main hall)
5. Link Gun +2 ammo packs (main hall)
6. 50 Health Pack (main hall)
7. Minigun +2 ammo packs (center of main hall)
8. 50 Shield Pack (main hall)
9. 50 Health Pack (main hall)
10. 50 Health Pack (main hall)
11. Linkgun +2 ammo packs (main hall)
12. Shock Rifle +2 ammo packs (main hall)
13. Rocket Launcher +1 ammo and lightning ammo pack (side entrance)
14. Flak Cannon +1 ammo and minigun ammo pack (side entrance)
15. Shock, link, flak (right side), rocket (left side) ammo packs (base of stairs)
16. Lightning gun (base of stairs in alcove)
17. Health Vial x3 (on stairs)
18. 50 Health Pack x2 (entrance to bridge)
19. Adrenaline Pills x4, 100 Shield Pack (right upper bridge entrance)
20. Biorifle +2 ammo packs (left upper bridge entrance)
21. Double Damage (CTF), Ball (BR)

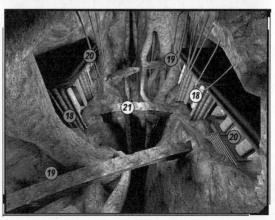

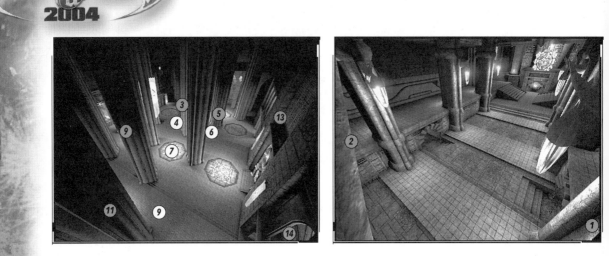

Overview

Bridge of Fate is a large but easily defended base. This gives many teams the sense that they can leave fewer defenders—don't make that mistake. All three entrances lead to immense hallways with pillars and floor octagons galore: your main translocation and combat zone. At the far end are three doors. The middle takes you to a central open rock walkway with a sheer drop on either side—and the ball. The two other entrances take you to upper walkways before the identical enemy encampment. The ball is in the middle of the central walkway.

Available Weapons*

Biorifle (at top of left side stairs overlooking rock walkway)	**Minigun** (outside base in main hall; middle octagon)
Shock Rifle (x2, outside base in main hall; near left and right octagon, BR only)	**Flak Cannon** (inside base, left side entrance)
Shock Rifle (x2, outside base in outer side passage, CTF only)	**Rocket Launcher** (inside base, right side entrance)
Link Gun (x2, outside base in main hall; far left and right octagon)	**Lightning Gun** (x2, base of side stairs leading to outer rock walkway)
	* For each side, double the total for the final number on this level unless otherwise stated.

Goal Patrol

The goal in Bridge of Fate is perhaps the easiest of the new Bombing Run bases to defend, as the area is almost entirely enclosed, with only three entrances. The first is the arched double doors at the opposite end of the base, while the other two are three quarters of the way down the main lower central corridor on either wall. These doors lead to side alcoves, each containing a weapon (flak cannon on the left, rocket launcher on the right).

The approach to the goal involves heading up stairs, turning either left or right, and running around the steps to the goal at the throne-like raised area. The enemies will try to score either by lobbing from the lower corridor, or by passing to a foe already up on the side balconies adjacent to the main corridor or at the goal.

Defenders have to stand in front of the goal to knock the ball away, or prowl the upper sides of this room, plugging anyone entering. If your adversaries aren't the sharpest, push outward and stand guard in front of the main doors, or at the weapon alcoves (each have ammo next to them), and bring the pain to them. Always use the columns behind the weapons as cover or ambush points. Finally, don't forget the 50 shield pack on the octagon adjacent to the main exit doorway. Everyone tends to dash for this, making it a good spot at which to aim.

> **NOTE**
>
> Find link, flak, and lightning ammo at the far end of the left upper balcony. There's shock, rocket, and minigun ammo at the end of the right one. Find minigun ammo near the flak cannon, and lightning ammo at the rocket launcher.

Midfield Machinations

The midfield area is composed of a giant hallway with nine floor octagons, numerous pillars, and a trio of exits in the far wall, allowing for multiple routes and madcap combat. Remember where you are! Look around. The side walls are smaller than the walls leading to the base and the middle of the map. The base wall has your team's colors flying, a large arch entrance, and two side entrances. The wall to the middle has three entrances (the two side ones jut out a little). Figure this out and you can quickly choose offense or defense plans based on your location and team help cries.

The hallway is the place for weakening enemies (even though most of your defenders should be inside the base as there's less room to lose your foes). Mainly, you'll be translocating the hell out of here, on your way to the ball and the enemy base. As you're difficult to tag while translocating, you're likely to be ignored, so use this as often as possible.

Translocate to the five different weapons placed in the center of octagons (two link guns with three ammo packs, two shock rifles, and a minigun each with two ammo packs), or the four health packs (two each between the center and outer octagons). Look at the map or rise up using the ghost function to understand how this hallway is structured.

The lightning gun is at the far end of this hallway, along with some extra ammunition in a narrow side alcove (lightning, rocket, and mini on the left, with lightning, flak, and link on the right). Head up the steps and around, nabbing three health vials on the way, and you'll reach the top exit. Turn around and look down on the lower doorway—this is a great spot from which to snipe, but the level is too big to spend time here. Head onto the rock platform area.

Head up the left stairs and grab a biorifle and two extra goo rounds. Use the goop on any entrances you can (such as the side exits in the base or the rocky walkways themselves). The walkway leads to the other side and the identical opposite base (you'll reach the 100 shield pack and four adrenaline pills). Head up the right stairs and you emerge onto the right side walkway; to the left is a 100 shield pack surrounded by four adrenaline pills. Pop these, and then cross to the enemy side, where you'll find the biorifle. Choose whether you want the shield or biorifle first—we recommend having someone sprint for the shield pack to prevent the enemy grabbing it.

The central doorway leads to the lower, main rock walkway. Before the walkway starts, there's a small alcove on each side (where you see your first translocating enemy). The right side has two health packs to grab. The ball's in the middle.

> ### TIP
>
> One of the most impressive sniping spots is on one of the corners, near the biorifle or the shield pack. You can look down the entire walkway zone. Plant a comrade behind you to avoid being ambushed from behind, and you can plug away all day! Want to be even more of an annoyance? Try shock-comboing foes off the walkways!
>
> Further annoy the enemy by translocating down into the bottomless pit, but aim the device so you land on one of the less-used snaking rock formations. Fire up from here to confuse as well as kill!
>
> Finally, when you're running along the walkway, double jump or dodge jump off the walkway, and then launch a translocator, aiming it at the walkway and teleport back on it. This is the perfect way to avoid incoming fire or enemies.

Going Balls Out

When you're crossing the three precipitous walkways, rely on your translocating skills. Fling the device onto the upper side walkway or the biorifle balcony to throw off an enemy. Translocate your team across and into enemy territory, picking up the ball, then lobbing it up to a mate on an upper walkway who can run down the steps, out into the huge hallway, and throw it back at you. Use all three routes to spread the enemy out and have a friend remain hiding in the enemy hallway to receive a ball thrown when it respawns on the central walkway.

Once you're inside the base, it becomes a game of skill and a little luck. Send in a friend to play interference with the enemy, approaching (for example) from the right side entrance while the ball carrier sneaks in from the left. When you're lobbing the ball, shoot it from the side entrance area of the main lower corridor, aiming just below the nearest ceiling roof section, and it will arc into the goal. Otherwise throw it in from the base of the steps.

TIP

Use the gigantic pillars in the hallway to help you. Carry the ball, lob it at the pillar, shoot an enemy that's causing you hassle, then catch the ball as it bounces back down. Skilled players only, please!

Capture the Flag Counterpoint

The main difference between the match types is the slight remodeling of the CTF version of BRIDGEOFFATE. Head out of either side entrance from the base, where there's a rocket launcher or flak cannon. This area is larger, with pillars. At the start of the hall, a wall turns the hall into an elongated cross shape. The reason for this is an additional outer passage in each corner of the map.

Out the side entrance, there's a door to the middle base doors and the main grand hall. Head to the map's outer edge to find a corridor with a shock rifle, two ammo packs, a health pack, and stairs up to an additional entrance into the lightning gun stairwells. The rest of the map is the same, except a double damage replaces the ball in the middle of the central bridge.

The additional outer passages to the sides make flag carrying and base protection difficult. Attackers now have a choice of three courses to take. They can move through the outer passages or the main hallway, switching courses by translocating at the bridges, or else stepping through the doorways into the adjacent areas. This makes the side entrances to the base more important, and pushes the choke points to the doorways in front of the entrances. There, you can keep watch of your own outer area and the middle doors. Have one teammate man each area (the left, middle, and right doorways) to ensure cover. Flag carriers can vary their route back so they aren't cut down in the main hallway.

BR-COLOSSUS

Recommended Players: 6–14

Legend

1 50 Shield Pack (top of side platform, left)	8 100 Shield Pack (CTF), Double Damage (BR) (inside cave)	14 Flak Cannon +1 ammo pack (ground level plate)	20 Minigun +1 ammo pack (ground-level plate)
2 Health Vial x5 (side platform, left)	9 Rocket Launcher +2 ammo packs (mesh walkway)	15 Link Gun +4 ammo packs (side platform tunnel, right)	21 Double Damage (CTF), Ball (BR)
3 Shock Rifle +3 ammo packs (base of side platform, left)	10 Assault, flak, rocket ammo packs (top of cave entrance)	16 Link, flak ammo packs (walkway)	22 Adrenaline Pills x3 (BR only)
4 Link Gun +4 ammo packs (side platform tunnel, left)	11 Shock, rocket ammo packs (walkway)	17 Health Vial x5 (side platform, right)	23 50 Health Pack x2 (under each side platform)
5 Shock and Lightning ammo packs (top of cave entrance)	12 Minigun +1 ammo pack (ground-level plate)	18 50 Shield Pack (top of side platform, right)	24 100 Shield Pack (top of side platform)
6 Flak Cannon +1 ammo pack (ground level plate)	13 Shock and minigun ammo packs (top of cave entrance)	19 Shock Rifle +3 ammo packs (base of side platform, right)	25 Ion Painter (CTF), Redeemer (BR), (top of side platform)
7 Lightning Gun (top of cliff)			

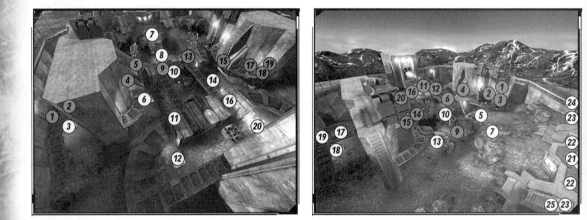

Overview

This massive level has two gigantic bases on each side separated by a hill with a walkway spanning left to right on the top. Double damage and a redeemer lie on either side of the central walkway with the ball on it. The walkway descends two sets of steps and a rocky drop, into a multi-entrance cave leading to the base interior. Players can traverse on the ground or on a large walkway sandwiched on both sides by a side balcony and small tunnel junction. Five air chutes allow trampoline-like movement across the level—for when translocation is outlawed. Watch out for snipers on this level, and try it on low gravity!

Available Weapons*

Shock Rifle (x3, one is on an upper platform, behind base; two are on extreme left and right rocky outcrops, down from middle stairs, overlooking base)

Link Gun (x2, each is in small covered tunnel above the sides of the base, reach via far side steps or side elevator platform)

Minigun (x2, on a metal ground plate to the side of the goal)

Flak Cannon (x2, on a metal ground plate midway between the base entrance and goal)

Rocket Launcher (x3, one is on the middle main base walkway after you land from the air chute; the other two are atop the steps on the far side wall entrance to the small upper junction tunnel next to the link gun)

Lightning Gun (top of rocky outcrop, between middle stairs, overlooking base)

Redeemer/Ion Painter (only one on entire map, on upper balcony opposite to DD, in middle of level, to the right [red] or left [blue]. Redeemer only available in BR. Ion painter only available in CTF)

* For each side, double the total for the final number on this level unless otherwise stated.

Goal Patrol

You face constant threat of snipers, so keep moving around your base and cover the main areas where the enemy congregates. It is impossible to completely defend your base, so grab the weapons with which you're happiest. The shock rifle behind the goal (with two ammo plus a lightning and minigun pack) is easy to reach and good at tagging from long distance. The minigun (plus one ammo pack) helps as the enemy closes, while the flak cannon (plus single ammo pack) is useful only when you're chasing an enemy or waiting on a raised walkway to lob a grenade you place in the foe's path.

Keep to the upper walkway of the base if you want a better view of the action. The rocket launcher on the sides, and the link gun, are useful if you can immediately leap back into the action or if you're following an enemy who is weaving around these side walkways and tunnel to avoid combat or well-trodden paths. Otherwise, it takes too long to nab ordnance from here unless you're quickly translocating.

> **NOTE**
>
> Health packs are scarce in Colossus. Find two behind the goal near the shock rifle, and two more on the ground under the rocket launcher (plus two ammo). Five health vials are on each side from the launcher leading across a platform to the tunnel junction and link gun (with four ammo). Other than that, the far area of the base is health free!

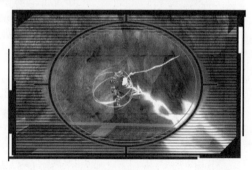

Because you and your foes will translocate across most of this stage, grab the lightning gun (from the midfield) and return to base to skulk around the top walkway and bottom ground level. Look off the sides of the walkway for enemies on the floor. Stand atop either of the supports flanking the goal (these are attached to the walkway, and you can walk under to pick up a flak ammo pack) as long as opposition snipers don't see you.

You also can stand in the middle, next to the jump pad leading to the goal to overlook the cave containing the jump pad, where enemies try to leap in from. That way you have visuals on foes all the way from the steps to the cave and the walkway. Of paramount defensive importance is the jump pad (to bounce up and into the goal), so knock away anyone who attempts to use it.

> **TIP**
>
> Keep the goal well guarded by using the jump pad to land on the edge of the goal and patrol it. This way, you can stop the ball from entering the goal from anywhere above the goal (but not below it!).

369

Instead of lurking around corners in your defensive monolith base, work out where the enemy tends to send in attackers and blast them from as far as possible, roughing them up before finishing them as they close. Other good camp spots are the link gun areas to the side. You can double jump onto the walkway, as well as cover it with link gun or rocket fire. Naturally, the main route to the goal is via the central cave, but there are four elevators and the ground area to worry about, too!

Have a spotter who focuses on the small elevator platform on each side, at the base entrance. If the enemies use this to reach the curved platform leading to the link gun junction tunnel, they can outfox you, so blast them as they arrive. Otherwise, train a patrol (either on the ground or walkway) to watch for enemies surviving the jog downhill who ignore the cave and just use the ground near the flak and miniguns. They can quickly turn and head for the goal (throwing the ball up and through) or step to either of the two rear elevators at the back of the base, and jog in from behind. If an elevator moves, have a rocket or two waiting for an enemy!

The air chutes are also relevant. Each base contains five, and the main one is inside a cave. This shoots you onto the rocket launcher on the walkway. Ignore the two on either side of the cave, suspended high in the air, unless you want to translocate into them and be shoved over and onto the side of the upper main walkway. If translocators are banned, you can enter the ground air chute in the base's middle far area, in front of the goal. It pushes you back out and onto the rocket launcher on the walkway. The final chute is behind the goal, accessed via translocator, and it

deposits you on the rocket launcher on the walkway (although usually you'll fly over that and into the chute exit from the cave). Chutes are a good way to clear large areas when the translocator isn't available.

> **TIP**
>
> When you've launched from a chute and are in mid-air, jump as you reach the top of your ascent and you'll rise even higher for a split second, enabling you to cover a little more distance, and control your fall more easily.

Then there are the translocating areas to camp out at. Some are spectacular, but you can't teleport to the side buildings' top as you'll be hit with depressurization damage and eventually explode. However, there are some classic spots to hunker down with a lightning gun, such as the floating air chute on either side of the cave entrance, near midfield. You can translocate into the chute (you'll be fired onto the middle of the walkway), but better yet, shoot yourself to the chute's top! It's flat, and there's a commanding view of the entire base and

midfield. Optionally run across the cables for another spot where you can see below you. Otherwise, translocate onto the sloped sides of the side buildings, above the link gun (and even the sloping arch above the lower arches) for another fine view. Lastly, try landing on the ledge next to the farthest air chute, overlooking the goal. This is a great sniping spot!

Midfield Machinations

The area between the walkway and the steps to the map's middle is known as "midfield." This zone is the base's gateway and has a central rocky outcrop with a lightning gun on it. This is the most helpful weapon on this map, allowing you to retreat and plug away at advancing foes, or stand your ground and wait for punks to come dashing over the central walkway. Translocate to the top or to one of the protruding rock sides where shock rifles await (go halfway up the steps, then turn left or right). From here, it's a quick dash up to the level's center.

The outcrop affords a great view of the base for both attackers and defenders, and makes a great shooting and ambush point if you stand in the shadows near the middle rock wall behind the gun. Below it is a metal ground plate with two health packs. If you need sustenance, check here. If you're attacking, pick up the health and guard this area.

On either side of the health packs are entrances leading to a cave under the base's beginning. This is a high-traffic area. Above the left entrance are shock and minigun ammo packs. Above the right are shock and lightning gun ammo packs. Through either entrance, you find yourself inside the cave with a 100 shield pack next to a jump pad. The pad is a great escape up to the walkway and the goal—but it's likely to be guarded. Have one or two of your team patrol this area to prevent enemies from taking the shield and running for the goal. Use the ground exit to mix up your attack; above this exit is ammo for assault, flak, and rocket weapons.

Games are won or lost in the midfield zone. Don't overstretch your team by chasing an opponent with a ball, only to find others waiting at the ball respawn point (a great tactic). Watch enemies when they enter your base (the foes must enter down the hill but then can dive into cover or a variety of locations detailed above), and watch out for foes dropping from the ball location. Patrol the walkway's edge, inform your team when a foe is entering the cave, and grab the lightning or shock weapons. Also try hiding in the shadows of the rocky hill.

TIP

Underneath the base walkway is an underused prowling spot. Hide in the shadows and blast enemies as they run past. They're preoccupied with heading to the goal, meaning you can tag them with less danger.

Going Balls Out

The nastiest action takes place at the zone's center. When the match begins, translocate and vault up to the sides of the main walkway. On one side (left or right depending on your team) is a small ledge with double damage. On the opposite side is a redeemer! Obviously, the team that grabs this first (and then counts down to the redeemer respawn and effectively patrols this location) will have the advantage. Don't necessarily head for the ball; lighting up the opposition with the redeemer or a lightning gun on DD is much more of a threat.

371

Bring your lightning gun (find two ammo packs on either side of the ball) and race to the ball in the walkway's middle, taking the three adrenaline pills on either side as you go. Judge whether the two health packs are needed (usually these are great to go for if you're translocating from combat, so remember they are under the DD or redeemer ledge), and then sprint for the lower portions of the hill.

Infiltrating the enemy base has already been covered (head up the elevators to mix it up a bit, or dodge jump and translocate into the cave and up on the walkway, or keep hugging the ground). Consider having mates already positioned on the side platforms, on the walkway, or on the ground to throw the ball to—making it to the goal yourself is almost unheard of.

When you have the ball and you're punting it at the goal, launch it from just in front of the rocket launcher on the walkway (it's possible to dunk it in from here) or from the minigun ground plate. Another great lobbing spot is the curved upper ledge near the link gun and ammo; this is a much easier shot to take, too. Dunk it by using the jump pad and flying up and into the goal, by sneaking around the back elevators and dunking, or (most cunning of all) staying on the ground and shooting the ball straight up and through the goal. Get your teammates to stand in these preferred spots and lob the ball at them, and victory is almost assured!

Capture the Flag Counterpoint

The only differences between the maps are the locations of three items: the redeemer is replaced with the ion painter, and the double damage and 100 shield pack switch places (meaning there's only one 100 shield pack on the middle platform and two double damage power-ups in the central cave on each side). Support your flag carrier just as you would the ball carrier, secure the ion painter early on; use it to demolish those chasing your flag carrier or snipe them from distance. Finally, the darkened areas around the flag make light work of leaving your translocator pod and warping back in for a quick second flag steal.

BR-SERENITY
Recommended Players: 6–10

Legend

1 Adrenaline Pills x3 (side grassy raised area)	**6** 50 Health Pack x2 (near base entrance)	**11** Double Damage (narrow ledge)	**16** Health Vial x4 (grassy bank)
2 Link Gun +2 ammo packs (base of grassy raised area)	**7** 50 Health Pack x2 (near base entrance)	**12** Minigun ammo x2 (grassy bridge)	**17** Redeemer (edge of wall)
3 Rocket Launcher +2 ammo packs (between trees)	**8** Link Gun +2 ammo (near ledge to DD)	**13** Health Vial x4 (grassy bank)	**18** Biorifle (red base) or Shock Rifle (blue) +2 ammo packs (near central bridge)
4 Flak Cannon +2 ammo packs (back of base)	**9** Health Vials x3 (near goal)	**14** Lightning ammo packs x2 (on hillock under tree)	**19** 50 Shield Pack (under bridge)
5 Minigun (bridge over base entrance)	**10** Health Vials x4 (near ledge to DD)	**15** Lightning Gun (on hillock between trees)	**20** Ball (top of bridge, in middle)

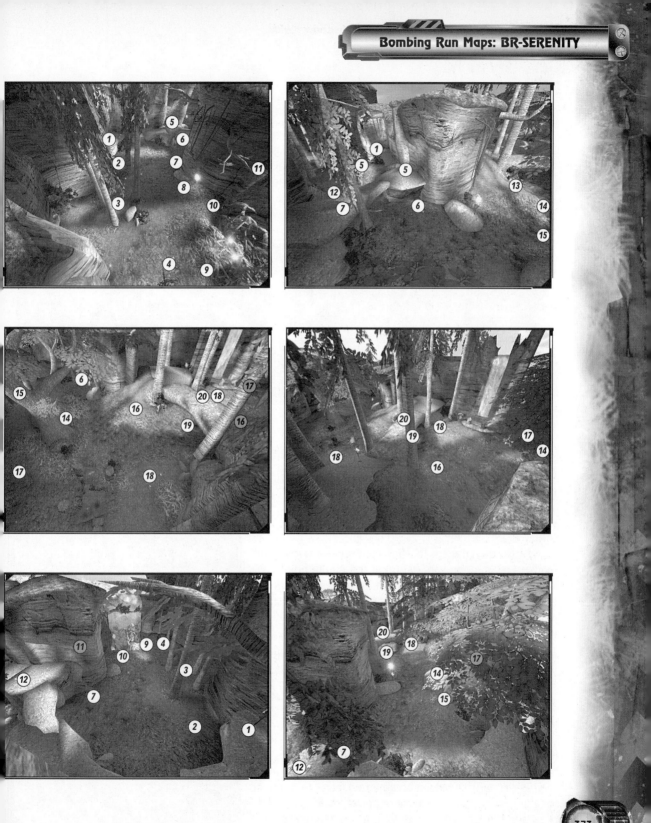

Overview

Serenity's goals are set next to a cliff and waterfall, giving you only one side from which to aim. From a clearing with a few trees and rocks, there's a natural bridge arc leading to a long left turn and valley, dotted by hillocks on the right, and tall grass. The center is a bridge spanning from left to right, with the ball on top. The blue base has a waterfall on its right side (looking toward the ball from the blue base), and a biorifle near the bridge to pick up (compared with a shock rifle on the red side). Don't forget the redeemer and double damage!

Available Weapons*

Biorifle (only one on entire map, raised hillock right of center bridge—blue side)

Shock Rifle (only one on entire map, raised hillock right of center bridge—red side)

Link Gun (x2, side of base, near team banner)

Minigun (left side of bridge, at base entrance)

Flak Cannon (next to goal)

Rocket Launcher (clump of trees in base)

Lightning Gun (top of hillock, right side, overlooking center of map)

Redeemer (low ground behind ruins, right side of map near middle bridge)

* For each side, double the total for the final number on this level unless otherwise stated.

Goal Patrol

Each goal is near a large and deadly cliff. Fall or jump off here and you'll die. Instead, concentrate on the trees on either side of the goal. These provide an area to bounce the ball into if aiming at the goal proves too difficult. On either side of the goal are three health vials—defenders pick these up.

Next to the goal are the flak cannon and two ammo packs. Flak cannons are useful at the choke point entrance to either base, at the natural bridge. Farther into the middle of the base is the rocket launcher (with two ammo packs). Nab this before the enemy does and patrol the entrance bridge or before a run to the opposing goal.

Also note the two health packs on the base's right wall just before the exit, and the three adrenaline pills on the short raised bank on the right. Grab the health to stop a wounded enemy from taking it, and snatch the pills only if you spend the match damaging others (rather than, for example, goal tending).

The most important weapon in each base is the link gun; find one on the right wall near the team banner, and one on the left, under the rise with the pills. Both have two ammo packs. This allows professional teams to keep a couple of defenders armed with chained link guns to decimate an incoming attacker. Finally, the double damage is partially hidden on a narrow ledge to the right of (and around from) the base entrance, overlooking the goal and cliff. Double jump to grab this before you push into the opposing area or if you're being swamped.

Midfield Machinations

From the natural rock bridge at your base's entrance, have your team grab the two health packs to the entrance's left (these help those guarding the rocky second and third entrance areas near the lightning or miniguns). The rock on the ground to the left, near the banner, is a good place from which to strike attackers, and you can drop behind it for cover or when you chase the ball carrier. Just behind and above this rock is the minigun, accessed either from the raised ramp near the adrenaline pills, or by looping around from the lightning gun (the long way). The minigun is a perfect close-assault weapon for ball carriers running under the arched bridge (otherwise, rockets or lightning shots work better). Dodge jump right, over the arch, to pick up the two ammo packs for the minigun.

Either move right from the arch, or run around the right wall from the minigun ammo and grab the lightning gun—it's one of the most useful weapons. Ahead is a tiny hillock next to a tree where the two ammo packs for the lightning gun rest. The hillock is great for sniping, and you can drop down and retreat to the tree for more cover as you follow and shoot incoming enemies.

The biggest prize is down and right of the hillock and tree near the lightning gun. On the grass to the right of the small patch of ruins (or waterfall and ruins on the blue side) is a redeemer! Make sure one of your team dashes for this (and your opposing side's redeemer location) when the match starts, and time the weapon's respawn to consistently grab it and use it to devastate the opposition. Once it's in your hands, make the single shot count, launching it to the base entrance, to the ball carrier (where the highest concentration of enemies is) or at the ball.

NOTE

Don't go too overboard with the double redeemer action! Even if you manage to grab the redeemer on your side and the opposite side, you'll still only have one shot. Fire one redeemer before you take the other.

375

Just in front of the redeemer is a patch of ruins (and a waterfall on the blue side). The protruding stone column ends provide reasonable cover and good tracking shots to blast the ball carrier and teams rushing in from beyond or over the central arch. Continue forward along the right wall to find a shock rifle and two ammo on the red side, and a biorifle and two ammo on the blue side. Spread the bio goop over the ball location atop the arch if you're first here, in front of a running ball carrier or at the top of narrow stepping stones on either side of the middle arch. Use the shock rifle to bounce enemies away from the arch's underside and the shield pack, to knock enemies off the arch's top, and to annoy an attacking team racing to the goal.

Finally, there's the middle arch. Those without the ball, on supporting role, or attempting to punch through defenses should run straight under the arch, watching for incoming rockets or other fire at this choke point. If you want to reach the ball, climb up the slope on the left (the easy way in) or up the stepped rocks on the right (slightly harder to achieve on the blue side). Then dodge jump to the arch.

Control of the arch is key to victory on this level. If you can set up snipers on the arch and defend this area well, you can demoralize the opposition and take the ball when it respawns. Use the darkened areas left and right as cover, and shout information on enemy movement to your team.

Going Balls Out

Make sure you understand the three entrances to this base. The first is simple; you can run under the natural arching bridge, so be ready with rockets to stall this goal run (which you'll see most often). The second is to dodge jump up the rocks. The third is via the slope on the left. If you have the ball, it's best to throw it to a teammate sprinting to the enemy base entrance, or to jump down and land amid the four health vials on the valley's right side. Set up a passing game until you reach the base entrance.

You can enter via the left slope near the lightning gun or through the hole, but both are heavily defended. If you get a teammate into the opposition's goal area, lob the ball over the entrance arch and run in to serve as backup. Once inside the base, lob the ball at the goal without overshooting the top of it, as you can make only one real attempt; the ball returns if you shoot it over the cliff.

Try mixing up your location with the ball to avoid being blasted in the base's middle. Run up the right side to the adrenaline and step in front of the banner, lob the ball so it hits the goal (if you're proficient) or stops in front, then finish the job. Also lob from the rocket launcher for an easy shot. If you're being chased into the base, dodge jump left around the wall curve to the other banner (to prevent some of the incoming fire from hitting you), then dodge jump right and lob the ball into the goal.

BR-TWINTOMBS

Recommended Players: 6–10

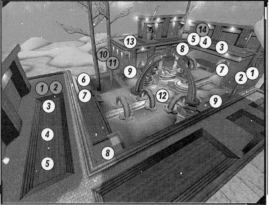

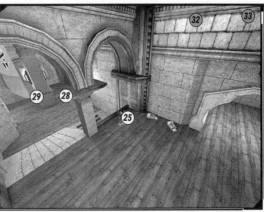

Legend

1	50 Health Pack (side ramp)	**14**	Double Damage (outer ledge behind base, in corner)	**24**	Assault and bio ammo packs (near corner of top corridor)
2	Link Gun (side ramp)	**15**	Lightning Gun +2 ammo packs (corner of base)	**25**	Minigun +2 ammo packs (top of stairs)
3	Rocket Launcher (outside balcony)	**16**	Shock Rifle (corner of base)	**26**	Biorifle (corner of top corridor)
4	50 Health Pack (outside balcony)	**17**	50 Health Pack (side of base)	**27**	Assault, Link, Flak ammo packs (under stairs)
5	50 Health Pack (outside balcony)	**18**	50 Health Pack (side of base)	**28**	50 Health Pack x2 (near side exit)
6	Flak Cannon (corner, near trees)	**19**	Adrenaline Pills x4 (top base entrance, left)	**29**	Flak ammo packs x2 (near side exit)
7	Rocket Launcher (outside lower balcony)	**20**	Health Vials x4 (top base entrance, right)	**30**	50 Shield Pack (lower corridor corner) and link ammo packs x2 (lower corridor)
8	100 Shield Pack (top base entrance, in corner)	**21**	Adrenaline Pills x2 (lower corridor, near base entrance)	**31**	Health Vials x4 (lower corridor)
9	Adrenaline Pills x4 (raised balcony end)	**22**	Bio ammo packs x2 (corner to DD)	**32**	Rocket ammo packs x2, 50 Health Pack (top of jump pad interior, side building)
10	50 Health Pack (side ramp)	**23**	Mini, rocket, lightning ammo packs (top corner of base)	**33**	Adrenaline Pills x4 (top of jump pad interior, side building)
11	50 Health Pack (side ramp)				
12	Big Keg-O-Health (random, CTF), Ball (BR)				
13	Lightning Gun +2 ammo packs (top of roof)				

Overview

The Twin Tombs are a duo of identical structures (a central main tomb and one to its right side) floating in the sea. Joining the opposite tombs is a courtyard with a variety of ornate archways and overhanging tusks in the middle. Each set of tombs has five entrances: two on the ground, two at a balcony, and a side tomb with an entrance on the top balcony. Inside each tomb is a maze of connecting corridors, with arrows leading to a main goal room. Beware of the hole in the ground as you reach your goal!

Available Weapons*

Biorifle (one end of corridor, near goal arrow and upper entrance)

Shock Rifle (to the right of the goal area)

Link Gun (dead-end ledge, near tree clump, BR only)

Minigun (near stairs in main interior side corridor)

Flak Cannon (corner of courtyard, near tree clump)

Rocket Launcher (balcony and top balcony outside base)

Lightning Gun (to the goal area's left and on the far top balcony of the side tomb)

Redeemer (middle of courtyard, CTF only)

* For each side, double the total for the final number on this level unless otherwise stated.

Goal Patrol

Starting at either goal, check the left corner for a lightning gun (and two ammo) and a shock rifle (plus two ammo) on the right corner. Move down either ramp, to a ledge with a health pack on each side of a hole. The hole leads to a waterfall and nasty demise, so stay away from it or shock combo punks into it from the safety of a corner. Following the health packs are two sets of stairs leading down to a large central lower entrance. There are stairs on each side also leading to a balcony with three exits: one on the left, and two on the right wall. The balcony also holds a rocket,  mini, and lightning ammo atop the left outer stairs. In the balcony overhang, the left exit is marked with four adrenaline pills and the right exit is marked with four health vials.

Defending the goal is made all the more fun when you're consistently bouncing enemies into the central pit, coating the lower entrances with bio goop, or waiting for the enemy to turn a corner—have a couple teammates waiting to throw ordnance. Don't be afraid to translocate; keep a friend on a high lip above the upper balcony, overlooking the entire base.

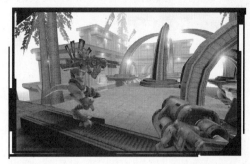

The upper left exit leads to a right corner and an open-air balcony with a rocket launcher. The upper right exit inside the balcony leads down some steps to a biorifle, ammo, assault ammo, and a left corner. Follow the corridor to the exit on your left. This leads to the rocket launcher balcony. You're under a 100 shield pack on the roof of this exit and can quickly reach the top level from here. The corridor inside continues past this left wall exit.

The corridor also has a doorway on the right wall. Take this into a small chamber with two jump pads. The right one shoots you up and left, to an upper side building with two rocket launcher ammo packs and a health pack. Near the hole you ascended through are four adrenaline pills. The left jump pad shoots you to the exit on the top balcony overlooking the entire base, and also near the double damage ledge.

Back down in the biorifle corridor, continue to a minigun and two ammo before a two-arched opening. At the far end of the corridor, there's a door to the left (take the two health packs and flak ammo). This is the farthest exit from the goal, to the map's side, opening up on the main courtyard.

Back at the descending steps, head under the minigun to grab link, flak, and assault ammo in a narrow corridor. Follow the corridor to the right corner for a 50 shield pack. Turn right. There's a doorway with pointed arrows on the left wall, and two link ammo packs on the right. Head left, turn right, plough through four adrenaline pills, and reach the lower entrance to the goal room. Back at the 50 shield pack, run straight, ignoring the left door; you pass through four health vials, up some stairs, and turn right. This leads to the ground level and the map's center.

Now for the final exit near the upper right, outside the balcony in the goal room. The corner has two bio ammo packs, and opens up on a square ledge with a double damage. Drop down here from above or translocate onto the top balcony.

Midfield Machinations

Check the upper left exit, leading to the rocket launcher balcony, and drop left. Turn 180 degrees and check the link gun and health pack to the base's side and a dead-end ledge. Turn back, and inspect the ground to the left. There's a flak cannon in one corner and a clump of trees. Across and left of that is another dead-end ledge, with two health packs. The cobblestones lead to the middle of the map and ball, overhung by four giant team "tusks." Left is the entrance to the biorifle/minigun corridor on your opponent's base, and four adrenaline pills.

Translocating or appearing out of the side building via the jump pads allows you to reach the top balcony. Here you can drop down or translocate across the yard to the opposite buildings, or pick up the two health packs and rocket launcher (a second one). Over on the far right end of the side building top balcony is a lightning gun and ammo. Hunt from this point or translocate up on the roof of either building!

379

Going Balls Out

Scoring a goal is a little dangerous if your opposition has installed defenders on the roofs, but the number of entrances and the wacky ways in the base can all work to your advantage. With a "tag" partner, pick up the ball and throw it to them (they may be up on a balcony). They can then enter through a multitude of entrances (detailed earlier), mixing it up each time. If you really know the level, have the ball thrower run into the base from a different door, then appear at the corridor's far end to grab the ball before the carrier is taken out.

The other method is a "convoy" of a couple of charging teammates clearing the way after planning the route, and the ball carrier following behind. Radio your friends if you want to change the course in mid-charge. Flexibility helps, as well as strength in numbers. After you make it into the base, or throw the ball up to an upper balcony and translocate up after it, you can lead your foes in a merry dance. One example is to throw the ball to the top balcony, translocate onto it, then move to the edge overlooking the double damage ledge. Now you're near the goal, so the enemy is likely to charge the goal room.

Step on the lip on the building's edge to the right, and follow it around to the building's other side, then drop down to the rocket launcher and entrance below. Or, double back if the enemy is wise to your actions. Once inside the connecting corridors, you must know the corners by heart and use the ground arrows to find the goal room. Fire from the lower or upper balcony. You can even double jump into the hole, and just before dying, throw the ball and score.

Capture the Flag Counterpoint

The strategy for Capture the Flag remains largely the same, except the entire team must translocate into as many different enemy entrances as possible. Or, you can all charge in one entrance at the same time and overpower the enemy. Defensively, the upper ledge above the balconies in the flag room is an excellent ambush point. Train a lightning gun sniper from any of the upper balconies outside to snag a foe or two; try having two snipers, each covering two entrances. Also translocate to the central tusks to drop down and attack, blast the flag carrier, or head off to an upper balcony. Defenders inside the base should coat the narrower corridors with biorifle ooze. There are a few changes to the map, such as jump pads at the lower entrance (use this to leap at the flag), at the DD (ascend to the top balcony), and the side ledge with the two health packs (ascend to the top balcony). All help the flag carrier, so find and use them on your way home. You'll also find a redeemer in the map's middle. Take two of your team and immediately secure it: one to grab the weapon and the other to destroy adversaries with the same idea.

Appendix

Appendix I: Loading Screen Hints

These hints appear on the Loading screen before a match starts.

- "F3" will bring up a personal stats display.
- If you miss a player's chat message, you can use "F2" to display a box of all chat messages you have received.
- Tip: If you receive a missile lock warning, try to get out of sight quickly
- Tip: The Raptor's missiles will automatically lock onto Mantas and other Raptors
- Tip: In the Raptor, press JUMP to fly higher and DUCK to fly lower
- Tip: The Manta can duck to smash your enemies by pressing DUCK or ALTFIRE
- Tip: Press JUMP to perform a 180 spin out in the Hellbender or Scorpion
- Tip: The Manta is the only vehicle that can jump
- Tip: The Leviathan is most vulnerable to air attacks when deployed
- Tip: You can heal a friendly vehicle with the link gun alt-fire
- Tip: You can heal a friendly PowerNode with the link gun alt-fire
- Tip: It is impossible to heal the final PowerCore
- Tip: Press "F12" to toggle the radar map on and off
- Tip: You can be hurt or killed by vehicles exploding near you
- Tip: Enemy spider mines can be destroyed but some weapons are better against them than others
- Tip: Pressing USE on a PowerNode allows you to teleport to any PowerNode your team controls
- Tip: You won't be able to spawn at a PowerNode that is under attack, even if your team controls it
- Tip: If you die, any spider mines or grenades you fired will die too
- Tip: Press "O" to voice chat with your team
- Tip: "M" will show the way to the nearest PowerNode or PowerCore the Red Team can attack, while "N" will do the same for the Blue Team
- When a new spawn area has been enabled, Press accent (`) to teleport to it instantly.

- Press "M" or "N" to highlight the current objective, show a path to it, and slide out the Objective list.
- The green icon over your teammates means you can use the alt-fire of your link gun on them to make them more powerful and share their damage.
- Pressing accent (`) after tossing the translocator allows you to view from its internal camera.

Appendix II: Easter Eggs

Below are examples of some of the game's Easter eggs—hidden messages, weird goings-on, and even a hidden gameplay mode.

- In AS-Junkyard, en route from the ironworks to the exit, there's a pile of scrap metal with a bathtub on it. The plumbing needs attention, as effluent flows in the wrong direction.
- In AS-Robotfactory, a large robot is trussed up in ceiling wires just the other side of the open tunnels near the entrance to the AI generator and final objective. It appears to be leaking oil from its nether-regions. Only the developers know for sure what these two Easter eggs mean….
- In DM-Deck17, check the area cordoned off behind the biorifle; it states that Deck16 is closed for repair and renovation. This adjacent deck is the classic *Unreal Tournament* map, now shrouded in darkness.
- Also in DM-Deck17 are screens with the following message: "If you're reading this, you're already dead. There is no reality, there is only this. This time. This place. This contest. Be the best. Unleash your power. Lead your team in a battle of the mind. Win the tournament. If you can't, step aside for someone who will. Keep your eyes on the prize, and your finger on the trigger."
- Both DM-DesertIsle and CTF-Moondragon have areas where wind-chimes gently jingle in the breeze.
- In DM-Morpheus3, check out the monitor inside each building, as the Liandri Corporation's marketing department shifts into high gear with an all-new set of figurines.

381

Unreal
TOURNAMENT
2004

- In many maps (such as AS-Convoy and DM-Rankin), the designers created tiny box worlds (impossible to reach) before constructing the real worlds. Check them out by entering the command prompt "ghost," then "slomo 5" to quicken your pace (the default slomo setting is 1.5), and float out of the map and explore the outer reaches....

- Wouldn't it be great if the mod community built Capture the Flag maps with all the antics of CTF matches, but with the firepower and all-new tactics of vehicular warfare? The new mode could be called "Vehicle CTF." We're sure that's hidden somewhere....

Appendix III: Console Commands and Cheats

Bring up the command prompt with the tilde key (~), or press "Tab". Then type in the following codes to add various interesting effects.

Cheat Codes

Code	Effect
CHEATSENABLED	Allows cheating commands in single-player mode (but disables unlockable characters from being obtained)
ALLAMMO	Full ammunition for every weapon
ALLWEAPONS	All weapons
FLY	Allows you to fly
GHOST	Allows you to pass through walls, known as "noclip"
GOD	Invincibility
LOADED	Bestows all weapons, ammo, and 100 adrenaline
TELEPORT	Teleports you to a random spot in the map
WALK	Stops FLY or GHOST command and drops you to the ground

Player/Bot Commands

Code	Effect
ADDBOTS [number]	Adds the specified number of Bots
BEHINDVIEW 1	Changes to third-person view
BEHINDVIEW 0	Changes to first-person view
DISCONNECT	Disconnects from current server
EXIT	Quits the game
KILLBOTS	Gets rid of all bots
OPEN [IP address]	Connects to a specific server IP
OPEN [mapname]	Opens specified map
QUIT	Quits the game
RECONNECT	Reconnects to the current server
SWITCHLEVEL [mapname]	Switches to the specified level
SWITCHTEAM	Switches your player's team
SUICIDE	Kill yourself
TEAMSAY [text]	Displays your message in team chat
PLAYERSONLY	Freezes/pauses the Bots
SAY [text]	Displays your message in global chat
SETNAME [playername]	Changes your player name
SET INPUT [key] [command]	Binds a key to a command, such as "SET INPUT L LOADED"

Statistics

Code	Effect
MEMSTAT	Displays Windows memory usage
STAT ALL	Shows all stats
STAT AUDIO	Shows audio stats
STAT FPS	Displays your frames per second
STAT GAME	Displays game stats
STAT HARDWARE	Shows hardware stats
STAT NET	Shows network game play stats
STAT NONE	Turns off all stats
STAT RENDER	Displays rendering statistics

Demo Commands

Code	Effect
DEMOPLAY [demoname]	Plays the specified demo
DEMOREC [demoname]	Records a demo using the demo name you type
STOPDEMO	Stop recording a demo

Admin Commands

Code	Effect
ADMIN SWITCHLEVEL [mapname?game=gametype?mutator=mutator]	Changes the current level to the specified level, game type, and mutators

ADMIN [command]	Performs the specified command
ADMINLOGIN [password]	Logs the administrator onto the server using the specified password
ADMINLOGOUT	Logs the administrator off the server
ADMIN SET UWeb.Webserver bEnabled True	Enables the remote admin webserver (after level change)
ADMIN SET UWeb.Webserver bEnabled False	Disables the remote admin webserver (after level change)
KICK [playername]	Kicks the specified player from the server
KICKBAN [playername]	Kicks and bans the specified player from the server using their IP address. To unban the player, edit the server.ini or use the web admin interface.

Other Commands

Code	Effect
BRIGHTNESS [number]	Changes the brightness level to the specified number
CDTRACK [number]	Plays the specified CD track number
CONFIGHASH	Displays configuration info
CONTRAST [number]	Changes the contrast level to the specified number
DEBUG CRASH	Test crashes the game with an error
DEBUG EATMEM	Tests memory allocation until full
DEBUG GPF	Test crashes the game with a general protection fault error
DEBUG RECURSE	Test crashes the game by infinite recursion
DUMPCACHE	Displays the memory cache contents
EXEC [filename]	Executes a file in the UT2003/system/ directory by default
FLUSH	Flushes all caches and relights
FOV [number]	Changes the field of view to the specified number
FIXEDVISIBILITY	For testing your own level. Fixes the engine's visibility from your current point of view. You can walk around and see exactly what is being drawn, check that antiportals are working, etc. Enter it again to turn it off.
GAMMA [number]	Changes the gamma level to the specified number

GETCOLORDEPTHS	Displays the maximum color depth supported by your hardware
GETCURRENT COLORDEPTHS	Displays your current color depth
GETCURRENTRES	Displays your current resolution
GETCURRENT TICKRATE	Displays your current tick rate
GETMAXTICKRATE	Displays the maximum allowed tick rate
MUSICORDER [number]	Change to a certain track in the song (0=ambient, 1=action, 2=suspense)
NETSPEED [number]	Sets the net speed, default is 10,000
OBJ CLASSES	Displays a list of object classes
OBJ GARBAGE	Collects and purges objects no longer in use
OBJ HASH	Displays object hashing statistics
OBJ LINKERS	Displays a list of active linkers
PAUSESOUNDS	Pauses all sounds
PREFERENCES	Opens advanced settings
RELAUNCH	Relaunches the engine
RENDEREMULATE [gf1/gf2]	Lets you see how your level will look on different cards (e.g., if some of your shaders are too complicated and don't have fallbacks)
REPORT	Copies a report of the current game to clipboard
SET [class variable value]	Sets a specified class and specified variable with the specified value
SETSENSITIVITY [number]	Sets the mouse sensitivity to the specified number
SETRES [WxHxD]	Sets your screen resolution to the specified width, height, and color depth
SLOMO 1	Sets the speed of the game back to normal real time speed
SLOMO 2	Sets speed to double. Increase number to go faster.
SLOMO .5	Sets speed to half. Decrease number to go slower.
SOCKETS	Displays a list of sockets in use
TOGGLEFULLSCREEN	Toggles full screen mode
TOGGLESCREEN SHOTMODE	Removes all HUD for screenshot taking
FREECAMERA [number]	Allows you to move the camera around your player
TYPE [text]	Displays the specified text on the console
UNPAUSESOUNDS	Un-pauses all sounds

Console Commands / Cheats list combined with the help of www.planetunreal.com.

383

NOW AVAILABLE

Unreal® II
THE AWAKENING

Prima's Official Strategy Guide

- **Complete walkthrough of all missions, including maps and all objectives**

- **Strategies to defeat each enemy—alien and humanoid**

- **Tips for handling each weapon, including the flamethrower, the sniper rifle, and the rocket and multi-mode grenade launcher**

- **Covers basic combat and evasive tactics**

- **Includes tips on using XMP**

PRIMA'S OFFICIAL — XBOX — STRATEGY GUIDE

Unreal® II
THE AWAKENING

primagames.com

This game has received the following rating from the ESRB

MATURE 17+

M

CONTENT RATED BY **ESRB**

Prima® GAMES

primagames.com®

The Prima Games logo is a registered trademark of Random House, Inc., registered in the United States and other countries. Primagames.com is a registered trademark of Random House, Inc., registered in the United States.

Unreal® II – The Awakening © 2003 Epic Games, Inc. All Rights Reserved. Unreal is a registered trademark of Epic Games, Inc. Unreal II – The Awakening was created by Legend Entertainment, an Atari studio, in collaboration with Tantalus Interactive. All other trademarks are the property of their respective owners. Manufactured and marketed by Atari, Inc.